THE FYLDE

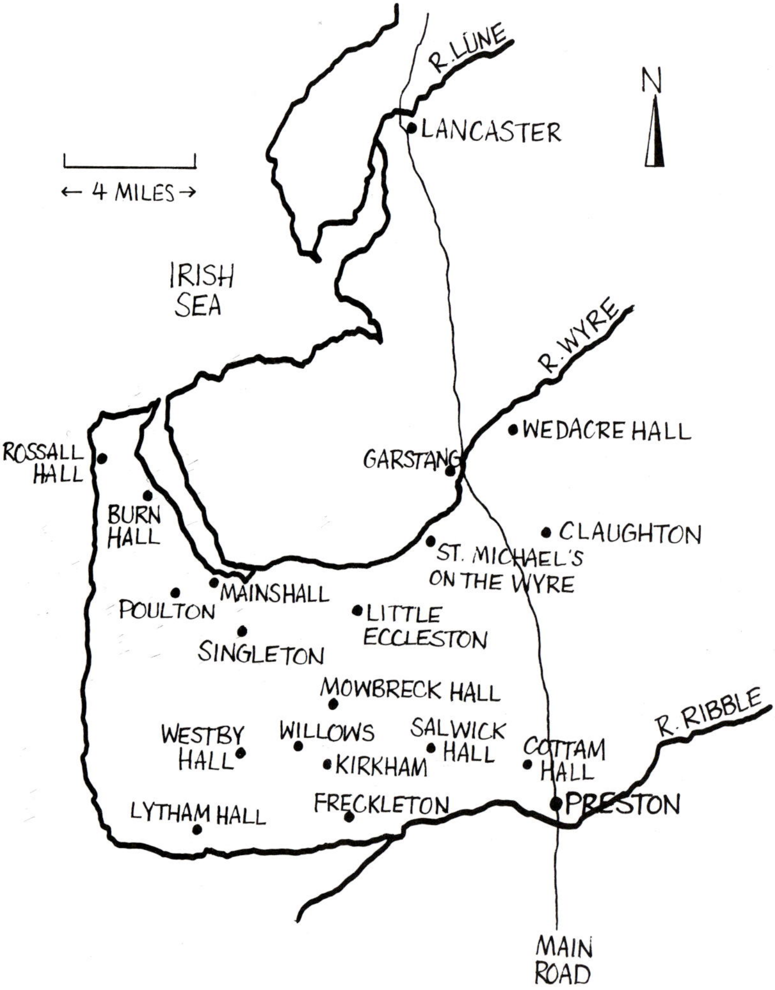
R. LUNE
LANCASTER
N
4 MILES
IRISH SEA
R. WYRE
WEDACRE HALL
ROSSALL HALL
GARSTANG
BURN HALL
CLAUGHTON
ST. MICHAEL'S ON THE WYRE
MAINSHALL
POULTON
LITTLE ECCLESTON
SINGLETON
MOWBRECK HALL
WESTBY HALL
WILLOWS
SALWICK HALL
COTTAM HALL
R. RIBBLE
KIRKHAM
LYTHAM HALL
FRECKLETON
PRESTON
MAIN ROAD

The Revival of English Catholicism

The Revival of English Catholicism:

The Banister-Rutter Correspondence 1777–1807

Edited by Leo Gooch

North West Catholic History Society
Wigan
1995

ISBN 0 9514615 5 9

North West Catholic History Society
10 Ellesmere Road
Pemberton
Wigan
Lancashire WN5 9LA
England

Printed in Great Britain
by T. Snape & Co., Ltd, Boltons Court, Preston.

Contents

Acknowledgments

The manuscripts of these letters are held in the archives of Upholland College and I am most grateful to the Rt. Rev. Mgr. J. Devine, Director of the College, for permission to publish them. Rev. Dr. Michael Sharratt of Ushaw College has been most cooperative in providing access to a microfilm of the letters and to the Rev. W.V. Smith's typescript of some of the early letters. Peter Doyle provided typescripts of Banister's letters in other archives; Sister Mary Gregory IBVM, Dom Aidan Bellenger OSB, Dom Geoffrey Scott OSB and Mr Philip Harris kindly provided information, and Mr Craig M. Rice drew the maps. I am also grateful to Miss Elizabeth Ward, Mr J.A. Hilton, Mr L. Warren and Mr J.W. Bamber for making sense of Banister's Latin, despite his poor handwriting and maddening habit of contracting words; I am, however, responsible for freely adapting their versions in the printed text. Professor Alan McClelland and Dr Sheridan Gilley gave valuable support.

Finally, I would like to thank the North West Catholic History Society for undertaking to publish these letters, and I am especially grateful to the following for their generous financial assistance, without which publication could not have proceeded:

The British Academy
The Rev. Dunstan Cooper
The Parish of St John the Evangelist, The Willows, Kirkham
St. Joseph's College, Upholland
The Josephan Society.

Editorial Notes

The letters are published verbatim although punctuation, spelling and layout have been modernised silently. Editorial interpolations, including translations, are given in square brackets. Footnotes have been kept to a minimum and are usually confined to explanatory material; unattributed biographical details as well as the locations of missioners &c. have been taken from works in the bibliography.

Abbreviations

DD	Doctor of Divinity
DNB	*Dictionary of National Biography*
FRS	Fellow of the Royal Society
FSA	Fellow of the Society of Antiquaries
GEC	*The Complete Peerage*
ipi	in partibus infidelium
OSB	Order of St Benedict
SJ	Society of Jesus
UM	*Ushaw Magazine*
WAA	Westminster Archdiocesan Archives

Introduction

Greatest attention in the history of post-Reformation English Catholicism has been devoted to the Age of Martyrs of the sixteenth and seventeenth centuries, and to the Second Spring of the nineteenth. Unaccountably, the intervening period has been found less sensational, yet it, especially the latter half of the eighteenth century, is marked by a number of events whose impact individually was important enough, but cumulatively represented nothing less than a radical transformation of the English Catholic body.

The recognition of George III as *de jure* king of England by the Holy See in 1766 allowed the English Catholics to drop what little remained of their Jacobitism, swear allegiance to the Hanoverians, and devote their entire attention to the repeal of the anti-Catholic penal laws. In deference to some worried members of the Anglican establishment, a parliamentary census of the Catholics was taken in 1767, and it showed that not only had they weathered two centuries of deprivation, they were even possessed of the sociological characteristics required for growth; to the horror of the more apprehensive Protestants, a second census taken in 1780 confirmed the English Catholic Church's capacity for expansion. It was with some misgivings, then, notwithstanding the extinction of the Stuarts, that acts of parliament were passed in 1778 and 1791 relieving Catholics of certain civil disabilities and permitting substantial ecclesiastical development to take place. Those measures fell well short of emancipation, however, and the Gordon Riots served to remind the Catholics that, as papists, their acquisition of full political liberty would always be fiercely resisted in certain quarters.

Various internal ecclesiastical difficulties added to the tensions created by the political issue. The suppression of the Society of Jesus between 1773 and 1814 had a disruptive effect on the English mission. The French Revolution brought the supply of newly-ordained English priests to a halt when the expatriate seminaries on French territory were forcibly closed. On the other hand, the nationalisation of the Church in France led to the involuntary exile of large numbers of French priests and some five thousand of them were allowed into England, although their pastoral role proved controversial among the English clergy. British patriotic sentiment against France sanctioned the return of English Catholic schools, colleges and religious communities but the relocation, status and accountability of the repatriated seminaries were disputed for several years. The deaths of one coadjutor and three Vicars Apostolic of the Northern District in the twenty years following 1769 created undesirable discontinuities in the leadership of the Church in the north, but the demise in 1790 of two of the four Vicars Apostolic (of the London and the Northern Districts) was particularly inopportune for the Church nationally. Negotiations over the second Relief Act were then in progress and the cisalpine tendency of many senior laymen, and some priests, had become the subject of public controversy. Their willingness to surrender various ecclesiastical prerogatives in return for political emancipation, and their attempts to elect successor-bishops to the vacant vicariates, were grave challenges to episcopal jurisdiction and almost led them into schism. The rupture between the two sides, which would take some time to heal, was the immediate cause for the uncoupling of the mission from the country-houses of the gentry where it had been established since Elizabethan times.

This, then, was a period of upheaval in English Catholicism, but it was ultimately beneficial, for it amounted to a renaissance. The English Catholics were passing through the intermediate stage between proscription and emancipation—a condition of legislative toleration but political exclusion. Their eventual recovery of a full place in national civic life was accompanied by a process of internal structural change. The re-establishment in England of the institutions which had been banished abroad for years facilitated a wider deployment, and the Church's greater visibility gave rise to slow but inexorable growth. At the same time, the Vicars Apostolic took control of the mission from the lay gentry and the era of clerical ascendancy began. Along with its newfound independence, the reinvigorated Church gained new patrons and a new ethos, for the centre of gravity of the mission was shifting from a rural to an urban setting, out of the old gentry fiefdoms and into the sphere of merchants and tradesmen, and the emergent industrial working-class. Hence, this was a time of reconstruction and development, and it became clear as events unfolded that this would be one of the most important chapters in English Catholic history. Indeed, the significance of the period is that it was truly the age of the Catholic Revival, for without its achievements the further expansion (or so-called revival) associated with Cardinal Wiseman, the Oxford converts and the Irish immigrants could not possibly have taken place.

That, in short, is the context in which this correspondence between Robert Banister and his nephew Henry Rutter should be read. It is quite exceptional for such a correspondence extending over some forty years to survive almost in its entirety, and the letters therefore provide a unique insight into this eventful period.[1] Both priests held strong views on all the controversial issues of the day and since neither of them expected the letters ever to see the light of day, they discussed events and personalities without reserve. But their letters have a further importance, for, in addition to high ecclesiastical politics, they touch upon a wide range of social and personal matters which fill in many details of daily life on the mission in the final years of the recusant era otherwise lost to us.

Little more needs to be said by way of introduction except to give a brief biographical sketch of the correspondents before they began to write to each other. Banister was born in October 1725, the second son of Robert and Mary (nee Bell) Banister of Hesketh Bank in the parish of Kirkham, Lancashire. He received his earliest education in Dame Alice's school at Fernyhalgh, near Preston; then, at the age of sixteen, he entered Douai College as a student for the priesthood. Simon George Bordley (chaplain at Mowbreck Hall and Salwick Hall from 1735 to 1746), later told him how this had come about:[2]

> Before you went abroad, your father (for whom I always had, and always shall have, the greatest value) inquired for some assistance to bring you up to our Trade. He found that the late Mr Martin, priest at Blackbrook, had left some money for that use. Mr Thomas Hawarden, priest, had the ordering of it. Your father applied to him. He said then, if Mr Bordley will send me his character and I like it, I will pay £40 towards his education. I sent your character and it was approved. So you had that £40.

Banister was ordained in December 1750. He stayed on at Douai as 'a Master 1 year of Rhetoric, 4 of Philosophy and 12 of Divinity'.

Banister went to the English mission in 1769, when he was forty-four years of age. The reason for this move is not known; his reputation suggests that he could have stayed on at Douai for the rest of his working life. It may have been that he genuinely wanted to become a missioner, but it may also have been that he could scent the winds of change that were about to blow through the college. As his letters show, Banister was a tough, humourless and unimaginative disciplinarian with rigid ideas. William Green had been President for the last twenty years; he was then at the age of seventy-four and about to retire. Henry Tichborne Blount, a member of an Oxfordshire gentry family and Banister's contemporary, both as a student and in age, was to succeed him. Banister disliked the gentry and he was no progressive; his knowledge of the new President might well have prompted his departure. At any rate, Banister was placed at Wrightington Hall, near Wigan, as chaplain to Mr Dicconson but he left after a year to take over the mission at Ladywell in Fernyhalgh, where he also opened a small school. Three years later Blount persuaded him to return to Douai as Vice President in succession to William Wilkinson, who had left to become President of the English College at St. Omer (which the secular clergy had taken over from the Jesuits in 1762). Banister was also appointed Professor of Theology and Prefect of Studies. These prestigious posts, however, could not hold Banister and in June 1774, after one academic year, he resigned, alleging that he was 'unable to stand the monotony of the routine'. He was, however, clearly unsympathetic to the changes introduced by Blount at Douai; as we shall see, his later letters contain many disparaging remarks about the management of his beloved alma mater then and later.

Banister went first to Thurnham Hall near Lancaster, but he moved the following year to Mowbreck Hall, halfway between Blackpool and Preston in his home parish of Kirkham. In 1767 there were about twelve hundred Catholics living in the parish of Kirkham, and they were served by five missioners, of whom Banister was now one. The Westby family had been seated at Mowbreck Hall from around the year 1300. They remained loyal to the old religion but Robert, who succeeded to the estate in 1729, was the last Catholic of the family to live in the Hall. He rebuilt the mansion and included within it a permanent domestic chapel and a set of rooms for the chaplain. He also established a capital fund of £1,000, the interest of which provided the chaplain's salary. Robert Westby died in 1762 without a male heir and his estates were divided between his four nieces. Mowbreck went to a cadet branch of the family who lived at White Hall. Mowbreck home-farm was leased to the steward cum tenant-farmer, and the priest continued to operate the mission from the hall.

Banister therefore went to Mowbreck Hall effectively as an independent missioner although he was living in a private house. Always the educator as well as the priest, and taking advantage of his situation, he immediately opened a day and boarding school in the Hall as a preparatory school for the Catholic colleges abroad. It need hardly be said that he would keep up the severity of his old manner, not least his readiness to pull the ears or cuff the heads of delinquents at catechism. His school was available to all, of course, but Banister was proud to have produced fourteen church-students over the following twelve years. Thus many of the secular clergy were educated by Banister at Douai and Mowbreck, and he came to be highly influential in ecclesiastical circles in England. Bishop Alexander Goss, his great-nephew, thought there was no more honoured name than that of Banister. Banister was elected to the Chapter and appointed titular Archdeacon of Norfolk and Suffolk in 1770. His name was on the *terna* sent to Rome as a possible successor to Matthew Gibson as Vicar Apostolic of the Northern District, but he was to remain missioner at Mowbreck until his retirement some thirty years later.

In 1761 Adam Banister received a letter from his brother Robert telling him that a vacancy would shortly arise at Douai College on the Winkley Fund and asking, 'Can you profit by this intimation', but his sons were all too young. It was not until September 1768 that his son Henry, then thirteen years old, was ready to enter the college. Adopting an old recusant security precaution, he took the maiden name of his mother, [Agnes] Rutter, and it is as Henry Rutter that he was invariably known thenceforth. Doubtless the correspondence between Banister and his nephew began in the latter's first days at Douai but nothing survives from the first nine years. The letters printed here begin when Rutter was twenty-two and in minor orders and when his uncle was fifty-two. Rutter's biography from that point on can be told almost entirely in his own words.

1. Although this correspondence has remained unpublished until now, the following articles are based on it: P. Doyle, 'Seminary Education: A Conservative 18th Century View', *North West Catholic History* Vol. 1 (1969) ; L. Gooch, 'Priests and Patrons in the Eighteenth Century', *Recusant History* Vol. 20 No. 2 (1990) ; L. Gooch, 'What shall we do with the wanton student?: Tutoring the Catholic Gentry in the Eighteenth Century', *Recusant History* Vol. 21, No. 4, (1994) ; W.V. Smith, 'Life at Douai College after 1750', *UM* vol. 76 (1966).
2. Upholland Mss., A/1/20 nd, c. 1783.

The Banister/Rutter Correspondence

1. Banister to Rutter — Mowbreck, 22nd June 1777

To Master Rutter,

I received your kind letter by Mr Daniel[1] and congratulate you for all the good progress you make in learning. I suppose Mr Burke, you quote so familiarly, is some old classical author lately discovered in the ruins of Herculanum. I need not send you advice, 'tis a commodity very cheap and easy to be found in your own house: discernment is indeed necessary to distinguish what is good from what is bad, but that is a gem of rare value and not to be found everywhere. 'Tis I believe like poetick fire, a gift of heaven, not acquirable by study, not to be taught by any scholastick methods.

If you could take some lessons very privately of a fencing master, I think it would open your narrow, bending breast and erect your chest into a decent attitude. I would give six livres for this end, not to make you ridiculous, but to do you good: Thursdays and play-days at the fencing Master's house are the only times and before you go to Divinity, not afterwards. I have desired Mr [James] Melling to give you six livres:[2] use your own wit and discretion and believe me to be always yours most cordially, R.B.

1. Three secular priests named Daniel were lecturing at Douai College at this time.
2. Melling was a professor. The annual pension at the college was 450 livres or £20; in 1781 Banister gives the rate as 600 livres, or 25 guineas (see No. 7).

2. Banister to Rutter Mowbreck, 16th November 1777

My dear Harry,

I wish I could send you some other token, besides a mere letter, of my affection. I know not how you bear the want of money; with impatience and inward repining, or with resignation and submission to your lot? This I know, that many arguments and motives might be alleged to persuade you to rest contented. Several have done so before you; some there are who spend nothing by choice, either to employ their money in better use, or to save it. All absolute necessaries are allowed you by the house, or if something more is wanting to make nature easy, it is but little. Then, your present situation will not be long; 9 years are past of your studies, 4 only at the most to remain. 'Tis best I think to say one has nothing to spend and so cannot join with your [Greek word illeg.]. I could wish you to learn a great horror of contracting debt: debts contracted are seldom but with great difficulty wiped off.

Your brother Robert continues to improve himself: you probably correspond with him. I live 3 times 9 miles minus 2 distant from your father, so do not often get news from thence, and Ribble is between us.[1]

Is it not a good entertainment to go on play-days in the afternoons a bookanisting? Not amongst the modern pamphlets, or comedies, or novels: nor amongst metaphysics, which young heads I think had better defer till more maturity of judgement descends upon them. But amongst old books at Bacque's, Simon's, &c, where sometimes books of great value lie in dust and may be bought for old paper. See then whether you can find the Paraphrases of S. Paul's Epistles (1632–40) by Antoine Godeau. These are excellent paraphrases, but hard to be found: you are not to ask for them, but hunt them from amidst lumber. I have several other books which I desire may be found for me, but will not mention them till I hear of your success in these.

Give the other side to Ralph Platt.[2] I desire you say some short prayer for me sometimes, when you are very fervent, and have received the Blessed Sacrament. You have heard that when kings and princes make a familiar visit, they are very gracious and hear and grant any humble petition; this is the reason why I desire you to prefer a petition for me when you have received the Blessed Sacrament. I remain your most affectionate friend and uncle R. Banister.

I desire you to take special care of the Saints Lives[3] which I left. And I think you may as well send me by some more careful sort of boy my Rollin's Ancient History. He may leave them with Mr [Joseph] Bolton at Mrs Hanne's in Gloucester Street near Queen Square, London.[4]

1. Rutter's family lived at Westhead near Ormskirk.
2. The second leaf is missing, presumably because Rutter tore it off, as instructed, for Ralph Platt, a clerical student at the college.
3. Armand d'Andilly (see N$^{o.}$ 7). The French authors cited in these letters can be traced in *The Catholic Encyclopedia* (16 vols. 1912).
4. Bolton, a Lancashireman, was Bp. Challoner's chaplain and a capitular in the London District (or Vicariate). Correspondence was usually conveyed by collegians travelling between England and Douai.

---

3. Rutter to Banister Douai, 25th February [1779][1]

Reverend Uncle,

If you are interested in my regard you will doubtless be a little surprised to hear that I am pitched upon to be Pedagogue to Esqr Clifton's son,[2] whom Mr [James] Willicey brought here some months ago. I am indebted for this honour to Mr [Gregory] Stapleton to whom he was recommended and whose kindness I can not sufficiently acknowledge.[3]

During the vacance I went with the young Esqr to Ghent where he has a good old aunt and 2 sisters. Here we stayed a week and during that time coached it about the town to all the public buildings and churches, some of which are very magnificent. We took Brussels in our way home where we met again with Mr Stapleton and Mr [Charles] Catrow, who had left us at Ghent to go to Louvain, where Mr Catrow is now Confessor in the place of Mr [John] Strickland.[4] We saw many curiosities at the Court, which, 'tis said, equals in many respects that at Versailles.

So much for my journey. But what is of much greater consequence is that I hope in time to be able by the bounty of Esqr Clifton to wipe off my College debt without being under the hard necessity of applying to my father. This you may be sure is a great satisfaction to me as doubtless it is to my Relations who I believe would not be in a condition to help me. The care, however, I am obliged to take of my young pupil is rather a hindrance to my studies and does not permit me to give all the attention I could wish to Divinity. For being now Sub-deacon and in the 2nd year of my Divinity I think myself almost at the end of my studies and ought therefore to apply myself more diligently to them. And having no capacity for the pulpit, I shall begin soon to prepare myself more immediately for the Mission and as you are experienced in it, besides teaching many years, I think nobody more proper to give me advice on that head. You will perhaps tell me to have recourse to Superiors. But, first, they have had no experience. Secondly, their advice is vague and general and consists in referring me to the Dictates[5] which ([with a better judgement]) seem not well calculated for the Mission and meaner capacities. I beg therefore that you will give me a short, easy plan adapted to my capacity so that I may know how to proceed, what to aim at, and by what means I may acquire at least what is essentially requisite and you will oblige your most obedient nephew. Hen. Rutter.

1. This can be dated to 1779 because Catrow left Douai in Nov 78.
2. Thomas Clifton (1728–1783) of Clifton, Westby and Lytham, married, firstly, Catherine Eyre, secondly, Anne Haggerston and, finally, in 1760, Lady Jane Bertie. He lived in some style at Lytham Hall, which he had rebuilt in 1764, and was known for the high standard of his stud and pack of hounds (to which Banister and Rutter always allude disparagingly). He supported a chaplain; John Talbot SJ (al. Mansell) was at Lytham 1743–1791; there was a congregation of 384 in 1767. Mansell's long tenure at Lytham was probably due to the fact that he was a first-class horseman. John Clifton (1764–1832), son and heir, was tutored privately at home [see No. 7] until he was fifteen, the point at which this letter was written. He was sent to the continent to finish his education under Rutter as his tutor and preceptor; he arrived at Douai College on 10 Jul 1778.
3. Willacy was master of Old Hall Green, Herts., a small school of twenty-five pupils for the under-twelves owned personally by Bishop James Talbot, Vicar Apostolic London District; Stapleton was Procurator at Douai.
4. Strickland, aged fifty-six, 'was eccentric in many things' and was being retired early.
5. Verbatim copies of lectures dictated in latin. On 9 September 1782 in a letter to an unidentified correspondent at Douai, Banister pointed out the disadvantages of printing Dictates as opposed to having every student copy them out; it would 'stifle or cramp future geniuses, put a bar to the study of improvement and make a dull sameness go on in the college . . . none but dullards can say that two hours spent in writing dictates per diem [is] time lost'. [WAA/XLVIII/110]

Note. The following two letters are badly torn at the margins. The incomplete texts are reproduced since the contents, which are of some interest, can be understood easily.

4a. Banister to Rutter Mowbreck, 9th May 1779[1]

My dear
I pray God that the charge, you give me on acco
Mr [James] Lawrenson may not puff you up with idea
& profit. I understand your pupil is not acri ingenio:
great knowledge and love of religion, of the firm,
grounds of catholick religion. Set before him the wic
and progress of the pretended reformation that he ma
detest it. It may be diverting to read and explain Wn
the missionary priests: some history of the reformation &
he will never be fond of reading, but an indifference to re
come to be bred in him several other ways. You will
an important service if you insinuate into him a ful
of one, true, holy, catholick religion, necessary to sa
In Bossuet's works in your library you will find "
between Bossuet and a Calvinist minister (I think D
about religion, in presence of a Lady & other persons
quality". See whether you can procure me that conference printed separately or with a few other opuscula. I dare say the volumes of Bossuet are to be bought separately too, to make up sets: so then you may procure me the volume in which you find the said conference.

Why do you lay by all thoughts of defending?[2] Do your best to speak plain, slow, concisely and sensibly. Endeavours will improve you, but none can do no good. Nor think your time lost, though you be not chosen to exhibit your talents. What need have I to give you plans of study, are you not at the fountain head? Mortify the obstacles to learning mentioned by Thomas a Kempis: ['If you avoid unnecesary talk and aimless visits, listening to news and gossip, you will find plenty of suitable time to spend in meditation on holy things'.][3] Pray do not lose your time in scruples, or fretting or repining, for they are incredible hindrances to all progress.

I desire to know Ralph Platt's dispositions as to a state of life, if you can procure me some information without much meddling? Also whether his hurt on his head was of much consequence? Also whether your brother at London corresponds with you? I remain most affectionately yours R.B.

Mr Melling will send you this from St. Omer. Desire Mr [William] Hull to say four Masses for my intention by August next; and tell him all his friends here are well, father, mother and sister.4

1. Sent under cover of another letter to Melling, Prefect at St. Omer College since Nov 1777; Lawrenson, a deacon, was sent home ill in February (taking N$^{o.}$ 3 with him).
   Robert Parsons SJ founded a college at St Omer in 1592 which remained under the control of the Society until its confiscation by the government at the expulsion of the order from France in 1762. It then became a French Royal College, i.e., it got a yearly pension from the French king; the Bishop of St Omer nominated the President; and it was to accept French pupils. The college was offered to the English secular clergy at Douai and, reluctantly, Henry Tichborne Blount, President of Douai accepted the presidency. Alban Butler succeeded Blount in 1766, and William Wilkinson was President from 1773 to 1787. The college gained a high reputation and was usually full; there were 114 pupils in 1786. [Ward *Dawn* I, 65.]
2. The public oral defence of a thesis given by selected students.
3. *The Imitation of Christ*, (Penguin Classics, 1952) Book 1, Ch 20.
4. Hull had gone to St Omer from Douai as a professor in Sep 1779.

4b. Banister to Rutter Mowbreck, 28th May [1780][1]

My dear Harry,

James Haydock is the bearer of this. You have probably
-pils enough, but I shall esteem it a great favo
the Prefect of Studies, whosoever he is,[2] will be p
at your request to recommend him to a careful Pe
Perhaps Harry Carter will be a very good one, I taugh
a little while at Fernyhalgh, and he was then a
tractable, ingenious boy. This newcomer will be
if I am not much mistaken, for low-figures, and re
high next S. Remigius. Four years Divinity are
in my judgement too much either for you or for any
nevertheless if your superiors at the end of
year destine you to teach, I know no remedy
patience and submission. I would have you preferr
way of conduct to all others, which shall be
likely to detain you the longest time in the Colle
one of my chief reasons is, because my proc

are very disagreeable to me and will be to you
you return. Therefore stay where you are and disch
the offices enjoined you as well as you can. I believe
temper is such that you can keep yourself
and easy, and give no offence to others. Mr John C
either sincerely, or in compliment to me, spoke l
of you the other day at Salwick.[3] God will dispo
his own good time of things and persons, that at you
-turn you shall not be mortified and shocked with
or hearing disagreeable things. Two or three y
I requested Mr [Joseph] Shepherd our Rector at Valladolid
eceive you into his house in quality of Master or
ct at the end of your Divinity. His regard to me
great, that he left the matter to my discretion.
efore if you are to be sent away next summer,
in 1781, let me know in good time that I may
you to Valladolid, if there be any want of you
e. Such a journey will do you no hurt, it may
for your great improvement, and the salary will
ble you to get something, that may do you good
soever you shall return. Mr Shepherd will for my
receive your own address to him very kindly, so if
see matters going so, that you are to be discharged,
not fail to write to him and offer yourself to serve
suppose that he cannot receive you, he
nevertheless return an obliging answer. The
ed you must put into the post for him, and if it be
ssary put it in a cover and direct it anew. I have
ed him to put his letter to me under a cover
on: let the postage be set to my account: desire
Stapleton to forward it to me. You neither sig-
ed to me when you was ordained priest, not that you was
but understanding it is so, I bless God who has crowned
desire and made you capable of daily approaching to his
ar. I desire you to say before next S. Remigius Six
sses to satisfy a perpetual annual obligation and have
acount of my education. Offer them for my Intention. If
many be inconvenient, ask Mr Davies to be so good as to say
three of them for me.[4] Assure the two Mr [Ralph & Richard]
Southworths of my love and constant remembrance of them.

I commend you to God and to the word of his grace and am your most affectionate friend and uncle R. Banister. I have received Bossuet.

1. This can be dated to 1780 since Haydock took it to Douai; he left Lancashire 29 May and witnessed the Gordon Riots when passing through London; he arrived at the college 18 June. James, Thomas and George Haydock all attended Banister's school in Mowbreck Hall; Banister had nominated James for the priesthood and was anxious about his welfare, hence his recommendation of another old pupil, Henry Carter.
2. Rowland Davies was Prefect of Studies and confessor at Douai; he had been a pupil of Handel and had played the organ at the coronation of George III.
3. Clifton returned to England because of ill health on 10 May 1779 accompanied by Procurator Stapleton.
4. Banister was confused about Rutter's ecclesiastical state. Rutter was a deacon and awaiting a dispensation from Rome to be ordained priest earlier than normal, so as to have the necessary status and authority as preceptor and be ready to move to St Omer whenever Clifton returned; he was not ordained until 18 Dec 1780; he left Douai next April.

5. Banister to Rutter — Mowbreck, 11th August 1780

My dear Harry,

I received your favour, dated 24th of July, the 7th of this month. I had heard, but I cannot recollect from whom, and some time since, even before my last to you, that you was chosen to be Tutor of John Clifton. As I believe the choice was made without any concurrence on your part, and much less on mine (for I have never been at the Hall, since I was settled here, but once, 4 years ago, when invited to a funeral) so I hope those who recommended you did it out of an honest persuasion, that it will be no detriment to you, and that you may be of service to him. The good education of a young gentleman of great fortune is certainly a matter of high importance: but the point of chiefest importance, viz. a sincere love of religion and the fear of God, is the most neglected. At least some modern tutors in our days have either overlooked that branch of education, or the soil on which they laboured was indocile and of a reprobate nature. I would not therefore wish you to make them models of your conduct over your pupil: let S. Fidelis of Sigmaringa and S. Vincent of Paul, who in their youth had the education of some children recommended to their care, be your patterns to follow.

I suppose you have already gained one chief point in this business, which is, you have insinuated yourself very far into the love and esteem of your Pupil, and as I hope that you acquired this without flattery, by your candour and sweetness, so will you preserve it by the same means. You cannot use this influence over him better than in imprinting on him a true sense of religion and of the fear of God: and to do this more effectually, endeavour to gain yourself a deep impression of them by some daily meditations. ['Every best gift and every perfect gift is from above, coming down from the Father of lights'.][1] Apply diligently to this Father of Lights for yourself and for your Pupil. Masters teach in vain, and catechists and preachers too, if God does not open the sense and heart to understand and love what is taught and preached. As your pupil has lost much inclination to study or [read] books, it will be easier to keep bad ones out of his hands. Locke's, Rousseau's, Bonnet's, Priestley's, Needham's, Berrington's, and universally all the tribe of modern idealists, metaphysicians and speculatists are to be avoided both by you and him.[2] If the late Prior of the English Carthusians[3] publishes his work Sur la Nature des Choses, it will be a tissue of ideas that never entered into any man's brains before his.

The gentleman under whose roof you are going to live, like the camaeleon, receives his colouring and species from the last book that he reads. He is very imperfect in theology, so do not apply to him for light therein: and he used to start out of the way propositions and maintain them as absurdly.[4] I do not think that your stay will be long at the place you are going because I apprehend your pupil looks upon all colleges as prisons and will invent some contrivance to obtain his enlargement. I must tell you what his Physician told me at his return from Douai College, viz. that whilst he was a boy at Salwick he could throw himself into a kind of convulsion whensoever he pleased: and the foresaid doctor, who is my neighbour, and where I often dine, suspected his sickness, that made him return, to be in some degree feigned. This I inform you of that you may better understand the genius and temper of your pupil, who was 16 years of age 25th of last January.

I do not think that you will be so independent as you suppose of the gentleman whose house you are to lodge in, for he was tutor to the father and will probably have a share in directing the son. You will find it a most irksome, tedious business to attend and teach a young gentleman but inexperience hides from you very happily future troubles. You will earn and merit superabundantly all that will be given to you: I wish you may have one half of what is given to a jockey. But real goods and trifles are seldom weighed with the same weights.

What can you read better than your Theological Dictate, your Epitome

Moralis, your Treatise de Ecclesia, your Decalogue &c. But how infinitely superior are your Dictates? They are a commentary on the holy scriptures and furnish you with abundant matter to instruct, direct, to defend and explain our holy faith. And as you will probably be soon promoted ad Presbytratu, 'tis a duty to learn the rubricks and to observe them exactly. When I see an old man inaccurate in ceremonies and rites, I am ready to excuse him, but when young ones, just come from the college, give themselves airs, and seem by their behaviour to slight accuracy and exactness in sacred rites, I cannot help conceiving an indignation against them. You may depend upon it, such are of a coxcomb-breed.

Besides your Dictates, the Conduite des Confesseurs and the Conduite des Ames will inform you of many necessary things: the author had great experience in the government of souls. Sacred history claims the first place; read it in the fountain itself, and if possible in Vitre's large folio, the chronology is marked in the margin, and in calce there are Lancelotti's most accurate, which being well read, digested and remembered, will exclude many long passages of Calmet's and such like dissertations. Ussher's and Lancelotti's arrangement of times is the best. You know chronology and geography are the eyes of history; it is groping in the dark without them. The black history of the reformation may be useful to your pupil, to give him an abhorrence of it. It is more proper for a mind like his than controversy and will effectually settle him in his faith. It converted the Duchess of York, first wife of James II.

Give the other side to James Haydock. I am sweet Hal most affectionately and most truly yours R.B.

1. James 1, 15.
2. Banister's antipathy to modern philosophy is discussed by P Doyle, 'Seminary Education: A Conservative 18th Century View', *NWCH* I (1969) 26–38.
3. Unidentified; possibly Joseph Williams (see N$^{o.}$ 14 n3).
4. William Wilkinson, President at St Omer, who had been preceptor to Clifton senior in the same way as Rutter now was to Clifton junior, except that whereas Rutter would be required to accompany his charge on the Grand Tour, Thomas Grimbalstone went as travelling-tutor to the father in 1746; he then became chaplain at Lytham Hall until 1751 and was now at Wigan. Wilkinson had been a professor at Douai teaching philosophy. In 1757 he gave a course on astronomy which was well abreast of current scientific thought, which was one reason why Banister thought little of him. [M Sharratt, 'Copernicanism at Douai', *Durham University Journal* vol. 67 (1974) 41f.]

6. Rutter to Banister — Douai, 6th February 1781

Dear Uncle

I received your kind answer and was glad to find you expressed yourself so freely and sincerely on the matter. I wish, however, your letter had descended a little more to particulars both with respect to pedagogue and pupil, as you may easily, I think, form an idea of our situation there. One of my greatest difficulties, in my opinion, will be how to keep him employed and out of idleness, especially as he is not fond of college plays. I therefore think riding will be very necessary for him and accordingly mentioned it to the father, but I fear to no purpose. I have reason to think the extent of his mind does not on all occasions answer that of his fortune. Last August I wrote to him to thank him for the honour he had done me and to settle with him concerning the pension. You told me, indeed, in your last that you did not suppose it would be above half of what is given to a jockey but I had the impudence and assurance to propose £50 p.a. without thinking the demand extravagant. The Esquire, however, was of a different way of thinking, startled at such a mighty sum and signified by Mr Grimbalstone that a less must suffice.

I was advised to leave the determination to his generosity and am now waiting to know its extent. Mr Stapleton signified to Mr Grimbalstone in his last that the best way, as he thought, would be for the Esquire to pay likewise for my clothing, washing &c. then fix what he thought proper merely for pocket money. I do not as yet know what Mr Clifton will say to it, nor what offers and conditions he will propose in his turn. Could you get me no sort of information from Mr [Robert] Wilson who, I dare say, could tell you what his salary was &c. when he lived at St Omer in the same capacity?[1]

I hear (is it true?) that young Clifton is somewhat changed for the worse by these two years of sport and idleness. To tell you the truth, dear Uncle, had I been guided by my own notions I should never have thought of undertaking the charge, being sensible how very unfit I am for it. I know nothing of high life, but that it is a state of slavery and should therefore have neglected the wise maxims of prudence whispered in my ears, for the peace and independence of a low and private life. I do not as yet, however, repent of my choice though I begin to doubt a little whether it was the best since your letter: quid tentare nocebit?

Supposing young Clifton does not stay above a year at St Omer I do not see what will hinder my return to Douai. It is slavery indeed to attend a young gentleman; but it is less so to be prefect where I am at present for that, I am told, will probably be the case if I stay. There I shall only have to take care of one, here of many. Mr Clifton does not send his son till Spring. In the interim I find myself perfectly happy: these are my ha[torn]ys in which I have nothing to disturb or disquiet me. [torn] employment is to approach to the holy altar and there to feast myself in that banquet of divine love. My wishes, my desires are crowned and I sing with Simeon: Nunc dimittis servum tuum.

But I must not omit telling you that Mr Platt is likewise to leave Douai next Spring in order to teach at Old Hall Green. He seems to enjoy a good share of Mr Blount's favour, who got him admittance there. He does not, however, lay aside his good intentions and is persuaded you would approve his measures if you knew the reasons of them.

Mr Wilkinson lately desired to know whether I would undertake to be confessor to the younger boys, but I answered him in the negative. Surely he must be reduced to great straits to apply to one so young and inexperienced as I am.

Would you, dear Uncle, have me carry many books over? If not I shall part with a few of those I have at present and trouble myself no more about buying others. I have 25 v of Sacy on the Scripture, 8 v of Lettres Critiques by Gauchat, Dic. des Heresies 3 v by Hermant, Vrais Merite, Meditations de Beuvlet, Stimulus Pastorum to pass over others. Are any of the above mentioned books worth carrying over? I must, however, have some good divine to supply the place of our dictates, which to my sorrow I have not completed, for as my breast has been but weak for these two years past I followed the custom of not writing them. What books of divinity would you recommend to me and I will procure them at any price.

James Haydock seems a solid, promising boy. Mr Stapleton is confined to his bed by the [torn] Great reformations expected from Mr [William] Gibson.[2] I am dear Uncle your [most] dutiful and affectionate nephew H.R.

1. Robert Wilson, nee Longstaffe, was tutor to Sir Piers Mostyn of Talacre, Flintshire, in the 1760s; they obviously got on well together for Wilson, now aged forty-five and missioner at Salwick Hall, enjoyed a life-annuity from Sir Piers if Banister is right (see No. 7).
2. William Gibson looms over these letters, firstly as President of Douai College and then as Vicar Apostolic Northern District, in which latter capacity he was

responsible for transplanting Douai to Ushaw in Co. Durham. Gibson was one of four priest-brothers: George (1726–78), missioner at Hexham; Richard (1739–1801) chaplain to Sir Walter Blount at Mawley Hall, Shropshire; and Matthew (1734–90) Vicar Apostolic Northern District. William (1738–1821) was not an academic (Banister taught him and found him lazy) so it was a surprise when he was appointed President of Douai College in Sep 1780 and installed in July 1781. Rutter's intimation of great reformations would not please Banister; indeed Gibson's modernisations led to resignations and pre-occupied the clergy in England as we shall see. Gibson was autocratic, had a rough manner and was given to blunt speaking, but, more pertinently, he was criticised on academic grounds. Firstly for introducing arithmetic, English and French into the syllabus. In September 1782 Banister wrote to an unnamed student at Douai: 'I often admire the conceit of some young men at the college, and of others too, that ought to have more penetration, in reading and recommending to be read, Spectators, Tatlers and such like books to learn fine English that they may become good preachers. Believe me, a spelling book is much fitter for several than a Spectator or Tatler. And whoever affects to speak fine English in harmonious periods will not be understood by far the greatest part in town or country. and to preach without being understood is beating the air'. [WAA/XLVIII/110]. French was undesirable because it would introduce students to the atheistic and deistic works of Voltaire, Rousseau, et al. Gibson was also attacked for his financial profligacy and 'execrable management' of the college, as John Barrow put it. Banister wrote an extended critique of Gibson in a letter to Thomas Eyre on 31 August 1799 which is reprinted in *UM* 24 174f.

---

7. Banister to Rutter — Mowbreck, 13th March 1781

My dear Harry,

I received yours dated 6 of last February in good time, but wish you had mentioned (unless you were enjoined the contrary by the bearer) the person who brought it over.

Mr Robert Wilson, when he was tutor or preceptor of Sir Piers at St Omer had annually 600 livres, i.e. 25 guineas, as his salary, and besides every other article of expence, clothes excepted. This he told me the other day. Sir Piers gives him now £40 sterling per annum, as I have heard, which is settled on him for life, but he attended on him several years. Undoubtedly your demand or expectation of 50 would startle the squire; I say not it is too much, especially if 50 are to find you with clothes, washing, barber, candles, fire and several other articles, but as you are advised to leave the matter to his generosity (what that is, or will be, I know not) so I suppose it will be the only way to come to a conclusion.

Master has a young man to teach him lessons of some kind, who was brought up with the Jesuits, till their suppression. But observe the difference between Alexander the Great and our petit squires: he honoured his master Aristotle as a father but young Master's master is ranked amongst servants and eats at the servant's table. Mr Wilson gave me the other day Master's character to this effect: "he is subtle, crafty, lying, pretending one thing and meaning another, one in whom a man can put no confidence etc." He is of Nimrod's order, of which S. Jerome never in his time knew any saints, but it is long since his time. I am entirely of opinion that in a month or little more he will be sick of some maladie inconnue at St Omer which will alarm you and make some write to his father to recall him with all speed. But I wish I may be mistaken in my opinion.

As to the duty of a pedagogue in the situation in which you are to be, one grand point of it is either to be always with him, or to be as certain and secure of his company as of your own self. You must be as a visible Guardian Angel; your conversation with him must be pleasing to engage him, serious to instruct him. You must instil a love of religion, generosity and humanity by proposing examples more than by precepts. But folly, as the Wiseman says, is found in the heart of a child, and the bewitching of vanity subverts the sense. How must these be eradicated? By gospel truths and examples. S. Ignatius often repeated to Xavier, whilst a young Professor of Logic, too full of worldly ideas "quid perdest hoc . . . patiatur?" I say you are to be always with him, even mediis noctibus; at least be certain that he neither goes out to another, nor that another comes to him. You are even to be present with the fencing, dancing, writing, designing, French etc. masters. One or other of these will otherwise, if you be out of their sight or hearing, tell Master of some charming Belle, and offer his service to procure her for him. And do you think a young heir of 17 or 18 years of age, having often ranged and romped with maids and servants below stairs, being likewise soft, full of excellent juices and meats, can reject an offer of that sort? Will he not rather seek opportunities unless carefully watched and dexterously diverted from such thoughts? Mr Wilson never let Sir Piers go out of his sight, and insisted on that as a condition when he took the care of him. But, my dear Hal, as I believe you have Jesus your true friend, so I hope he will make all things succeed in your hands, as God made all things go well which Joseph undertook in Pottiphor's house or in the prison. Mr Wilson and I are both of opinion that young

Master's father could do nothing better than procure for his son a proper partner to marry.

To be General Prefect where you are demands care and vigilance to hinder ill weeds from growing and rankling; for your house is as a garden, if careful hands are not ready to watch and pull up thorns, briars and bad herbs (zizania), the good ones will soon be spoiled.

I wonder how you got so many books, I think Gonet is the worst; truck away the lumber for Estius in Sententias in 2 vols. folio. Then you may buy Coleti in 5 vols. octavo to serve you for Moral Divinity, or some other of like merit. You may (when you go a bookaneering) perhaps meet with Cornelius a Lapide in Ecclesiasticus or in Evangalia; they will be worth your buying for they contain abundant matter for instruction etc. You have Biblia Sacra, I wish it were by Vitre with the chronological dissertations of Lancelotti at the end. That is a book I want above all. The following is an excellent book, but scarce. Analyse de L'Evangile selon l'ordre historique de la concord avec des dissertations sur le Lieux difficiles. Par le R.P[illeg.], Pretre de l'Oratoire, 1695. Also his Analyse des Epitres de S. Paul et des Epitres canoniques avec des dissertations sur les Lieux difficiles, 1693. I want a good latin edition of S. Jo. Clemacus, item of the Practum Spirituale; the old one is by Michael Isseltius Colonia 1685. Rosweyde has given a good collection of the Fathers of the Desert, it is worth your buying if you delight in such conversation.

The following I should be very glad of. Les Vies de Saint Peres des Desert et des quelques Saintes ecrites par des Peres de l'eglise et autres antiens ecclesiastiques traduites en Francois par Monsieur Armand D'Andilly, Nouvelle Edition 3 tomes Paris 1668. In which last is the whole Scale of S. Clemacus translated into French. Procure for me Histoire de Croisades par Pere Louis Maimbourg 4 tomes 1685. Item Histoire de l'Heresie de Iconolistes et de la translation de l'Empire aux Francois, 2 tomes par le Pere Louis Maimbourg 1675. If you can find these editions they may come in cheap and are probably the best and most genuine. There are other works of Maimbourg I should covet but I will mention no more at present.

Find if possible the following: Causes celebres et Interessantes avec les jugemens, qui les ont desidees. Reconcillies par M. Gayot de Piteval Advocat du Parlement de Paris 1735. In the fifth tome you will find Histoire de Francois Harronard disavoue par son Pere et sa Mere. Item Histoire de la Marquise de Gange etc. To supply the place of a voluminous Morcen you may buy Nouvonau Dictionaire Historique Portaatif par un Societe de Gens des Lettres in 4 volumes Amsterdam 1769, though I believe the authors are partial to Jansenists.

I received January 9th 1776 two guineas from Mr Ralph Watt[1] to be sent to Mr Ralph Platt, which I remitted February 18th 1776, idem desired Mr Stapleton to set them to my Debitor and place them to Mr Platt's Creditor. Item I received from Mr Watt June 24 1777 two guineas for Mr Ralph Platt which I sent September 12 1777 in a letter to the said Mr Ralph Platt, idem I told him to get them set down on his Creditor. Be sure to see whether things were, as I suppose they are, yet done or not, and see whether Mr Platt acknowledges the receipt. If Mr Stapleton finds me in debt to the College-book by my drawing too much, be sure to let me know that I may send the balance.

Be so good as to say eight intentions for me between this and next August. In your next let me know how many of the following boys at Alma Mater or elsewhere are in via ad ordines sacros. James Gage, James Gentil, James Akers, Mr Leigh, Joseph Hodson, Robert Taffe, John Earle, John Gregg, Matthew Sharp, John Rayment, John Hawke, Peter Leigh, James Howard (vere Quin) N Hart.

Bringing books over and down to Lancashire is very expensive. If your gettings or savings of money will allow it buy half a dozen silver forks and as many silver spoons. Buy a neat painting of our Blessed Lady holding our Saviour in her arms, and some others of like taste and beauty.

It is certain some one must preside over the Squire, and if they continue to desire you I would not be understood to deter you. But see that this and my last letter never fall into hands where it should not. Give the bottom to James Haydock. I remain ever yours R.B.

1. Unidentified; not a priest.

---

8. Rutter to Banister — Douai, 2nd April [1781][1]

Dear Uncle,

Your kind letter, which I received on 22nd of last month, gave me entire satisfaction in every particular. I intended indeed not to have answered it till my establishment at St Omer, but as I know not when that will take place, I could not let slip the present opportunity without sending you a few lines by Dicky Rimmer who has been for some time past in a bad state of health. As his departure was very sudden I could not procure all the books mentioned in your last. I have only sent Gayot de Piteval in 23 volumes and, though the edition be not that mentioned by you, it is,

I believe, more complete at least and far preferable to any French edition. I could have sent you, moreover, the two first volumes des Croisades by Maimbourg, but thought it better to stay till I could get them entire, as likewise his History of Arianism and Lutheranism, had I known they would be acceptable. The above-mentioned work cost 44 livres, which I fear you will think too much. Upon examination I find that you are still creditor about 5 livres, and whatever money will be requisite to pay for other books I will readily supply. Mr Platt received in 1776 and 77 2 guineas and there is no doubt but it must have been from you.

Out of the 25 mentioned by you, the following 9 succeed: Mr Earle, Jos. Hodson, [John] Wright, my school-fellows, who are now priests; Francis Leigh, [William] Poole, [Alexander] Matsura, Gregg, Sharp and, perhaps, Quinn.[2] Upon computation I find that not a third part attain the end for which they came. This surely argues a defect either in those who choose or in others. But fine regulations are soon expected.

I have received a letter from the Squire and wonder his son is not yet arrived. He allows me 20 guineas p.a. and finds me with everything. I am much pressed for time and am your most dutiful and obliged Nephew, H. Rutter

1. Dated to 1781 because Richard Rimmer left the college on 3 Apr 1781.
2. James Akers and Raymond [Benedict] Rayment in Banister's list were also ordained, the former in Lisbon.

9. Banister to Rutter — Mowbreck, 27th April 1781

My dear Hal,

The bearer of this, Mr Lawrenson, conducts to you Mr Clifton junior. I have your last sweet letter, brought by Mr Rimmer, but he has given me no account of the books, yet I will hope they are safe somewhere in reserve for me. I have money to receive at London in August if remitting it then will suffice.

I have a long history of Arianism, so need not Maimbourg's. He is, I apprehend, too severe upon Charles V in his History of Lutheranism, but you may procure it for me. Item, Histoire de la decadence de l'Empire apres Charlemagne par Louis Maimbourg 1686. When you get all the tomes of the Croisades, read them, for they are peculiarly entertaining. Take down on paper the authorities and resources he refers to in his margin, you may probably find them in St. Omer Library. If you can become master of the subject, you shall offer it in English, not translated throughout (for he is too censorious upon our English crossbearers) but modelled and moulded in a new form, as Mr Manning has done by the History of the Iconoclasts.[1]

Ven. Bede in his History of the Saxons, about the beginning, remarks of us English that we are fond of changes and always changing. The humour prevails in every class and society of men of this veering-about nation. This accounts for the fine regulations you hinted. They will be fine whilst new, a little age will make them be valued like old tinsel.

I am glad my last letter gave you satisfaction. If you keep it, seal it again with care that no one may pry into it. Be careful of your health and set out your breast that your lungs may suffer no compression, which is very hurtful. Remember me in mementoes. I am ever yours truly, R. Banister.

1. Robert Manning (d. 1730) author of several works of controversy. Kirk 157; Gillow IV 456 item 9. Banister in No. 10 refers to item 6.

10. Banister to Rutter — Mowbreck, 24th August 1781

My dear Sir,

Your letter came near 20 days after its date, 'tis probable it might lie in the post office at London for some days.

You are therefore in an employment which would be far above my ability or talent, but I believe God has given you a talent for it, because he has placed you in it. Your great object is to form a good man. The first and chief means, then, which you have is to humble your soul exceedingly before God and to beseech him to make the youth of a docile mind and to give him his fear. The next means is your longanimity and soft insinuations and persuasions. A third means is to remove far away all occasions or opportunities of danger and sin. You are therefore to be with him at all exercises, and with all his masters whensoever he walks out, or rides, or visits &c.

I believe you are not able to study much, for which reason totally decline the office of confessarius in the house. It would hinder your necessary attendance to the charge you have undertaken; you would often be forced to leave him in his own hands, to suffer him to seek company which might be dangerous and to undo in an instant what you are daily labouring to do. However, your prudence must direct you how to decline Mr Wilkinson's solicitations; you may do it softly yet firmly; you are under no tie of obedience in this point, yet your refusal may be in the way of entreating. The office you have is of such importance that if all your attention is given to it, 'tis not too much. Perhaps one great reason why so many pupils have become bad men is the supineness and inattention of their preceptors, who frequently are pursuing their own amusements or business or connections, whilst they ought to attend only to the education and conduct of their pupils. S. Francis of Sales takes notice that some are for reforming the exterior part in the very beginning, but he is for reforming the heart which is as the root from whence springs the branches and leaves of all our outward actions.

You will not therefore be offended at some vulgar phrases by which he expresses his dislike of things. If you can but make religion fasten hold of his heart and influence him, you will gain an important point. [But a fascination with worthless thoughts subverts judgement], too frequently and in too many. As for riding out with him at your own cost or expense, it appears to me a clear case that you are not to do it but at his father's charge only. You are both preceptor and guardian; you are to be with him to guard his frail youth from corporal and, above all, from spiritual injuries.

In writing an account to Lytham say what good you can without flourishes or exaggeration, and complain not without good consideration and very softly. The father, I understand, is very firm but is under difficulties to please the mother; 'tis mothers who frequently ruin their children. When he was at home this last year he had a boy, or a boyish young fellow, to teach him something, the Lord knows what, to read perhaps and write. You desire to know my thoughts of your plan or your regulation of the day; where nothing more perfect can be followed it must serve. I am sorry that Geography does not please his taste, and much more of a want of generosity.

The man you esteem most both for his virtue and experience is, I hope, greatly improved and deserving of your esteem; but open not your heart too soon to any man. S. Vincent of Paul had a friend whom he valued much but in the end found him very unworthy of his esteem and so totally broke off all connection with him. If so wise a man was overseen, how much more a young one like you. Nevertheless be sure to profit by his good advice and continue to esteem him as long as he deserves it. You may let me know what topic he dwells on from time to time, or chiefly.

I wish you had Mr Manning's England's Conversion and Reformation Compared, that your pupil might learn to love one and hate the other, or some such book in the historical way. Mr Rimmer (who was here a week) left the 22 vols. of Piteval with Mr Bolton and they are there still. I expect a letter from him every day, to inform me both of them and of les Vies des SS. PP. I wish for the folio edition of Vitre. And, although you expect to have money enough at the end of the year, and so I need not remit any to you, yet, my sweet Hal, you may want it when you come over to stay and I shall hold myself accountable to you for it. Therefore 44 liv. for Piteval; 15 liv. for les Vies de SS. PP.; 24 liv. for Vitre in folio; which comes to 73 livres; let it be set down in your Memorandum book.

Your brother John is dying of a consumption. I went to see him the 24 of July and stayed all night at Ormskirk; he then kept his bed except when he rose to have it made. He wears away by spitting; at present he takes a little whey for his nourishment. I saw very small hopes of recovery when I was there and now there can be none. Your mother, too, was very much out of health when I was there but is well again, as I hear, for which I bless God with my whole heart. I gave her half a guinea and charged her to let none know of it, but at the same time I thought it should be your gift too in the following manner. I have ten intentions on account of that half guinea; be pleased therefore to say them in 5 or 6 weeks. I need not name the ten different persons for whom you are to celebrate, you may offer them in the same order as they are in my paper.

Your brother Richard went home this morning; he had been here about 3 weeks to bathe in the salt flood for an ulcer in his breast which is now nearly healed. Your cousin Robert Hodskinson went 6 years ago to Jamaica; we have all reason to fear he is dead, so my sister Helen, his mother, who sends her love to you, begs of you to celebrate for him. She also desires you to go to the Discalced Carmelites (you have a house in town[1]) and get her name enrolled in the Confraternity of the Scapular; also to ask whether her ordinary confessarius may not change the obligation of fasting on one meal, on church-fasting days (which she cannot do, although she abstains from flesh, and on Wednesdays too, by the prescription of the rules of the scapular) into another good work. The next time you write mention you receiving of this.

What are the changes at Alma Mater?[2] I wish I could hear of a change from great dissipation and expensiveness to fervent studies, much retirement and the learning to bear a denial. I recollect nothing more to write at present but that I am and shall always be your most affectionate Uncle and Servant, R.B.

1. Not an English house; it was at Lierre.
2. Or sometimes Alma: Douai College.

11. Banister to Rutter Mowbreck, 2nd November 1781

My dear Harry,

I received your last, dated 13th, on the 20th, and was surprised at its coming so soon by a private hand, whom you do not name.

I cannot yet learn how long Master is to stay; it is probable that all such matters are as yet undetermined. I would have you attend him wheresoever he goes if it be at your option, and Mr Wilson is of the same advice. Do you imagine that several tutors or preceptors of young gentlemen, whom I could name, had all those qualifications which you specify: "perfectly acquainted with high life and the world, an agreeable and entertaining companion, well stocked with patience and much esteemed and respected by others?" Such men are not easily found, and fewer such are to be prevailed on to accept it with its burden. S. Vincent of Paul and S. Fidelis Sigmaringa, who had not the science of high life but of the Saints, were infinitely better qualified to be preceptors than men high made. Wherefore, taking them for your patterns, oppose his abuse and cultivate an invincible meekness. Have an unwearied patience, for patience hath a perfect work. Negotiate your affairs with our Lord in prayer, for he has all hearts in his hand.

I own the insensibility he shews about religion affects me grievously, for it is now exceeding common in almost all ranks, and especially in people of fortune, so that it seems by how much the more plentifully they enjoy the gifts of fortune, by so much the more hard and insensible they are in relation to God and to their eternal welfare. But this bad symptom is so far from being a reason why he should be confided to a man who perfectly knows high life and the world that, on the contrary, he ought to be kept out of it as much as possible. And you must use the best and most prudent means which our Lord will, I hope, put into your mind, to inspire him with a fear of God and of his dreadful judgements. One might say to him: if your having no fear of hell or of a bad death were the best means to escape both, then I would advise you not to fear them, nor ever to think of them, but 'tis certain that living without fear of them is the sure way to incur them, and therefore we ought always to fear them, and the fear of them will keep us from sin and consequently from those horrible misfortunes, a bad death and eternal torments. It would be proper to read and explain to him the history of the rich man and Lazarus, Luke 16. 'Tis the word of God which converts souls and which penetrates to the division of soul and spirit and is keener than a two-edged sword.

If his father has not given you an absolute authority over him, he ought to do it. Item, if all his money does not come through your hands, it ought to do. If these two points are not in your power, I must own your situation is not proper, either for him or for yourself. If you cannot represent, in a proper manner, the necessity of having such authority, to the father, desire Mr Gregory Stapleton to do it for you. He was [the] one who engaged you to undertake this office, as I understand, and therefore will, I hope, procure you the necessary powers to execute it. Again I entreat you to bear everything for the love of our Lord; pride does not overcome pride, but humility can. So meekness conquers wrath, patience long-suffering, piety irreligion, charity rancour and spite.

When you go to Paris you will find Maimbourg's Croisades, so defer your search for a while. That new author you mention I know nothing of, so I will not have him.[1] By all means secure me Vitre.

I think it is the fittest way for me to put Douai College quite out of my mind. If under that word politeness they understand one of the eight beatitudes, or any other virtue which the Gospel recommends, then it cannot be too often inculcated in dire circumstances. Although he who should undertake to harangue his people only about faith, which the Gospel undoubtedly requires as a foundation for all good, and make little or no mention of other Gospel virtues, would be but a poor preacher. But if by the word politeness they understand, as the rest of the world commonly does, nothing but an external shewy behaviour, it is a very empty, senseless accomplishment. All great masters of Spirit with St. Francis of Sales begin with reforming the interior not the outside. Let the mind be instructed in solid gospel truths and principles; let the heart learn Christian charity, meekness, mildness, self-denial and a supporting of others' defects and frailties, and then the outside, the leaves and the bark, will participate of the root and shew forth its nature and excellence. When empty accomplishments are recommended and inculcated in youth, they readily conceive that all consists in them, and what an education will that, think you, be? Politeness is established by law in China, the people are most ceremonious and polite, in so much that the omission of ceremony is a greater crime than exposing a child to be devoured or drowned. But what do they cloak under their ceremony and polite behaviour? The most insidious malice, the craftiest frauds and most odious vices, inimical to society. And are not our people in the world much better? Are they not perfect strangers to probity, candour, self-denial, supporting one another &c. But of this enough. Please to write what follows to Monsieur Blacoe at Douai College:

> Dear Robert
> My Uncle Mr Banister has desired me to write to you [torn] you know, they have to-day received your letter from Douai and are overjoyed to hear of your safe arrival. Your father and mother and family are all very well as you left them, but your mother has been in great sorrow for your going. So in your next at Christmas say something to comfort her; let her know how well you like the college and that you want for nothing. Mr Banister, my Uncle, desires you to have a good heart and to think no lesson hard, for then you will learn better and faster. And you must remember that a city is not built in a day, and so you cannot be a scholar but with time and patience.

To this you may add your own conclusion. 'Tis my neighbour's son, come with Mr John Gillow.[2]

Your sister Ann lives with her Aunt Dorothy at Preston. I believe all are well at Westhead at present. You will write again to me and believe me your most affectionate uncle R. Banister.

1. In fact many of the works Banister asks Rutter to get for him are of comparatively recent date.
2. Robert Blacoe's father was a tenant-farmer on the Mowbreck Hall and Westby Hall estates; John Gillow's parents lived at Westby.

12. Rutter to Banister — St. Omer, 4th January 1782.

Dear Sir

I take the opportunity of sending this as far as London by Mr [William] Fryer from Valladolid who, with two others, is going on the mission. I intended indeed to have sent it before by one Mr [Gabriel] Bate, who had likewise undertaken to carry your Vitre which, however, he found too cumbersome and sent it back from Dunkirk.[1]

Yours of the 2nd of November came to hand in good time, in which your advice is to continue in the station I am in with patience and perseverance. I will therefore for the present endeavour to make myself easy and content under its cares, which certainly are none of the lightest, but their weight would be much diminished were I persuaded they would be of any benefit to the young man under my care. For such are his dispositions that I have great reason to fear that all I can do or say will be lost on his stubborn mind, which is so callous and hardened that the more I try to inspire him with sentiments of religion, the more he seems to turn a deaf ear to them. Hence when I talk to him on serious things, he will burst into a great laugh, speak with contempt on everything and tell me that the more I inculcate such nonsense, the more he will be averse to it, adding sometimes that if he has a mind to go to the d–l it shall not be in my power to hinder him. Now, how can I be of assistance to such a one unless by praying for him, for persuasion and exhortation seem to do more harm than good.

The two points you mentioned, however important in themselves, seem not to be so with respect to him. The father, I imagine, has given me an absolute authority, but to what purpose if the son will not submit to it. Again, how easy it is for a young gentleman of his fortune to procure money by running into debt, &c? Add to this that the contemptible idea he has of me, lessens me very much in his eyes and makes him regard everything coming from me as the effect of ignorance, prejudice and a low, contracted college education. The consequence is plain, my company and conversation cannot be very acceptable to him, he thinks himself more fit to give than to take advice from me and I have less authority over him than another person would have in the same situation. The fondness he shows me sometimes extends, I'm sure, no farther than as he finds me indulgent to his will and pleasure, and therefore were I to attend him elsewhere it could not be with the least hope of doing him service or keeping him under proper subjection. If, then, he is to make any considerable stay at Paris the best way I think both for him and me will be to decline accepting any offer that way, but I hope the father will only send him to have a short view of it, in which case I should have no objection to bear him company.

I cannot say much of his improvement under me during these eight months, on the contrary, his behaviour is certainly worse than it was at his first arrival, especially since we have another young gentleman amongst us on the same footing as himself. In the next letter I write to the father I will begin to acquaint him how matters stand, but this will not be till I am favoured with your thoughts on my situation as here described.

I heartily join you in your good wishes for Alma and hope the solid and essential part of the old plan will not be changed for the little recommenditory arts of the graces. I have not, however, been able as yet to tell how far the latter deserve my attention and wish I could settle my notions on this head. Politeness, 'tis said, makes virtue amiable, sets her off to the greatest advantage and, by engaging the senses, easily puts us in possession of the heart. Whereas without it everything is rough, disagreeable and disgusting to the last degree. What quality therefore more necessary for Society? On the other side, the idea of a good Christian seems to exclude that of a social, agreeable and pleasing companion. For how can he who is disgusted with the world, who loathes its pleasures and pastimes, is fond of solitude, and whose conversation is in heaven, I say how can he laugh and be merry with others, enter into their little concerns and interest himself in their foolish and [torn]ant discourse, &c?

Joseph Berington's book is translated and published at Paris; they accuse him [torn] his religion &c.[2] I recommend myself to your good prayers, wish you all that is good and am with all respect yours, H.R.

1. Fryer was Vice President of the English College, Valladolid, on a visit to Paris and London. He did not stay in England but returned to his college as President in June 1782. Bate was a lay student in Philosophy at Douai.
2. Joseph Berington (1743–1827) a distinguished priest-scholar and author; a liberal and cisalpine. He was Professor of Philosophy at Douai until 1771 when he was removed for propagating progressive ideas. Banister and Rutter attack him throughout these letters. Rutter refers to *The State and Behaviour of English Catholics from the Reformation to the year 1780* (1780; 2nd & rev. ed. 1781), parts of which were censured by the bishops. Gillow I 189; Milburn 10–12.

13. Banister to Rutter — Mowbreck, 25th January 1782.

My dear Hal,

I received on the 21st yours dated the 4th. The reading filled me with grief, both for you and your pupil. Yet I am more grieved for him than for you because the dispositions of his mind and heart seem to be precipitating him to ruin. But your sufferings, though I condole with you, yet put me in no fear for your soul, but rather make me confide that, by the grace of God, they will be an instruction to you and a matter of merit. As to his despising and ridiculing you, 'tis not, in my opinion because he undervalues you personally in particular, but he hates books, teachers, instructors, monitors &c. Idum totum genus [He is one of a kind]. You therefore seem to me to be under an erroneous opinion when you imagine that another tutor or instructor would have more authority over him than you have. Give him one for his preceptor who has power to deprive him of his fortune, the basis and foundation of all his present hopes and of all his future worldly treasures and glories, and then you should see him tractable and submissive. But where must such a preceptor be found?

You say he sometimes shows a fondness for you but you are sure that 'tis only whilst he finds you indulgent to his will and pleasure. And are not many, very many children of the same behaviour to their own parents? Is it not highly probable that he had the same at home? The idol of all who are born to wealth and worldly glory is their own will; everything and everyone that indulges and humours it is agreeable. Now, though we have reason to fear that his dispositions being so bad he will become eminently vicious, yet there is one thought which gives me hope of something better [and nearer salvation].

For I perfectly well remember his father at Douai College. He came thither about the age of 14, after hunting, sporting, without control (for he lost his father at the age of 7 or 8 or sooner) indulged, caressed &c., hating schools and books and studies. The Prefect went almost every morning to call him up; he lost his breakfast therefore, was compelled to steal it or send out for it or get a friend to bring it from the Refectory (for it was necessary to be dexterous to get one). As he had money, as often as he pleased, two or three often hung on him. They nick-named him Justice Brude hall, and Broody oftener, to intimate his frowning, huffing, passionate behaviour. He was very fond of hand-ball, but he could not endure to be overcome. He had every day a second portion at dinner, but mumped it up by himself, seldom invited any one to partake. Mr Wilkinson, your present Principal, was his pedagogue, but I dare say he made very little of him. After a stay of 2 or 3 years he left the college nearly as he came, and was conducted to Paris by his Preceptor. I have heard that formerly he would fly out into great rage and passion on the hunting ground if men or dogs did not perform according to his mind. But at present he is a great deal more calm, although the last year, if I mistake not, he lashed his own son with his whip for making some wrong evolution in hunting. Now had you been his tutor at Douai College 'tis likely you would have foreboded nothing but ill of him, yet, thanks be to God, he is at present (as those assure me who know and converse with him often, for I never do) a very sensible man, loves and respects religion, hates all drunkenness and profaneness, never speaks ill of the absent, and cannot endure to hear any ridicule or satire upon the absent, has kept the same priest in his house near 40 years, and has a well ordered family. In fine, it were to be wished that all our Catholics of fortune would tread in his footsteps and follow his example. Do not therefore, my dear Hal, entirely despair of the youth whose education you have undertaken. You sow your seed now in tears, but God can make you reap with joy.

I am not against you opening the matter softly to his father, provided you can gain thereby a word or two from him to his son to make him more tractable and more willing to learn. But, believe me, his father has not an entire, independent and uncontrolled authority, effectively I mean, although he has it radically. Do but consider how much wives, especially of high birth, expect to be humoured and to have their own will; and if they cannot obtain this directly, will at least extort it indirectly by frowns, fits, teasing, fretting &c. A certain person, who is often there, has signified to me that this is the case and that the father, whose intentions and designs are the best, is notwithstanding in great difficulty to execute them. As to your going with him to Paris, say nothing of that as yet, let time show what is to be your pupil's next situation. And you need not fear that you will be blamed for his making so little progress.

And it is wrong to say I could spend my time and labour upon him more willingly if I knew it would be beneficial to him. For did not our Lord preach to the obstinate, blind Jews three whole years, although he certainly foresaw that his preaching would be not only unprofitable to them but would even, through their malice, become their ruin. Read Rodriguez Part 3, Treatise 1st, chap. 18, page 96.[1] However, as he shows a dislike to pious or grave subjects, I would not affect to speak of them. 'Tis said of the Earl of Rochester, a profane debauchee in the time of Charles II, riding out one day met an old woman and asked her the way to hell. She answered: by Rochester, which pricked the nobleman to the quick. But I fear the monsters of our days believe no hell nor future torments nor future accounts.

I understood long ago that your pupil was allowed the liberty of choosing his preceptor and that he made choice of you. Suppose, then, that on a proper occasion you remind him that he oftentimes scorns you and shows a great contempt of you, and that 'tis likely he is tired of you and would be glad of another, and so, if it is agreeable to him, you will join him in writing to his father to appoint another. For my part I am of opinion that he will deny that he either scorns or contemns you and that, as to preceptors, all will be alike to him because all of them, if they do their duty, must keep a constant eye upon him and move him to some study and application.

In my last I advised you to apply to Mr Gregory Stapleton, but you take no notice of it in your last. I suppose you cannot make the Principal your confidant and it is not convenient to trust many or any. 'Tis a country saying; the least said is soonest mended.

Be pleased to say six Masses for my intention by the end of April. Your brother Thomas was here in Christmas and is very well. I hope this will find you so too. I pray my good Jesus to give you longanimity: ['Patience is necessary that you may inherit the promises']. I remain yours most affectionately R.B.

1. A. Rodriguez SJ, *The Practice of Christian and Religious Perfection* (1609), an immediately popular manual, translated into English in 1612 and again in 1697; reprinted frequently until 1846.

14. Rutter to Banister St. Omer, 22nd April 1782.

My dear Uncle,

I received your favour about two months ago and beg pardon for not answering it before this.

Though I do not entirely despair of the young man under me, yet I am far from thinking he will ever resemble his father. As he is young, giddy and inconstant, I cannot pretend to ascertain at present his real character which is not formed but appearances are much against him. So they were, you say, against his father, but, in my opinion, the nature of Abingdon and Clifton is here blended together. You know Lord Abingdon's history and character.[1]

I easily believe what you say concerning the limited authority the father has over his son, though I am pretty sure it is greater, effectively not only radically, than all the rest put together have. Perfectly indifferent to all others, he fears him alone. I dare not however say much to him, as that would set them at a greater distance than they are already. In my last letter indeed I just mentioned that his aversion to study was as great as ever and that the authority of a tutor was not sufficient always for young men of his age and condition. And though I am persuaded another would be more proper than I am, yet I am determined at present to follow your advice and say no more on that head. Had I not been guided by you, I believe I should before this have given up my charge, as a very fine opportunity occurred of retreating genteely. The case was this.

Mr [George] Witham, either desirous of being Vice President, or at least thinking the priests were disregarded (for 3 of the council are seculars) endeavoured to remove Mr Mumford from his place. On the other hand, the seculars, knowing this, get him away, and accordingly jointly insisted on it as necessary for the good of the college. George therefore is to go in a month or two's time and they are very pressing that I should succeed to his place.[2] Fine things are promised me: I may have the choice of my school, 600 livres a year, every reasonable gratification, nay, I believe, even a place in the Council. Mr Wilkinson would undertake to disengage me from my present charge and settle matters with Esq. Clifton. All this, added to my own inclinations make me seriously think what to do. However I told them not to depend on me, being not yet resolved to change my place. In case I do, I am half inclined to try the Mission, which perhaps would not be more difficult now than some years hence.

I made use of this occasion to convince the young Esquire that it was not through necessity that I stayed with him but only that I might not irritate his father who would be displeased with him to the last degree in case of a separation. He accordingly promised to be more tractable and to change his behaviour, but words cost nothing. Upon the whole I think it best to stay where I am; one year is now over and two only remain. Disagreeable they certainly will be, not only on account of what I have already mentioned to you, but likewise from the want of money. Mr Clifton instead of advancing money into some banker's hands to be drawn for as occasion requires, has forced me hitherto to borrow it from Mr Mumford or others, who do not always choose to lend it. You may easily conceive that I am not a little embarrassed on this account, especially as the allowance he gives is but small. I have endeavoured indeed in several letters to represent the case to him, but to no purpose. I hope Mr Stapleton will be more successful, for he is going over shortly. You told me to apply to him and I am of your opinion that he is the most proper person, for he is acquainted with the family and would do anything for me that lies in his power. But what can be done? He may indeed set the father right in money affairs, but setting the son right is the point. If you see him you can talk over matters together, for he knows all the secret and has, I believe, a great regard for you.

I understand you are no great favourite at Lytham, nor do I think you desirous of being one. The squire was saying today at dinner that he saw you once at Salwick but that he left your company abruptly before dinner was half over. His story altogether appeared so false that I could willingly have lashed the coxcomb on the spot.

Some time ago I made an excursion as far as Ostend. My first intention was only to go see cousin [James] Finch who had pressed me very much to pay him a visit before his order should be abolished. He and the Prior were exceedingly kind and seemed very happy and content in their calm retirement. We do not hear of any success the Pope has had at Vienna, so that 'tis still doubtful whether the suppression of Religious Orders will not take place in the Low Countries. If it does, Fr. Bruno proposes to become a fellow-labourer in the vineyard.[3]

As I despair of sending your book by a private hand, I think the best way will be to venture it with 50 or 60 of my best books by sea from Dunkirk to London, from whence they may easily be conveyed to you. If you approve of this scheme I will let you know in my next what bookseller to apply to in London for them. I have said the 6 Masses you desired and am ready to do the same again wh[en you wi]ll think proper.

You are right when you imagine that I have little to do with our Principal. He keeps his distance and I am [determined] not to make any advances. Of late indeed he has smiled on me a little but I take no notice of it, well understanding his designs. I am more inclined to follow Mr [Francis] Hind[4], whom I take to be no bad judge of men and things. In a former letter you did not seem to approve my choice, but why not? Indeed his success in life does not speak much in his favour, but perhaps age and experience have made him wise. I have observed that he has not any favourite topic of conversation; he talks of this, that and every thing indifferently and tells a story admirably. He may perhaps carry his snug principles too far, but you know him better than I do.

You see dear Uncle how freely I write to you; 'tis to you only I talk without reserve, being fully convinced of your kindness and love for me. I recommend myself to your prayers and am your dutiful and loving nephew, H.R.

P.S. This letter has been ready some time ago, but the person I designed to have sent it by, did not go. I kept it therefore for Mr Witham or Stapleton who go together. I have prevailed on the former to carry your book. Clifton seems resolved to leave the college this summer. Commissaries have been examining the English Carthusians' effects. The English nunneries are not to be suppressed, but many others are already.

1. Lord Willoughby Bertie, 4th Earl of Abingdon, Clifton's cousin: 'A singular young man, not quite devoid of parts but rough and wrongheaded, extremely underbred but warmly honest' [Walpole, *Journal* Sep 1777]. Lord Charlemont said he was 'a man of genius but eccentric and irregular almost to madness' [GEC I 48 n (b)].
2. Witham was teaching at St Omer but, having been forced out, went as chaplain to the Stapleton family in Yorkshire. Mumford is unidentified.

3. Pope Pius VI (elected 1775, d. 1799) went to Vienna in March 1782 to confer with Emperor Joseph II about the latter's Gallican policy and suppression of innumerable monasteries. The conference was inconclusive and, inter alia, the Charterhouse of Sheen Anglorum at Nieuport, Flanders, with a community of six choir monks, was suppressed by the Emperor in 1783. The last Prior of the English Province was Joseph (Francis) Williams who died at Little Malvern Court in 1797; James (Bruno) Finch (1748–1821) was the last surviving member of the province. [Bellenger (1984) 13, 59]
4. Vice President at St Omer

---

15. Banister to Rutter — Mowbreck, 1st June 1782.

My dear Hal,

Your pupil did not leave dinner abruptly but stayed the greatest part of the evening and was very chatty. But you may easily conceive that Mr Wilson and myself wanted many thousands to be agreeable company to him, who rates all by their wealth and opulence. I never go to his father's, but I believe I am no less esteemed for that. I was invited and went to his daughter's funeral as pall-bearer. I never went to Mr Brockholes's[1] but was called to assist at his funeral.

If your pupil is determined to return this year, I suppose he will act over again the scene of an hectical or convulsive patient. You see his genius is admirably calculated for dissimulation and romancing. I have by me a hasty poem, the title of which is Catiline's Conspiracy, a Mirror of the Times.[2] In this the earl your pupil's uncle is said to be delineated in these verses:

Beneath his elbow of unequal size,
when bold thought witty and when witty wise,
the Spendthrift Piso, who had sold his land
and household gods, now figured in the band.
Free was his person and his folly free,
streamed out in nonsense uncontrolled as he.
So famed for riots, that as yet a boy,
when insurrection found him no employ
at home, he left the nation of his birth
and led rebellion in a foreign earth.
But, shipwrecked all his wealth at last
he took a method to subsist and wrote a book;

Harangued the publick on it's sunk affairs,
which then absorbed his wisdom and his cares;
and hoped to manage, if his book were known,
the publick fortune as he had his own.

Though you receive slow and scanty remittances of money, I dare say the 3 jockies, grooms and dog-keepers have full and punctual salaries. But this, and many other like things, you must necessarily swallow and keep so closely down in your stomach, that they may never transpire either by tongue or pen. Likewise, if your pupil is pleased to represent me in any ridiculous form, let no resentment swell your breast.

If those 3 secular powers had gained your consent to accept the offer, in my judgement, you would have taken a very wrong step. 1. Because you cannot with your credit and honour abandon the care of your pupil. 2. Because I can scarce recollect one who has not been some way duped at that house. Who seemed more secure than Mr George Witham, and yet he is compelled to quit, to his no small heart-burning, as I suppose? Therefore keep off from Babylon and be not deceived by transitory smiles, which will be followed by frowns and some clandestine dimittimus. I have hardly a doubt but you will be wanted as a preceptor to some one or other when you have finished your present care. Say not, I will never take another, but act like many a prudent widow in these parts who, having buried a sottish, savage husband try a 2nd and a 3rd, hoping to find a better. As you are every day most feelingly taught the absolute renunciation of your own will, and are often reviled and scorned, you will be most excellently qualified to teach true wisdom and philosophy.

I am very much obliged to Mr Witham for bringing over with him my Vitre. When I returned in 1774, I left my trunk of books to be taken to the Custom-house at London and desired Mr Coghlan Bookseller to get it out, which he did paying 30s. for ten or twelve different articles. I have still the bill by me. Whence I conclude that you had better keep your own books to come with you and see them yourself out of the Custom-house, or make some running venture of them.

Mrs [Elizabeth] Henneage, widow of George Henneage Esquire, has desired and obtained Mr Robert Wilson, my neighbour at Salwick, to be her chaplain.[3] This has hugely offended your pupil's father who, notwithstanding, is but a very partial patron of the place, allowing the house and a bit of ground, yearly worth £10 or £12—the rest of the salary is £5 from bench-money, and the interest of £300, which is by an old country-trustee lent into many hands, chiefly farmers and poor artificers.

If the German Henry the 8th suppress our English Chartreuse he will surely allow each of them an annuity. If Father Bruno comes over, this Salwick [chaplaincy] would perhaps be very acceptable to him. But the squire, I am told, will let none come on his premises but one of his own choosing; and the elected must likewise please the rustics of the place, who, you know, are always admirable good judges of men and merits. I will, please God, write to Fr Bruno for he ought not to take upon him a new state of life without very mature deliberation. Mr Wilson is not gone yet from Salwick, nor is to go till an express permission comes from Mr Matthew Gibson B[ishop][4].

Be pleased to say one Intention for each of the following deceased: Matthew, Thomas, Dorothy, Edward, James, Isabell, Jane, Elizabeth, Ann, Richard. In all ten, for which I will present your mother half a guinea, or remit it to you, as you will. Then please say two, viz, one for one Mr Martin,[5] and the other pro omnibus fidelibus defunctis.

Mr Gregory Stapleton is not, as I have heard, come into Lancashire. I will make it my business to see him if he comes not to see me. In the meantime I beg of you to hold on with courage and patience. Who knows but God, seeing your longanimity in suffering the most mortifying things for his sake, may show mercy to the graceless one. Read the life of St. Abraham in the Fathers of the Desert, who preached and laboured 2 or 3 years in a heathen city and received no other return but the most shocking insults and barbarous treatment; but, bearing all with invincible courage and perseverance, did move God to open their ears and hearts and to work their entire conversion. May this be your success. Amen, Fiat, fiat.

I have not been over Ribble since last July, but as I hear nothing from Westhead, I hope all are well. Your sister Susan is still at Torre Abbey [Devon] with George Cary Esquire, who has married Frances Stonor, widow of the late Thomas Giffard of Chillington, his 2nd wife. They both know me very well; and for his part he is a very well-meaning, good man and perhaps has some little more regard for Susan on my account. Your brother Robert has not written to me this long time. If an opportunity to answer does not come soon, write by the post. [Let us remember one another at Mass]. I remain most affectionately ever yours R.B.

1. The Brockholes family lived at Claughton, Lancs.
2. Not traced.
3. When Thomas Wright moved to Stratford and West Ham in Essex at Mr Henneage's death; Wilson did not take up the post because she died shortly after (N*os.*27, 32).
4. Matthew Gibson (1734–1790), Bishop of Comana ipi and Vicar Apostolic Northern District, 1780–90, in succession to Bishop William Walton. He was

a forty-six-year-old Northumbrian and the older brother of William Gibson, President of Douai College, where Matthew had taught before coming onto the mission in 1768. He was resident at Headlam Hall, near Gainford, Co. Durham, with the Maire family. Rutter and Banister usually refer to him as Comana.

5. Unidentified; there were several priests of that name.

---

16. Rutter to Banister — St. Omer, 25th June 1782

Dear Uncle

I received your kind letter the 16th of this month and conclude therefore it did not come by Bruges as I had expected; for I think I desired you to send it to Mr [Matthew] Burgess to forward it to me; if not, you know that he lives in the Rue des Carmes.[1]

Your letter confirmed me in my opinion of Master's inclination to romancing, in which he so much excels, that I am at a loss when to give credit to a single word he says. Those two verses quoted in your letter agree to him admirably:

free was his person and his folly free
streamed out in nonsense uncontrol'd as he.

I have been favoured with a letter from the Squire, who tells me that our stay in this place is to be till next Spring, but does not intimate where we are next to go to. He says I seem to think money very plentiful in your parts, though I am sure I never had any reason, from what he sends to these.

I do not know what grounds you can have for thinking that I may be wanted as a preceptor for some one or other after the expiration of my present charge. At least, if I continue in the same mind as I am at present I shall be very loath to accept another; neither my disposition nor capacity are suited for this way of life. You know I am of a silent and dull turn of mind and fitter to keep company with Fr. Bruno at the Chartreuse than young people of so contrary dispositions. Besides, the life of a tutor seems to be a very indolent one, without any advantage either to himself or his pupil who, considering him as an enemy to his ease, pleasure and satisfaction, keeps out of his company as much as possible. Master is at present more civil than ordinary and does not show that scorn and contempt of me which he used to do.

If I had accepted of a place in this house, I am entirely of your opinion that I should not have enjoyed it long. I have seen myself too much to think otherwise; but then, I should not have desired to stay above a year to prepare myself for the mission. I do not think this last an easy employment, but I hope its difficulties are not so great as to make me imitate Mr Rimmer's example who, I hear, is returned to Douai, probably to succeed Mr Physick [Richard Fishwick] as General Prefect. I understand I should have been in that capacity had I remained at the college. Mr [John] Griffith I hear is going to Valladolid, from whence I imagine I might have been admitted there, as you had desired it of Mr Shepherd.[2]

Old Mr [John] Hankin departed this life the 24th of last month; he had been infirm for a long time but kept up his spirits to the last. I ever admired his generous dispositions and great philanthropy, which made him sensisble to the wants and necessities of all. I suppose you have heard of Mr [Henry] Peach's death long ago; it was occasioned by a violent cold, which he imprudently neglected.[3]

I hope Mr Wilson will have a successor at Salwick to your liking; it would doubtless be very acceptable to Father Bruno if he goes on the mission, in order that he might be near you. If a suppression takes place, 'tis said his annuity will be about £30 a year, with which he proposed to come and live with you for a time, to be instructed in his new way of life.

As to the half guinea you make mention of, you may give it to my mother, if you please, for it is at your disposal. Pray tell me, when you are able, whether things go on the same way at home as formerly, 'tis seldom that I hear from thence. I am concerned for Brother Robert, as he has not written to any one for this long time, neither home, nor to you or me. Does he succeed in his business?

As I have a little leisure time on my hands, I think I cannot employ it better than in qualifying myself for the pulpit. Having an impediment in my speech, and other difficulties to overcome, I cannot expect any great success this way, but endeavours and practice may perhaps do good. For this end I propose by and by to speak a few sermons for the instruction of the boys who, I believe, stand in need of it. Our Principal indeed is sometimes pleased to read a little to them, but I own I do not admire his talents in this line, nor indeed in any other. I wish you would tell me what method you would have me follow. Many seem to think that it is sufficient to read a good book without being at the trouble of composing a sermon and getting it by heart, and indeed I do not see the necessity of adding to the great number of excellent sermons that are already made.

I desire to be remembered to my relations and remain your dutiful nephew, H.R.

1. Burgess, chaplain to the English Augustinian nuns at Bruges, left that year having been 'ill-used' by the prioress.
2. Rimmer came to the mission in 1781 but returned to Douai later that year to succeed Fishwick who had left for England. Rimmer came back to England in 1784 and served at Sheffield until his death in 1828. Griffith left Douai to teach philosophy at Valladolid in June 1782.
4. Hankin served at Sunderland until he was driven away shortly after the Forty-five; he then served at Witton Shields in Northumberland until 1778 when he returned to Douai and died in 1782 aged seventy-six. Peach died at St Omer on 24 Dec 1781.

---

17. Banister to Rutter Mowbreck, 13th September 1782.

My dear Hal,

I send you this by Mr Gregory Stapleton who will himself give you some account of his negotiation with the Squire.

Mary your sister displeases me very much by admitting one Moorcroft, a hatter, into her small apartment as a boarder and lodger and sweetheart or wooer. He is, moreover, a Protestant. Her mother's remonstrances, as I hear, have no influence upon her. You cannot well conceive the obstinacy, blindness and precipitation of a girl when she is once engaged in such a connection. They pay no regard at all to religion or its dictates; they have no fear of putting either themselves or future children either totally out of the way of heaven, or at least into eminent danger of missing the road. When she lived at Tarleton she began a connection of the same kind; Richard and Jenny Mawdsley and my sister Helen, and I too, urged to her parents the absolute necessity of taking her from thence, which was happily done. Now, I suppose, she looks upon herself entirely emancipated from all obligation of hearkening to her father or mother. Indeed, such girls are deaf to every voice but that of their seducer. However, I will make some essay upon her, but if I find it in vain, I shall cast her out of my mind as a thing not fit to occupy it. You may also try your own efforts, but say nothing personally reflecting on the man lest she show him your letter. Rather, shew her what most unhappy consequences will follow from following her own counsel against the advice of her best friends. He may possibly tell her that he will become a Catholic but no credit is to be given to words; nay, an actual convert is often nothing but a hypocrite and falls back again.

For my part I now ask all young persons: 1. Whether they woo or are wooed? 2. Whether their sweetheart be a Catholic or a Protestant? If the latter, I tell them in resolute terms to come no more to me nor look for any Sacraments from me unless they desist immediately from such connections. And if one is not on the watch to ask frequently, they will be plunged over head and ears in the puddle of sensual, carnal love, and the chain will be so strong that no advices nor threats nor predictions of future miseries can break it. It is a deplorable thing to see what a deafness is in the ears of the hearts of worldlings, young people, &c.[1]

I have received Biblia Sacra by Vitre, 23 tomes of Piteval and 3 tomes of the Lives of the Saints by d'Andilly together in a box from London.

Father Bruno wrote to me concerning his future situation when their house is dissolved. I answered him last Tuesday. He says that he will let me peruse the Croissades but I choose to have them only as propria bona, not borrowed, for how can I return borrowed books at so great a distance?

On Wednesday the 11th the Squire's 3 year-old won the race against 4 or 5 others. On Thursday, yesterday, his horse called Tommy won with ease against two. Great acclamations and shouts of joy echoed throughout the whole stadium to the banks of Savock and Ribble; the river Gods started from their oozy beds and the nymphs of the field danced in chorus. Kirkham bells proclaimed the victory and our Kirkham Pindar, the Author of Kirkham Churchyard, may perhaps celebrate the glory of Tommy in a Grub Street Sonnet.[2]

I beseech you to possess your soul in patience: ['Patience hath a perfect work'.][3] It brings all to a good end on one side or another. I am, my sweet Hal, your most affectionate Uncle, R.B.

1. Banister appears to allude to his questioning in the confessional.
2. Not traced.
3. St. James, ch.1.

18. Rutter to Banister [St Omer,] 16th October 1782

Dear Uncle,

I received your last by Mr Stapleton by which it seems that mine never reached you, or perhaps you did not think it worth mentioning. I own indeed that I am not master of the Epistolary Style and I hope you will excuse any defects in that respect, especially in this letter, which I must scrawl out as fast as I can for want of time.

I am much grieved at Sister Molly's obstinacy and blindness which I hope you will find means to overcome, but this change must be the work of God. I have written a few lines to her which may in some measure prepare the way.

I have committed my books to the care of an English Captain sailing from Dunkirk to London, which method I find has hitherto succeeded very well, and which is much less troublesome and expensive. He is to send them down to Lancashire, being directed to my Uncle Wearden, afterwards to be delivered to you, as I hope you will be able to put them in some corner of your house till I want them. Many of them you will probably think not worth the carriage, but they were such as I had and which could only have been sold for waste paper. There are some, however, which I think you will approve of and which I beg you will make use of as you think fit. I have desired Mr Stapleton to remit you three guineas which I designed for my mother but pay first, if you please, the carriage of the books which, I imagine, cannot be above a guinea, as they are to be sent by the wagon.

One reason why I sent my books was that I expected soon to follow them, as I apprehended some one would succeed me in my charge. For, about 2 months ago Esq. Clifton wrote me a letter which did not please me and which I answered in his own style, telling him that I was ready to resign the care of his son to whomsoever he thought more capable of governing him. This I thought was saying enough to an Esquire of Lytham but Mr Stapleton assures me he does not think of sending another in my place, so that I must jog on as well as I can. However, I cannot but think that another would have more authority and therefore wish he would make the experiment. I am therefore tempted to write again to the Esquire, especially for I find I can do nothing with him.

Fr. Bruno has been here, but fell sick on the road and continued dangerously so during his stay. Being something better, I went back with him to Nieuport, but hear since that he is in a very poor way. The suppression, according to Abbe [William] Mann[1], was to have taken place at the beginning of this month, but we hear nothing of it.

You have probably heard of Mr Mumford's death, which is much regretted by the English in this town. 'Tis uncertain whom we shall have as a Vice President. Mr [William] Gibson had indeed agreed to send Mr [John] Daniel, but he cannot now be spared, as Mr Ralph Southworth is to go to

Louvain in the place of Mr Blount, who, I hear, is returning to England.[2] I am dear Uncle, Your most dutiful Nephew, H.R.

1. An English Carthusian.
2. Southworth left to assist Charles Catrow at the English Augustinian convent. Although Blount had resigned as President of Douai College on 30 May 1781, he had remained in the locality for some time, to the new president's chagrin, before going to Louvain as a convent chaplain. He was now to retire to Mapledurham.

19. Banister to Rutter Mowbreck, 1st November 1782

My dear Hal,

I return this answer to your last, dated October 16, sooner than otherwise I intended for two reasons. First to assure you that I took no notice of yours dated June 25 because another object possessed my thoughts, the conduct of Mary. As to the value and esteem I make of your letters, I keep them all and think those the best which are the longest. To me therefore at least use no prefaces or apologies of any kind. Indeed, when I find prefaces and long reasons of silence in the beginning of a letter, I begin to read it at the middle or towards the end.

Another reason why I write speedily is to prevent your writing to the Squire, at least in the manner you seem to intend. Yesterday Mr Wilson of Salwick was here at dinner and we talked of you and your charge a good while. We are both of one mind, viz., that you are not to give up your office of tutor, but hold on patiently, whatever it costs your poor sweet soul. to endure the indignities of a shallow, proud, indolent pupil. The Squire has no design of sending one to succeed you, this you may depend on. His grand object is pareatur sumptui, and I defy him to get one (unless it may be some hackney Irishman) at a less charge and expense than you. You undoubtedly keep accounts of recepta et expensa which you will show when you come to Lytham.

If Master will do nothing, or behaves ill, Mr Wilson says, you must write an account of him to his father, in a moderate way (which will be black enough, I dare say, without colouring), but before you send it, let Master peruse it. If he is unwilling for you to send it, and promises amendment, throw it into the fire; but if he is unabashed, send it, and you may add that Master has perused it. Mr Wilson assures me that this was his method.

When Mr Wilson with Sir Piers lived at St. Omer, their quarterly expenses (all comprised) amounted to between £40 and £50, that is, near £200 a year. What do yours amount to? And Mr Wilson adds that Sir Piers was then a child. If you be ordered to Paris, or Brussels, or any academy, the expense will be at least £500 p.a. Then he is never to go into any company what-ever without you. To do otherwise is to send a vessel to sea without sails, compass or rudder to a certain shipwreck. When Mr Wilson took up Joseph Blount, he made this a primary, fundamental article to which the father and young ward assented.

I wrote my sentiments some time ago to Fr. Bruno. I compassionate his illness, but if God takes him I shall not doubt but it is to reward his early, constant piety.

I gave your mother the half guinea and shall give her the rest when it comes, except disbursements for the carriage of your books.

I think the best preparation for speaking to the people is meditation upon The Sinner's Guide. St. Charles Borromeo used and recommended that book. He had also an impediment in his speech yet overcame it. Fine words neither make those saints who use them, nor those who hear them.

Your letter brought me the first news of Mr Mumford's death. If they invite you to take his place, do not accept it. I would not take the last place in the house unless they would give me an indemnifying bond that, if the council discharge me, I should claim, by virtue of their bond, a very considerable sum of money. Do you think Mr Daniel had also agreed to come? He is a bold man if he did. I heard long ago of Mr Hankin's and Mr Peach's deaths.

I have not as yet attacked your sister Mary. Her change must come from God, as you truly observe. Your sister Fanny has been here 6 weeks. My brother is in some moderate way yet makes his sallies sometimes. Their whole family is but three.

Mr Wilson, as well as myself, is of opinion that you are as fit a person to have charge of Master as any other. He hates all restraint and all learning. I mean solid and substantial, and therefore hates all the whole tribe of preceptors. I do not know of any one who has a design of choosing you for a tutor after you have finished your present business. Yet such persons are wanted, and not so easily found, I see some probability that you may be sought for. This day I begin my 58th year being born a sinner on the day of All Saints. Remember me in your devout mementoes and believe me Your most affectionate and dearest Uncle, R.B.

20. Banister to Rutter Mowbreck, 7th February 1783

My dear Hal,

Parson Gill did not bring your letter to London.[1] By some means it was put, as it seems to me, into the post office at Paris; 'tis certain it cost 10d. to London and 5d. to Kirkham, total 15d.

Your box of books arrived here a month or more before last Christmas. Indeed, my sweetheart, you stuffed it with too much trumpery; the carriage from London cost 13s. You have sent plenty of commentators but the most useful is Corn. a Lapide in Evangelia. I find nothing of ecclesiastical history. Young's Night-thoughts are rightly entitled; night and darkness reigns throughout each piece.[2] But now I have not time to give you my judgement of all your books. No Saints' Lives amongst them.

You desire me to answer a query for which I am not duly circumstanced. When you are at Paris consult Mr [Charles] Howard or some other judicious person who will weigh all things duly.[3] Neither Master nor you should go to indecent plays. As for assemblies, I believe none go amongst the French but the invited. And as far as I have heard, our English are not easily nor commonly admitted into French company; I mean, company of great honour and quality. If then, your pupil will be for rambling sometimes out of your sight, I affirm that he had better come home and run after hares and hounds than go to Paris. You will insinuate to his father that you cannot answer for his son's behaviour unless you have him always with you and that, as Paris is a place where occasions and opportunities of ruin abound, it will be best and most advisable to let his son stay there a very short time, and send him to some other city in France or Italy or Lorraine.

You tell me that harshness and severity make your pupil still less docile and tractable, therefore you are bound to use sweetness, mildness and patience. And to show these exteriorly, heartily and cordially, you must have them prepared beforehand by meditation and prayer, especially by looking upon the great pattern of all meekness, our Blessed Saviour.

Your sister Mary was married to one Moorcroft before last Advent. I never wrote to her and am glad of it. Let us not rail at her or against her; by giving a good and kindly countenance to her and to her husband, one may be able to gain him. 'Tis certain, anger and resentment will not. I have not heard of Robert this long time, but there is a cousin of ours in

London to whom I have lately written and desired him to find out Robert's present state and circumstances.

'Tis late in the night. I must conclude by assuring you that I am, with singular esteem for you, your affectionate Uncle, R. Banister.

1. Gill is presumably an Anglican clergyman.
2. Edward Young, Anglican Rector of Welwyn, poet and playwright; *Night-thoughts on Life, Death and Immortality* (1742–5) probably went into more editions in the century after its publication than any other book of the day. Boswell called it 'a mass of the grandest and richest poetry that human genius has ever produced' and George Eliot thought it 'a Juggernaut made of gold and jewels, at once magnificent and repulsive'. [R Stock, *The Holy & The Daemonic from Sir Thomas Browne to William Blake* (1982) 189]
3. Banister was unaware that due to ill health Charles Howard had resigned as President of St Gregory's College, Paris, in 1782.

---

21. Banister to Rutter — Mowbreck, 10th April 1783

My dear Hal,

Mr Marsh, who was formerly butler at Lytham, and is therefore known to your pupil, brings this to Bruges, from whence Mr Burgess will forward it to you, for now I know not where you are.

Mr Wilson, my good neighbour, always bids me to charge you to continue your office. And to the quaere whether you should accompany your pupil a la Comedie at Paris he answers, 'tis suspension ipso facto for one of your character to go on any pretence. And as to your pupil, if your authority cannot restrain him, his father's must and ought. This you may be sure of, that if his father allows him to go wherever and with whomsoever he pleases, the youth is ruined, debauched, poxed, and utterly lost to reason, humanity and religion. Write and insinuate these truths to his father to the end you may have the same power of restraining him which Mr Wilson had with regard to Master Joseph Blount. He received him on this condition that he should go no whither, nor accompany any one unless he were with him. But if the old Squire, insensible or deaf to your insinuating counsels, will permit his son the liberty of rambling and of connecting himself with whomsoever he pleases, then he alone must anwer for the consequences. You will be no more than a nominal tutor, more for parade than use, for ostentation not for instruction.

In my last I was too severe, I fear, on your collection. Sacy's Commentaries are admirable, and so is the Analyse de Evangiles & des Epitres, though I cannot agree with the author in several dissertations, particularly in the 30th. Ceillier's great work on the Fathers and ecclesiastical writers is become very cheap, and so is Tournon's Vies Illustres of Dominican Fathers. Mr [Alban] Butler's Lives of the Saints[1] are too copious and too learned for vulgar people. I could wish some select lives were published in a very plain style and such as may be patterns and models for people living in the world. The account of old and young Toby is a perfect model I would endeavour to follow in writing for the vulgar. So I would choose to publish the lives of Homobonus, of Guy, called the poor man of Anderlecht, of Zeta, a servant man, of Isidore, a ploughman, of Servulus, a beggar mentioned by St. Gregory the Great, and several others who lived in low life and sanctified themselves and their vocation, not by converting nations or directing grand councils, but by fidelity in little things. Yet all these lives are greatly abridged in Mr Butler; nothing of the simple, humble style of Toby's life appears in them, very few particular actions are recounted. They can not therefore be so instructive to the vulgar, nor make that lasting impression on their minds. Therefore when you go a bookanisting, if you can pick up any authentic lives of the saints I have mentioned, or such like, buy them up.

I pray you to say 8 Masses for my intention before the end of next July. I understand your Brother Robert is also married at London.

My sweet Hal, remember what St. James says: ['patience is a perfect work'], and the wise man: ['the patient man will tell of his victories'], and our Blessed Saviour: ['in patience you shall possess your souls'], and St. Thomas a Kempis: ['bear accusations through all']. Remember Horace speaking of poetical faults: ['I am not offended by a few spots'] which you must apply to the case of your pupil.[2] If you can keep him out of notorious mortal sins, wink at all his venial ones, though ever so gross.

I must conclude in haste my dear sweet heart that I am ever yours most affectionately, R. Banister.

1. Alban Butler (1710–73), priest-scholar, had taught Newtonian science at Douai; he was later Vice President; then chaplain to the Duke of Norfolk; and then President at St Omer until his death. He spent thirty years compiling *Lives of the Fathers, Martyrs and other principal Saints, &c.* (5 vols. 1745, and many subsequent editions).
2. St James 1, 4; Luke 21, 19.

---

22. Banister to Rutter Mowbreck, 19th April 1783

My dear Hal,

The near prospect of what you have long wished for ought to give you much satisfaction, but if nature is apt to move you to resentment, either for past ill-usage or any other cause, I hope you will not listen to her suggestions. From those who refer all things to themselves you must never expect anything. Wherefore on this occasion exert yourself so as to signify no kind of resentment or complaint or dissatisfaction. Divine providence over-rules all events and ['we know that to them that love God all things cooperate for the good'].[1]

I have heard nothing about the matter on this side. Last Friday but one, the 11th instant, I sent you a letter by one Mr Marsh and, as I did not know but you were removed, I ordered him to drop it at Bruges with Mr Burgess to be forwarded to you. This Mr Thomas Marsh was formerly butler at Lytham Hall. When I came hither he was innkeeper at Kirkham and broke like many others of the same business. He told me that he has orders to see Master before his return. But you may be sure he is not designed your successor. If the event happens as you are informed, stay at Douai College if invited, nay, invite yourself, and if you dare not speak to the President, break the matter to Mr Stapleton.

Mr Robert Wilson at Salwick Hall is to go and live with Mrs Henneage, widow of George Henneage, Esq. Now, if you come over and this place be offered you by the Squire, I must assure you that you want two great talents to fill it. 1st, age and experience in the ministry. 2. A competent independent fortune of your own. To which add that the person must be acceptable to the heads of the congregation the Squire's tenants. The whole salary is but £36 p.a., much too small to live on. The people conceited and niggards, but you are not to understand these terms of all. But if you observe in reading the lives of the saints you will find that the servants of God never studied or courted the favour of great ones, but always sought to lie hid in obscurity, forgotten and unknown.

In the letter I sent you by Mr Thomas Marsh, I desired you to say 8 times for my intention before the end of July. If either you return, or see Mr Marsh, bring me or send me a long white night-cap of Segovia wool, or two short ones of the same manufacture. Mr John Orrell, College Agent in Lancashire, sent me the 3 guineas you ordered, two months ago. Please also to send me 6 pairs of white linen socks. Item, two scapulars of the same sort you sent before.

At Salwick there is the interest of £500, £6 bench money, which niggards would rather keep to themselves, £5 from the Squire, instead of which he gives a house and ground sufficient to keep two cows and a horse. But an incumbent cannot till the land. Mr Wilson has been at great expense to make it worth something, for before him it was of little value. I again entreat you to be perfectly easy and indifferent whether you have a successor or none. But stay at Douai College if you can; the professors' table will be good enough for you. If you get the study-place you may save some money. I remain, Sweet Hal, your most affectionate servant, R.B.

P.S. 'Tis best to keep your mother's name, Rutter.[2]

1. Romans 8, 38
2. The use of his mother's maiden name was a throwback to the years of persecution when priests commonly adopted aliases.

Note. Rutter was relieved of his post a year ahead of time, no doubt as a result of the ex-butler's report to Thomas Clifton. As it happens, the post would have lapsed shortly afterwards because Mr Clifton died on 11th May 1783, aged fifty-five, and John, nineteen years old, would have had to return home to take over as the new Squire of Lytham.

Despite Banister's strong advice about obtaining an academic post in one of the English colleges, Rutter did not (or perhaps could not) get one and he joined his uncle pending his disposal by Bishop Matthew Gibson. He wanted to stay in Lancashire but he was presently made chaplain to the Silvertop family at Minsteracres in Northumberland. Appalled at the prospect of repeating his recent experience as tutor to more young gentlemen, Rutter tried to get out of it but the bishop was unmoved and the disgruntled Rutter went over to the north-east to join his new family at Benwell Hall (or House), their summer home, near Newcastle.

At the beginning of the eighteenth century, Albert Silvertop became a successful Tyneside coalmaster, firstly as agent to Lord William Widdrington and then on his own account. In 1721 he bought Minsteracres, a farm some eight miles south east of Hexham, which became the nucleus of a large estate built up over the next twenty years by Albert and his son George. In 1758 George Silvertop described himself as Esquire, obtained a grant of arms and began the process of transforming Minsteracres into a gentleman's residence. The *nouveaux riches* Silvertops soon gained social acceptance from the old Catholic gentry; George's heir, John, married Catherine, daughter of Sir Henry Lawson of Brough; George's daughter Mary married Sir Thomas Haggerston, the richest Catholic in the region; and Winifred, George's youngest daughter, married John Wright of Kelvedon, the Catholic banker.

George Silvertop established a mission at Minsteracres in 1765 with his distant kinsman William Gibson as chaplain and tutor to his fifteen-year-old son John. Gibson left to become President of Douai College in 1781 to be succeeded by John Daniel. It may be that chaplain and squire did not suit each other for Daniel left after only two and a half years to go to Stockton; Rutter, then aged twenty-eight, took over.

The family comprised George Silvertop (I) aged seventy-nine and a widower of six years. He had handed the family's coaling business over to his son John, thirty-three years old who had been married ten years to Catherine Lawson who was three years older. There were five children: George (II) aged nine; Mary, seven; John (II) six; Henry Thomas, four; and Charles, two.

---

23. Thomas Eyre and Rutter to Banister — 1st September 1783, Stella Hall, near Newcastle

Dear Sir,

I am happy to inform you that Mr Rutter arrived in this neighbourhood on Saturday 23rd in better health than spirits. I hope that his place will become daily more agreeable, at least nothing shall be wanting in me to render it so. He has the charge of a small but dispersed flock which will only give him just as much employment as he would wish. As he is situated in the midst of the country, and few of his people possess clocks, I foresee that he will be at a loss how to measure out his time to his poor people so as not to trespass upon his family hours, and consequently the want of a watch is a great inconvenience. To remedy this I must beg the favour of you to bespeak a good watch from Mr Tarleton of Liverpool, who is an acquaintance I understand of yours, and a relation of my brother Vincent's[1], and to desire him to forward it to Newcastle for your nephew. I hereby hold myself bound to answer his demand for the same.

I most sincerely thank you for the countenance you are pleased to give to the new edition of The Instruction of Youth.[2] I hope this will find you in good health.

I remain with very great respect and esteem,
Your most obedient Servant,
Thomas Eyre.

1. Vincent Eyre, a lawyer of Lincoln's Inn and estate manager to the Duke of Norfolk.
2. Eyre published a translation from the French of Charles Gobinet, *The Instruction of Youth in Christian Piety* (2 vols. 1783) which sold 4,000 copies in a year. He also edited John Gother's *Works* in 16 vols., including *Instructions upon the Sacrament of Confirmation* (1783).

23a. [Benwell Hall]

Dear Uncle

To save expense I take the advantage of writing a few lines to you in Mr Eyre's letter.

I arrived at Minsteracres Saturday 23rd. As to the particulars of my journey, you will have learned them from Cousin Billy, though indeed nothing occurred worthy of notice. Our expenses were greater than I expected, for I could have travelled for less in the public coach. I had indeed the pleasure of Billy's company, but he is too great a friend to those of his <u>own profession</u> to make me wish to travel with him for the sake of economy. I met with great civilities on the road, especially at Lartington, and Mr Maire, with a politeness peculiar to himself, sent his horse and servant with me to Minsteracres.[1]

The air of this place will, I hope, agree with me better than I apprehended; at least I must say this, that hitherto all is civility and attention. They know, as everybody else does, that I came much against my will and I am sorry that I expressed myself so freely and unfavourably of the place. I am vexed at myself for being so imprudent and unthinking.

Minsteracres is not so near Newcastle as we imagined, for it is 20 miles off, and half that distance from Stella Hall. Mr Eyre was so kind as to come and see me last week and to go with me yesterday to Newcastle to buy a few little necessaries. He is indeed exceedingly civil and I hope to find in him a true and sincere friend. The commission he desires you to do for me is a very good proof, as I find myself very much distressed for want of a watch. Mr Tarleton will, I hope, easily find means of conveying it to Newcastle.

I wish I had brought my black suit with me for I want it much. Could you signify this to my father that he may send it by the carrier as soon as possible. They all tell me that unless I economise I must run into debt, which is what I hate as much as you can do. I have at present near two guineas left of what I brought with me, and when I am in want I shall make bold to apply to my Patron. I am sorry I did not buy a horse in Lancashire, but we must grow wise by experience.

Be pleased to remember me in the kindest manner to my cousin Crook, likewise to my guide and to all. Have you seen the new edition of The Instruction of Youth, it is chiefly owing to the care and labour of Mr Eyre, and as it is a book you approve of, I hope it will be supported by your countenance and recommendation. The Instructions for Confirmation are by the same hands and will, I hope, be of service in preparing your flocks for the Bishop's coming amongst you. We are all peace and concord here and wish it were so with you. Adieu, Your most dutiful Nephew, H.R.

1. Rutter usually called on fellow-missioners for a meal and/or a bed when travelling. He was often accompanied on his journeys by a relative or a servant; the reason for Cousin Billy's unsuitability does not emerge; he may have been too convivial for Rutter, or a publican, or both.

---

24. Banister to Rutter Mowbreck, 19th September 1783

My dear Harry,

I received yours in due time after its date, viz., the 1st of this Instant. You say you are sorry for having expressed yourself so unfavourably of the place and I wish you may not be sorry again for your sorrow. However, endeavour to comport yourself so prudently that if a rupture happen it may not originate from you. Laelius de Amicitia says that some held an opinion that friends must be friends, as if they were to be enemies. This indeed he does not approve of but probably, with me, he would approve of it in you towards your high and mighty.

They tell you that you must use economy; 'tis very wholesome advice in all times and places, but I tell you to shape your coat according to your cloth, or rather more literally, make your coat, waistcoat and breeches of that kind of stuff which your salary will afford. Ten pounds a year will not afford a broad cloth or silk breeches or ruffled shirts, or to lay aside your stockings when they want darning above your shoes. Therefore be sure to get your stockings darned, as long as darning is good, both in and above the shoe, your shirts patched and your elbows too, and breeches if necessary. I know that servants who wait at tea or dinner in the parlour must not dare to appear in a stocking darned above the shoe, nor in a patched elbow, or with a silk handkerchief about their neck, but that is no rule for you; fine clothes on your back will but make you a heavy heart if the shopkeeper and tailor are unpaid. And if a coat of good plain at 9s. p. yd. displeases the eyes of your quality, you can insinuate the true reason why you have no better.

Therefore instead of sending you your black coat and waistcoat, the carriage of which will cost almost as much as they are worth, buy a plain of 5s. or 5s.6d. p. yd. and get it made into a coat and waistcoat and breeches. Pray do not be ashamed of such gear; 'tis a greater shame to wear clothes above our ability. Many a good missioner never wore better, nor perhaps as good. For solemnities and gala days you have a super fine suit; a suit of plain will do for every day. And if you cannot pay immediately for it, undoubtedly the shop-keeper will readily trust you; your credit is yet untainted.

In my opinion you may buy a Scotch Galloway[1] for much less money there than a horse here. On no persuasion would I buy a fine horse; you may almost be certain that your horse will be a hack-about, either day or night, or both.

I wrote last Saturday to Mr Tarleton for a good watch (as Mr Eyre expresses it) for you. He has done a good work in printing The Instruction of Youth. I wish he would print The Sinner's Guide, but this when The Instruction of Youth is in great part vended. I have just received a letter from Mr Tarleton in which he tells me that he will make as good a watch as he can, and as soon as possible, for you. He sends his compliments and respects to Mr Eyre and you.

Though you are now (as you write) all in peace and concord, yet it is but a few years and there was the hottest contest in your parts about saying Vespers in English before the congregation. The seamless coat was almost rent.[2]

I am glad you missed our meeting.[3] We dined in peace and drank a glass or two; then Mr [Simon] Bordley distributed his printed Rules, then proceeded to propose the officers appointed by the Rules: "Let them (says he) lay their hands on the table". He then proposed Mr [John] Barrow[4] for

Treasurer: 15 laid their hands on the table, 13 were motionless. Then he proposed me for Secretary: 15 on the table, 13 stiff and still. Then he proposed Mr Marmaduke Wilson for Procurator: 14 on the table, 13 not. Then he began to propose one in each Hundred, whose office is to transmit all legacies and donations to the Treasurer; Mr [William] Fisher was accepted for Blackburn Hundred, Mr John Orrell for Derby Hundred, but, when he proposed Mr [Michael] Wharton for Lonsdale Hundred and Mr Barrow said no let use propose Mr [William] Pennington, the schism began. The 13 motionless gentlemen began to rise and after some words and altercations went off, I suppose, into another parlour. But the noisiest man was Mr William Earpe, commonly called Dunn; he received nothing of the dividend, and yet, as he said, was inscribed in the Fund last September 1782. But his inscription was contrary to a practice which has been for some time observed in regard of others, viz., that no one is to be received into the Fund till he has been a year on the Mission.

You will perceive by this that there are two parties, but why or wherefore, I think 'tis difficult to discover, except that Mr John Chadwick[5] (notwithstanding that he gave his vote for funding our monies) aims at nothing so much as keeping our monies in the hands of his relations, who owe £665—if the truth could be discovered. I look on it as certain that he never wrote a single line to the bishop about your staying in Lancashire; 'tis not worth your labour to investigate it but use all your experiences to be wiser.

I began this letter the 19th but did not finish it till today the 21st because my eyes became bloodshot and sore by reading Foote's Minor, a very small print, one night by candlelight.[6] He concludes it extremely well and truly:

For foremost rows in side-boxes you shove,
Think you to meet with side-boxes above?
Where giggling girls and powdered fops may sit?
No, you will all be crammed into the pit,
And crowd the house for Satan's benefit.

As St. Paul says that Callimachus, whom he styles the Cretans' own prophet, gave their true character in one verse [Greek phrase] &c., so Foote is in these verses a true prophet; players and spectators will all be crammed into the pit, &c.

You have left behind the best of all your books, saving the Scriptures and Thomas a Kempis; 'tis a small brochure giving admirable short documents to a young parish priest. I never found it till the other day. You will write me your Nouvelles from time to time and be assured that I am your most affectionate Uncle, R. Banister.

P.S. On the 6th of this month cousin Crook and his wife were all night at Westhead and found all at home and well. I hear nothing of Robert that I like, and yet hear no positive ill.

1. A small but strong working horse.
2. Charles Cordell published *The Divine Office for the use of the Laity* (1763; 2nd ed. 1780). Bishop Challoner, among many others, disapproved of such innovations and Bishop Hay told Thomas Eyre that if English were allowed in Vespers, 'the next step would be to ask the same for Mass' and Hay 'would not expect many real conversions from it'. [Gooch, thesis, 186]
3. The clergy lived on the charitable donations of their relatives, friends and congregations, but many bequests were made to the secular clergy in general rather than to an individual, and so a Common Fund had to be established to adminster the money, invest it and distribute the income, especially to sick and aged priests who may have had no other means of support. By the end of the 17th century funds of this kind were well-established in every part of England, such as the Northern Brethren's Fund in the north-east and the Secular Clergy Fund in the north-west; Rutter and Banister became officers of their funds. Banister here names many of the Lancashire secular clergy at one of the periodic 'fund meetings' called to elect officers and discuss policy. Until the passage of the Catholic Relief Act of 1778 it was illegal for Catholic clerics to hold property and their assets were held in trust by layfolk. But the clergy then began to reorganise church-finances and regain control of the church's and their own funds. (See also No. 29)
4. Missioner at Claughton noted for his plain speaking. He had been seven years a press-ganged sailor in the Royal Navy
5. Chadwick, whom Banister distrusts, had been named second on the terna for Bp. Walton's coadjutor in 1780; the list became redundant at Walton's death and Matthew Gibson, the first-named, was appointed Vicar Apostolic Northern District.
6. Samuel Foote (1720–77) actor and dramatist, known as the English Aristophanes to his contemporaries. *The Minor* (1760) was a satire directed against the Methodists. [*Oxford Companion to English Literature*]

---

25. Rutter to Banister Minsteracres, 19th November 1783

Dear Uncle,

I received your favour in due time, for which you have my hearty thanks.

You give me good advice about clothes, but I hope it will not be necessary to follow it exactly. For though I have bought a plain coat, yet a patched one will never be allowed of, I imagine, in my situation, nay it might, for ought I know, give Ladies the hysterics. My salary is £20 p.a. which, as times go, is not too much. I have no Galloway of my own but ride the Esquire's, who has occasionally mounted me on his own horse but this, you may suppose, is a great favour and not often to be expected.

I have heard nothing of my new watch and therefore am under apprehensions about it. I hope to have it as soon as possible for we are all clockwork here, such regularity and exactness is observed. Prayers[1] are at 8 and a half, but I say them no oftener than I think proper.

The family have been absent for near a month on a visit to their friends in Yorkshire so I have been Lord and Master here, but the sweets of liberty are for persons in your situation, who are happy under your own roofs without fearing the frowns of an angry and imperious Lord. But it is too soon to begin this language and therefore I will not as yet trouble you with complaints. Things are really better than were represented and, though the Gentleman is not so easy and amicable in his manner as could be wished, he possesses other qualities that make that deficiency less remarkable. He has testified some regard for me more than once, but I do not place much confidence in the favour of Great ones.

They have five children, 4 boys and a girl; the two eldest are at school and I am preparing the 3rd for the same place. I came indeed with a resolution of declining this honour but her Ladyship's eloquence has overcome me. However, the novitiate I have gone through has in some measure prepared me for any future difficulties I may meet with, which will now appear far lighter when compared with the past.

The old Gentleman has just left us for the winter; he is in his 79th year, and though his body begins to be infirm, his mind is as vigorous as ever it was. He is much attached to Alma and will not suffer anything to be said in her dispraise. I was witness the other day to a dispute in which he maintained his ground most resolutely against 2 or 3 of the opposite side. The Lady is a great Jesuitess[2], and I am so far the Jesuit as to conceal my sentiments from her on this head.

Mr Silvertop desires his respects to you and says he shall be pleased to see you here if ever you come into these parts. Indeed, it is allowed that persons of our character are nowhere in the county better received than here. I do not despair therefore of seeing you, some time or other, in these parts, for you have many acquaintances here and such a jaunt would do you good. The Bishop has given me an invitation to Headlam, but I doubt whether I shall ever comply with it.

I hope, dear Uncle, you will not fail to write to me from time to time, and the longer your letters are, the better, for I only correspond with you, except that now and then I shall write home.

The Miss Cliftons[3], I hear, have been flashing away in Yorkshire in a manner that does them no great honour, at least their conductress, and I fear Lytham will appear but a dull place at their return. They have been the general topic of conversation but opinions are different as to their beauty. One of them very innocently was like to have occasioned a duel at Stockton by dancing with a different person than she had engaged with.

You say I have left behind me one of my best books, but I hope next year you will send it to me, together with my other books, excepting such as you may like yourself.

Be so good as to remember me to cousin Crook, Billy, &c of my relations. I wish to know your opinion concerning a common practice of poor people here who suffer their infants to be laid in the same bed with them. Can this be overlooked?

Pray how do affairs at Liverpool go on?[4] The two Dunns[5] have been here and gave an account of your dissensions at the meeting, so as to throw the blame on your side you may imagine. They returned home, I believe, poorer than they came. I hope you will give me some intelligence concerning the Esquire of Lytham, for I feel myself a good deal interested in his regard. I am, dear Uncle, your most affectionate Nephew, H. Rutter.

1. The term commonly used in the penal era for 'Mass' and, like the use of aliases, redundant.
2. The Lawsons kept Jesuits at Brough, hence Rutter's not entirely jocular reference to his patroness's devotions. This may also be an allusion to the IBVM nuns, by whom Mrs Silvertop was educated, who were sometimes known as Jesuitesses.
3. Eleonora, Sophia and Catherine, John Clifton's sisters.
4. At the suppression of the Society of Jesus by the Pope in 1773, Raymond Hormasa SJ (al. Harris), a Spaniard, moved from Walton Hall to St Mary's, Liverpool, to join Joseph Gittings, SJ. They fell out some five years later over the management of the mission and the congregation took sides. Hormasa only submitted to the bishop after being suspended thrice. The affair, which gained a great deal of publicity, is treated fully at Gillow III 392–5; IV 369]
5. Joseph Dunn SJ, missioner at Preston; William Dunn, (DD St Gregory's, Paris,) secular missioner in Blackburn. Both were born at Brough and used the alias of Earpe.

26. Banister to Rutter Mowbreck, 19th December 1783

My dear Hal,

On this day I was ordained priest 33 years ago, being then 25 years and 48 days old.

Last week I received a letter from Liverpool which tells me that your watch is very nigh ready, and would have been so before this if the finisher had not been ill; as soon as he is able to work again it will be done in 4 or 5 days. Mr Tarleton says that he has made you one from the beginning entirely on purpose, which will be as good a one as can be worn both in neat workmanship and soundness. But my watch is often sick and unsound.

Your stipend being £20 p. annum, I expect you will save one half every year, and put it out to fructify, except this first year, which will take it all to accoutre you complete. I was at Wrightington my first year and did not spend £10 in all that time. There is no need of your wearing a fine clean shirt with ruffles every day; 2, or at least 3, in a week is sufficient, and sleeves to slip on as occasion requires. Nor is there any need of wearing and tearing your clothes in shooting or hunting. Prayer, study, exact temperance and moderate sleep, are enough to keep body in health and the spirits vigorous.

I am glad you have undertaken to teach that little boy. Often teach him the first leaf-side of his catechism, the grand import of it; I mean the little catechism, not that of Douai.[1] Read a note on St. Frances Jane Chantal, Dec. 23, page 992. It may move you to a resolution of never wasting your time or money in cards. I would not be a Will Wimble[2] or a lady's implement to make up their parties.

If Madam holds equivocation to be lawful, or the less safe and the less probable, I could not forbear proving them unlawful and very pernicious. But I suppose all her Jesuitism consists in a sort of bigoted partiality towards them, and why should you or anyone besides disturb her? It is often great discretion to conceal our sentiments but the maxims and certain truths of the Gospel are never to be concealed, but preached in the light and on housetops.

I can see no cause but only perhaps some scruples or fears why you should not celebrate every day. I advise you to it most earnestly, for it will engage you to keep a constant watchfulness over your mind, heart, thoughts, words and actions. And if suggestions or impulses arise you will repel them by reflecting and saying within yourself: I cannot consent or agree to you because I must celebrate tomorrow. St. Gildas,[3] in his work De Excidio Britanniae Liber Querulus, says the priests were slothful, seldom celebrated and came to the altar unprepared. They are almost sure to be ill-prepared who are slothful and who seldom eat the bread of life. Therefore beware of these faults from your first setting out. As far as I am acquainted with, or have heard of, the priests now living in these our days seem to me to be but of a secondhand sort, most of them having their oddities, whims, playthings, and are more or less warped to self, or to some creature. I do not doubt but your patron and patroness are very good people, yet have their oddities, &c.

I hear nothing of the youth at Lytham but that he is a keen hunter, rides impetuously after the dogs, and leaps undauntedly over hedges and ditches. He has lately bought two hunters. I have heard that since his return out of Yorkshire persons of our order and quality are more hospitably received. I hear too that Sir John Webb's daughter is talked of for him, which of the two I know not. No fewer than 8 gowns are actually in making at Kirkham for his sisters. Probably the poor, busy things are so overwhelmed that they cannot find time to take a single stitch for themselves.

You have surely heard of the truly holy man who died lately at Rome; Mr Melling tells me many miracles are worked and conversions of heretics.[4]

Mr Morgan goes out ahunting with his charge.[5] Do you not envy his noble employment? I asked him if he followed the example of the younger Pliny [who] took his books and writing tackle so that he might return home either with game or with some composition of genius. A hare at Lytham must be sold for 2 guineas at least to indemnify the cost and charges in taking her, viz. a stable of 8 or 9 hunters, two huntsmen, 3 hunting grooms, a dog-kennel of 60 hounds and a dog-man &c., &c. This is the invention and custom of barbarous nations and all our civilization has not yet rooted it out.

When you hear and are sure that poor women over-lay their infants, then use your best endeavours to deter them from the practice of letting the child lie with its mother or nurse. The women assure me in these parts that their infants would perish with cold if they were not to lie with their mothers or nurses. However, I always read out of the Ritual the instruction after baptism

I know nothing of Liverpool affairs, but all former productions of their witty or waspish pens are aprinting in numbers, price 3d. each, to be continued weekly at Liverpool. I know one who is of opinion that our

Right Reverend will appear to be one of as much duplicity as Mr [Nicholas] Sewall of Preston.[6]

I hear Robert talks of going again to London; if he does I can hope no good from it. You should not seal your letter on your writing. If my compliments can be agreeable to your patron pray make them in my name with thanks for his kind invitation. Mr Melling is come from Aberford ill in health and has been unable to celebrate a considerable time. A spitting of blood, nervous fever and doctors, &c. He complains of their mistaken erroneous treatment of his case.

I wish you a good Christmas and many of them and remain evermore your most affectionate Uncle, R. Banister.

1. H Turberville, *Abridgment of Christian Doctrine* (1649), commonly known as the Douai Catechism, was adapted and abbreviated many times, most notably by Bishop Richard Challoner in 1770, which version has remained in use ever since. [Cf. Bossy, 272ff.]
2. The good-natured and obliging friend of Sir Roger de Coverley who boasted of having 'a pack of dogs better than anyone in the country'. Cf. Addison's *The Spectator*
3. A 6th-century Scot, educated in Wales, served in Ireland and became a monk in Brittany. He was the earliest British historian, quoted by Bede and Alcuin.
4. Benedict Joseph Labre. His life was written in Italian by Giuseppe Marconi but the Rev. James Barnard used the French version of it for his English translation: *The Life of the Venerable Benedict Joseph Labre who died at Rome in the odour of sanctity, 1783 . . . together with an appendix giving an account of several miracles said to have been wrought by his intercession soon after his death* (London 1785).
5. Philip Jones used the alias Morgan; he was at Holywell at the time, not far from Talacre and he may have been tutor in the Mostyn household.
6. An ex-Jesuit who wrote about the Liverpool affair; he left Preston in 1783.

27. Rutter to Banister — Benwell Hall, 26th January 1784

Dear Uncle,

I received your favour the 22nd of last month; it was directed to me at Minsteracres but we are now at Benwell Hall, about 2 miles from Newcastle. This is our winter residence as it was formerly the summer one of the Prior of Tynemouth, whose kitchen is now our dining room. The situation is very agreeable and remarkably healthy, from which we have a fine view of the river Tyne and the coal trade that is here carried on.

I often see Messrs. Warrilow and Cordell at Newcastle, oftener, I believe, than they do one another, for light and darkness are scarce more opposite than these two singular characters. The latter has undertaken to translate Muratori on the Sacrifice of the Mass; he has the cacoethes scribendi and I am sure Warrilow has that of loquendi. But you must know them both.[1]

I am still anxious for my watch. Is it finished and does Mr Tarleton know how to send it? Let him know my address and be so good as to acquaint me when it will set off. You will think me impatient, and so I am.

I understand affairs at Liverpool are in a worse situation than ever. I have lately read the bishop's Mandate and MacDonald's[2] own account of the affair that occasioned it, and shocking it is. The bishop himself seems to apprehend that the charge of duplicity will be brought against him. But no wonder, says he, if my letters are to be mutilated, changed and misrepresented.

You have too good an idea of my economy if you think that I can do with £10 p.an. I shall be content if I can but save two guineas, which I mean to send annually to my mother for her tea and other little necessaries. I am glad to find by your letter that they are all well at home, for I have not heard from them since my departure.

You seem to think that exercise is not necessary either to keep the body healthy or the spirits vigorous, but I apprehend I should soon feel the want of it were I to lay it aside. I have always been a great advocate for exercise and attribute to it the good state of health I have always enjoyed. I think it peculiarly necessary for me in my present situation to prevent the bad effects of high living, for I must confess that I am not sufficiently master of my appetite to observe always the exact rules of temperance and moderation. But though I am fond of exercise, yet I would not have you think me a Will Wimble in the manner of taking it. This, however, seems to have been the case of William Gibson, who has left behind him the reputation of being an excellent marker [marksman], an honour I do not aspire to. He always accompanied his patron in this capacity and on all other occasions showed a flexibility greater than my pride will submit to. He was indeed a most worthy man, but his humility in this respect not a little surprises me.

You say you would not be a Lady's implement to make up parties, and surely you know me better than to think that I can be such. I am not of a nature to gain the favour of ladies; I have something too heavy, too stupid and sombre about me to enter into their light and frivolous amusements, to laugh, play with and flatter them. Indeed, I find that I am not formed for society and this defect I attribute chiefly to Education. I went to the college a tabula rasa, capable of receiving impressions of any kind, gay or serious, vicious or virtuous. My mind being there fixed on grave studies or still graver duties of religion contracted a bias that now turns it from all that is sprightly and modish and that gives it a hardness ill-suited to the pleasures of society. My habits of reserve and sheepishness made me entirely mute and exclude me from sharing in the conversations of any company. So I have one perfection, at least, requisite in a chaplain, that of being silent, a poor, stupid thing that cannot open its mouth. You will say, and perhaps with more reason, that the fault is in myself and not in my education. However it be, and with all my reservedness, I am free enough to lodge all my weaknesses in your bosom and shall always think myself happy in your counsel and advice.

Pray did the Doctor of Burscough obtain a redress of his grievances at Preston?[3]

Does the death of Mrs Henneage fix your neighbour Mr Wilson at Salwick, or is he to make room for some greater favourite at Court? My compliments to him and to all friends and am your dutiful nephew, H.R.

1. William Warrilow, SJ, was the only member of the order in the north to protest publicly about the suppression, which he did in a letter to the press in Newcastle. He was reprimanded by Charles Cordell, his secular colleague in the town; relations between them never recovered, [cf. Gooch thesis 118]. Gillow does not list Cordell's translation of Muratori.
2. Archibald (Benedict) MacDonald, OSB, took over the ex-Jesuit mission in Liverpool during the troubles.
3. Burscough Hall, Ormskirk, where James Brown was missioner; but this is presumably a reference to Richard Morgan who took charge of the ex-Jesuit mission at Preston in succession to Nicholas Sewell in 1783.

28. Rutter to Banister   Benwell House, 14th March 1784

Dear Uncle,

I shall forget how to write unless I sometimes take up my pen and this I seldom do but when I write to you. Besides, I am now in haste to write to you to recall what I said in my last which, I think, was written in a bad humour. I do not recollect what it was, nor am I much concerned when I reflect it was to a person on whom I can rely with an entire confidence.

I have just received my watch after having given it up for lost, for it was above a month on the way. I hope it will prove as good as Mr Tarleton says, for in that case 6 guineas will not be too much. If you have an opportunity you may let Mr Tarleton know that I have received it and that he may depend on Mr Eyre for the payment of it and so you will have no more trouble about it.

I hope Lent agrees with you, it does with me perfectly, and I hope the body will be benefited by it as well as the soul. However, I have no great idea of the merit of modern fasting, which seems to be only a name, for who would desire more than a good dish of chocolate at breakfast, and yet this seems universally allowed and taken in the best families. What are your thoughts on this subject?

To be sure, you have amongst you his Lordship's Pastoral for Lent, and doubtless your congregation was much edified with the elegance and force of expression, the sublimity and grandeur of thought that shines forth in every period.

I have lately accompanied Mr Silvertop and Mr Warrilow as far as [North] Shields to dine onboard the Good Luck, a new ship, ready to sail, in which he has no small share. This place is the port of Newcastle and consequently a very great trade is here carried on. I wish there was a good foundation made for a chapel, for there is a rising congregation which, if properly encouraged, would soon become very numerous. Mr [James] Johnson indeed attends there, but only now and then, for he has business enough on his hands at home, whereas one of the Gentlemen at Newcastle might easily be spared.[1]

I do not know how it is, but I do not find so much time for study as I could wish, and yet I seldom play at cards or ramble abroad. Probably you contrived it better when you were so happy as to live in a family.

The first excursion I shall make will be to Brough, as Sir John [Lawson] and his Lady gave me a very kind invitation. They were here on a visit not long ago with their 2 young ladies and propose going to France after Easter. They mean to make some stay there, as everything will be new to her Ladyship who never was in those parts. Our family has likewise determined on the same expedition to conduct Master George Silvertop to Douai College, which I am heartily glad of. I was always indeed partial to a college education, but since I have lived in a family I see the absolute necessity of it, at least of sending children from home as soon as possible.

There are still 3 boys at home, and fine boys they are, but I should fear very much for them from the fondness of servants did not the father maintain his authority over them.

I have just received a letter from sister Mary, which tells me that she has a fine girl, baptised by Mr Crook.[2] I desire you will acquaint me with any domestic news that you may hear, for I need not expect any from home as my father, I find, is displeased with me. I pray for them and wish them all well. Be pleased to remember me to all friends and to believe me your ever dutiful nephew, H. Rutter.

1. Johnson served at Pontop Hall and was one of several priests who supplied the North Shields mission. The first resident priest went there in 1821 when a church built by James Worswick, missioner in Newcastle, was completed.
2. Unidentified; possibly a Protestant clergyman.

---

29. Banister to Rutter Mowbreck, 21st March 1784

My dear Sir,

I received your last yesterday, and the other some time ago in its due time. Nothing that you write will ever displease me, so spare all apologies. Upon receiving your last but one, I wrote out of hand to Mr Tarleton, and find by your last that it had its effect. He tells me in a letter I received to-day that he sent it off the 4th of last month. I shall inform him by this or next post that it is arrived safe and that Mr Thomas Eyre will indemnify him.

Taking chocolate in the morning on fasting days is certainly an abuse, but I cannot say that it is gravis abusus in parva quantitate. 'Tis now the fashion to dine in gentle houses at 3 or 4 o'clock, the hour or past the hour of None. 'Tis morally impossible to fast so long without some little sustenance, especially for us English who are so used from our infancy to take a breakfast. Many gentlemen take no supper the year round, at least it is a morsel of bread or some other small trifle. The French take no breakfast, dine at 12 or 1, and sup largely. 'Tis easy for them to go without a breakfast in Lent, but not easy to relinquish supper. Hence their collations are set out with salads, fruits, pisciculi (in some places), butter, cheese &c. And because some of them cannot sleep without a full supper (and I dare not go to bed after) their easy casuists allow them one, and the rigids allow dinner or a full meal at night and a collation at noon. This will nearly do for our people of quality who, rising at 10 or 11, collate on chocolate, take their full meal at 4 or 5 and a morsel of bread and wine at 11 or 12 at night.

But, as to writing for, or instructing persons of quality or fortune, 'tis to little purpose; no way will please them but that which is broad and easy. Yet I would venture to answer for their chocolate in the morning and their tea in the evening, their dipping a small biscuit in wine, and licking up a teaspoonful of sweetmeats in Lent, or on other fasting days, provided they would extirpate that pride which is ever predominant in their hearts, that idle and unprofitable life of carding, visiting, dancing, going to plays and balls, and making la frivolite the sole end and object of their thoughts and time.

As to your part, if you fast from everything in Lent or on Ember days till 3 or 4 o'clock in the afternoon, you will ruin your health and constitution; you will not immediately feel the consequences, but it will nevertheless operate upon you. If you have to visit the sick or infirm, never go fasting if you can avoid it. You will perhaps think me lax and indulgent. But, as princes, who are prudent and foreseeing, take great care of the health and nourishment of their soldiers and mariners because they consider their lives as very precious and necessary to the State, so because the lives of missioners are exceeding precious and necessary for the faithful, they ought to be preserved with all due care and prudence. Yet when God pleases to send us a Baptist, that is one who comes neither eating nor drinking, we must not say with the Pharisees, he hath a devil, but be roused up and animated by his example to do penance, if not by rigorous fasts, at least by prayer, recollection and meditation and the flight of the world.[1]

Mr Barrow read to his people the whole Pastoral Letter (though it had not the least signature of the Pastor, nor even the initial letters of his name). One of them said to him afterwards: "It is a high-penned piece". Indeed, it is so highly penned that I was certain not one of my people would understand either all or even half of it; so I read most part of it but let it down, as a distiller does with his strongest spirits, and substituted plain words, more fit for understandings which are to be fed with milk and honey and not solid food.

Our Fund affairs are running into a right channel at last. All legacies and donations in future are to be remitted to one man, called our Treasurer, who is, by the general vote of 1781, to place them in the stocks: Item, the said Treasurer to call in our monies, which Rural Deans have time out of mind lent to farmers, yeomaners, tradesmen, gentlemen, &c., and often lost, and often mismanaged, and place them in the stocks, except the money that has been lent to the Chadwicks, viz., £600, the interest whereof making £24.6s., is yearly to be divided amongst 8 members, who thereby are divided and separated from the other Brethren.

My sister Dorothy departed this life on the 19th of January which had been, I think, to her a long [torn] of trouble, affliction and slavery. Sir Robert Gerard1[2] died the 6th of this Instant. My brother did not come to Preston to sister's funeral but was there with your mother the 18th of February. That same day I was there too, and we were very loving; at parting we embraced and kissed very sweetly. Yet I have heard since that he lays at my door your going so far off, which you know to be entirely false. But transeat: his error in this is of little moment; may God open his eyes to see things of infinite concern. I heard no good things of Robert last Christmas; I apprehend he is idle. Let not this afflict you too much, rather adore God's justice and judgements, yet entreat his mercy who does not will the death of a sinner.

I yet owe your mother 3s. or 4s. of the money you remitted me from St. Omers. Please to say for me the following Masses: 1. Richard. 2. Thomas. 3. William. 4. James. 5. Robert. 6.John; for each one Mass, in all six; and I will give your mother at opportunity 10s. 6d. But, moreover, I pray you to say 8 Masses for my intention: all may be said my midsummer, I hope, without your inconvenience.

Young Mr [Thomas] Eccleston of Scarisbrick is to be married to Miss [Eleonora] Clifton soon after Easter. May all blessings attend you. Do not admire Mr Warrilow: a pompous man, I hear, omnia magna loquens, I suppose. I am all yours in God. Amen. R.B.

1. Banister's sound advice reflects his preoccupation with medical practice. In May one of Banister's pupils at Mowbreck would die. Banister was sorry but blamed the doctor's prescription of bouillon clair and the boy's confinement to bed; he wrote to one of the boy's relatives: 'Last year many persons died at Preston and Eccleston in the Fylde of a kind of malignant putrid fever, and chiefly the poor who live in filthy houses, have no change of sheets or linen, very poor nourishment or attendance. Nothing of which was ever wanting at the college and yet by the good doctor's orders boys have been many times almost stifled by the noisomne fevers and exhalations of their own bodies, bathed in sweat in sheets and shirts impregnated in contagious morbid particles. Even in the small pox no change of linen was allowed which above all things seems most necessary in that loathsome distemper. All which conduct appears to me now very contrary to reason and the re-convalescence of patients, esp. since I saw what Dr Tissot and Dr Buchan of Edinburgh have written on the treatment of persons in fever and such like diseases'. [WAA/48/129]
2. Sir Robert Cansfield-Gerard (IX) married Catherine, daughter of William

Anderton and Mary Clifton. The family was hardpressed to keep the dynasty going at this time; the seventh baronet died young, the eighth died in 1780, the ninth in 1784 and the tenth in 1791.

---

30. Rutter to Banister Minsteracres. 8th June 1784

Dear Uncle,

I am now got back to Minsteracres where I live in the greatest solitude, almost as much retired as any of the ancient hermits. For it is a wild, uninhabited place and the family is from home. The old gentleman and his son are gone with Master Silvertop to Douai, and Madam is gone avisiting with the other children into Yorkshire. However, I would not have you imagine that their absence preys much on my spirits.

I have lately been at Brough to see Sir John and Lady Lawson before their departure for France, as they had given me a very kind invitation. I met there with several of our rank, especially of the ci-devants who have not forgotten their old haunts. It is a time, I perceive, when all our Gentlemen are on the wing, young and old, so that my acquaintance has been much enlarged by it. Among the rest I was glad to see Mr [John] Coates, who is the oldest Douatian we have, being in his 84th year, and still in perfect health and spirits.[1]

The bishop has been in these parts to see his friends and relations. He paid us a visit at Benwell and means to settle, I believe, on the banks of the Tyne, probably at Stella with Mr Thomas Eyre, his particular friend. You have heard, I imagine, of his patroness, Mrs [Mary] Maire, leaving him £40 p.a., besides a thousand pounds to him as bishop, which, with former benefactions, should afford him a decent maintenance.[2] You may soon expect him in Lancashire, if he dare trust himself amongst you. Who lives at Salwick?

I am sorry to hear of the death of my Aunt Dorothy, not for her own sake but that of the family which must feel the loss of her very sensibly. I have had a letter from my father to tell me how much he is displeased with me for not letting him know the day I meant to leave home. He seems hurt likewise that I preferred your advice to his own on some occasion or other. But I hope we shall still be friends, at least more so than if we were neighbours, and on his account I do not regret so much my distance from Lancashire.

I am glad to hear that your Fund affairs are settled to your satisfaction;

ours are entirely in the hands of Messrs. [Nicholas] Clavering,[3] Coates and Eyre, who, I hope, will admit me next August.

You seem to have no very favourable idea of persons of quality and fortune, and I still less so of their servants, who are given to idleness and what not. I am frequently at a loss how to act, how to reconcile indulgence to them with safety to myself. You have been in my situation and what is the result of your experience? I have no reasons, however, to complain of our servants in particular, as they have a master who takes pretty good care of them, and who is more remarkable for his severity than indulgence to them.

After the next winter we are to live here always and therefore at present they are concerting a plan for an additional building. They promise me a change in my apartments and I have reason to expect it. For there is a shocking little chapel and the way to it is through my room, which indeed makes part of it on Sundays and Holydays. Moreover, there is no Sacristy, which makes it very inconvenient at times, and as an additional recommendation, it is in the garret. As a step to this I wish the coal trade may mend, for it has been very bad these six months past, and I fear will continue so, all is confusion and disorder. In this you may suppose me as much interested as a coal-owner, when I see and feel his looks and thoughts as black as the coals he thinks on. I am, dear Uncle, Yours, H.R.

P.S. I had forgot Mr Eyre's respects, who desires you will apply to Doc. Rich. [Morgan] at Preston for money to pay Tarleton for the watch, which seems to be a good one. I have said the Masses. I would willingly have my books if you could insure me 5 or 6 years here. At any rate, you may send them but not till you have received the others from my father.

1. Missioner at Witton Shields, First Superior of the Northern Brethren's Fund from 1739 to his death in 1794.
2. Mrs Mary Maire, widow, had died at Headlam, leaving £4,000 in charitable bequests.
3. Missioner in Durham city and Treasurer of the Northern Brethren's Fund. His was the third name on the terna sent to Rome when Bishop Walton sought a coadjutor in 1780.

31. Rutter to Banister — Minsteracres, 11th October 1784

Dear Uncle,

I have long expected the favour of a letter from you and am sorry to find myself so much disappointed. I have broke off all correspondence except with you and this, I hope, will last as long as our lives. I write home indeed occasionally but they seldom answer me, so I shall not be over-burdened with the additional postage of a letter.

Mr Silvertop went in the Spring to Douai with his eldest son George, as likewise his nephew, one of Mr Wright's sons[1] of Kelvedon, who is desirous of his being under the care of Mr Gibson preferably to the monks, amongst whom he himself was educated. I often hear, as you may suppose, the praises of Douai College now raised to the highest pitch by the vigilance and superior abilities of its President. But while he is so agreeable to the gentry by his condescension and politeness, I wish he would show himself a little more so to persons of a contrary stamp such as Mr Bordley, who is, I hear, much displeased at him. Unless the clergy can humour the old man more than they do at present, I fear the monks will come in for a good share of his money, they seem to entertain hopes.[2]

I presume you have heard of the wretched death of Sir Thomas Tancred at Paris who, it seems, died as he lived.[3] Our family is in black at present for the late Mr [Stephen] Tempest.[4] We have had a full house for these last 3 months, for very few see more company than we do. As to my part, it makes very little difference to me, for I am as mute as a cat at table, and after a bumper to the coal trade, take myself off to my room very quietly, unless the fineness of the evening invites me to a solitary walk. I have still a relish for study though I believe neither myself nor the world will ever be much wiser by it. It is sufficient if I can amuse myself agreeably without pretending to high things, which I leave to your great Geniuses.

I imagine the bishop is amongst you. Though he be fixed at Stella with Mr Eyre, my acquaintance, I dare say will never exceed a little outward formality and ceremony. His assistant, Mr [John] Taylor, I frequently see here as he is on a most familiar footing with the family, having been their chaplain for 5 years.[5] He lives at Hexham the nearest market town, distant about 9 miles. If you see him he will describe this rude and uncultivated country so as not to make you envy much such a northern situation.

I am sorry to hear that brother Robert is gone off again. I was in hopes adversity had cured him of his juvenile follies, but now I fear a relapse into the same bad courses. Agnes, I understand, is married. Do you approve of the match?

The Jesuits have had a general meeting, but I have not heard the result of their debates.

I have just been reading the life of the humble [St Benedict] Labre, as given by Marconi, the holy man's confessor, which Mr Eyre lent me. His life being hid with Christ's does not abound much in adventure and may not perhaps please curious and frivolous minds: "yet the eye of God hath looked upon him for good and hath lifted him up from his low estate and hath exalted his head; and many have wondered at him and have glorified God."

Pray who is at Salwick and at Townley? How does my uncle Wearden go on since the loss of my aunt? What is your opinion of smugglers? Would you suffer yours to buy commodities of them?

Mr [Ralph Peter] Clavering, whom you must remember, has left England with his family and means to settle at Liege. His affairs are in the greatest confusion, but I hope some part of the estate can be saved by the management of my patron, who is appointed one of the trustees.[6] The shocking death of young Webb is often talked of and the judgement and discretion of the father is often called in question.[7]

You are now in my debt two letters and I hope to hear from you soon. How does our young Actaeon come on and what are his sister's fortunes? Remember me in your prayers and believe me with all affection, Your dutiful Nephew H. Rutter.

1. Thomas Wright. John Silvertop's youngest daughter Winifred married John Wright of Kelvedon.
2. Bordley (1709–99), a priest-schoolmaster, was the son of a yeoman. He had served the mission at Salwick Hall and Mowbreck Hall where he had a school in the 1740s and was often in straits but he had saved a considerable sum since.
3. Sir Thomas Tancred (V) of Brampton; Gray's Inn 1772, DCL (Oxon.) 1773, barrister 1775, died in 1784 in Mayfair (not Paris). By 'wretched' Rutter probably means 'apostate' since Tancred's career hardly corresponds to that of a contemporary Catholic.
4. Stephen Walter Tempest of Broughton (1719–84) married Frances Meynell of Aldborough. Their daughter Frances married Thomas Wright referred to in n1 above.
5. Chaplain at Benwell Hall.

6. Ralph Peter Clavering had become so indebted after thirty years of expenditure in the improvement of the Callaly Castle estate that he was forced to flee abroad, where the living was easier. His brother, the Rev. Nicholas Clavering, moved up from Durham to Callaly to take over the mission and act as caretaker of the estate.
7. Sir John Webb (V) of Odstock, Wilts., married Mary Salvin; she died in 1782 but it is not clear why his son's death two years later was shocking. At any rate Sir John sold Odstock to a Protestant and moved away after it; he died in 1797 and was succeeded by his nephew.

32. Banister to Rutter — Mowbreck, 14th October 1784

My dear Sir,

I received your last letter dated 8th of June and have been in your debt for it an enormous length of time, for which I must crave your pardon.

Our bishop began his progress in this county at Hornby, proceeded to Lancaster, Claughton, Great Eccleston, Lytham (but no Squire there), and arrived here for dinner on Tuesday the 21st of last month. The day after, he confirmed and dined again with me and, as it set in for a constant heavy rain in the afternoon, he was easily persuaded to stay another night. The morning after was fine and I conducted him to Mr [John] Carter's[1] where he confirmed and dined, and between 4 and 5 o'clock went to Preston. I suppose he is still in our county for I have not heard of his return. The Vicar General [Chadwick] had marked out his stages so as to pass by me, but Mr John Barrow changed them, by which means he was my guest two days and received several heads of important enquiry which I wrote for him in his book of memorandums. I know nothing as yet of the issue.

Whilst he spoke to the confirmandi I prayed in my mind that God would please to make his words fructify in their hearts but I greatly feared their understandings were too gross and dull to comprehend his language. Daily experience teaches me that one cannot speak too plain to the vulgar. Our style ought to be altogether of the simple kind which nevertheless may be sublime as the masters of eloquence affirm. For sublimity, they say, consists not so much in the turn of phrase as in the thought. I therefore entreat you never to study for fine phrases and fine language, grand metaphors and tropes, but study to convey the sacred truths of the gospel in the plainest and easiest manner possible into the minds of the simple and illiterate; doing otherwise is labour lost.

The bishop's man told Mary, my housekeeper, that the good chaplain at Stella preaches long sermons and better than his Right Reverend guest. Which I can readily believe because assiiduity will improve more and more even a very indifferent beginner, and the want of practice will disable good talents. If you have not yet begun, delay no longer; propose to yourself to speak for ten minutes, or a quarter of an hour at most, you can certainly furnish good matter for so short a time. Propose to yourself to speak of, and to prove and inculcate, but one point without exordium, partition or division, useless things in a short discourse, and of modern invention introduced into sermons; the homilies of the Fathers have nothing of that kind. As for action or gesture, if there be no oddity, nor stupidity, nor affectation, nor flourishing, 'twill do. Modesty and gravity, an exterior of piety, but proceeding from some little interior fund, best recommend a pious discourse. We should speak not only to be understood by attentive hearers but to be heard and understood by the dull and the inattentive.This is a very short, imperfect instruction for a young preacher, but it comes from your affectionate well-wisher and friend and therefore let none see it besides yourself.

You ask me concerning servants, how far you may indulge them? I suppose you mean in the church-precept of fasting, to which I answer that they ought to make a distinction between fasting days and no fasting days. Their something in a morning and at night must not be a whole breakfast or a whole supper, unless their labour require it, and even our day-labourers will not grudge to pinch their morning and evening meals, in Lent at least. But servants in great families are often pampered, epicurean fat hogs. You can do nothing with them in foro externo [publicly], but when they come to your forum internum [Confession], deal roundly and plainly with them. Sit not with a great handkerchief before your face like one that is ashamed of himself or of his employ, but as much as possible show your countenance full of serenity, gravity, piety and compassion; and when you see people going in that broad road to perdition, [Cry aloud, never ceasing, raise thy voice like a trumpet-call, and tell my people of their transgressions . . .][2] Read the life of Mr [William] Webster in the Memoirs of Missionary Priests and follow his spirit.[3]

Mr Wilson is still at Salwick and will, I hope, continue there, for the death of Mrs Henneage has set him at liberty. I hear nothing from Westhead. Agnes was married in August to Robert Rimmer, a joiner in Crosby, a promising youth and of her own household. Robert is again emigrated to London; never more expect your money till he fall heir to Westhead or, which is more probable, you yourself become the heir, for I cannot think that he will wear to a great age.

The carriage of books is so dear that I am not willing to send you many; what provision has your Squire? Perhaps of novels, plays, romances, not fit for you. But if of a better stamp he surely will not debar you from reading them.

I hear Mrs Eccleston of Scarisbrick has had a miscarriage. Mr William Gibson, President of Douai College, [who] desires his compliments and respects to me, has received one at my recommendation on a fund gratis, and will take another recommended by me for £9 p.a. whom, life accompanying, I shall send over next Spring. I suppose your young Argentea fastigia are placed there; may they become pennae columbae de argentatae.[4]

The last time I saw my brother was at Preston in February. We were not long together but we kissed with great cordiality, your mother was with him; they paid their visit of condolence. Is your time keeper exact? Do you mind what I said, never to visit the sick while you are fasting? That you may live to the age of Mr Coates is the prayer of your most affectionate Uncle, R. Banister.

1. Goosnargh. Bishop Gibson's 'progress' was, of course, a Confirmation Tour of the western half of the District.
2. Is. 58, 1
3. By Richard Challoner (2 vols., 1741/2). The book's title proceeds: . . . *and other Catholics of both sexes that have suffered death in England on religious accounts from the year 1577 to 1684*. William Webster, alias Ward was martyred at Tyburn 26 Jul 1641, the first victim of the Civil War. Challoner says he had the reputation of 'a rigid ghostly father; and albeit many great persons made use of him in that way, nevertheless he yielded nothing to their greatness but was rather more severe to them than to meaner persons &c.'
4. This is one of Banister's rare jokes; 'Argentea fastigia' puns 'Silver tops', meaning the two boys at the college; the other phrase continues the allusion to height: 'wings of a silver dove'. Bishop Milner later took the opposite line in referring to George Silvertop as 'Copper bottom'.

---

33. Rutter to Banister Benwell House, 9th January 1785

Dear Uncle,

I received your very acceptable favour of the 23rd October and am glad to find you begging pardon for your long silence and neglect. You cannot write too much, or too often, to one who is ever glad to hear from you and whose youth and inexperience entitles him to your advice and instruction. Your short plan for a young preacher is, I think, well suited to my capacity and therefore by degrees I will endeavour to reduce it to practice. A great deal, to be sure, depends on practice and perseverance, but I despair of ever arriving at the perfection of speaking ex tempore if I may judge by the great want both of words and ideas that I experience at present when I speak on any any subject whatsoever.

I fear that simplicity you recommend will be wanting in Mr [James] Archer's sermons, now preparing for the press. However, for acquaintance sake I must be a subscriber. I knew him perfectly well at the college and always thought him a genius of the first class, not less solid than bright. He is indeed too young, but the reason of his appearing so soon in print is in order to get the start of one Mr [James] Appleton who is going to make public his composition. He was before my time but probably you can form some conjecture as to their merit.[1]

I mentioned in a former letter what a vigorous, healthy old Gentleman we have, and as a proof that he himself thinks so, he is going to be married to a widow 40 years younger than himself. Her settlement must necessarily take a good sound sum from the family (I hear £400 or £500 per annum), and therefore this affair has occasioned no small vexation to the son, whose behaviour has been too tender and dutiful to have given the least occasion to so juvenile a step. But such is the weakness of man![2]

The Lady will bear it much better for she is of an even temper, and likewise a very good Christian, but much given to the Jesuitical devotions. You have read and perhaps made use of her uncle Lawson's book on devotion to the Sacred Heart, "the manifestation of which", he says, "was reserved by God to these latter times, as a means of drawing the Faithful out of extreme tepidity into which he foresaw they would degenerate".[3] Now, in what consists the excellence of this devotion about that to the Blessed Eucharist, for he says they are really distinct. But I do not see clearly in what except that the latter is addressed to the sacred heart of Jesus without any relation to the other parts of his adorable body, and to what purpose?

The Abbess at York[4] was cured, I am well-informed by a good Jesuit putting down her throat a scrap of paper on which were two lines addressed to the Blessed Virgin which I have forgot. What say you to this?

I desire to know your opinion as to smuggled goods; our books do not seem to authorise the common practice on this point.

I hear Gregory Stapleton is come over and is not to return, likewise his friend Mr Rimmer.[5] Pray if it is his brother that my sister Agnes has married?

As the carriage of books is so dear you need not send me all my collection at present, but I could wish to have the following and any others you may think particularly useful for me. Namely, Massillon, Pensees de Bourdaloue and anything else belonging to the pulpit. Nicole, 2 collections of instructions on how to spend the year, Bible, Combat Spirituel, His. Cat. by Fleury &c. The Squire has a good many books of his own collecting, some very expensive ones, chiefly in relation to the English History, but I seldom ask him for the key.

My watch seems to be a very good one. I wish you many returns of the season as likewise to all friends and remain your ever dutiful Nephew, H.R

1. Archer published five volumes of sermons beginning in 1787; Appleton's translation of *Pious Lectures* by C. F. Lhomond did not come out until 1794.
2. George Silvertop's second wife was Jane Selby of Earle in Northumberland. This was her third marriage; the first was to a Quaker; the second to an Anglican; now she had taken a Catholic. Moreover, as the *Gentleman's Magazine* pointed out in February, each husband was half her age. (See also N°. 35.)
3. Thomas Lawson, jun., SJ, *The Devotion to the Sacred Heart of Jesus &c.* (Bruges, 1767). There were eleven editions by 1816.
4. Mother Anna Aspinwall; she died in 1789 and was buried in the chancel of Holy Trinity church, Micklegate.
5. Procurator Stapleton and Vice President Richard Southworth opposed Gibson's rebuilding programme and day to day administration because it brought the college close to bankruptcy. Southworth hung on but Stapleton resigned and became travelling-tutor to Thomas Stonor in place of Henry Tichborne Blount who felt unable to undertake the journey. Rimmer opposed Gibson's modernisation of the syllabus and also resigned; he returned to England. It must be said that Gibson's plans were not universally condemned; the students were most enthusiastic about his changes, which were generally agreed to be long overdue.

---

34. Banister to Rutter — Mowbreck, 11th February 1785

My dear,

I received your last, dated 9th of last month, in due time. On 25th there was at Lytham Hall a grand banquet and entertainment for the birthday of the Squire who then was at age. 32 dined with him and 33 with his steward. Messrs [Thomas] Cuerden, Orrell, Wilson and Barrow of Claughton were only invited amongst us [priests]. Item, Parson Harrison of Clifton the only one of that stamp. On the 27th all the chief tenants were entertained; a glass holding 2 gills circulated round as a bumper to his health immediately after dinner. My neighbour, a farmer of some tithes in Wesham, came off sound and well, not staying till the punch-bowls were brought up, for many were slain by that potent adversary of health, sense and reason, and taken off and laid in straw. However, the dead revived again. I am told that near on a thousand dined there on the 27th. It could not cost much less than £300. Gibson, the Lytham parson, has held forth (I am told to-day) two Sundays upon this riot. The son, following the example of his father, allows him no admittance under his roof.

As to Mr Archer's sermons, I can frame no certain judgement of them. For my part, if I continue in the same mind I shall neither purchase nor read either his or Mr James Appleton's, or any other modern productions of the sort. Not because they are modern, (for Horace shows that to be an invidious exception against contemporary geniuses) but because I love the fountains rather than small rivulets which often swell and froth and make a bubbling and yet afford but little water to quench one's thirst. I knew Appleton perfectly well; he was Mr Wilkinson's grand pet. His health was not very good, on which account he had but a small pittance of theological learning, but abundance of indulgence and a journey to England at the college's expense with recommendations to all Mr Wilkinson's acquaintance. I will, however, believe that retirement, prayers and study, and wisely borrowing, may have enabled him to make a tolerable production. I know nothing so easy as setting forth an edition of new sermons. Even Sterne, author of Tristram Shandy and of The Sentimental Journey, has published his Sermons, and others of his stamp theirs.

I saw many years ago Uncle Lawson's book The Devotion to the Sacred Heart and thought it a very mean performance. I wished to see several extracts from the Fathers and Saints, if not explicitly at least implicitly, teaching and recommending the said devotion. Mr [John] Jenison,[1] then of Preston, showed me his Office and Lessons of the Feast which he and all of his order recited, but I was much disappointed in finding it so little pertinent to the subject. Our Office for the Sacred Name of Jesus is admirable. St. Bernardin in the 14th century was the ardent promoter of devotion to the Sacred Name; I wish any one of the Jesuits were like him and would propagate as ardent a devotion to the Sacred Heart. You ask me "in what consists the excellence of this devotion above that to the Blessed Sacrament?" I answer that in recommending or treating of devotions and forms of prayer, it is foreign and impertinent to say one is more excellent than another. It is enough to show that the devotion is good, is either expresly or implicitly taught and recommended by the Fathers, or that several saints and great servants of God have used it. I think, too, that there is a difference between devotion to the Sacred Heart and that to the Blessed Sacrament. St. Teresa says her father was much devoted to the mystery of our Saviour carrying his cross. St. Jerome was devoted to the Sacred Manger. We have an Office and Feast in honour of St. Peter's Chains, though none in honour of the nails or thorns of our Saviour. The Most Sacred Heart of our Saviour was filled with infinite love for us, with extreme sadness in the garden, with an ardent desire to suffer and die for us; it was pierced with a lance for us, and the wound is open to receive us and to protect us from the wrath which will fall on us impenitent sinners. I therefore think that meditating on the Sacred Heart under the foresaid and many other considerations must be very good and very profitable. But to say it is better than devotion to the crib, or to the carrying of the cross, or to the Blessed Sacrament, I will not pretend.

If that good Lady uses Jesuitical devotions with simplicity and pious intention, without bigotry and prepossession against all other kinds, and without censuring others who do not use them; if likewise she join true and solid Christian virtues and conforms not to the common ways of people in high life, then she ought not to be told that her devotions are empty and unprofitable.

My opinion of smugglers is that they are defrauders of the public customs so never admit a trader in smuggling. But as for poor sailors who bring over perhaps a few gallons of rum, or a few pounds of coffee, leaving them to their bona fides, may be best, as it seems.

I find by a letter of Mr Ralph Platt[2], dated 26th of last November, but I only received it last week, that there is some revolution at Douai College. He writes thus:

Mr Rimmer, who gave up his office of General Prefect on 14 Instant, a happy circumstance indeed, comes with Mr [Matthew] Sharp to England. He has many good qualities, but those of a General Prefect were among the least. Our worthy friend Mr [John] Gillow still continues Prefect of Studies, and a zealous good man he is. I was terribly afraid our President had not courage to support him in some late struggles. I am very warm in support of Mr President's party, if I must give it so unbecoming a name.

Excuse me from saying more, I am afraid of saying something uncharitable. Mr [Isaac] Bellass is a Deacon and from Warrington succeeds Mr Rimmer.

So far Mr Ralph. Mr Sharp is only come to see his relations before he sails to Lisbon. I sent thither two boys 12th last October, who arrived there safe in 9 days sailing from Liverpool. But the captain and his son and a boy and ship are all lost off Holyhead in Anglesey in their return home.

Mr Richard Rimmer is not brother, nor cousin, to sister Agnes's husband. What age is your old Miner? You say the widow is 40 years younger but your data are insufficient to know her age. I will look out some books for you after Easter.

You described yourself in one of your letters to be paucoru sermonum altio silenti: 'tis very well, you will consequently be a more accurate observer. You will not bubble and let all run out as fast as it enters, but like a basin which emits no water till it flows over the brim or margin.

Your Squire is then curious in English history; we want one very much for the use and perusal of Catholics, who would not be led into errors and prejudices and false notions and sentiments about many important points and characters. Therefore, begin whilst young and vigorous, make collections and extracts from every writer of note of our English history; this will be like gathering materials for an edifice. We once were proposing to Mr [Alban] Butler to write an English history which others, as he told us, had desired too. He said it would cost him 3 or 4 hundred pounds to collect printed books and manuscripts for commencing such a work. But you need be at no charge; your squire has a valuable assortment for you, and if you desire more, go to Mr Marmaduke Tunstall[3] at Wycliffe on Tees.

Make my compliments to Mr Silvertop, junior, and to Mr Eyre and Mr Taylor when you see them. Your squire gave Miss [Elizabeth] Riddell for his toast on his birthday, do you know her? I hope all are well at Westhead, for I hear nothing contrary. I remain your most affectionate dear Uncle, R. Banister.

1. John Jenison (alias Thompson) SJ, at Preston 1768–75.
2. Procurator at Douai but he soon fled, pleading incompetence. He was succeeded by Thomas Smith, who was ordained for the purpose after only two years study of theology.
3. (1743–90), Catholic layman; antiquarian and naturalist; FSA (1764); FRS (1771). Tunstall held that 'Banister, though he carried matters too far otherwise, was right in being an advocate of laying in a solid stock of knowledge in the work of the ancients as a basis to build on'. [*UM* 24 (1914) 69]

---

35. Rutter to Banister Benwell Hall, 18th March 1785

Dear Uncle,

I received in due time the favour of your letter, dated the 9th of last month.

You give me a fine description of the rejoicings at Lytham for the birthday of the young Esquire. I ventured to write him a line or two on the occasion, which he civilly answered giving me an invitation to Lytham if I had any design of coming to Lancashire this summer. Now, as a jaunt will be of service to me and I never can have a better opportunity, I propose soon to make you a visit and hope to be with you at least in a fortnight's time. Mr and Mrs Silvertop are going to see their friends in the south and, as we are about to quit Benwell entirely (to my sorrow), I shall make use of this opportunity and so avoid the confusion and disorder that must necessarily be the consequence of it. The only objection that occurred was the expense of the journey, but this, I hope will not be greater altogether than I was at in coming hither. However, as I am not very fond of rambling, I may perhaps be induced to change my mind if you have any very strong reasons to offer against it. But you must write immediately or else it will be too late, for I mean to set out either next week or at latest the week after. Unless indeed the weather continues as unfavourable as at present, for it is snowing very heavily and looks more like Christmas Day than Easter Sunday. The severity of the winter has been greater here than was ever remembered, and has been particularly felt in this family, both in regard to the coal trade and the plantations at Minsteracres, which have suffered exceedingly. But I wish everyone could bear his losses as well as we can ours.

I assisted last Thursday at the consecration of the holy oils at Stella. His Lordship is very well at present, but I fear he will not long continue so unless he changes his ethos of life. He has a good appetite, yet takes no kind of exercise, never stirs out to work off the gouty humour which the doctor says he is full of. I saw there Nicholas Clavering who is going to conduct Mrs Clavering and his brother's family abroad to Douai.

The old Gentleman's Lady (whose age you would know) is in her 42nd year and has, I find, been very severely reflected on in the newspapers for her matrimonial taste, having had 3 husbands and each of them double her age. She is, however, a most generous, disinterested woman and a very good Christian and has made it her study to bring about peace and concord among us, which she has happily effected.

You need not send my books till I see you, when we can settle much better than by letter. I am now in haste to set out for Minsteracres to my little flock, and remain your most dutiful Nephew, H. Rutter.

P.S. You talk to me of writing and collecting, but I wish you would set me the example and not bury the talents entrusted to you for the good of others. We agree here that there is no one more fit to follow the plan you suggested, of writing the lives of the saints. Mr Eyre will undertake to print them for you. In case you cannot be prevailed on, I understand Mr Gother's are to be reprinted just as they are without any alteration.

---

36. Banister to Rutter — Mowbreck, 17th June 1785

My most dear Sir,

On Saturday the 28th of last month your box of books, directed in very legible characters, both on the top and side: To You with John Silvertop Esqr, to be left at Mr Adam's Office, Newcastle, Northumberland, was carried by Robert Blacoe's cart to Preston. William Wearden sent if off by the York carrier on Monday 30th. It is probably at Newcastle by this time. If not, let me know. It cannot be lost for it was entered in the carrier's books at Preston.

I pray you to excuse my silence, and I beseech you, for the love you bear to our Lord, and to me for his sake, do not attribute it to any displeasure I have taken against you or about you. For indeed there is no such thing.

I have been greatly depressed in mind, the reason of which I will not mention at present, but may inform you at another time. All our relations are well, cousin Crook has a son, born the 20th of last month. Mr Wilson is at Talacre on a visit to Sir Piers Mostyn.

Last Wednesday Mr [Joseph] Higginson came hither to see me; he is Prefect of the Study-place and is to be at Douai College again the middle of next month. He seems to own that there is a great torrent of pomp and grandeur. He says the two Yorkshire bankrupts[1] are likely to stay where they are. I told him that now they seemed at Alma to be convinced of [Joseph] Berington's assertion, viz., that our missioners have hitherto brought nothing home but a lumber of scholastic divinity. Therefore scarce one goes through a whole course, and there has been no universal defensions in divinity since Mr [John] Gillow and [John] Griffiths.[2]

Pray write to me soon and let me know how you got home, and your Galloway. Oremus pro nobis met invicem. Tomacini sailed from London May 19th. I am ever your most affectionate Uncle, R. Banister.

1. Obscure. Possibly a reference to Procurator Stapleton, who was born in Yorkshire, and President Gibson, a Northumbrian but could as well have been a Yorkshireman to someone on the other side of the Pennines.
2. Gillow and Griffiths were ordained on 18 Dec 1779.

37. Rutter to Banister — Minsteracres, 1st January 1786

Dear Uncle,

I have been long expecting to hear from you and am not a little concerned at your silence. Pray tell me the reason of it, if arising from any fault on my part, that I may ask pardon and reform it if in my power.

Since my last to you I think nothing very particular or interesting has occurred; indeed, my way of life cannot abound much in adventure and, as to others, I should know almost as much on the mountains of Siberia. We are not as yet entirely blocked up by snow but this I expect will be the case very shortly. We have far more snow here than you have, but Providence has provided us plenty of fuel so that it is our own fault if we are starved with the cold.

I suppose you have heard that Charles Berington is chosen as coadjutor to Thomas Talbot[1], and I hope he will prove as good a bishop as he has been a tutor. His success with Giffard has gained him universal praise. I hope they will next proceed to choose a coadjutor for these parts; for his Lordship's health, I believe, is in a far more precarious state than that of either of the other two. I dined with him not long ago and he enquired after you, but I could give him no satisfaction.

I understand they are going to republish the Ritual and, I hope, with some of your amendments and additions; If you choose a greater work, there is the Holy Bible, a new edition of which is expected to come out, by and by; and though that of Bishop Challoner be much approved of, yet some persons think that it might be corrected in some places and improved with a few more annotations, the want of which I daily experience.

The establishment of a new school seems as far off as ever, though it is often spoken of and much wished for in these parts.[2] Mr [Ferdinando] Ashmall has of late been very ill and in all appearance cannot live long.[3] We have had here a most solitary Christmas, in comparison of Benwell, where we had always a full house. It is difficult entirely to prevent dissensions amongst servants and not even to be entangled in them, but I hope to be more wise for the future. What advice have you to give me on the subject? You must have heard of Mr [John] Bolton's commitment to York Castle for converting a Protestant. If the only effect of this prosecution be his leaving England it will be a great happiness and what has been long wished for. Lord Fauconberg who, I believe, repents that he did not get him hanged heretofore (as he might have done), is said to have a hand in the affair, but he himself denies it.[4]

Sir Carnaby Haggerston's marriage with Miss [Frances] Smith [Smythe] afforded great joy and satisfaction to all his friends. He had long figured away in the first circles and is particularly intimate with the Duke and Duchess of Rutland, but I never heard how far he exerted his interest in our favour. However, I know of one instance of his zeal and that was preventing a certain very unworthy person from being made Bishop of Quebec, but at the same time, he would not nominate to that dignity, not choosing to meddle in such concerns.

I could wish, dear Uncle, to have your profile taken the first opportunity at Preston or Liverpool, and that you will send it me in a letter. The expence would be very trifling and therefore I hope you will not deny me this favour.

I am exceedingly glad that Mr Clifton is settled, What do they say of his match in Lancashire? Is he still on the turf? Are matters agreed upon between him and Lady Jane? Did you see sister Susan and how do all friends and relations do?[5]

I have got a Jesuit's bean but am at a loss how to send it you. I imagine you are acquainted with its virtues, but pray do not forget that it is itself a strong poison.[6] Which are the best books and directions for catechising? I think I shall write down something as a help that way.

I do not like the accounts from Douai, but there are some, especially monks, who make things far worse than they really are. Is Mr [Richard] Southworth in England? How many boys have you sent abroad altogether? Pray write me a longer letter than your last and believe me, with compliments of the season, to be your ever dutiful Nephew, Hen. Rutter

1. There were two Bishops Talbot at this time: James (1726–90), Bishop of Birtha, ipi, and Vicar Apostolic of the London District; and Thomas (1727–95),

Bishop of Acon, ipi, and Vicar Apostolic Midland District. It is not always clear which our correspondents refer to when they omit the Christian name. Berington (1748–98) took his DD at the Sorbonne in 1776 then came to the English mission at Ingatestone, Essex. Immediately before his election as Bishop of Hierocaesarea and to the coadjutorship, he had spent two years as travelling-tutor to Thomas Giffard of Chillington, with whom he toured through France, Italy and Germany.

2. Small Catholic private and dame schools existed unofficially. The Catholic Relief Act of 1778, while abolishing the prosecution of Catholics for the practice of their religion and permitting them to own real estate by inheritance or purchase, did not precisely authorise Catholic schools. But, since the use to which buildings could be put was not specified in the act, Catholics went ahead, rightly confident of toleration, although Protestant pupils were not admitted until 1829.
3. The ninety-year-old missioner at Newhouse, Esh, Co. Durham; he would live on for another twelve years.
4. John (Anselm) Bolton OSB (1736–1805), the domineering chaplain and estate steward to Anne Fairfax of Gilling Castle in the North Riding. Evidently to Fauconberg's fury, Bolton's trial collapsed when a witness was found to be a perjurer. Henry Belasyse, fifth Viscount and second Earl Fauconberg (1743–1802), MP and a great favourite of George III. His father, Thomas, apostatised and embezzled the bequest to the mission by a previous chaplain on the grounds that the money had been left for superstitious uses. It is said that he was reconciled to the Church before his death in 1774. Henry did not follow suit but his younger daughter Mary married Thomas Eyre of Hassop and he had other Catholic connections, including the Norfolks and the Fairfaxes. His kinship with the latter perhaps explains Henry's dislike of Bolton's influence over Anne's business affairs. Henry was the last of the direct line; the earldom passed to a kinsman; the seventh and last earl was a Catholic priest.[Kirk; G R Smith, *In Well Beware* (1978) passim; G Scott, *Gothic Rage Undone* (1992) 94/5]
5. John Clifton was engaged to Elizabeth Riddell of Swinburne Castle. He was negotiating the sum of the jointure of Lady Jane Clifton, his mother.
6. A poisonous seed of the plant *strychnes ignatii*, akin to *nux vomica*. Banister used it with alegar as an oral prophylactic [No. 48].

38. Banister to Rutter Mowbreck Hall, 12th January 1786

My dear Hal,

It is, I think, impossible for you to displease me, unless you first displease

God by ill-conduct, which I hope will never happen. I had been, about the time I wrote my last, very much troubled at two things.

First, a poor woman came to Kirkham (her husband remaining at Liverpool), very sick and far gone in her pregnancy. I hoped and prayed that she might live till she was delivered but greatly feared for her and in that fear I was continually thinking by what means I could procure the caesarean operation to be performed presently after her decease. She was lodged in a poor cottage, in a chamber of four beds, all the family Protestants maintained by the town whose overseer was very rough and harsh. At last I discoursed with the man-midwife who, at my desire, visited her, and told him that it would be a horrible thing to bury the living with the dead, that for our parts we look upon baptism as absolutely necessary and that if he would open her side after her death and save the child I would recompence his trouble. The man, though a Protestant, is very humane and good-natured, and promised to do what I desired if he were at hand at the time of her death. She died on a Sunday, an hour or more before I heard of it. I immediately hastened to Kirkham but the man-midwife was gone to Lytham town. I sent for Thomas Swarbreck, a Catholic apothecary. I entreated him to perform the operation, told him I would bear all the blame, if any could arise, and offered him a guinea. He examined the corpse again and again and still confidently pronounced that the child was dead. I know these asseverations of chirurgeons and doctors would not have satisfied Cangia mila, but what could I do, I had no other resource. This is a heathen country, we cannot compel anyone to perform such operations. If entreaty and the offer of a reward will not move the surgeon, we are to rest content as far as I can see.

The other thing that mortified me was of little importance in comparison of the first, and I cannot give any reason why it made such an impression on me. It was the proposal Mr Thomas Eyre made me of undertaking the administration and presidency of a new school, and affirming that if I refused it, the design would be dropped. I commended the design as exceeding useful and pious, but never consented to engage in it but, only at most, to deliberate on it, forseeing that my deliberation would always conclude in the negative. I have asked two, Mr Wilson and Mr Barrow, what their advice is? They bid me reject it; they remind me of Douai-affair. They tell me some gentleman or other will run down my conduct and then I must decamp. Mr Wilson is of opinion that the bishop wishes to get me out of Lancashire. I said to Mr Eyre that I confidently trusted in his pure, sincere and most candid intention, but if his Lordship (said I) has any sinister motive, depend upon it, the scheme will never succeed. I knew his

Lordship so well at the college, and his ways of prescinding, arguing, splitting, doubling &c., that I cannot easily trust myself to him and never implicitly. But Mr Eyre is a true and sincere good soul, and I hope he will never learn duplicity nor acquire any tincture of it. Can you imagine it a method proper to begin, or promote God's honour or glory, who is truth and delights in nothing but truth? My dear Hal, let your tongue and heart grow together. Did ever man in our memory do greater things than St. Francis of Sales or St. Vincent de Paul? and can you find in all your, or in all their, letters, the least tincture of duplicity or double dealing?

So, by your account (which I suppose you received a fide dignissimis) Sir Carnaby hindered an unworthy person from being nominated Bishop of Quebec. If that unworthy person be Mr Raymond Harris, I pray you to read his character and encomium in an authentick letter sent him by Bishop Gibson, given at length in the printed Appeal. But perhaps you may have it not, or dare not read it. For my part I was never near the state of the question till I had read it, and now I am persuaded both from the whole tenor of the account, and even from what I observed at Preston when the parties met the bishop there in December 1782, and from some other anecdotes, that the grand central point aimed at was the removal of Mr Harris from Liverpool. And is not this manifest too from the tenor of his suspension: if he will go to Ugthorpe he may have all parochial faculties; if he stays at Liverpool, he is suspended even from celebrating. A bishop in France cannot deprive a man of his curacy so and pack him off to a little pittance in a corner of his diocese.

But we must not scrutinise or criticise the conduct of our superiors. No by no means, but one may, I hope, without offence pity the oppressed. One may wonder why a man so praised and extolled in April or May is totally suspended in September or October after. I believe Mr Harris to be by far the ablest scholar in the defunct body; his sermons and publications show him to be an exact and acute reasoner, and I admire a foreigner so perfect a master of our language. His study must be almost uninterrupted; it certainly allows no time for the theatre, assemblies, card-tables, drinking-bouts, races, cock-fights, dangling after ladies &c., all which deserve to be Ugthorped infinitely more, in my opinion, than this object of his emulous brethren.[1]

They say Lytham wears a new face very unlike the old one, but I cannot learn precisely in what the difference consists. However, all the cats are hanged and many hounds, but to make room for a new sort, called fox-hounds, from Puddington. His hunting horses are all of high blood but I hear of no race-horses. Lady Jane has agreed to take £800 p.a. I hear old

[Thomas] Riddell has tied the young squire out from giving a lease for lives. If so, our Fylde people will be much displeased. I fancy he is a true enigma.

When my nephew Thomas can take my face I would rather recompense him for it than a stranger. Susan was here one night, for she hastened to Swinnerton to Basil Fitzherbert's: £16 p.a. and her tea. I desired her to write to me at Christmas but have received nothing from her as yet. No one has been here this season from Liverpool or Westhead, but I believe all are well. Did you take my Cabassutius among your books by mistake?

Mr John Barrow set out on Christmas Day for Douai College to take away Mr Miles [Stapleton's] son [John]. William Gibson has sent to his father a vile account of him, I wonder he would write so, but they think at Clints that he is for rooting out every twig of Stapletons. You will live to see every Gibson extirpated too on some revolution.

I received your letter this morning; it has roused me from a kind of lethargy and hastened this half answer. I must now desire you to pray for me and am ever yours most affectionately R. Banister

1. Harris was the main protagonist in the Liverpool affair (see N° 25, n3). Ugthorpe in the North Riding was known as 'purgatory' because it was the poorest mission in the District and was where the bishop sent any missioner proving unamenable to the episcopal will.

39. Banister to Rutter Mowbreck Hall, 27th February 1786

My dear sweet Hal,

This is the second part of an answer to your letter dated Jan. 1st. I hope it will reach you through your blockades of snow. So, Charles Berington has catched a mitre by his renowned travels with Master Giffard!

What do you look for by your labours on Master Clifton? Had you told me that he had acquired an universal reputation by learning, remarkable piety and contempt of the world by pathetic sermons which had worked wonderful conversions of hardened sinners, you would have given the character of a man truly worthy of a mitre. Of if you can inform me that Master Giffard is not walking in the paths of other young squires of great riches and estates (as one hints to me that he does) but on the contrary is truly poor in affection, uses his wealth to relieve the distressed and to do actions of universal beneficence; not to clothe himself in fine linen and purple and to feast sumptuously every day. If you can inform me that he is most chaste, most sober, that he spends a considerable time every day in holy meditations, that his connections are very few, and with persons of sincere and undoubted piety, and if, in short, he is another St. Elzear [of Sabran] in all his conduct and government of his house, then I will attribute a good part of this to the lesson and examples of his tutor. But, alas, I apprehend that the renown of Berington arises from nothing more than the outward accomplishments of his pupil, his genteel personage, his polite carriage, easy access, ready and free conversation, relating his travels and observations, modes and fashions in a facetious way &c. And do you think that educating a pupil for the polite world ever made a man worthy of a mitre?

I have nothing more to say about the Ritual, but it were to be wished that our bishop would publish again the Instructions set forth in 1752 by Bishop [Francis] Petre[1] with injunctions and precepts drawn from the canons, to repress the pride, worldly spirit, continual dissipation and worldly manners of his missionary priests. As to annotations on the Scripture, I think the same intention should be pursued, as the old translators and annotators of Rheims had always in their eye. They everywhere make observations on those texts which confute the then new-broached heresies, and explicated in a true Catholic sense such others as the heretics wrested to themselves. Now the grand reigning system of religion is that any mode of external worship will do, and any faith suffice, provided men live moral lives. Nay, there are, I question not, too many Catholics who cannot be persuaded but [that the] Protestant faith (which, in fact, is no faith but variable opinion) will do with a moral life, that is, a life free from gross, palpable sins of adultery, theft and the like. Whereas the necessity of divine faith of all and every article proposed by the church and its unity are clearly shown in the holy scriptures, and to show this in a good light will be an object worthy of the editor and annotator.

When charity demands your intervention to conciliate peace then you must not decline her call. I believe the greatest art and address is necessary. Nay, I know not how it is possible to reconcile people who breathe nothing but a spirit of the world, to whom the precepts of Jesus Christ are no more than an old song and who know nothing of submission or self-denial. Wheresoever, therefore, you perceive that to attempt to reconcile people is scarce less difficult than bringing the east and west together, be silent, yet receive no such obstinate spirits to the sacraments.

I had understood long before that Mr Bolton was not what he ought to be; pray, is he out of jail and gone to his convent?

Your brother Thomas came very lately on purpose to see me. I like him very well and conceive great hopes of him. When he has made himself more perfect in designing and painting he will draw me on a piece of canvas for your inspection.

I long since wrote with my own hand my last will and testament, and bequeath everything to you, and appoint Mr Wilson and Mr [Joseph] Orrell my executors. Yet I intend to leave you directions how to dispose of some money and other things. I came hither ten years ago 21st of last October, and on that day one year's subsidium charitativum (as Mr Vincent Eyre allows it to be called) was due to me, viz. £40 or guineas, and the two last remittances were £50 each. If I do not live till Thomas Hodskinson2 returns a priest from Valladolid, I must necessarily charge him on your goodness. For I know not what his father ever will or can do for him, and there is no one in your family in any prospect as yet of going to college or monastery.

Susan has written home that she likes her place very well. Robert came from London home last month dressed in very good clothes, new boots, with a box full of goods, suits and shirts, the carriage of which cost 15s. Yet he was not for staying but returning soon and talked of getting a place in the post office of £50 p.an. with the privilege of pursuing his art of designing and drawing. Thomas asked him to come and see me but he turned a deaf ear to that. Keep the Jesuit's bean for some lucky opportunity.

Mr Barrow was at Stella last week had you but known. Get Bishop [George] Hay's works in 2 vols., 3s.6d. each, you may see their titles in any Directory.[3]

James Marsh, Joseph Ratcliffe, Thomas Hodskinson to Valladolid. Joseph Hull, Henry Parkinson to Lisbon. Ralph Platt, James, George and Thomas Haydock, Thomas Barrow, Jo. Hall, John Woodcock, James Newsham, Robert Blacoe to Douai College,4 where all but a lickspittle disapprove the carryings on of the polite Mr Gibson.

God keep you in his holy fear and love and pray for your most affectionate Uncle, R. Banister

1. (1692–1775) Bishop of Amoria, ipi, Vicar Apostolic Northern District 1752–1775.
2. Thomas Hodskinson, a kinsman, does not appear to have been ordained.
3. George Hay DD (1729–1811), was a doctor and chemist. He became a Catholic in 1748 and was ordained priest in 1758. He was made Bishop of Daulis, ipi, in 1769 as coadjutor to the Vicar Apostolic of the Lowland District in Scotland whom he succeeded in 1778. A list of his works is given in DNB, including *Letters on Usury and Interest, &c.* (1774). Banister here refers to

The Sincere, Devout and Pious Christian (1781–6). Cardinal Wiseman advised JH Newman to study theology in Hay's writings.

4. The list of his pupils Rutter had asked for in N$^{o.}$ 38

---

40. Rutter to Banister   Minsteracres, 25th April 1786

Dear Uncle,

The business of Easter being now over, I am at liberty to acknowledge your two very kind and acceptable letters which I received in due time.

By the first I find there is no prospect of your coming to settle in these parts in order to undertake the direction of a new school and, though I should have been glad to have had you a little nearer, yet I cannot but think you were perfectly right in declining the honour of it. For I entertain the same opinion (and perhaps with better reason) as Mr Wilson in regard to his Lordship's manoeuvre and that he wishes to get you out of Lancashire not solely for the purpose of making you President of his school. The matter does not seem to be any great secret; for a gentleman here was speaking of it the other day and of you as being appointed to the administration of it, but the whole design will, I dare say, be now dropped.

My sentiments of Mr Thomas Eyre do not exactly coincide with yours. I have indeed a great regard for him and am indebted to him for many favours, but believe me he has more the cunning of the serpent than the simplicity of the dove. I assisted on Maundy Thursday at the blessing of the holy oils with Messrs Taylor, Johnson and Clavering. Mr Cordell, though much nearer, is not invited on these occasions for he would make confusion. I am glad you rectified the ill opinion I had of Harris, but he was not the person I alluded to but one Abbe Tr. I don't remember how I expressed myself in regard to [Charles] Berington but I never meant to say that travelling with Giffard had qualified him for his high station, especially if we may judge from the extravagance of the pupil. A letter from London says Dr Thomas Rigby is to be coadjutor bishop.[1]

I am glad to hear sister Susan is happy in her new place. I never heard much of the name of Fitzherbert till of late when nothing else has been talked of on account of Mrs Fitzherbert's connection with the Prince of Wales—a fine topic this for the ladies. It seems certain that they were married by a priest all present being disguised. What think you of such a masked marriage?[2]

I thought Cabassutius belonged to me and as such put it amongst my other books; shall I send you it back?

I was at Brough before Lent, our family being there. Sir John Lawson is perfectly recovered. Mr [Arthur] Storey of Tudhoe (formerly your neighbour) went with me. I can see nothing extraordinary in this genius, who once made such a noise at the Sorbonne. We dined at Cliffe, which is near the road, and found Mr [John] Billington in good spirits, at last reconciled to his situation, and it to him.[3]

Have you seen [Joseph] Berington's new work against Hawkins? I find it pleases the gentry as an amusing agreeable performance, but I cannot suppose it will meet with your approbation.[4] [Arthur] O'Leary's[5] name alone is sufficient to recommend his production on the same subject. Mr Thomas [Eyre], I understand, has laid aside his design of republishing the holy scripture, but Geddes is still labouring at a new version from the Hebrew. He has lately set forth another Prospectus of it, which was shown me by his particular friend and encourager Charles Cordell, who says he is equal to the task, being a person of unremitted study and well skilled in biblical learning and, as such, is encouraged by the Scotch bishop and many learned Protestants. Kenicot had a particular esteem for him and introduced him to the notice of others.[6]

Mr Bolton was acquitted at York, but the judge expressed himself on the occasion in harsh and severe terms. He is therefore now returned triumphant to Gilling Castle where he is sole lord and master and I fear there is no hope of his ever going back to his monastery. I heard his body blamed for not keeping him in when they had him there a few years ago but interest in worldly policy has great influence sometimes even with religious.

I had a letter lately from brother Tom, but he did not mention any commission you had given him concerning your portrait, and I fear he would not be equal to the task. I still wish therefore to make sure of your profile when an opportunity offers. Tom writes about his watch which he says brother John left to him. Did you give it back again into my father's hands?

Clifton's marriage articles are no secret here, he receives £8,000 with his wife, and her jointure is £800 p.a. I ought to have sent him a congratulatory epistle on the occasion, but did not.

I am at a loss what to say to that part of your letter where you are pleased to mention your will so much in my favour, and if ever you will alter it I hope it will be only on account of my death and not of any displeasure my conduct may give you; as it shall be always my study to prove myself your most dutiful nephew, H. Rutter.

1. Missioner at Lincolns Inn Fields; he was never a bishop. The abbe is unidentified.
2. Maria Fitzherbert, eldest dau. of Walter Smythe. At the age of seventeen she married Edward Weld who died within a year. Three years later she married Thomas Fitzherbert but he, too, died shortly afterwards, leaving her a substantial income which enabled her to enter London society; she became involved with the Prince of Wales, whom she also out-lived.
3. Billington was chaplain at Cliffe Hall, near Piercebridge, home of the Withams.
4. J. Berington *Reflections addressed to the Rev. John Hawkins* (1785). John Hawkins, an ex-Benedictine who, having taken a wife, wrote 'An Essay on Celibacy' [Gillow I 192].
5. An Irish Franciscan in London of liberal and pro-British views. He had been recruited in 1784 by the British secret service to spy on the Irish Catholics. [M Buschkuhl, 23]
6. Alexander Geddes (1737–1802) expatriate Scots priest; in 1765 the Earl of Traquair invited him to live at his home in Tweed-dale. Geddes helped to establish the Society of Antiquaries of Scotland; two years later he fell in love with a female relative of his patron and deemed it his duty to leave; he had, in any case, fallen out with Bishop Hay. Geddes went to London and gained the patronage of Robert Edward, 9th Lord Petre (1733–1801). Geddes translated the scriptures during this period; the first volume appeared in 1792 and was censured by the Vicars Apostolic; it was generally doubted if Geddes could be considered a Christian let alone a Catholic. Kenicot is unidentified. [Ward, *Dawn* I 42; Gillow II 410; *DNB*]

---

41. Banister to Rutter — Mowbreck, 28th April 1786

My dear Hal,

As you are a much better correspondent than I, and more exact in answering letters, and as none of yours has reached me since that which was dated the 1st of last January (to which I replied by two subsequent letters), I have been thinking that you either are sick or embarrassed in some domestic broil (something of which you insinuated in your last) or in fine that you have made some false step and set on foot, either to the right or the left, awry, and so Mr Silvertop or his wife, or both, look black upon you, and you think yourself in distress on that account. Well, suppose this be your case, what can the consequence be? Suppose you be Ugthorped by Comana; Ugthorpe itself will be a paradise to an innate freeborn mind that hates servitude and cringing and flattery. You will not leave at Minsteracres either your good sense, learning or books. You may say with the old philosopher, omnia mea mecu porto. One or two shirts will fit you a week, a patched coat and darned stockings. You will be no more a slave to the pride of life.

I wish they would send for their old excellent marksman, before he has totally ruined Alma Mater. 'Tis not monks or ex-Jesuits that say it is tumbling down; I have just received a copy of a letter wrote this month by Mr Ralph Platt, in which he avers that, though it may appear strange and incredible, yet it is a matter of fact that her finances are exhausted and that one man has had it in his power for a year past to reduce her to bankruptcy, and it is owing to his generosity that Alma Mater and the President still subsist. (I suppose this man to be the butcher.) Item, he avers that he finds on the book of private expenses of professors and divines £2,000 and wishes £500 may be recoverable. And what wonder, says he, whilst there is such high life, jaunting abroad, riding post from one end of the country to the other. Neither the General Prefect nor Vice President can hinder these abuses for the President permits, and his permission (says Mr Platt) is good in law. Mr Platt can see nothing to rescue Alma and the President from this load of debt but selling some of the college revenues; and yet all whom Mr Platt has consulted declare he has no power to do it. He adds that he could write a folio of smaller abuses and that his very soul heaves for vexation. Mr Southworth and Mr [Isaac] Bellas, General Prefect, are determined to quit; and he, too, unless things be speedily remedied. He says the President has made, more than once, magnificent promises to redress and reform what is amiss, but goes on in the old train.

Comana, I suppose, believes all at Alma to be in a flourishing state; for when Mr Barrow of Claughton was there in February, Comana said he had received a letter from thence, and seemed to express a great satisfaction. But Mr Barrow sat as one deaf and opened not his mouth, nor asked even how does your brother do? Does he who sits at Comana's right hand, or at bottom of the table (I know not whether) know anything more of the real situation of Alma? But however, if Mr Platt stand to his word, he will inform all the College Agents and they will acquaint the principal Brethren. But I foresee no remedy will be put to these dilapidations and the ruin of good manners and discipline till Douai College becomes like Paris Seminary in a late President's days, or like Lisbon College, which for a term of several years could not maintain a dozen students. But how can I foresee this? Because the Gibson faction will endeavour to support itself, and because the bishops can do nothing without application to the 7 hills[1]. It will however be a most impudent mendicity to go about England imploring succours to redeem the dilapidations incurred by high life, pomp and vanity. Sed haec hactenus.

You do not, I suppose, make Mr Eyre privy to the sentiments I send you, his connections with Comana make it unsafe. On receiving this I shall hope for your speedy answer. In the mean time I remain your most affectionate Uncle, R. Banister.

1. Rome: another anachronism.

42. Rutter to Banister — Minsteracres, 9th June 1786

Dear Uncle,

My last letter, I think, would reach you about the same time that I received yours.

The account you give of Alma Mater is indeed most deplorable and I wish some remedy could be applied before it is too late. How far Comana is acquainted with the true state of affairs there, I know not, but this I know that the Brethren in these parts all agree in thinking Mr Gibson the President is unequal to his charge, and they form this judgement of him from their own personal acquaintance with him. But to say this in the house I am in, would be high treason and is therefore a subject I never touch upon. Comana was here not long ago on a visit and, though we drank his brother's health in a bumper of the best Douai Burgundy, yet nothing transpired in my presence relative to the present situation of affairs. He indeed mentioned the enhanced price of provisions and, as a proof of it, said the butcher's bill was now £100 more p.a. than it used to be by the mere addition of a farthing per pound. After reading your letter this needed no comment to be understood.

According to the last accounts received from there, he (the President) was in a bad state of health and is therefore, by the advice of Comana, expected over very shortly for the benefit of his native air. I am confident myself that a little moorish air will be of great service to him and told them so here. So, perhaps he may resume his old place of honour, the ensuing season, and become once more an humble chaplain in the family.

I have been expecting to see Mr Eyre for this month past and would not write till I had seen him, but I can get very little information from him and at the same time am on my guard how I speak your sentiments. He has heard the dismal account Mr Platt sent to Miles Stapleton and says he will discuss the subject freely with Mr President when they meet but he does not take that liberty with his Lordship. However, he has occasionally given him hints of what he has heard concerning the college, but the bishop, upon writing over, has received accounts entirely different and contradictory; so both sides should be impartially heard.

You must have heard of Sir Edward Swinburne's eldest son renouncing the errors of popery with a view, as it is believed, of sitting in Parliament for this county, for there is now a vacancy by the death of the Duke of Northumberland. From the little I saw and heard of him, I could not be surprised at any step of this nature, nor if his father had showed him the example, or his uncle Harry Swinburne, for they are all of a piece.[1] Indeed, I have a most despicable opinion of our Catholic nobility and gentry in general, as they seem to surpass the rest of the world only in extravagance and the fashionable vices of the age. I could mention an accomplished young gentleman just returned from the Grand Tour now figuring away in the metropolis (Giffard) whose ruin both in regard to fortune and constitution is, I fear, at no great distance.

I received a letter from my father the other day (the first he has sent me since I was in Lancashire) requesting me to lend him £10, for which he would pay me interest. But I have it not, and if I had, should be loth to put it into his hands unless I had some prospect of his making a proper use of it.

You judged right in concluding that I had been engaged in a domestic broil, the consequence of which was that the house-keeper with another left the house, but all is now peace again.

Mr Cordell's new translation of Moeurs des Chretiens is in the press, but I fear it will not sell.[2]

Miss [Mary] Silvertop is returned from the York school[3] in so poor a state of health that there is little hope of her recovery; being the only daughter, it will be a great affliction to Madame.

I wish you would give me a method of catechising and instructing children, for at present I seem to labour in vain. What author do you recommend on the subject as containing the clearest and most orthodox exposition of Christian doctrine?

I hear Mrs Clifton is in a family way? Does old Riddell make any great figure amongst you? There is a great want of rain here and little prospect of it. I remain Dear Uncle, your ever dutiful Nephew, Hen. Rutter.

1. Sir Edward Swinburne (V) (1733–86) had been a wine merchant in Bordeaux of whom it was said, inscrutably, he 'did not practise his religion but kept the faith'; he was, however, closely involved with the Catholic Committee (see No. 49 n 4). At the end of his life he expelled the chaplain from Capheaton Hall and instructed him not to attend the chapel unless specifically invited. His son Sir John (VI) was born at Bordeaux in 1762 where he was educated and came to know Mirabeau and Wilkes. On succeeding to the baronetcy he renounced his Catholicism and closed the mission at Capheaton (See No. 53). He married Emilia Bennett, a niece of the Duke of Northumberland by whose interest he got into the Commons as a member for Launceston, Cornwall, one of the duke's pocket boroughs. (Henry Howard, Charles Brandling, and Thomas Giffard who is mentioned in this and previous letters, also apostatised around this time to enter parliament). Henry Swinburne (1743–1803) of Hamsterley Hall, close by Minsteracres, was an inveterate traveller; he too was liberal in outlook and criticised the Catholic clergy in his two bestknown works: *Travels into Spain* and *Travels into the Two Sicilies*. He died in Trinidad. [Kirk]
2. *The Manners of the Christians*, (1786) translated from the French of Claude Fleury.
3. The Bar Convent school run by nuns of the IBVM. Mary Silvertop entered the school in 1783, aged seven.

---

43. Banister to Rutter — Mowbreck, 17th July 1786

My dear Sir Hal,

Your last letter to me was dated the 9th of June. Soon after that I had received it Mr Barrow informed me that Comana was set out (on 22nd of June) for London to meet his brother William there, and the two Bishops Talbot, to discuss the affairs of Alma Mater. I am of Mr Barrow's opinion that matters will be patched up through the influence of Comana. William (he says) denies all, calls Mr Richard Southworth wrong in his head and affirms that Platt and the rest act and write through sinister motives. I expect in some little time to see Mr Thomas Horrabin who will be able perhaps to inform me of the issue of this meeting. Mr Barrow's strong, nervous letter would not arrive at The Star before Comana set out.[1]

I had also designed to write, and promised Mr Barrow that I would do it, but after writing a copy of a letter in which I endeavoured to show a very striking resemblance between William Gibson and Elias of Cortona, second General of the Franciscans, I laid it by; again I wrote a long letter to Mr Richard Southworth but still keep it by me. Upon mature consideration it is no farther any concern of mine, but inasmuch as it is of very great importance to the mission and to religion, for both of which I must believe our Vicars Apostolic and several other Brethren have more zeal and love than I, and much more prudence and conduct in exerting it.

As to the method of catechising children, I know no other than to imitate mothers and nurses who feed their infants with milk, and chew the meat before they put it into their mouths. Messangue has written a long exposition of the Christian doctrine, pretended to be catechetical lectures, not for children, I am sure, but for divines who have run through no small part of divinity. I wish every Sunday to inculcate into children to say their prayers with mind and heart, not with their lips only, like chattering birds, but because they speak to God who made them. To fear displeasing God by swearing, stubbornness, by bad songs and words and actions, by stealing, lying, &c, because he can cast them into hell, where they must burn for ever. I see no profit in making a long and fine exposition of an Article or of a Sacrament to children; what will they remember, think you, when you have done? Not even the subject or theme you have so eloquently dilated. This brings to my mind two verses in Young's Universal Passion[2]

The very best ambitiously advise
Half to serve you and half to pass for wise.

Such catechists think more of making connected discourses with flowers and figures of speech, than of beating plain, easy, but necessary truths into the giddy, heedlesss, inattentive minds of poor peasants.

What numberless times have I asked: Why is Jesus Christ true God? and have been answered, Because he is the only son of the Blessed Virgin Mary. How few children know what Pontius Pilate is or was? How few know the meaning of the word Trinity? Several will name the 7 Sacraments, but do not know when asked, whether they have received any of them, or which of them or all of them? How many say hallowed be thy name and never reflect on its meaning which is holy be thy name, id est, to me and to all men as it is in itself? How many say Hail Mary and know no meaning of it; how many put Jesus in the vocative case and so make nonsense? When these and such many like things, which learned and pompous catechists may call mere balbuties, are inculcated as they ought to be, I believe peasant children will receive as much as the capacity of their intellects is able to retain. Sed usus to plura docebit: I shall fall under Young's satirical lash.

I pray you to say ten Masses as soon as you well can for the persons following: Dorothy, Helen, Ann, Elizabeth, Susan, James, Betty, Henry, Mary, John, and when I can conveniently I will send to your mother ten shillings which were given to me by persons requesting the foresaid anniversaries.

I hope my brother at Westhead will at least reform when he neither has, nor can borrow money, nor run on tick. Yet if by misfortune any fool should lend or trust him and then, in order to recover, arrest him and compel him either to go to jail or to pay, we must join all together to keep him from such disgrace.

If William Gibson should, by a new revolution, quit the college, do not offer him your place. Not that I think the famous marksman would be there desirable, if it be true as Mr Barrow assures me, that he would most certainly have been expelled the premises, although he had not been named to be President.

I am really sorry to hear of Mr Eyre giving up a new edition of the holy scripture; it would go off in this county infinitely sooner than the Instructions of Youth.

You will not be long before you write. I remain your most affectionate cousin, R.B.

1. Horrabin lived with the Vicar Apostolic London District and was the London District Agent for several of the English colleges abroad. The Star was presumably the inn at which the meeting was to take place. As Banister predicted, the meeting did not resolve matters; Southworth and Platt resigned and left for England together on 25 August. John Daniel became Vice President and Thomas Smith Procurator. Smith was ordained for the purpose although he had completed only two years of theology; he would later become Gibson's coadjutor bishop.
2. Edward Young, *The Universal Passion* (1725–8).

44. Rutter to Banister Minsteracres, 3rd September 1786

Dear Uncle

I received your favour in due time and am rather afraid you will think me too long in answering it. The tedious illness of Miss Silvertop has been a great confinement both to the family and me, as we could neither stir from home or see company here. She departed this life on 27th of last month and was buried on Wednesday without much pomp and ceremony.

She was the first I have assisted at the hour of death and the impression made on me was greater than I could have imagined on this occasion. Have you any advice to give me besides what the Ritual prescribes de modo juvandi morientes?

I have heard no particular account how matters were discussed by our Vicars Apostolic. Nothing transpired at Comana's return, not even the most distant hint to our family, but it was said in the south that William Gibson was to be made bishop and Mr [John] Douglass to succeed his place. However, I received the other day very different information from Mr Taylor who has been supplying at Stella in the absence of Mr Eyre. He tells me that Mr Southworth is indeed leaving the college, but that things are now amicably settled there and peace and harmony perfectly restored. This is the substance of two letters which Comana has received from thence, one of which was written by Mr [Thomas] Varley[1] who accompanied the President back. In this case, the Petition of the Lancashire Clergy[2] will only serve to make them laughed at by those of another side, and may probably be no great recommendation to the person to whom it was addressed. Is it true that you have taken your money out of his brother's hands?

You will have heard of Miss Barbara Webb's marriage with Lord Shaftesbury, and how Spearman was served on this occasion.[3] But it is said that he means to bring an action against the noble lord for false imprisonment. Joseph Berington was to have been her Ladyship's chaplain but he refused it unless £100 p.a. were settled upon him. I wish he may not give a tincture of his brilliant ideas to the newly elected bishop who, I hear, is consecrated.

I thank you for the hints on the method of catechising and beg you will not be afraid of Young's satirical lash whenever you write, for I would have all your letters as long as they can be as well for the profit as the pleasure they afford.

I am sorry to hear that Mrs Clifton does not please in your parts; her father is dangerously ill and cannot in all probability hold out long. You would hear of the Duke of Norfolk's death.[4] Is it true that Miss Clifton is going to be married to Sir John [illeg.][5]

I have not yet procured the two works of Bishop Hay which you recommended to me. Do you adopt his sentiments on usury, which seem indeed to be universally adopted in practice.

On ne prete plus a usure,
Mais tant qui on veut a interet

Pray remember me to my relations and believe me your ever dutiful Nephew, Hen. Rutter.

1. London District Agent for Douai College.
2. The draft of a petition of the secular clergy in Lancashire for the removal of President Gibson.
3. They married at her father's house in St James's in July. Barbara was the daughter and heir of Sir John Webb (V) of Odstock, Wilts. Anthony Ashley Cooper, fifth Earl of Shaftesbury (1761–1811), 'long resided in France and does not appear to have made any mark in the world' (GEC). The reference to Spearman has not been traced.
4. Charles Howard (1720–1786) of Greystoke, Cumb., 10th duke, married Katherine Brockholes of Claughton. He was a scholarly recluse, an FRS and FSA and, like many other Catholic gentlemen, deeply interested in horticulture. He died in 1786 and the dukedom passed to an apostate.
5. Whoever he was, he lost Catherine Clifton to John Talbot, brother of the 10th Earl of Shrewsbury, or was rejected by Sophia Clifton who remained a spinster.

45. Rutter to Banister — Minsteracres, 23rd October 1786

My dear Uncle,

It is now some time since I have heard from you and my other friends in Lancashire, but I hope you are all well. Of late I have flattered myself with the hopes of having you a neighbour at Durham, for this is one of our best places and you would have been as independent there as you can be in Lancashire. Mr Nicholas Clavering leaves it this week and is succeeded by Mr [John] Lodge from Sheffield, to the no small satisfaction of Mr Rimmer, who will now be Lord and Master.[1] Mr Clavering's intention is to manage both the temporal and spiritual affairs at Callaly, an undertaking too great for him in the opinion of some who are well acquainted with him. For, considering that he begins to be infirm, he will find employment sufficient in settling his brother's concerns without the charge of a large congregation. He is one of our Fund-Superiors, but I think an improper one as being much in the same predicament as Chadwick. We have had no meeting this year, which I suspect to be a manoeuvre of his lest he should be discharged from his office. But we are all at peace as yet, and rather than not continue so I would even part with a little of my right.

How do matters stand with you? I hear there is a change of ministers and that Mr Barrow is knocked off the perch, as Bordley expresses it.[2]

This must be a great triumph to the Chadwickians, and perhaps the Gibsons may share in the joy of it. Comana in consequence of it went to meet Chadwick at Carlisle, but this was a grand secret in these parts, whatever it might be in yours.

I hear nothing lately respecting Alma, and hope that peace and good order are restored. Platt has been much blamed for his imprudence, and Varley has entirely acquitted the President of the charge of bankruptcy. Moreover, his conduct has been approved of by the Propaganda, and we are soon to see him at the head of the list of College Benefactors, for he is in a fair way of increasing its revenue a thousand p.a. by means of the Pope's Nuncio, his particular friend. Another friend, who is an archbishop, will engage to make St. Omer dependent on him if he pleases. All this I shall believe when I see it come to pass.

I have not seen his Lordship since his return from London, for he seldom stirs from home. Mr Cordell's new translations are published, viz., of Fleury's Manners of the Jews and Christians, and his short and larger historical catechisms.[3] This last I should think an excellent work for both young and old, and very proper to give them a full and thorough knowledge of religion. What is your opinion of it? I hope it will sell well, otherwise the translator may be involved in difficulties, as many of his former works are still on his hands.

What method do you follow in instructing converts? To learn the catechism is a long and tedious task which persons grown up are scarcely capable of. Pray give me a plan for this purpose. Do you make a long trial of them? Protestant converts think it quite sufficient if they come to the chapel, and I am at a loss whether to exclude them or not.

Mr Thomas Eyre desires his respects to you. I would willingly send my mother a guinea if I knew how to do it. I am glad to find that all the places belonging to the Duke of Norfolk are secured by being put into the hands of Mr Eyre's brother. Joseph Berington is still scribbling; a most learned work is about to appear (unless he has actually published it), Eloise and Abelard, the subscription I am told a guinea.[4]

I beg you will write to me when convenient for you are my only correspondent, and, though I have little to say to the purpose in writing to you, this can never be your case in my regard. I commend myself to your good prayers and am, dear Uncle, your most dutiful Nephew, H. Rutter.

1. Lodge had shared the mission in Sheffield with Rimmer for a year or so.
2. Chadwick had been instituted Vicar General in place of Barrow.
3. C. Cordell, *The Manners of the Israelites; The Manners of the Christians; A*

Longer Historical Catechism; Short Historical Catechism all translations and published in 1786.

4. *The History of the Lives of Abeillard & Heloisa* (1784); the 2nd edition (1787) included their letters and an author's introduction.

---

46. Banister to Rutter Mowbreck, 27th November, 1786

My dearest Sir,

I have now received two letters from you, the first dated 3rd of September, the other 23rd of October, to which this shall be an answer. But I conceive not how your letters are 12 days in coming hither.

You say the death of Miss Silvertop made a great impression on you; was it of fear, or of compassion, or both together? One cannot but fear for a soul just going to the grand tribunal, but that fear ought to be tempered with hope both in the penitent and director. 'Tis, however, proper and even sometimes necessary to teach the moribund on what he ought to ground his hope, not like the pharisee, because he has not been unjust, an extortioner, or an adulterer, or like other men or because he has fasted twice a week and paid tithes of all his goods. The illusion of the pharisee I can often discover in the words and sentiments of some people but our hope rests solely on the infinite power and goodness of God, on the death and merits of Jesus Christ, on his promises, &c. As to compassionating the sufferings of the sick, 'tis not amiss to hear the detail of their pains and pity their sufferings, but then a good director will endeavour to alleviate their anguish by motives of faith by shewing the necessity we all lie under of suffering, that by dying on the cross with Jesus Christ we are to reign with him in glory &c. St. Augustine on his death-bed often repeated the penitential psalms, and with many tears, and used to say that no-one, after having fallen into actual sin, ought to quit the world without repentance which, when true, includes all the three theological virtues, and humility, compunction, patient suffering, resignation, &c. But you have the Lives of the Saints; their holy deaths will teach you how to conduct both yourself and others in that great crisis. Read l'Esprit de St. Francois de Sales in several numbers.

Bishop Hay, as far as I recollect, starts nothing new in his treatise upon loans[1], except that it is his opinion that in a commercial country like ours there will always, or almost always, occur in the loan of money and the receipt of [a legitimate addition above the capital sum], a title excusing from usury; which title will either be [delayed income], or [expected loss], or [unusual risk]. It seems also that lenders and borrowers of money thoughout the nation enter into an equivalent contract of society; the dangers are mutual but unequal, yet the greater danger of losing often rests on the lender. The profits too are unequal, the greater profit ought to go to the borrower, or he will never repay what he borrows. Suppose now to yourself that no one man in the nation will lend a sum of money for fear of the sin of usury, except a trifling sum of £9 or £10 to a poor man. What would follow but an universal stagnation of all trade and commerce; not even farmers could be able to stock and till a farm. Thomas Shuttleworth of Lancaster (father of Mr Shuttleworth, President of Douai College[2]) bought a ship one night. The morning after, some Lancaster merchants asked him saying, Well, Tom, you have then bought a ship, and with what, pray you, will you freight her? With credit, says he, as you do. A smart but true word, for merchants in a general way must either borrow or buy on credit. I therefore believe that the general practice of our missionaries is to leave everyone to his own conscience and bona fides in the loan of money. Yet if usury be discovered in any contract, whether ouverte or palliated, it must be corrected. There is a fraud which I apprehend is very common; people run into debt beyond all ability to pay their creditors, then make an assignment of all their substance to two or three assignees to pay their debts. These pay perhaps 10s. or 12s. in the pound; the creditors give an acquittance in full, so by law can never recover more. Thus the debtor is unjust 1. by running into debt beyond his power of paying. 2. too often in secreting a large share of his substance from the assignees. 3. in often bringing up false creditors who make themselves his accomplices in injustices. 4. in thinking himself acquitted of all obligation to make up all deficiencies to his creditors. Beware how you admit such insolvents if any of that kind address themselves to you.

If a convert can read so well as to make sense of what he reads (which they cannot do who spell half their word, nor they who call words wrong), give him a Double Catechism, a Garden of the Soul, The Catholic Christian, or some such book.[3] But if he cannot read, or at least can make no sense, and is grown up, and has a poor memory, then teach him to say our Lord's prayer, the Hail Mary, Creed and ten commandments correctly, minding stops and pauses. At every conference give a very short exposition of the foresaid prayers and commandments, or rather of one only at a time, lest their memory be confused and so they will retain nothing. The exposition should be constantly in the words or nearly so. Hallowed be thy name is little understood, but holy be thy name is easily explained. Forgive us our trespasses &c. is unintelligible to illiterate peasants, but forgive us our debts &c. may soon be expounded. The relative (who) in the creed must be explained and referred to Son.

The commandments must be expounded by showing what they command and what they forbid. I believe there are several who have no idea of the words adultery, fornication, pollution, &c. I say idea of those words not of the things. 'Tis therefore requisite to explain the meaning of those words, as modestly as possible, yet so as to be understood, adding at the same time a lively description of the torments prepared for those who do such things.

As to Protestant converts, as you style them, 'tis not advisable, I think, to exclude them from the chapel but from the Sacraments only. Who knows but that by hearing they may conceive a serious resolution of working in earnest for their salvation. Converts are to be proved and tried according to circumstances. If the occasion or motive of conversion be something extraordinary and, as one may judge, immediately from God, inspiring a new light with an ardent desire, then a short probation will suffice. But if the occasion be nothing particular, if to gain a husband or wife, or because their master is a Catholic, or because they think it fit to follow some mode of religion &c., then the trial and probation ought to be long and exact. Then it is necessary to inculcate 1. the two eternities, heaven and hell, death and judgement, shortness of life, that few are saved and millions more damned, &c. 2. the necessity of true faith where true faith is to be found &c. For, you see, that persons must have a sincere desire of saving their souls, before they will search for the true means of saving them.

You say (3rd September) : "in this case the petition of the Lancashire clergy will only serve to make them ridiculous and laughed at by those of another side and may probably be no great recommendation to the person to whom it was addressed. Is it true that you have taken your money out of his brother's hands?" At our meeting on 29th August Mr Bordley showed and read to all Bishop James Talbot's letter in which he says a dismission or abdication was first proposed but absolutely rejected by the two Gibsons. I cannot recollect many other things of the said letter but he allows Mr Bordley and his brethren to pursue and obtain Gibson's deposition if they judge proper, although he himself is of opinion that he may be tried a while longer. I left the meeting very soon, seeing our party going to be overpowered, but I declared to several that I would in no manner sign any petition for Gibson's removal. No petition or address has been made as far as I know. But explain what person it is you mean to whom the supposed petition was addressed: item, who the said person's brother is?

Your letter of 23rd October contains very pleasant apocrypha; pray write some more and tell me your authors. I am ever yours &c., R. Banister.

1. *Letters on Usury and Interest &c.* (1774).
2. John Shuttleworth was never President of Douai College.
3. Richard Challoner, *The Garden of the Soul* (1740? and innumerable editions subsequently); *The Catholic Christian Instructed &c.* (1737), a form of catechism.

47. Rutter to Banister Minsteracres, 6th January, 1787

Dear Uncle,

Your letter came to hand the 2nd of last month and afforded me much pleasure and instruction. I hope therefore you will not be very long before you favour me with another of the same kind.

At present I am quite in solitude and retirement, our family being gone to see their friends in Yorkshire. They are to pass their Christmas at Brough in company with Mr and Mrs Eccleston and Miss Clifton, &c. They have left the two children with me in order to learn to read, a task tedious enough. They are fine boys in presence of Papa and Mama, for they know where they can take liberties. The former has them in proper subjection as a parent ought to have his children, but the Lady manages them more by dexterity and the winning arts of her sex than by any exertion of arbitrary authority. Is not this a wrong method with children? As there are few who have had more experience than you in regard of youth and who can more easily convey instruction to their tender minds, I hope you will communicate such lights and hints as may be necessary and profitable to me as a master and teacher.

We are busy in making preparation for our new building. The intended addition is a chapel, offices and servants' rooms, all of which are much wanted. The weather of late has been very favourable for the masons, it being extremely mild and open, which perhaps is not so suitable for us at this season as frost and snow. People say this is the cause of the fever which has been at Newcastle for some time past and which has carried off many.

As to the Petition which I mentioned in a former letter, it must have been Mr Barrow's letter to Comana, which was virtually one; at least it was called such in these parts and severely reprobated by the opposite party. Their great argument is that it is unfair and unjust to condemn a person before he has been heard in his own defence and that Mr President had not so much as heard of the accusations that were brought against him before his arrival in England.

I have not as yet seen my neighbour Mr Lodge and wish he may be as acceptable to his present congregation as he was to that which he left in Sheffield. But I hear the Genteel part of it think his morality too rigid and severe, and will doubtless therefore prefer that of the Jesuit [Edward] Walsh[1] as more agreeable to flesh and blood. I wish in regard of morality as well as faith that we were all of one mind, that we said the same thing and that no divisions were amongst us. But how little do we see of this unity, though directed by one and the same rule of the Gospel. The Jesuits, however, seem to have the advantage of us in having found out an easier way to heaven than we pretend to.

Have you seen the life of Ganganelli published last year by Thorp and Jones in vindication of their body?[2] To effect this, their sole aim is to vilify our most holy Father and supreme Head of the Church, whom they represent as a most infamous and abandoned [torn] devoid of principle, of religion and of every good quality. In a word, if I want to see how much passion can get out of reason, I have only to turn to this work.

As to Religious in general, I respect them exceedingly as the chiefest ornament of Christ's Church, but I find in this age they are considered in a very different light, not only in Germany but likewise in France, where I hear a petition has been sent up by the Clergy, headed by the Archbishop of Paris, to have them subjected to new regulations and their numbers diminished. I wish to read an apology for religious orders if I knew where to find one.

Pray remember me kindly to my relations and friends about you. I wish you many returns of the season and am, dear Uncle, your most dutiful Nephew, H. Rutter.

1. The ex-SJ missioner in Durham city.
2. John Thorpe & John Jones, *A Candid and Impartial Sketch of the Life and Government of Pope Clement XIV* (1785). Clement [Ganganelli] had suppressed the SJ; Thorpe and Jones were ex-Jesuits out to do him down. [For the full history of the book and its aftermath see Gillow I 567; III 666; Kirk 58.] Pope Clement was well liked in Britain; he confided to an English friend in 1748 that he had 'a passion for your brave poets and philosophers'. He was especially fond of reading Newton and Berkeley. The pope invited the Duke of Gloucester to Rome in 1772 and ensured that the king's younger brother was lavishly entertained. The duke attended Mass in the Sistine Chapel

on Ash Wednesday after which he and the pope conferred privately in the Vatican Gardens. Clement presented Gloucester with paintings and prints; the duke gave the pope a gold-embossed bible (presumably the Authorised Version). The duke left Rome on Easter Tuesday; Prince Charles Edward Stuart entered the city two days later only to find that his royal pretensions were no longer to be taken seriously by the Holy See. Pope Clement presently sent Monsignor Caprara to London to thank Gloucester and to explore the possibilities for Catholic relief. Caprara was well-received and this exchange of visits may be said to have initiated the process of emancipation.

---

48. Banister to Rutter Mowbreck, 19th February 1787

My dear Sir,

Your last was dated the 2nd of last month. The fever at Newcastle, which you mention, is, as I suppose, of the nervous, putrid kind and has a long time raged in Kirkham, and carried great numbers (considering it is but a small town) to their graves; a Catholic man died of it the 2nd, and another the 19th of January. I have a St. Ignatius's bean and for the first time used it when I visited my last patient. I held it in my mouth whilst I was with him and frequently held to my nose a small linen rag dipped in alegar, and when I came from him washed my hands, although I abstained from touching either him or his bed-clothes as much as possible. Almost all believe it infectious although, for my part, I have frequently said it is not. For it does not agree in its symptoms with those of a true putrid fever as specified by Dr Buckhan. However, ad majorem cautelam I generally comported myself as above.

You do not know perhaps as yet that I have had in my tuition this day 5 months, the two eldest sons of Vincent Eyre of Sheffield, Esquire, nephews to Mr Thomas Eyre; the older, Vincent, is past 12, the younger, Charles, past 8 years of age. Shall I now give you their character? But you must not even hint it to Mr Eyre your neighbour. Vincent the elder has been 3 years at the Park[1], and a greater blackguard never entered my house; a fair face, very comely and a smiling countenance, but no bashfulness, no respect to anyone, no blush can ever be seen on his front; addicted to lying; will eat as much or more than any plough-boy; wit enough and memory, but hates serious studies; fears the rod and ferula (for I have used both, yet sparingly) as death, but no fear of, or reverence for, his master. In short, as my man Richard Billington expressed it, he seems to think that whatever he doth is right. I have reproached him in the most severe terms with pride, conceitedness, lying, obstinacy, contempt of superiors, and with having neither fear, love, or respect for God or for prayer. I have applied to him the character of a Cretan as given by the poet Callimachus and by St. Paul. Truly, folly is bound up fast in his heart, and whether my documents, ferula and rod will eradicate it or not, God knows.

I have now a very mean opinion of the Park, and Mr [Vincent] Eyre told me he would never send another boy thither, but I fear he resented more the want of clean shoes (for he specified them) and stockings and such like things than the want of good breeding, good impressions, bashful behaviour, knowledge of duty, &c. After all these bad beginnings I will still hope, for I now can draw tears from his eyes by bitter reproaches which I could not do at first. I have frequently told him that he is proud and high-minded, and puffed with conceit because he has seen letters addressed to his father with the title of Vincent Eyre Esquire, and that he will not learn because he expects to be heir of a few clods of earth; that eldest son and blockhead are words signifying the same thing; that proud, illiterate and blockish are the common titles of the firstborn son of a gentleman's family &c.

As to Charles, he did not know his letters when he came, but he knew perfectly well how to be in mischief. We have not, as yet, in these five months gone through the monosyllables of Dilworth's spelling book, but we have been repeating again and again the 1st and 2nd table, 3rd and 4th, ba be bi bo bu &c. I teach every boy to call and pronounce the five vowels as they are pronounced in the latin tongue at Douai College. At the Park my master Vincent learned to pronounce the first vowel as we pronounce the 2nd in latin, and he can hardly be corrected.

You have to teach two little boys; I dare say they are like my Master Charles, as giddy as if they had no souls, no attention, no application, an invincible repugnance to everything but play, eating and sleeping. Also as full of pride as their parents and think all below stairs, and all in rags, of different flesh and blood. It will be absolutely impossible for you to teach them humility whilst their mother teaches them pride, not in words so much as by her behaviour and comportment. You read in the Lives of the Saints of mothers of high nobility who nevertheless taught their children, both by words and examples, true humility, true poverty of spirit and the fear and love of God. But I neither know nor hear of such in our wretched times.

If one may judge by their fruits, that is, by the gentlemen or noblemen's sons sent to Douai College, they never learned anything else of their mothers but pride, conceitedness, an eternal love of vanity, folly and amusements. Teach your boys, if you can, to pray with their heart and not with their lips only. Teach them the greatness and majesty of God who made them; tell them frequently that a rich man will hardly be saved; show them frequently the rich man in hell, Luke, 16. Do not all our gentlefolks live, or strive to live, as he did? They will therefore receive good things in this life but be tormented for ever in the next.

As to the morality of the Jesuits, it has made above these 100 years very much noise in the world. The book you left behind containing the Provincial Letters[2] and very many other pieces against the lax casuists convince me that morality has been excessively depraved; and although 'tis reprobated by the church, yet I fear 'tis much followed in the practice of blind guides qui consuunt pulvillos sub omni cubito.

Beware of counterfeit Catholics and penitents. On Saturday evening, the 10th instant, a woman was taken up at Weeton, 3 miles north-west from me, in a dying condition. The morning after, Sunday, a Catholic woman of the said Weeton told me how she really believed her to be a Catholic and desired me to visit and assist her. In the afternoon I went, found her pulse very weak and low, could not speak but in a whisper, swallowed her saliva with difficulty, said she had a great oppression on her breast, had taken nothing from the time she was found lying on the bare ground till that time. I therefore believed her to be in danger of death and began to examine whether she was a real Catholic. She told me that she had lived at Holywell, knew Mr [Philip] Jones and Mr [Joseph] Tyrer [SJ] the two priests of that place; that her husband, William Hall, a Presbyterian and silversmith, had two years ago taken her to Edinburgh, died there 9 months before, as also 3 or 4 of her children; that last Easter she confessed to Bishop Hay. She said an Ave Maria very well, professed the Holy Sacrament to be the body and blood of Jesus Christ &c. I therefore administered to her all the rites of Holy Church, leaving nothing to be done, because at that distance I could not come and go every hour. On Monday the 12th I wrote to Mr Jones at Holywell. He communicated my letter to Lady Mostyn of Talacre who informed me yesterday that this woman, who calls herself Mary Hall, is an arrant hypocrite; that the last May she played the same tragic farce near Talacre, was taken up for dead or dying, desired Mr Jones to assist her and in some space of time recovered. Lady Mostyn did everything to bring her to health, gave her a guinea and clothed her decently. She told Lady Mostyn that she had a brother in Exeter, but told me that she had a brother and sister in Holywell, viz., William Johnson and Peggy Williamson, which is absolutely false. She has a little girl with her, pert enough and ready at her lesson; undoubtedly can lie like her father the devil.

I pray you to write to me before Easter. John Hodskinson is at London and, as I heard, with Mr [Thomas] Langdale, Distiller.[3] Robert his brother is at Jamaica, or in the Bay of Honduras, on the Mosquito shore.

A certain brother, whose sayings, however, are not with me very authentic, told me lately that Comana is in no esteem with our gentlemen. As to William Gibson has he the face, or rather effrontery, to say that he never heard or knew of the charges against him till he came to London? But why should I concern myself about these matters which are entirely out of my sphere; I have more than enough to answer for myself and for my people. Pray for me and believe me ever your most affectionate friend, R. Banister.

1. Sedgley Park, near Wolverhampton, a preparatory school for one hundred boys founded by Bishop Challoner in 1763. Pupils usually went on to the English colleges on the continent.
2. Blaise Pascal, a Jansenist, directed his *Provincial Letters* (1656/7) against Jesuit casuistry. A brief treatment of the consequent and interminable controversy in England is given at Gillow III 51. It will be evident that Banister has a Jansenist frame of mind—on at least two occasions he refers to 'we who follow the stricter laws'.
3. His distillery in Holborn was burned down in the Gordon Riots.

---

49. Rutter to Banister — Minsteracres, 29th March 1787

My dear Uncle,

I received your favour the 25th of February and return you many thanks for it. The character you give of Mr Eyre's two boys is such that I do not envy you the honour of being their tutor, but I am still disposed to think favourably of the Park-school, perhaps on account of its President, my old friend and pedagogue, Mr [Thomas] Southworth.[1]

As to Comana, I fear it is but too true what a certain brother said of him, viz., that he is in no great esteem with our gentlemen, nor do I think he courts much their favour and friendship. His conduct after Mrs Maire's death gave offence to the Lawson family, which I take to be the greatest in the north in point of interest and consequence, and which had been particularly attached to his Lordship. However, I believe there was blame on both sides, as usual on such occasions. At present he seems covered with a thick cloud on every side, but I hope it will soon break and serve only to make him shine with greater lustre than ever. Perhaps you know what I allude to and are better acquainted with the present situation of affairs than I am myself. However, you may perhaps like to hear what I have to say on the subject, which may be depended upon as authentic as coming from Comana's secretary.

His Lordship wrote to the Congregation de Propaganda Fide to consult them how he was to proceed in regard of the funds belonging to the Ex-Jesuits, to which he received an answer from Cardinal [Leonardo] Antonelli dated July 1786 which I have read. The Exs (amongst whom [William] Strickland[2] is the leading man), finding that the bishop, in consequence of the Rescript, would never suffer them to dispose of, alienate and transfer their effects to the Regulars, take refuge under the wings of our Catholic Committee at London, as if his Lordship meant to enforce the Pope's jurisdiction in temporals. The gentlemen take up the matter hastily in this light, as if Mr Gibson had perjured himself, and write to him in a high style to know what he can say in his own vindication. Nay, some of them at London went so far as to talk of summoning him to Westminster Hall. In short, the spirit of party was revived; letters upon letters were sent to the old friends of the injured body and even some of the clergy (amongst the rest Charles Berington) were weak enough to espouse their cause. Perhaps the intemperate warmth of some of the Committee was owing to a pique they had conceived against Comana in consequence of the letter he sent them upon being requested to subscribe to Berington's analysis of faith. Whilst all things are thus in a flame, and the bishop almost universally condemned without being heard, Mr Thomas Eyre goes to Lartington and gives a true statement of the case to Mr [Henry] Maire, a person whom for his virtue and polite accomplishments I esteem above all our other gentlemen. He was open to conviction, in spite of old prejudices, and has succeeded in removing those of his brother Sir John, whose sway, no doubt, will be very great in the business.[3]

The scene therefore at present begins to brighten up and the Stella may blaze out with greater lustre than ever. He has wrote lately to the Committee, who were impatient for an answer and just on the point of epistolising him a second time. His letter, I am told by one who has heard it, is candid, moderate but firm, and will, I hope, meet with as good a reception from the Committee as those of the other two bishops.[4] A letter from London says there will soon be two sorts of Catholic there, some admitting the Pope's superiority, others rejecting it entirely. We have got Berington's new book which I think is the worst and most dangerous of his publications. He truly appears to be "unshackled in his thoughts and free in his expressions", which is a new character, he observes, for a Catholic writer here in England. In a word, in the character of Abelard he seems to have portrayed his own, that of a vain, self-sufficient innovator.

You say that a depraved morality is still much followed in the practice of blind guides; but I pray you to tell me in what particular points, that I may not be of the number. You know my situation and disposition, and therefore can best tell me what practices I am to avoid, and what dangers to guard against, and a letter on this subject will afford me more light and instruction than I should acquire in years by my own industry.

It is the fashion in the south to cry down the Douai Catechism as containing nonsense and not fit for children, such are our enlightened times! I am at present writing down something by way of explanation of the catechism and think I shall go on, if you will but favour me with your corrections, additions and amendments hereafter.

Pray remember me kindly to my relations and believe me dear Uncle, your most dutiful Nephew, H. Rutter.

1. Second President of Sedgley Park.
2. President of Liege Academy, a Jesuit school and seminary, 1784–90. See G Holt, SJ, *William Strickland and the Suppressed Jesuits* (1988).
3. John Maire died in 1771 leaving his property to his nephew Henry Lawson on condition that Lawson assumed the name and arms of Maire; hence Lawson and Maire are brothers. The Silvertops, Withams and Wrights, among many others, also adopted the practice of name-changing as the means of preserving the old Catholic dynasties. Notwithstanding these efforts, however, the names of Witham, Lawson and Maire became extinct in the 19th century.
4. A Committee of the Catholic gentry negotiated the first Relief Act (1778). A second Committee was formed in 1782 to press for the repeal of the remaining penal laws but in the uncertain political situation it was deemed inexpedient to pursue the matter. Although various discussions took place between them, the Committee was more or less permanently at odds with the bishops, as these letters show, because the laity were deemed to have 'interfered' in theological matters which were properly the preserve of the bishops. In general, and bearing in mind that there were dissidents on each side, the dispute arose because the bishops sought to maintain the autonomy of the Church while the Committee was prepared to sacrifice a number of ecclesiastical prerogatives to achieve political emancipation. Issues raised by the Committee which offended episcopal sensitivities included: the restoration of the ordinary hierarchy so as to alleviate prejudice against papists, arising partly from a perception that the Vicars Apostolic could not act without consulting the Pope; the

creation of a school which would exclude boys intended for the priesthood; and support for the ex-Jesuits in their dispute with Bishop Gibson over the disposal of the Society's property. The final act of the 1782 Committee was the publication of an *Address to the English Catholics* in April 1787 which, inter alia, questioned the Pope's spiritual jurisdiction in Britain. A protest, got up by Sir John Lawson, was signed by some fifty of the gentry in the north.

Note. Political prospects brightened in 1787, and at this point in the correspondence a third Catholic Committee was formed on 3 May, for the next five years. Many of the members of the old Committee were elected and Charles Butler continued as Secretary; Sir John Lawson and John Townley represented the Northern District. Relations between the Committee and the clergy did not improve although two bishops and a Benedictine became members in 1788. Indeed, as will be seen, at one point the English Catholics were brought to the brink of schism over the terms of a draft Second Catholic Relief Bill. Banister and Rutter, of course, deplored all of the Committee's proceedings, which were issued as 'Blue Books'.

---

50. Banister to Rutter — Mowbreck, 7th July 1787

My dear Sir,

I received your letter dated the 29th of last March in due time. My obligation to answer it has very frequently come into my mind, but by deferring it, I have received more information and intelligence concerning the principal part of it, viz., the affair between the Cappadocian bishop[1] and the Exs. I have seen the Rescript: 'tis nothing more than a direction. It says that the [Goods, money, chapels and houses] of the Exs are spiritual, i.e.,[annexed for spiritual use], and therefore are not to be alienated to profane uses, but to go in the same channel of the mission and that Comana is to see this done, and compel them if necessary, by ecclesiastical censures, and, if I remember well, not suffer them to transfer to Regulars their goods and properties. I cannot find in it any new powers given him. It approves the execution of a power which he had before. When I had done reading it, I said that if I had been in the place of Comana I would have concealed Antonelli's answer and proceeded by my own authority until such time as it might appear necessary and proper to produce the approbation of higher powers in my justification. I can see not the least reason for resentment either from the Committee or the Exs.

I am told that the Committee has printed and circulated their letter to Comana, which is said to be most virulent and indecent. Undoubtedly they learn their catechism, if they learn any, from our modern Abelard, whose spiritedness and rancour against papal jurisdiction knows no bounds. As to the Exs, I believe them to be at the best genus irritabile, but if Comana has lost their confidence, as I fear he has, it will probably exceed all his powers either of rhetoric or logic to bring them to his terms or proposals.

My elder Eyre gives me every day more presages of his becoming a noble gentleman, one of the mode. Master Clifton and his bride[2] are supposed to fear want, so order and dispose their affairs to the greatest gain and profit. You know him to be a mere niggard and hidebound; yet when the frolic allures his fancy, none more lavish. His bride is of a skinflint race, and will probably check him in his flights, when he is for soaring.

Mr Edward Kitchen[3] was at Preston last week but I never saw him. Mr Arthur Storey gave me a short call in his way from Singleton to Preston. I suppose all to be well over-Ribble, for I hear nothing to the contrary. All at Preston and on this side are in good health, thank God. Please to say six Masses for me, viz., for James, John, Thomas, Richard, Mary, Ann.

Continue your studies of morality and divinity. Lose no time in news, novels, gazettes, magazines, &c. They are indeed amusements, but they fill the head with useless ideas and leave the heart very dry, empty and ill-disposed for prayer and serious consideration.

When you see Mr Thomas Eyre, you may assure him of my great affection for him, but not a word of his nephew. I do not intend to gain hatred by telling truths that will avail nothing. Do not follow my example in deferring to write to me, who am always your most affectionate Uncle, R. Banister.

1. Bishop Gibson—Comana is in Cappadocia.
2. John Clifton married Elizabeth, daughter of Thomas Riddell of Swinburne Castle but became estranged from her in later years. [Gillow *The Haydock Papers* 237/8; Bence Jones 144/5].
3. Chaplain at Lartington.

51. Rutter to Banister Minsteracres, 23rd August 1787

Dear Uncle,

I received your favour dated the 7th of last month in due time. I had been impatiently expecting it, and was not a little disappointed to find it so short and concise. Its brevity I consider as a censure on my long and tedious letters, which are with difficulty scratched out, in hopes of receiving yours in return of equal length, because they always afford me much pleasure and instruction. I am glad to find that all my friends and relations are well and beg you will remember me kindly to them and let me know more particulars of them.

I waited on Mr Clifton when in our neighbourhood, and he seemed glad to see me. Both he and his bride gave me an invitation to Lytham, and in private he offered me the choice of his places in case of a vacancy. But I should have been much better pleased with an offer of a few guineas in order to have enabled me to have bought a horse, which I was then in want of. I am really sorry to hear that he loses himself by story-telling and romancing. The reception he met with in these parts was such that I shall very much wonder if he pay a second visit to Swinburne [Castle] as long as old Riddell lives.

Comana is gone to Sheffield, to see his patron Mr Eyre, as it is said, but I dare say he has something else in view and that he will proceed much farther south. My neighbour Mr Taylor is removed from Hexham to Nuthill in Yorkshire and is no longer to have the honour of attending my Lord Bishop in his journies. I am sorry to inform you of the very sudden and unexpected death of Mr [Luke] Potts, one of the brethren in this county, which happened on 16th of this month. He was in perfect health to all appearance, and in remarkable good spirits half an hour before he expired.[1]

This is the Octave day of the Assumption of the Blessed Virgin Mary and, though I profess myself one of her unworthy clients, I could wish for more positive proof of her body being taken up into heaven. How account for the absolute silence of the first ages and primitive Fathers of the Church in regard of this wonderful event?

Mr Arthur Storey would probably acquaint you with his design of setting up a school at Tudhoe, about 4 miles off Durham. The undertaking, I hear, is encouraged by Sir John Lawson, but I have some doubt of it succeeding.

I could wish much to see you here in the north, where you will find many friends glad to receive you. Our autumn, I think, is a finer and more settled season than any other, and I would meet you where you please to appoint. I made a visit to Lartington very lately and Mrs Maire enquired kindly after you. The new chapel there will exceed everything of the kind I have seen in England, for Mr Maire has an exquisite taste, formed in the Italian school. I wish our religion kept pace with the exterior marks of it, for we are all building chapels, at Tudhoe Mr Storey, Darlington Mr Daniel, Sunderland Mr [William] Fletcher, &c.[2]

I am sorry to hear that the Brethren in Lancashire are still full of complaints, which I fear will answer no purpose. I am dear Uncle, your dutiful Nephew H. Rutter.

1. Potts had been imprisoned in York Castle during the Forty-five having been refused shelter by his congregation at Egton Bridge, NRY. He then served at Thropton in Northumberland until his death.
2. Strictly speaking, although the 1778 act allowed Catholics to own real estate, these chapels were still illegal since it was only under the second Catholic Relief Act (1791) that Catholics could obtain a licence to open a chapel. (See also N$^{o.}$ 37 n2)

---

52. Banister to Rutter — Mowbreck, 1st September, 1787

My dear Sir,

A great and deplorable laxity to be avoided by all who desire to be faithful dispensers Mysterium Dei consists in giving absolution indiscriminately to all, [after confession is scarcely half through, in which some trivial thing is mentioned while something truly more grave and much more perilous is either omitted out of deep ignorance or too much haste, or concealed out of malice. It is also a very grave laxity and imprudence to absolve all indiscriminately with either a brief admonition, or none at all. If ever there is ever any hope of warning or of advising sinners fruitfully and effectively then it is certainly much more likely when they come to the tribunal of justice with some desire at least of penance and of emending their lives. In most cases, a pious and fervent admonition therefore ought not be omitted so that their vices are corrected and they may try harder. Most of them know the ten commandments, that is, they can recite them from memory, but many of the poorer people do not know what they mean, and they commit mortal sins without any bridle of conscience or remorse. The prudent and dutiful priest, therefore, will gently show penitent sinners the penalties for the enormities which they have committed. That will be as if to open the eyes of the blind that they may see the precipice towards which they rush that they may flee back with all their strength. And since priests stand not only as judges but also as spiritual physicians, it is their duty to take care and prescribe, indeed strongly inculcate, especially in the lower classes, the most apt and easiest remedies to check their wicked and sinful habits and more readily bring them back to the practice of the faith.[1] What is he who neglects this but a dumb dog who cannot bark. But I should be unwilling that you should think there is one remedy for habitual sin, and that is to delay giving absolution. It is indeed sometimes useful—even necessary—but I would wish you first to try many other things which prudence and the circumstances of the sinner suggest.

Now I shall copy out a letter which I sent to the Rev. Mr William Husband while he was resident in Singleton, dated 7th March, the feast of St Thomas Aquinas, 1772:[2]

[Since next week the necessity recurs of administering the sacrament of penance that the faithful may gain a plenary indulgence, it came to my mind to prepare for you a reply concerning recidivists. You will easily understand the various kinds of recidivists; there are those such as St Paul deals with: argue, entreat, reproach them with patience. The experience and practice of the wise is constant: crimes are common where the sacraments are frequented rarely. Where, however, it is difficult for the confessor to grant absolution, people go less frequently and more unwillingly. The administration of the sacrament of penance must, therefore, be weighed carefully, viz., that the good of the community of the faithful is taken into account; that souls do not despair or think there is no pardon for those who slip back; that they do not abandon themselves to even graver sins; and that they do not pitch themselves beyond the thought of repentance. Indeed, even if the head of a household having children does not wish himself to return to the sacrament of penance, it is gravely offensive to delay absolution, whether or not it is feared and notwithstanding the ruin of the family, for children are easily led to imitation in this miserable state of affairs where the exercise of religion is neglected by the parents. You therefore ask if absolution is to be given as required on all occasions. Not in the least. If a priest summons someone to confession then it must be heard outside the time of Indulgence or of a Feast, secretly and without others knowing. This could be a procedure more suited to serious recidivists—although I have my doubts. Then you may easily induce them to agree to a delay if it is necessary. If they come to confession on the vigil of a feast or on a Saturday night, they consent more easily to a delay. But, however much they seem to consent to the delay, it is necessary to weigh carefully what will be useful for the future, not only for the individual but also for the good of the community of the faithful. The sacrament is not a remedy for those who are not well-disposed, so make them well-disposed by not delaying but by inspiring ardour in the penitents, by recalling the multitude of their sins, the depths of their ingratitude, the impending vengeance of God, the fire of hell, the demonic torments, the severity of punishment, etc. The good of the community of the faithful demands that as efficacious a barrier as possible is placed against habitual sin; penitents will frequent a confessor who is most zealous for God and who most sweetly inculcates the horror of sin and adds new threads to effect a reconciliation. He does not launch into the conclusion and proof of the treatise concerning grace and final perseverance, as a special grace of God. Rev. Mr Gandy[3] probably meant that when he said it is useful to give absolution to these persons 3 or 4 days later. Cardinal Toletus, confessor to Clement VIII, assumes almost the same, viz. it is useful to absolve the recidivist and to do it often since the death of the absolved can be happy and blessed; that of the unabsolved is truly miserable and unhappy. But the saints and servants of God have promised no such thing, and being daily in a circle of relapsing and absolution presages the worst. Truly they lay up for themselves wrath on the day of wrath. How therefore to counsel the salvation of recidivists? Privately and publicly and through inculcating the suggestion of the necessity for truth, and sincere internal emendation of life and habits. The Father of Mercies is most forgiving.

In catechising it is often necessary to define the proof of the need for true repentance, that the young may learn at least that God has not imposed a kind of empty punishment. Vulgar persons of a slow and low-spirited disposition can be put off by this and so divine truths must be frequently inculcated in them by being specific about those words and actions which are always mortally sinful; and that only by humbly repenting every mortal sin may they stand firm against the devil, for few are saved while many more perish in their guilt.

Amongst your recidivists are the shameless young of both sexes who frequently enough slide back into unchastity (of an imperfect form) and may have to be treated circumspectly. If they are unwilling and delay returning to you, then they are certainly exposed to graver sin. If they can be brought back to [illeg.] indulgence and they confess their faults either willingly or when accused then there will be hope that you can succeed.

Vehemently exhort, expound the peril and the fear of hell, but especially of public infamies etc. to put a check on shameless license erupting into grave scandal and notoriety which can be repressed by a prudent confessor. You will see fornication is frequent where confession is infrequent, or where the priest is a dumb dog or a strong barker.] [One sentence largely illeg. but seems to stress the need for strong but sympathetic treatment of recidivists.]

My dear Sir, I received your last wrote this month, in due time. Although I have long delayed the conclusion of this letter, yet scarce a day has past without a thought of you and of my obligation to write to you. [As pastors we are most certainly obliged under pain of grave sin to give fraternal correction, but only under certain conditions, one of which is if the correction is judged to be to some extent effective; that is, if it is [one line illeg.] for sins that are only venial, unless they lead into mortal sin. I was not confessor to Mr Dic . . . son[4] nor to his wife, though privately esteemed. They governed their house their way, I keeping silent and winking at it. I neither rebuked them nor reckoned myself a proper person to whom they should listen. But you certainly [illeg.] the noble spouses and the whole household and you can and ought (if it is necessary) to correct fraternally. If they do not wish to follow private correction, what more can you or ought you to do? Certainly, correction made outside the confessional can be profitable. Correction of a certain kind can be applied while preaching or reading; but it is necessary to take care that no-one should suppose that we have acquired knowledge through private confession.]

As to setting flesh meat on the table for their Protestant guests, it is coming into vogue, as I hear. It is a very unnecessary complaisance for Protestants will go to a Catholic gentleman to dine on fish being glutted at home with flesh dinners. But consult the bishop on this point; you probably have done it and he has sent you an answer full of unmeaning, equivocal, ambiguous terms, which leave you in as much doubt as before.

For what purpose are you coming to visit us after Easter? I do not ask because I shall not be exceedingly glad to see you, but because I imagine there is some dolus malus in your fine fanciful quality. You are a piece of old furniture which they wish perhaps to exchange for new.

At Westhead all are well. Thomas was here two nights this Christmas. Nothing has been heard of Robert these two years. Mrs Clifton is on the point of lying-in. Master's behaviour makes the loss of his father much lamented.

Say ten Masses for me as soon as you well can, viz., for John, Alice, James, Margaret, Elizabeth, Dorothy, Isabel, Jane, William, Ann. I gave last July 10s. 6d. to your mother and at some opportunity will do as much on occasion of your saying these Masses. I pray you let me know soon that you have received this and that you will say these Masses. Sweet Jesus keep you in his holy fear and love. I remain most truly your dear and affectionate Uncle, Robert Banister. 24th January, 1788.

1. Isaiah 56, 10. All in this letter in square brackets was in Latin.
2. William Husband (1743–79) missioner at Great Singleton, Kirkham, immediately after his ordination in 1768. He moved to Salwick Hall in 1771 and died eight years later from smallpox, caught when visiting the sick.
3. James Gandy (1698–1761)
4. Mr Dicconson of Wrightington Hall whose chaplain Banister was in 1769.

53. Rutter to Banister Minsteracres, 10th February 1788

Dear Uncle,

I received your favour in due time and return you many thanks for it. I am glad to hear that you and all my friends are well and hope to have the pleasure of finding you so sometime this summer. My intention indeed was to set out immediately after Easter which is the time Mr Silvertop fixes on for his journey to Douai with Master Jacky his second son. But I cannot with propriety leave Mrs Silvertop at home by herself, and I do not hear that she means to stay long with her friends in Yorkshire as I had expected. In regard of my journey, I do not apprehend any dolus malus on the part of this family who did not propose it to me, and flatter myself that I am as much in their favour as ever.

Your letter, which I have read over and over again, is a treasure to me of which I will endeavour to make a proper use; but what use can I make of the obscure and ambiguous oracles of our Apollo? His Lordship's answers, I am told, are now clearer and more intelligible than formerly, but I shall still have recourse to you in my doubts and difficulties to receive that satisfaction which I in vain look for elsewhere. However, I will not often trouble you hereafter after you have given me some directions in regard of the two following points.

The first is in regard of prints and paintings, of which Mr Silvertop has a tolerable collection. Now, I know that indecent ones are neither to be looked at nor kept, but I am at a loss to determine which are to be esteemed such, and whether those can be tolerated which are covered only in one part, like a crucifix, when the subject does not evidently tend to raise impure images, or those which are naked about the breast and shoulders.

My second difficulty is in regard of those who keep ale-houses; for how can they comply with the duties of religion and live so as becomes Christians amidst the dangers of their state? How can they avoid partaking of others' sins, when they suffer them to drink to intoxication, and how can they refuse liquor when called for, especially by clubs and societies that meet at their houses? What laws are to be laid down to such persons?

I suppose you have heard of Mr Arthur Storey's undertaking a new school at Tudhoe; but it does not seem to go forward, because gentlemen are sensible that one person cannot at the same time take proper care of his scholars and attend a wide and numerous congregation. The bishop hitherto has had nothing to do in the matter, but I believe he soon will have and then probably you will be the person to preside over it.

Mr Gregory Stapleton is now at Clint, but I hear that he is to return to St Omers to be President of the Royal College, but this is only report.[1] I will say your masses as soon as possible. Sir John Swinburne has sent off his priest, one Mr [Andrew] Ryding, [OSB] and seems to be making preparation for the next election when it is thought he will be brought into parliament by the Duke of Northumberland.

It is certain that Lord Newburgh will recover at least part of his estate this session on condition of paying yearly a certain sum out of it to the Greenwich Hospital. I wish he would rebuild Dilston, the family seat, about 6 miles from us, now a heap of ruins, but formerly noted for the charity and hospitality of its possessors.[2]

I began this letter last week but was called away to attend a Solemn Dirge at Stella for the late Lady Catherine Belasyse[4], Mr Eyre's sister-in-law, who died lately at Brussels. The bishop is very well and was civil to me. His brother writes that there is great confusion in the Imperial Flanders, you would see some account of it in the public papers. The Emperor seems to aim some fatal blow at religion by being so resolute on having the management of the Louvain Seminary in his own hands. All the bishops, it is said, are firm in refusing to entrust the education of their clergy to any persons but such as they themselves approve of. Only one has subscribed to the Emperor's demands, viz., the Bishop of Tournay.

Pray do you ever hear from James Finch? I beg you will excuse haste and believe me most sincerely your ever dutiful Nephew, H. Rutter.

1. Clints, near Ripon; the report was true.
2. Anthony James Radcliffe, succeeded as 4th Earl of Newburgh in 1786 and

claimed the restitution of the ancestral Radcliffe estates lost as a consequence of the attainder of his great-uncle the 3rd Earl of Derwentwater in 1716. The claim was dismissed in 1788 but he was granted an annuity of £2,500 out of the estate-revenues. Dilston Castle was beyond repair by this time but Rutter hoped that the chapel, which had been reordered for Anglican usage in 1733 and was in good repair, might be restored to the Catholics of Corbridge. Cf. L. Gooch, *The Desperate Faction?* (1995)

4. See N°· 37, n4.

---

54. Banister to Rutter — Mowbreck, 14th April 1788

My dear Sir,

Your last favour to me was dated February 10th and received it due time.

As to prints and paintings, their attitudes are worse than their nudities; for if they express a certain lasciviousness they will be very apt to raise the same passion in the spectator. But if there be nothing of a lascivious, wanton gesture, the nudity of the breast, shoulders, arms and legs may be tolerated: as S. Mary Magdalene in her grotto, Daniel in the den of lions, Hercules and Anteus in fight, are, I believe, represented with very little drapery. Infants are often painted quite naked, but of the male sex. The divine infant in Correggio's drawing is so, of which I have a fine engraving by Robert Strange. As I never have seen Mr Silvertop's prints and paintings I cannot pronounce sentence upon them specifically, but if there be any Venus's, Lais's, Sappho's, or suchlike representations, he certainly ought not to expose them to the view of everyone, but to keep them concealed in his closet. And if he resents your admonitions, fear him not but show him that to occasion sins in others is a heinous scandal and he had better have a millstone tied about his neck and be cast into the sea than scandalize even one person.

All alehouse-keepers are not alike. There is one in Weeton, two miles from hence, who encourages and promotes drunkenness in a shameful manner. I lived a year or more in an alehouse when I went to Kirkham school and never saw one man drunk in it, and the doors were shut and all went to rest by 9 or 10 o'clock. But the scene is much changed in Kirkham in these times. I do not believe that you have more than one innkeeper in your congregation; if he harbours an habitual drinker day after day he is guilty of many enormous sins by favouring, abetting, &c. If clubs of colliers meet at his house he will never be able to rule them, they never will desist from drinking till they be completely made brutes. I know something of the manners of colliers by what I saw in Wrightington; they are in general a most sottish, incorrigible race of men. After due advertisements and instructions to them and to the innkeeper, if your endeavours are ineffectual shake the dust off your feet in testimony against them. Do not cast your pearls before swine: Matt. 7.6.

Genteel clubs are not, I believe, to be compared with colliers. There are clubs formed in this town, and in many other places, for the relief of members when sick. They have meeting-nights and each pays a small sum per month and is allowed a gill or two of ale, and no drunkenness, nor obscenity, nor swearing, nor quarrelling is permitted amongst them; their rules at least are good and commendable. A man may possibly drink too much in an alehouse without any fault of the innkeeper, but how many were made dead drunk, gentle and simple, at the birthday feast of your ancient pupil? An infamous Bacchanalian rout! And how many in gentlemens' families are daily drunk? Comana, when at the college, would needs make me believe that drunkenness was entirely laid aside among gentlemen. He talked off book, surely he knows better now. Our Kirkham quality drink hard, I am told, but at home snugly; one indeed will load himself in an alehouse and pretty often too. But enough of this, I think.

Master Clifton had a son [Thomas] born some little while ago.

My neighbour, Mr Joseph Orrell, told me very lately that he dined at Lancaster with Mr [John] Rigby who informed him, "that he had received a letter from Mr [John] Bew in Paris who says, on the authority of Mr William Hurst, that William Gibson has run the college in debt £600 since his return from London, July 1786".[1] Although this seems incredible, yet there are many examples in common life of persons who instead of redeeming their shattered fortune by good economy continue to sink deeper in debt. Is not one of your very near relations an instance of it?

I have heard nothing lately from Westhead; your brother Thomas was here at Christmas and then all were well.

My two Eyres are to go home in some little time; the elder to Douai College, the younger, with his brother Thomas, may perhaps come hither. But as I am now affected I think to send my excuses, that my avocations are so frequent, and my health not very steady, that I am not able to teach boys as they ought to be taught. Indeed these two have been so indocile, so rude and void of all grace that I am extremely disgusted with them. The elder is in his fourteenth year, yet, as far as I can see, there is in him so little fear of God, so little piety, so little respect at Mass and prayers, that I think him very unfit to be admitted to his First Communion. At Christmas they were with Mr Orrell at Singleton 4 days and 5 nights and showed their genius so well that he told me "they out-do all in lying, cheating and stealing". All admired how we got on our time with them. On Sundays in the morning they are dressed up, clean and neat; before night their stockings resemble boots well-bemired. All the week after we let them go on like blackguards. Yet Mr Eyre, when here last October, told me he would never send another son to the Park, and for what fault think you? He mentioned no other but that his son's shoes were not cleaned scarce once a week. To keep him decently clean, a man and maid ought to attend him constantly and new clothes be bought for him every month. I wish your friend Mr Thomas Eyre knew all this, but I shall not inform him unless some just provocation be given me.

I am so disgusted with boys unless I choose them myself that I shall never undertake a promiscuous school on any consideration. Let neither Comana nor Mr Thomas think of me. Your very mentioning it affected me; if it was from your own fund, just say so in your next and use no excuse or apology, be short and concise. The salaries I receive for children's board wage scarce indemnify me for their maintenance; I take nothing for teaching. How foolish then to think of erecting a school, e.g., of 50 scholars, at £14 for each p.a., and out of £700 pay house rent, masters' salaries, servants wages, meat, clothes, fire and candles &c. for the scholars. Besides scarce less than £300 or £400 will furnish a house for their entertainment. Sed haec hactenus. I remain your most affectionate friend and uncle, R.B.

1. Orrell was missioner at Great Singleton and Rigby at Lancaster; Bew was President of St Gregory's College, Paris; Hurst was confessor to the English Augustinian nuns in Paris.

---

55. Rutter to Banister — Minsteracres, 30th June 1788

Dear Uncle,

I am, God be thanked, got safe back to Minsteracres [from Lancashire], but find the house in great disorder and confusion, and nothing finished.

At Blackburn I saw Mrs Saltmarch for the first time and drank tea with her, being introduced by Dr Dunn, who insisted on my lodging at his house. It is a very elegant one, but unless the bishop had advanced money for the purchase, the doctor must either have left the country or perhaps have been lodged in Lancaster Gaol.[1]

I reached Skipton on Sunday night without stopping at Broughton. From Skipton it rained all the way to Cayton, about 24 miles. I stayed there till Wednesday and met with great civilities. Mr [Robert] Bullen, a Roman priest, has been obliged to leave Nidd, where he had lived above 20 years, and is now settled at Cayton, where Mr Messenger is fitting up a chapel for the congregation.[2] Dr [Charles] Howard, who was drinking the waters at Harrogate, dined with us on Tuesday.[3] I was surprised to find the Parisian Doctor rusticated into the farmer and the learning of the Sorbonne laid aside for that of the plough. Both at Cayton and Brough I heard of Mr Gibson's quitting the college, but I still think he will maintain his ground in spite of all Mr Talbot's efforts to remove him.

I arrived at Brough on Wednesday drenched in rain and should have set out for Lartington the day following had Mrs Silvertop been there, but she was to leave it that day to come to Brough. Besides that, the way over the moors would have been very bad after such heavy rains. At Brough I met with Mr [Rowland] Davies,[4] who is now thin and meagre and has as little to say as myself. On Friday I set out for home and was accommodated with Sir John's returning chaise as far as Durham, where I found Mr Lodge confined to his room by rheumatism.

I must not forget to tell you that Mr Storey gets forward with his school, and the two Eyres, who are soon to be his scholars, will doubtless establish its reputation. But, in my humble opinion, no master could be found less qualified to finish what you have begun in their regard than Mr Storey, for I am fully acquainted with his easy and good-natured disposition.[5]

Mr Silvertop was advised by the faculty not to take his son to the college this year on account of his sore eyes. He has left him therefore at Sutton Place[6] till his return from Douai, when he will bring him back again to Minsteracres, to my great sorrow and disappointment. Had I foreseen this, and that I must resume again the tedious task of teaching, I should have put many queries to you on the method of teaching the Latin tongue.

Pray remember me to all friends and assure them how sensible I am of their civilities to me when amongst them. But my chief obligations are to you, dear Uncle, for which I shall ever remain your most dutiful Nephew, H. Rutter.

P.S. I had not an opportunity of sending off the above written according to the date, since I have been at Stella. Mr Thomas Eyre was kind enough to advance £5 for me and will write to Mr Kitchen next week that it may be remitted by his steward to Ann Wearden. The report of Gibson's resignation groundless; Comana enquired after you. The elder of the Eyres is gone to Douai, the other two are at Tudhoe. They amused themselves the first night with breaking Mr Storey's windows. You will let me know when I am to expect my books.

1. William Dunn, missioner at Blackburn since 1782, built the first chapel and house there at some expense. Mrs Saltmarch was one of the benefactors.
2. Bullen, an alumnus of the English College, Rome, (known as the *Venerabile or VEC*), a pre-Reformation institution. The Jesuits held the rectorship, but at their suppression in 1773 it was given to the Italian secular clergy, although the Vicars Apostolic pressed for an English rector through the college's Protector, Cardinal Corsini. [M Williams, *The Venerable English College Rome* (1979).] Rutter is confusing about the details of his journey. Nidd is about twenty-four miles from Skipton, as the coach travels, and it seems that he stayed there, not at Cayton, which is south of Scarborough and well out of his way. It is not clear why Bullen left Nidd but he found a new lay-patron in Mr Messenger, who took him in until his death in 1792.
3. There were two priests named Charles Howard at this time and both were DDs of the Sorbonne. The one meant here was chaplain at Burton Constable.
4. Chaplain at Clints.
5. Despite Banister's pessimism and Rutter's disdain, Tudhoe Academy became popular because it allowed parents to keep those children not intended for the priesthood at school in England until the age of fourteen. Like many public schools, the Academy offered a wide classical education with particular attention being paid to 'morals, behaviour and mental improvement. £22 p.a. Dancing 2 guineas extra'.
6. Residence of the Weston family near Guildford.

56. Banister to Rutter Mowbreck, 20th September 1788

My dear good Sir,

The last letter I received from you gave me an account of your safe return to Minsteracres. I began to be ill a day or two after the Assumption of Our Blessed Lady, and the first week had a fever during the night, and presently angry sores broke out on my chin and left side of my face, which continued a considerable time, and their marks are visible yet. I had, moreover, a frequent pain in my left ear and left side of my head which is still very sore to the touch, and never fails to wake me 3 or 4 times in the night; and after sleep is the most painful. In some space of time it mitigates and suffers me to sleep again. I am otherwise very well and can eat with a good appetite, but refrain almost entirely from ale and wine. After the example of the best physicians, I have used no medicines except a little rhubarb and nitre. Whey is my cordial, which Dr Arbuthnot affirms to be the best cure for rheumatisms, and I suspect this pain in my head to be nothing else.

I have heard nothing from Westhead, nor of their goings on.

Young Vincent Eyre was not gone to Douai College when you wrote to me for I received from him a handsome, grateful letter dated the 12th of last August in which he makes not the least mention of his going abroad. I sent his father my accounts the 10th of last July, and have long waited for his answer and a bill for £18.2s. Being in great want of cash, I wrote to him again last Thursday. I wrote to the proud steward with as great a deference as if he had to give me the money out of his own substance. But we ought to say with David: bonum mihi qia humiliasti me, ut discam justificationes tuas.

When I can conveniently pack up your books and send them to the carrier, I will advertise you. Are they not to be addressed to Mr Adams at his office in Newcastle?

Mr Rimmer at Sheffield has just received a coadjutor, one Mr [Francis] Crathorne from Valladolid. Mr Joseph [James] Marsh came over with him and is now with his father in Kirkham. Next Monday he intends to go to Mr Chadwick to learn his destination. Two others, who also left San Albano[1] this summer, stay in the London District.

I could not go to our meeting the 26th of August. Mr Barrow read his phillipic against President Gibson, but I am told it was not generally liked it was so caustic. He never consulted me, nor gave me the least hint of it; and yet very probably I may be thought by some to have had a hand in it. Indeed I believe him a fit object of a severe invective, but it ought to be founded on truth, on matter of fact, on a good evidence, which we at this distqance cannot well obtain. He has rid himself of the three best witnesses of his conduct and proceedings and has only his creatures about him, whom he can blind and lead into his measures with a bravading grandiloquence. For I never heard of a man, though loaded with debts, who could not demonstrate (if you please to believe him) that he is able to acquit all with ease in a short time, &c. Did he not blind Varley, poor man, and make him exclaim against Platt? Whereas Platt, when here in 1786, showed me certain and undoubted documents of his dilapidations, which how they can be repaired I know not, even though he demand £30 p.a. for each student, a thing going to be done as Miles Stapleton averred to me 17th of last May.

Mr Marsh cannot at any rate get a Ritual; is the new one gone to the press or still under correction and amendment?

My best compliments to Mr Thomas Eyre when you see him. Does he continue to improve in duplicity and finesse. I am mistaken if they be not contrary and incongruous to his nature, and so not easily acquirable by him. He had much better make this sacred text his motto and rule of action and expression: He walks secure who walks pure, Prov. 10 v.9.

How have you managed with your innkeeper? They will surely make you fair promises to concur with no drunkenness, and how can you get more than promises, which will perhaps be bent or broken four times for one they are kept.

William Wearden is in a dying condition, past recovery. We have received a letter from my sister's son Robert Hodskinson, dated the 21st of last March, from Honduras, a province of Mexico in America. He is there ahunting inconstant fortune, following a parcel of negroes to cut down mahogany and send it, I suppose, to England. His cousin Robert is, I hope, at London, at least in some part of the kingdom. I pray you to say six Masses for me, viz., for Ann, John, Richard, Isabel, Thomas, Alice.

Master Clifton's two grand agents have put on Mr Wilson's farm a valuation of £12 a year. So, for ought I know, Mr Wilson will have to pay master £7 yearly; his place will thus be reduced to a poor pittance. One is hearing almost every day some thing or other of his pettinesses. He offered his wife's male midwife 20 guineas, looking upon his demand of a guinea per day, during 5 weeks attendance, a great deal too much, for 7 times 5 is 35 guineas. How matters are compromised between them, I know not.

Our harvest here is good, and the weather has been seasonable for housing it.

Memento mei, and believe me your most dear and affectionate Uncle, R. Banister.

1. English College of St Alban, Valladolid.

---

57. Rutter to Banister Minsteracres, 16th November 1788

My dear Uncle,

I received your favour in due time and was extremely sorry to learn that you had been so much indisposed; but your complaint, though an obstinate one, will I hope be removed long before this.

Little has occurred material since my return home. Old Mr Silvertop has had lately a stroke of the palsy, which seized only his brain, and it is well if he ever recovers the use of his intellects considering his great age. Mr [Thomas] Eyre of Derbyshire is gone to the south of France for the sake of his health.[1]

I am told that Mr Rimmer of Sheffield has signified that he is in no want of a coadjutor and therefore Mr Crathorne is expected in our parts to assist Mr Ashmal, who is almost past service but still unwilling to resign. Mr [Robert] Himsworth,[2] a young priest from Douai, is settled at Thropton where Mr Potts lived. Mr Coates still continues to enjoy good health and spirits, and to exert them wonderfully in looking after his flock.

The new Ritual is gone to the press under the inspection of Mr Talbot at London.

Mr Barrow's phillipic against President Gibson must have been caustic indeed to have been so generally disliked, as I hear it was. Mr Silvertop's panegyric of the same person at his return from Douai was, I believe, as much in the opposite extreme, and yet he says that it is founded on truth, on matter of fact and the best evidence. As to the college debts, which he does not deny, he says they are unavoidable by reason of the advanced price of provisions to be proved from the Procurator's books, and the testimony of the other colleges, who are going to increase the pension as well as we. When he laid open to the Seniors assembled together the complaints he had heard against the college, especially at London (some of which were most scandalous), they were shocked, he says, to hear Alma traduced as a place of riot, dissipation and irregularity.

As to the charge of partiality, Mr Silvertop thinks the tattered condition he found his own boy in, a sufficient refutation of it, for his shoes were full of holes, his cassock threadbare, &c. However, though I suspect there is a good deal of misrepresentation and exaggeration against Alma, I am still of opinion that the President is no way adequate to the place he holds and I could learn that his measures are not altogether approved of by one of the leading Seniors, who must be a much better judge of their tendency than his flaming panegyrist.

Mr Talbot, I heard, was resolved on his dismission but probably will not have courage to pursue his determination. As to his brother the bishop [i.e. Matthew Gibson], I see him but seldom, but he is always civil and obliging, as well as his Secretary, Mr Thomas. I was perhaps mistaken in the opinion I formerly had of his finesse, which was owing probably to the secrecy and close manner he generally observes as to his motions.

I hope the good effects of your oratory were not confined to your own congregation, I mean in regard of the theatre. But the Prestonians, I observed, did not relish your zeal, appealing to the conduct of their own pastors. We have a new play-house at Newcastle, which has been honoured this year with the abilities of the great Mrs Siddons. You will probably have heard of what happened to the famous pickpocket Barrington on this occasion, viz., that he was apprehended by the Reverend Mr Warrilow in the playhouse. When I compare the conduct of many of our brethren nowadays with that of the missionary priests a few years ago, I am struck at the great contrast between them and am at a loss how to account for so extraordinary a change.[3]

I have said the Masses you desired me. With my books I shall expect to see yourself in miniature. You may address them to me at Mr Adam's office, Newcastle.

I am informed from Westhead that my father is hugely offended because the money we raised for him was deposited in Alex. Moorcroft's hands, but what could be done?

Young [John] Wright is going to be married to Miss Elizabeth Lawson, which gives much pleasure and satisfaction to his friends and relations.

The finest weather this year ever remembered in these parts. Our housekeeper is going likewise to enter into the matrimonial state. Do you know of any you could recommend in her place; she must be elderly, &c?

Poor Billy Wearden! I beg you will remember me to him and to all friends. I desire likewise my respects to Mr Wilson and am dear Uncle, your ever dutiful Nephew, H. Rutter.

1. Thomas Eyre (1743–92) of Hassop, who married Lady Mary Bellasyse. He kept in touch with the Committee's affairs through his cousin, the Rev. Thomas Eyre, at Stella.
2. He was later deprived of his priestly faculties for immorality; he left under protest, was refused ordination in the Anglican church, and practised as a man-midwife; he died in a lunatic asylum in York in 1811.
3. Rutter deprecates the attendance of priests at the theatre in contravention of canon law. Mrs Siddons heard Warrilow preach and declared that had he

taken to the stage he would have immortalised his name and realised a splendid fortune.

---

58. Rutter to Banister Minsteracres, 25th March 1789

Dear Uncle,

This is to request of you the favour of a few lines informing me of your state of health and whether you be still troubled with rheumatic pains. Your long silence makes me apprehensive that something is the matter with you that hinders you from writing. As for my part, I continue to enjoy good health as usual, God be thanked, and find this Lent agrees with me better than I expected. Are you still able to fast? And do you allow buns with butter in them in the morning to our Gentry and what quantity?

Old Mr [George] Silvertop, who never properly recovered his faculties since the first stroke, departed this life on 11th of this month, in the 85th year of his age, universally regretted in the neighbourhood. His wife is now with us and showed him so much attention during his long illness that her son in law has settled £100 p.a. upon her more than she was entitled to. The old man has left by will £500 for a fund at Douai, £500 for the poor of his parish, £200 for prayers for himself and wife, and last before he was taken ill he has agreed for the purchase of a field to be added to the Thropton Fund.

Comana is at present in a very unpleasant situation and at a loss how to act. [Charles] Butler has repeatedly written to him in the name of Lord Petre and his Committee to subscribe to certain propositions which have been signed by 3 bishops and most of their clergy in the south. But Comana does not approve of them and wished to know the sentiments of the Irish and Scotch Bishops whom he has consulted on this subject. He thought the matter of great moment and such as required mature deliberation and advised that the bishops should take a little time to consider it and agree amongst themselves. But our Gentry are impatient of delay, and as they have obtained the signatures of so many respectable persons, condemn Mr Gibson's conduct as absurd and ridiculous. Bishop [John] Geddes[1] is on the side of Comana and so was Bishop [Charles] Walmesley[2] at Bath, but he has since deserted him and subscribed. How our Bishop will proceed I know not but I shall be much surprised if he submits to what the Gentlemen require of him. Most probably you know all this and I shall be very glad to hear your sentiments on this subject which I shall certainly adopt as my own and follow accordingly.[3]

I beg likewise Dear Uncle that you will favour me with your sentiments on another subject in which I am more immediately concerned. I mean in regard of first communicants. You will be so kind as to give me a few hints for my direction in regard of their age and what knowledge you require of them and a short plan of instructions for them. I am exceedingly distressed at present with respect to such as live at a distance in Protestant places and who seldom come to prayers.

I hear my father has had a sale of his effects and is gone to live at Ormskirk. The money was put into Alex. Moorcroft's hands, for his use and benefit, either to buy a cow or pay off the debts he had contracted, but he had too much spirit to accept of it in that manner; he would either have it in his own hands or not at all.

Mr [Thomas] Sanderson, the Prefect at Douai, has been over in these parts for some time and seems to speak of the college like an unprejudiced person who is of no party. He allows right on both sides and that discipline was much relaxed at the beginning of Mr Gibson's administration owing to his imprudence and indiscretion, but that experience has made him wise and things are now managed with the utmost order and reularity.

Mr Crathorne is going to live with Mr Tempest of Broughton.

The enclosed piece of veil comes from the chapel at Loreto, duly authenticated; the indulgence was lately published at York by Mr Thomas Lawson.

You once mentioned to me a work entitled Exposition de la Doctrine Chretienne which I believe Mr Wilson has. Do you approve of it? I beg my compliments to him and to all friends and remain, Dear Uncle, your dutiful Nephew, H.R.

1. John Geddes, coadjutor to Bishop Hay and elder brother of Alexander; he was a highly cultured and popular man who was described by Robert Burns as the finest Christian clergyman he had ever known.
2. Charles Walmesley, OSB, DD, FRS (1722–97), consecrated Bishop of Rama, ipi, in 1756 to be coadjutor in the Western District, to which he succeeded in 1763. The mob would gut his chapel in Bath during the Gordon Riots later in the year.
3. In February 1788 the Catholic Committee presented a *Memorial* to Prime Minister Pitt reciting the remaining civil disabilities under which the Catholics laboured. Consequent upon a meeting with Pitt in May the Committee drafted a Relief Bill. Lord Stanhope, leading the campaign for the relief of Protestant Dissenters, suggested that the Catholics should formally disclaim those tenets falsely attributed to them, and which were commonly supposed to prove that

Catholics could not be held to their allegiance. He drafted a paper to that effect, the essence of which was that Catholics did not hold that an excommunicated prince could be deprived or murdered; that the Pope could not order Catholics to rebel against their government and that he could not dispense with the obligations of oaths. The Committee embodied the suggestion in a public *Declaration*, also known as the *Protestation*, which they issued for general approval by clergy and laity. On 21 December 1788, however, Bishop Gibson told Bishop Walmesley that he would not subscribe to the *Protestation*, and reiterated his decision on 20 March 1789.

---

59. Banister to Rutter — Mowbreck, 2nd April 1789

My dear Sir

I have now received two letters from you, the latter of them this week. This must be an answer to both and a long one so you must not think that I shall be able to send it to the post on the day it is dated above.

To begin with buns: we eat them here in Lent bona fide; you make no scruple of eating apple-pies or tarts which are not made without butter in the crust.

Last week but one Mr Miles Stapleton sent me a letter which was the first information I had concerning the Declaration of the Catholic Committee at London. He desired my opinion upon the third declaratory answer. The objection, as I may call it, runs thus: "We have likewise been accused of holding as a principle of our religion that the Pope, by virtue of his spiritual power, can dispense with the obligation of any compact or oath taken or entered into by a Catholic; that therefore no oath of allegiance or other oath can bind us and consequently that we can give no security for our allegiance to any government". To which the Committee answers as follows: "There can be no doubt but that the conclusion would be just if the original proposition upon which it is founded were true. But we positively deny that we do hold any such principle; and we do solemnly declare that neither the Pope, nor any Prelate, nor any Priest, nor any assembly of prelates or priests, nor any ecclesiastical power whatever can absolve us, or any of us, from or dispense with the obligations of any compact or oath whatsoever".

I was very much grieved to see my opinion required on such a matter. Notwithstanding, I recollected and wrote down two or three modes in which I though the proposition contained in this Declaration might be explained and understood in sensu sano et catholico. Mr Wilson happening to come hither, I showed him what I had written. He advised me to write a concise answer without interpreting the proposition or speaking of imaginable hypothetical cases in which oaths are dispensable. The grand quaere is, says he, about the oath of allegiance and about compacts and oaths between man and man. I therefore sent Mr Miles Stapleton the following answer which he will, as Mr Wilson says, undoubtedly show to others his friends and familiars:

Mowbreck, 23rd March 1789

My dear, Honoured Sir,

I received your letter the day before yesterday and, because I bear a great respect and affection for you, I have used great diligence to answer it, for I have been very much hindered and unavoidably. The declaratory answer to the 3rd objection with which you present me is not very accurate, but supposing it to be reducible to this plain position, viz., that neither the Pope nor any ecclesiastical power nor any power on earth can give me leave, or a dispensation, to break an oath of allegiance, or any lawful compact confirmed by oath between man and man, it is certainly true and you may sign it a thousand times if necessary. Observe my reason: allegiance or fidelity to our Sovereign Prince, as honour, love and obedience to parents, is commanded both by the law of nature and the law of God and therefore is indispensable, even without an oath; an oath superadded strengthens the obligation. Compacts between man and man, supposing them lawful, are binding by the law of nature and, in virtue of natural justice, are therefore indispensable; an oath superadded strengthens and confirms them and binds the party or parties in virtue of religion. Justice and religion are eternal obligations. The Protestants make much ado about papal dispensations, and interpret them to be nothing else but a leave to break oaths and compacts, whereas you may most confidently assert that neither any power on earth or in heaven can give anyone leave or permission to break or violate an oath, for that would be to make God witness to a lie. I hope the authors of the declaratory answer to the 3rd objection had no other meaning than that which I have given it. Therefore you may, I think, sign it without hesitation. But I submit my sentiment in this and everything else to better judgements to be corrected if found defective. I remain, dear Sir, yours &c., R.B.

So far to Mr Miles. You see I make no hypotheses nor imaginable possible cases in which the bond of an oath may be relaxed by dispensation.

Propositions are oftentimes couched both in Scripture, Fathers and Divines in terms of universality and yet some exception may be found in which such propositions may not stand true. For example, it is said universally: children are to obey their parents in all that is not sinful. Yet there is one case at least in which they are not bound to obey them, although it be no sin but in itself good and ordained by God, viz., marriage. Divines teach that [promises made on oath through fear or extorted by force oblige in conscience but often merit dispensation. Do they oblige by virtue of justice or religion? By virtue of justice, it seems, for in this case it is possible to give a dispensation. Things which oblige by virtue of religion, out of reverence for divine authority, are sworn before a witness. In these and other cases, we Catholics have recourse to superiors or to bishops or to the Supreme Pontiff for a relaxation from the bonds of an oath which, when lifted, ceases to be obligatory. Both Protestants and non-Catholics seek to release themselves from the bonds of an oath; they seek no dispensation, which they rather mock as superfluous, but we are permitted thus to be loosed. We who revere the more severe laws], a parody from Martial.

Now I pray you, do not read or show this to your squire. If he has any scruples let him consult Comana and indeed, I suppose, he will have no recourse to any but to him. I believe Butler and his comrades of the soi-disant Committee are very mean theologians but self-sufficient to a high degree. What, do you think, they want to get by the repeal of penal laws, to save us from the gallows? Do you think several of them would be sorry to see us hanged? For we but disturb them sometimes in the spacious flowery road in which most of them roll and dance along: 'So, full of ease this life passes and they go down at last without a struggle to the grave', Job, ch. 21, v13.

Now to say something of the admission of young persons to their first Communion, some instruction must necessarily precede it. The shortest Catechism is too much for some and several who say it off book by heart have little or no understanding of it, that is, of its meaning and import. What can be done with such terrestrial beings? I begin with hearing them say the Our Father, Ave Maria and Credo, then explain in a few distinct easy words the meaning of each petition. I endeavour to explain the petitions at every clause in the same concise plain words, for, if you are diffusive or vary your expressions, they will retain nothing. In like manner I explain the Ave Maria and every article of the creed. And, because the life, miracles of Our Lord and the number and manner of his sufferings and death are not sepeculative, but facts most wonderful and most affecting, the meanest capacity may understand them and the dullest heart be moved. It may be then very proper to relate them but clearly and concisely, not to overwhelm the memory of unthinking creatures. The ninth article deserves to be inculcated in a very particular manner in order to fix young novices firm in the belief of one true saving faith. For in these corrupted times the detestable doctrine of Alexander Pope, in his Essay on Man is very much propagated:

> For modes of faith let greaceless zealots fight,
> His can't be wrong whose life is in the right.

It was a singular providence, as [Thomas] Ward[1] takes notice, that suffered not the first pseudo-reformers to change the words Catholic Church in the ninth article although they everywhere changed it into General Congregation in their translations of the Scriptures. It remains unchanged in the creed to bear witness that as often as they say it, they lie to their Maker.

Having often explained in the manner above the Pater, Ave, Credo, the ten commandments come next which everyone should say by heart. I explain how they may be broken and by what mortal sins, I mean the most usual not rare or uncommon ones. It is necessary to tell them what mortal sin is, how great an evil, how much to be feared, and yet very common and into which unthinking people often and easily fall, &c. Moreover, it is necessary to specify in what thoughts, words, deeds and omissions or negligences it is found. Many think themselves very regular because, like the proud Pharisee, they are not unjust to men, nor extortioners, nor swear, nor steal, nor break a house; whilst they live in a continual violation of the first and greatest commandment, viz., by taking more care of their bodies than of their souls, by living in mortal sin and thinking little, or not at all, of repentance, which is the sin of presumption; by saying no more prayers than a hasty Pater, Ave, Credo morning and night, which is the same as if you should sprinkle on a dry garden three drops of water morning and evening. The vulgar make no distinction between swearing and cursing, they declare all in one word, I have swore, seeming to think all either mortal or venial. It is, therefore, absolutelyu necessary to ask them what they say when they swear and to mention the different modes in most use that they may recollect those they have used; and ask too whether they have rapped out some thundering words as G..d's zounds, G..d's b..d, by G..d, I'll be d..n'd, the d..l take me, &c. All which I reckon mortal sins. As I would write on other matters I must quit the subject of catechumens.

Young [Thomas] Clifford[2] of Tixel came here on Maundy Thursday in the evening with the Declaration and a long list of signatures. I told him

I could not sign till our Bishop had signed. He then produced a letter given him by Comana to Mr Butler in which he says that there is nothing in the Declaration but some speculative matters or some equivocal terms which withhold his signature, that he has consulted the Irish bishops, that he reprobates all the imputations which are falsely laid to the charge of Catholics, &c. I cannot well recollect the words of the letter, but it seems that he might as well have signed as wrote it. Mr Edward Eyre, Mr James Johnson, Mr [John] Silvertop did not sign. However, I put my name to it, induced as much by Comana's letter as by my own judgement.[3]

Your old pupil is gone to Newmarket Races. Last month he had a second daughter born. His old aunt Miss Julie died on Christmas Day, I was one of the mourners on the 30th, stayed all night at the hall by express invitation, lodged in the best guest-room, &c. He speaks of you in a panegyric style to me. I remain, my dear Hal, ever yours &c., R. Banister

1. A 17th-century controversialist. Banister probably refers to his *England's Reformation* (1710 and numerous subsequent editions).
2. (1762–1829) of Tixall, Staffs. He was created a baronet on 22 May 1815 at the especial desire of King Louis XVIII of France.
3. Eyre and Johnson were priests. On 12 April Bishop Gibson told Bishop James Talbot that if the Protestation was generally and impartially understood to refer only to temporals then his name could be added to the list of signatures if Talbot thought it necessary for the common good. Talbot appended Gibson's name but withdrew it later considering it was unnecessary. 1,770 Catholics signed it, including 240 clerics.

60. Banister to Rutter — Mowbreck, 22nd May 1789

My dear Sir,

My sisters, your aunts, Helen and Ann were both seized with a fever the 28th of last month. Ann only continued 11 days and departed this life the 9th of this month about 6 o'clock in the morning. Helen continued 3 weeks and a day and died a little before midnight on the 20th. I hope you will pray for them and offer up a Mass for each. There now remains of the old stock only my brother and self. Helen was 12 years and a half older than me and Nanny 11 years older; my brother will be at least 72 in August 73.

John Gillow's[1] wife died in April after a long consumption of a year and a half and has left him 3 infants.

I am going to keep a horse for my own riding but they are very dear to buy and horned cattle very cheap. Master Clifton's horse won two plates at Chester Races. I am told that Bernard Howard, heir apparent to Norfolk, has married one of Lord Fauconberg's daughters and will probably imitate his brother.[2]

The petition for the repeal of the penal laws will meet with no success, I am told. I am no way sorry for it, nothing could be worse conducted and managed, as I am informed. It brings to my mind all the past miscarriages and ill-concerted schemes of our Catholic ancestors.[3]

Mr [Edward] Daniel of Croston has published The Outlines of a Trial of the Roman Catholics of Great Britain with a view to Union, Liverpool, printed for the author, 1788. It is nothing but incoherent scraps, I never in my life saw anything to parallel it.[4]

I hope you received my last long letter; this must be a short one and conclude with desiring you to pray for me and to believe me, Your most affectionate Uncle, R. Banister.

1. Tenant of Salwick Hall farm.
2. Bernard ('Barney') Howard, 12th Duke of Norfolk, married Lady Elizabeth Belasyse. As a Whig and a cisalpine, Banister expected him to apostatise from Catholicism, but he did not.
3. In May the *Protestation* was presented to parliament in the form of a *Petition* in which the petitioners were described, at the suggestion of Lord Chancellor Thurlow, as the 'Catholic Dissenters of England'.
4. Not listed by Gillow.

61. Rutter to Banister Minsteracres, 22nd June 1789

My dear Uncle,

I received your two letters in due time, the latter of which brought me an account of the death of my two aunts. I shall not fail to remember them in my prayers, and have said Mass for both of them. For I always had a regard for them, especially Aunt Nanny, who was likewise my father's favourite.

Your other letter relative to the Committee business was very acceptable, as your sentiments on that subject had been very ill-stated to me. However,

I could wish your observations had not been confined merely to the third declaratory answer concerning oaths, but that they had been extended to some other parts which appeared to me to be equally objectionable, especially as every part of the said Declaration was to be taken in the plain and ordinary sense of the words without any evasion whatever. What I hint at regards the power of the Church, satisfaction and, I may add, the papal infallibility, which I did not think you would have given up so easily. For I had always imagined this to have been your private opinion.

I accompanied Mr Silvertop to Stella Hall to meet Mr Clifford and, not having received your letter, followed the example of my bishop in not signing. I think I told you in my last that he was at first extremely averse to the Declaration and had written to his Vicars that none of his clergy should sign it. He likewise corrected and expunged the objectionable parts and had it reprinted in Newcastle, but I hear his emendations were much criticised and rejected by some as worse than those very parts he wished to rectify. What surprises me is that he should at last follow the crowd and that all this bustle ended in sending up his name to Bishop Talbot. But in this he was not singular; Bishop Walmsley and Mr Lodge, who at first said it could not be subscribed to, acted the same part. Little, I believe, is to be expected from Parliament this year, owing, as I hear, to the indiscretion of some leading persons in the Committee.[1]

I am informed that Mr Douglass is to be coadjutor to Bishop Talbot, at least he is the first on the list of those whose names have been sent to Rome.[2] I am sure I envy him not.

Old Riddell is at last released from his long and tedious illness. His eldest son[3] settles at Swinburne, but the chaplain must live at a distance from the house. Mr [Thomas] Trafford[4], I am informed, has made the same application, and how Comana will supply all these places, I know not. Mr Billington, I fear, will not long be able to do the duty of a missioner; he is indeed very pious but is of the Kendal line and so troubled with scruples as to be almost unfit for any of his ecclesiastical functions.

Mr Silvertop has had a very severe attack of the gout for the first time. All the children, thank God, are now from home. Jacky, who is the second, is gone to try sea-bathing, for he has still a complaint in his eyes. The other two little ones are at Mr Storey's school, Tudhoe. Sir John Lawson is now enlarging the house so as to contain about 30 boys, for several applications have been made which could not be attended to for want of room. Pray, what boys have you at Mowbreck, or have you any? I ask, for report here says in laughing way that you are attended at the altar by two fine misses. I mention this to show how ready some are to catch at anything in your regard that can possibly be turned to ridicule.

I am glad to hear that you begin to be in favour at Lytham. Pray, has the squire raised Mr Wilson's rent? Mr Thomas Eyre desires his respects to you; he is now busy reprinting The Garden of the Soul. I hope you will not forget your promise of sending me your profile when an opportunity offers. Pray remember me to all friends, and believe me, dear Uncle, your ever dutiful Nephew, Hen. Rutter.

1. In June John Mitford MP gave notice of the Catholic Relief Bill, but its introduction was postponed because of the King's illness. A new oath based on the Protestation was, however, published.
2. John Douglass (1743–1812) was not consecrated as Bishop of Centuria, ipi, until December 1790. Bp. James Talbot died in January that year having recommended Richard Southworth as his successor.
3. Thomas Riddell of Felton Park and Swinburne Castle.
4. Of Trafford Park, Manchester, he married Elizabeth Tempest in 1773 and inherited Trafford in 1779. The necessity for chaplains to be resident with their patrons lapsed after the 1778 Relief Act and many of them were required to, or chose to, set up as independent householders.

62. Banister to Rutter — Mowbreck, 27th July 1789

My dear Sir

The bishop has so engaged me to take a journey to Stella that I cannot but comply with his request. So I propose, Deo volente, to set out from home next Friday and take my route in a single-horse Whisky, which my young man Richard will conduct, through Lancaster to Dodding Green, from thence to Penrith and Greystoke Castle. From Greystoke Castle back to Penrith, from whence on Sunday in the afternoon and Monday the 3rd of August I hope to cross the country to Hexham. I do not promise to come to visit you at Minsteracres, but you will, I hope, contrive to visit me at Stella on Wednesday or Thursday the 5th or 6th of August, although I shall not probably leave Stella till Monday the 10th.[1]

In your last letter you suppose that I have given up the Pope's infallibility, but your supposition can only be your inference drawn from the premises. But I hold the inference to be unduly drawn and that the premises do not contain the conclusion you make. It is not an article of faith that the Pope, per se, is infallible, therefore he is not infallible is an undue inference. He is not infallible in everything, e.g., in factis personalibus, therefore he is not infallible in anything is also a false illation.

Two very elegant young girls, the daughters of one Mr Hall, a Protestant surgeon in Manchester (but his wife is a Catholic), one 10 the other 9 years old, for the first time were my acolytes last Christmas Day, being dressed up in fine muslin frocks and very nice tippets, and blue silk bonnets, and red merroquin slippers. They officiated in the same dress on three or four other festivals. And when I told Mary what you had written concerning them, she assured me that several of the congregation were much pleased to see them serving me so becomingly and elegantly. But last Friday their mother took them away to place them at Preston after a year's stay here at Mowbreck.

Yesterday I went to see Mr Wilson and he advised me to take my route as above, but in pursuing it I may change my mind. I hope this will find you well. Ora pro itinerantibus [Pray for the traveller] and believe me your most dear, affectionate Uncle, R. Banister.

1. Bishop Gibson wished to consult Banister on the terminology of the new oath. He afterwards issued a circular prohibiting anyone in the District from taking the oath proposed by the Committee. Greystoke Castle was the residence of the Howard family.

63. Banister to Rutter — Stella, [October 1789]

My dear Sir,

We set out for London either tomorrow morning or this morning, for, at my writing this, I do not know whether it is still Sunday or Monday morning.[1] I fear you was ill-wet before you arrived at Minsteracres.

I send you eight intentions, viz., John Ryley, Isabel Johnson, Eliz. Carfoot, Ann Sharples, Thomas Carfoot, Ann Suddall, Richard Holmes, Margaret Posnet.

When it pleases God to conduct me back to Mowbreck (which I hope for before All Saints) I will write to you.

[Unless the Lord builds the house &c., unless the Lord directs the counsel &c.][2] Pray for me and believe me, your most dear affectionate Uncle, R.B.

1. The Vicars Apostolic held a crisis-meeting in London 19–21 October to discuss the new oath in the *Protestation*. Banister was theological adviser to Bishop Gibson.
2. Psalm 126.

---

64. Rutter to Banister Minsteracres, 27th December 1789

Dear Uncle,

I have been long waiting with impatience for the letter you promised me after your return to Mowbreck but which never reached me. However, I am glad to hear by another way that you got safe home and that the business you went upon was so happily concluded, which I think is to be ascribed in a great measure to the active part you took in it. I have not seen the bishop since his return to congratulate him on his triumph, but hope to do it very shortly, especially as he may perhaps inform me of some particulars concerning yourself, which you are not pleased to communicate to me.[1]

We have had a letter very lately from Mr William Gibson at Bristol who says the waters seem to agree with him, but there seems little prospect of a speedy recovery, or of his returning back to Douai College. I am not sorry for it on Alma's account, for, without reference to the complaints lodged against him, I am convinced from the little acquaintance I have had with him since he came to England, that he has neither learning nor abilities adequate to the government of such a house.

It is now a fortnight since I began this letter, since which Mr [Thomas] Riddell is come from Bristol, who says Mr President has been so unfortunate as to be overturned in his carriage as they were returning from Bath, by which his feet, his head and breast were hurt, but that Riddell escaped unhurt. This misfortune must render his recovery still more uncertain and difficult. His brother, My Lord Bishop, has likewise had a severe attack of the gout, which still confines him to his bed. I have seen him since his return and then thought he looked remarkably well.

Our wise Committee seem determined to carry their point and I was extremely hurt to find their impudent letter to our Missioners signed by Berington and [Joseph] Wilkes [OSB].[2] This shows that nothing is to be expected but mischief and dissensions, unless a vigorous stand be made against them by the body of Catholics at large to annul their proceedings and take away their power, which will probably be the case.

I have received a letter from my brother Robert and am glad to he hear that he is married but he says nothing of his wife's religion and family. I have answered his letter begging to be informed of these particulars and advising him to settle and think seriously of his salvation.

I have said Mass for those you desired me and wish you much joy at this holy time and many returns of the season. I am dear Uncle, your dutiful Nephew, H. Rutter.

P.S. Be pleased to send me directions to sister Susan.

1. At their meeting in October, the Vicars Apostolic unanimously declared that: (1) the term Protesting Catholic Dissenters was highly objectionable; (2) the new oath was unlawful (the oath in the 1778 act being sufficient, in any case); (3) that they would instruct the faithful accordingly. An encyclical letter to this effect was issued on 21 October. The Committee was undeterred, however, and the lesser clergy remained divided; but on 1 January 1790 fifty-five priests in Lancashire signed a Petition supporting Bishop Gibson and entreating him to seek a way of avoiding schism among the English Catholics. He complied by issuing a pastoral letter on 15 January. Ten days later, however, fifteen of the Staffordshire clergy publicly approved the new oath and at the beginning of February ten priests of the London District did so.
2. Missioner in Bath. He was said to lead an extravagant way of life, unbecoming in a monk, but was so pleasant in conversation that he enchanted everyone. [Ward, *Dawn* I 124]. Wilkes was elected to the Catholic Committee in 1788, with Bishop Charles Berington, and became its chief theological adviser. Hence he was a target of the anti-Committee elements in the church.

65. Banister to Rutter — 18th January 1790

Dear Sir,

As soon as you receive this, carry the 2 enclosed sheets to Mr Thomas Eyre—do not trust them to a post. I have sent him 4 such sheets, 2 the last week and 2 the week before, but he has not acknowledged the receipt of them. I shall finish my work in two sheets more, at least in 3. If they are to see light I wish to be totally concealed and my name not even whispered. Next Wednesday I shall, if I am not much hindered, send you 2 sheets.[1]

Rigby at Lancaster has written to his brother Thomas at London that the Committeemen's letter has convinced him, and he joins their sentiments. I have not heard what Dunn of Blackburn thinks, but as he is a Paris Doctor, I scarcely doubt but he joins in sentiment with the purple pamphlet.

You must not show the enclosed to your squire—his brother in law the Baronet [Sir John Lawson] is, unless converted, an abettor of Committee proceedings.

Direct to Susan with Basil Fitzherbert Esquire, Swinnerton, Stone, Staffordshire.

I have not time to write more at present, only that I am ever your most affectionate Uncle, R.B.

P.S. Coghlan sent me the act of parliament and oath of 1778, which he procured from the King's law-printer. So the 7 Committeemen are convicted of fallacy in asserting that the clause of 1778 is the same, excepting the word heretical, as in the oath condemned by Paul V. They will scruple at nothing to gain their point.

1. Gillow remarks that Banister's 'pen was probably engaged, directly or indirectly, in the controversy concerning the oath of allegiance'. This and subsequent letters confirm Banister's anonymous literary role in support of the Vicars Apostolic in that and other disputes. Eyre was Bishop Gibson's secretary.

---

66. Banister to Rutter — 1st February 1790

My dear Sir,

I sent you 19th of last month, as I think, two sheets enclosed and desired you to carry them to Mr Eyre, which I hope you have done long since. I then promised to send you two more, in like manner enclosed in a cover, but I could not get them ready for the day, so I have sent now all to Mr Eyre; the last went to Preston post-office on Saturday 30th of January. If the lucubration be to go to the press, I have proposed you to Comana to go to Newcastle and to choose the form and type, to correct the proof-sheets, &c. For I believe you have much less to do than Mr Eyre. Besides it is not proper that he should be suspected of having a hand in it, much less Comana, and I wish you, and much more myself, to lie concealed. There will be no need for the printer to put his name to it, nor the name of the place where it is printed. If that be necessary then a feigned name, and

Glasgow or Aberdeen may be put, though that will look to be a bare-faced lie.

The junto will be now exceedingly occupied in electing their bishop.[1] To be sure, our Rigby at Lancaster will stand foremost amongst the candidates because he is gone over to the Committee, and probably with that view. He explains the oath with great facility: you may swear the Pope has no spiritual jurisdiction here if it interferes, directly or indirectly &c., and yet his jurisdiction will affect your conscience; you give up his jurisdiction but not your consience. The Mahometan Mufti has no jurisdiction or authority to make laws to interfere here in this kingdom, therefore he cannot bind your conscience; and, in like manner, if the Pope has no authority to make decrees or constitutions, that interfere, &c., he cannot bind conscience. So Rigby's interpretation or explication is a plain fallacy. But it will, I fear, deceive many because it is accommodating.

Bishop Talbot proposed Mr Richard Southworth to be his coadjutor but, because he was rejected, he would choose no other.

1. Bishop James Talbot, Vicar Apostolic London District, died on 26 January 1790 without a coadjutor to succeed him. (James Barnard administered the District as Vicar General.) On 18 February the Committee despatched a letter to Cardinal Antonelli extolling the merits of Bishop Charles Berington, one of their number, hoping to have him translated from the Midland District where he was coadjutor to Bishop Thomas Talbot. A group of priests who did not want Richard Southworth also nominated Berington; John Douglass was their second choice and Peter Browne third. The latter was a capitular and a missioner in London and would die four years later.

67. Rutter to Banister — 19th February 1790

Dear Uncle,

I received in due time the two sheets which you enclosed in a cover for Mr Eyre, and which, according to your desire, I carried to him on the same day. Since that, I have received another favour from you on the 7th of this month. As to your lucubration, I believe it will go to the press, but I am to have nothing to do in the business, as Mr Thomas will settle everything relative to the form, type, &c., which I am very glad of, being totally unacquainted with such matters. I understand it is to undergo some few alterations before it be sent to the printer, and whatever these may be,

I hope they will be submitted to your judgement and approbation. For without this precaution I fear your work will fall into the hands of some mar-plot who, by attempting to change a part, may possibly spoil the beauty of the whole performance.

I ardently wish to see it made public, and wonder it is not in greater forwardness, considering how long it has been at Stella. But perhaps they expected that the new oath would be abandoned and that Comana's letter would set everything right. But it is quite the reverse, and I am well assured that the number of those who defend the oath and Committee proceedings is daily increasing. Even Strickland himself, who certainly professed himself an enemy to the oath, is now become an advocate for it, and I fear his example will have no weight with many of his brethren.[1] We have hitherto had little information concerning the late proceedings of the Committee. Coghlan writes that nothing is yet finally settled by them, that they may have dropped the new oath in its present form and substituted in its place The Declaration and Protestation of English Catholics.

As to his Lordship's Pastoral Letter, I hear it is commended by some in the south as a judicious, sensible performance, and condemned by others as a bitter and malicious invective. There is an answer come out to it, by an unknown hand, which seems truly deserving of this harsh censure. If you wish to have a specimen of it, here it is. "The popish religion has often encouraged her children to commit almost every sort of crime", and a little after, "I make no hesitation to affirm that the popish religion has been mediately or immediately the cause of almost all the political disturbances in Europe since the days of Gregory the 7th".[2] He afterwards mentions his Lordship's "bringing poor Cadwallader[3] on the stage . . . he fell a victim to his own prejudices; he died a material traitor to his country". He asserts that Bishop J. Talbot was not able at the time "to do any business either temporal or spiritual", and then, "it was most cruel in your Lordship to take advantage of his then situation". As to his grammatical observations, I fear they are but too well-founded and, if I might judge in your own style, perhaps you yourself will think that his Lordship has too much of the "syllabub", &c.

The substance of Bishop Walmesley's letter to Comana is as follows: 'that the majority of the Committee had agreed to drop the oath. The old bishop insisted that any new oath ought to be submitted to the Apostolic Vicars but, so far from this, they will not allow them to have a peep at it, except Bishop Talbot, who says it is the same as the other excepting one alteration.' That part of the Pastoral Letter which regards C. Berington the Committee declared to be false.

The post is just going off and I have only to add that I am most sincerely your dutiful Nephew, H. Rutter

1. Strickland, President of Liege Academy, was, in fact, only trying to solve the problem of the oath. [Holt, *Strickland* 34–7]
2. Saint Pope St Gregory VII (Hildebrand), c.1020–1085, who subdued his temporal opponents. He was canonised in 1728.
3. Roger Cadwallader, martyred in 1610. He thrice refused to take the oath of allegiance saying that while he freely acknowledged James I as his King, the oath went on to deny the Pope's spiritual authority.

---

68. Rutter to Banister Stella Hall, 17th May 1790

Dear Uncle,

It gives me great concern that I am to inform you of the death of his Lordship, who departed this life about 9 o'clock this morning after an illness of 7 or 8 days. Mr Chadwick is appointed Vicar General. Mr Thomas Eyre, Mr William Gibson and Mr [John] Lonsdale[1] are the executors. I have only time to add that I am your dutiful Nephew, Hen. Rutter.

1. Missioner at Linton upon Ouse.

---

69. Rutter to Banister Minsteracres, 24th May 1790

My dear Uncle,

On the 17th Inst. I wrote to you in great haste from Stella to inform you that Mr Gibson our bishop had departed this life about 9 o'clock that morning. I will now give you a more particular account of his illness, and confidentially disclose to you what appears necessary and proper in the present critical situation of affairs.

His Lordship's disorder began on 5th of May with a cold which seems to have been accompanied with something of the gout and jaundice. He was confined to his room on the 8th and Dr. Hall, an eminent physician of Newcastle, was afterwards sent for, who visited him 4 or 5 different times without ever seeming to apprehend any danger. Nay, the very night before he died he gave Mr Eyre great hopes of his recovery, and the day after, examining the dead body, declared the cause of his death to be a perfect mystery, which he could not explain. His Lordship, during the whole time of his sickness, was perfectly in his senses, asked for the Sacrament, the Benediction, &c., and at last gently expired almost without a sigh.

I trust in God he has made a happy exit and is safely arrived at the port of eternal peace and quiet after the storms and tempests to which of late years he has been exposed in his episcopal character. I have no doubt but that his death was at least hastened by the opposition he met with on every side and the many perplexed and disagreeable affairs which he has lately had on his hands and which seem at last to have overwhelmed his mind and spirits. I sincerely regret his death as a public loss at the present very critical period, though others I know will consider it in a very different light.

But who will now come forward in his place and stand in the gap to oppose himself as a wall for the house of God against the present set of Innovators? The sole management of affairs will, for the present, be committed to Mr Thomas Talbot, or rather to his coadjutor C. Berington, and what can be expected from such guides? The Committee, I believe, will now conceive hopes of succeeding in their attempt of translating C. Berington to the London District, especially as they have so powerful an interest at Hilton. Mr [Robert] Smelt is our Agent[1] there and he sends the following information in a letter dated April 8th, 1790

I informed Cardinal Antonelli of the method used at the meeting in London. He said it was new, nevertheless he approved of it, not seeing any other in the present circumstances. I told him the names of the candidates, &c., and the reason why they were not formally presented. He enquired how long Mr Talbot's will was made prior to his death. On hearing two years, he instantly rejected Mr Southworth, saying there was time more than sufficient to publish his intention and send a Postulation hither. To Mr Berington he had some objections: being already fixed, why was he to be removed? Besides, his name was in the Committee, whose proceedings he had procured from England and got them translated into Italian. It is true, upon enquiry, it appeared that Mr Berington was not the author. Mr Berington, he said, must be much beloved by his brethren to have two thirds of their suffrages. To the other two he said nothing, but when the Postulation came in proper form, it would be laid before the Congregation of Propaganda, enquiries made concerning the qualifications of each of the three, one of them appointed and recommended to higher powers &c., as usual in such cases.

Mr Clifford of Tixall about a fortnight ago presented a Memorial to Antonelli, on behalf of Mr Berington, signed by all our peers. Tuesday last, when I presented your letter, he told me the Nuncio at Paris had transmitted a Memorial in favour of Mr Berington, signed by four peers and several baronets, which was put into his hands by the Spanish Ambassador there. How far the first Memorial may succeed, I cannot pretend to say, but if the other is effectually supported by the Spanish interest (of which I have some doubt) the memorialists will probably obtain the prayers of their petition . . .

The Spanish interest is very powerful here, indeed, the only one that prevails. It is the only country except Portugal that is not, at least in some degree, at variance with this court. For this reason great attention is paid to the Spanish Minister here, who is said almost to command what he pleases. It will be some time before the affair can be concluded . . . In the meantime you may send your objections, and I will present them; this appears to be the best way.

So far Mr Smelt. From whence it appears still doubtful whether or no C. Berington will be translated to the London District, but every step in my opinion ought to be taken to prevent it.

For this purpose I earnestly entreat you to draw up a Memorial in latin to Cardinal Antonelli supported by solid reasons, instead of interest, and enforcing the objections which, I hope, Comana has already alleged against him. You can refer His Eminence to the proceedings of the Committee, which he got translated into Italian. You can dwell particularly on his scandalous opposition to the Vicars Apostolic after they had formally condemned the oath. And pray do not omit the shining paragraph in which they inveigh with such rage and virulence against Pope Paul V.[2]

I would likewise explain the reason why our nobility and gentry and their dependent priests are such sticklers for him because he is accommodating, and an advocate for the oath. I hope you will likewise mention that he lives in the same house with his cousin Joseph Berington, whose scandalous writings show him to be an Innovator, tinctured with pride and deviating from a sound form of words at least, if not from faith. And what if you put down some of his rash, objectionable propositions as extracted from his works?

But I beg your pardon for suggesting my ideas on this subject when I am sure your own will be far more to the purpose. Only commit them to paper that they may be sent to Hilton as soon as possible. Before I left Stella I asked Mr Thomas whether such a measure would not be proper on the present occasion, and he seemed to approve of it, and moreover said he would send the said Memorial, if you pleased, to Mr Smelt to be presented by him to Cardinal Antonelli. It must not be sent to Mr Stonor, for he certainly favours C. Berington, and I think would not present it. Moreover, I would not (for certain reasons) have it signed by yourself, or in your own handwriting, and therefore I will transcribe it or have it done by some other person. I beg you to answer this and believe me always yours affectionately, Hen. Rutter.

P.S. His Lordship's instructions concering the person whom he recommends as his successor were left in writing and have been, according to direction, sent to Bishop Talbot, who I hope will faithfully execute the trust reposed in him

1. Hilton is Rome where Robert Smelt had only just arrived as assistant to Christopher Stonor, Roman Agent for the English Secular Clergy.
2. Saint Pope Pius V (1504–1572), an austere and reforming pontiff, the friend of St Charles Borromeo. He excommunicated Elizabeth I and, in the bull *In Coena Domini*, proclaimed the traditional principle of the supremacy of the Holy See over the civil power.

70. Banister to Rutter — Mowbreck, 26th May 1790

My dear Sir,

I received your letter on the 22nd Inst., and the news was so sudden and unexpected that it gave me a great and heartfelt sorrow, and caused me many tears on several accounts. For losing a good friend, for I cannot think otherwise of him, and in these present circumstances whilst people are so fluctuating and such endeavours are used to promote the unworthy, thieves and wolves to rob and devour the flock of Jesus Christ.

Mr Barrow of Claughton informed me the other day that the Spanish Ambassador had written from Rome in favour of Charles Berington. He adds that he is retired to his cousin Joseph Berington on account of the many reproaches thrown out against him of idleness, sloth, eating and drinking too much, &c. "London", says he, "would be a dainty morsel for his insatiable cravings, could he finger the immense sums that would then pass through his hands. Like Lucullus he would then be enabled to dine every day in the hall of Apollo". There is not any doubt of Committee men stretching every nerve to promote him, as he is a fervent abettor of their new oath. I fear they will likewise make themselves exceeding busy to give us one of their own principles.

Can you inform me whether his Lordship expressed a wish before his death that any particular person of sound principles might be his successor, and whether he ordered Mr Eyre sigillatim, or any number of you together, to recommend in his, and your own names, any determinate person? I ask not this on my own account, but because a certain busybody, who visits me often, and with whose notions I do not perfectly accord, was here on Monday last. I informed him of his Lordship's death on the Saturday which, he said, had filled him with various thoughts that rushed into his mind successively and turmatim, and hindered him both from meat and sleep. He therefore came to me on Monday in the afternoon to communicate one of those thoughts to me, viz., that it would be very proper for a certain number of us priests in this county, i.e., of the ancient and wiser sort, to hold a meeting. I asked for what? Nay, says he, when you are met together you will see that. I again replied that there could be no meeting without Mr Chadwick the Vicar General. Why then, says he, someone must write to him. I answered that for my part I would not write to him. You know, says I, his extreme taciturnity; he unbosoms himself to none but intimates. I never learn a syllable of him but what I glean from Mr John Lund[1] sometimes. Then I told him that we know not whether his Lordship did not give some orders about the choice of his successor before his decease and, if so, why should any of us hold a meeting in this county. Upon this he was willing to drop the scheme of a meeting until I had written to you and heard from you if you can give me any information or surmises about the matter.

I therefore pray you to let me know, if you can, the particular circumstances of his Lordship's death and whether he wished a particular person to be his successor. You must signify what is to be a secret, and what I may venture to notify to my busy visitor, Mr Joseph Orrell, who, having first set afoot the address to his Lordship, which was so agreeable to him, is now brim full of ideas for the welfare of this district. But he constantly and severally censures our Hammersmith meeting, not for declaring the new oath unlawful, but for not making a new one, and principally for not conferring with the Committeemen, and hearing their arguments and pleas in defence of their admirable fabric. He also censures his Lordship's nomination of Mr Chadwick to be Vicar General, and says Mr Lonsdale is the properest person. But perhaps if you ask a Yorkshire missioner he would flatly deny it and choose Mr Chadwick.

I wrote to Mr Eyre last Saturday, only to express my sorrow and condolence, and told him that his Lordship had one good mark, at least, in a servant of God in suffering persecution, not by corporal instruments but by tongues and pens, which are even keener than swords. My visitor is one, and I could name some others, and you know not a few.

Mr Orrell's oldest son died at the Park-school two hours after his arrival. Mr John Orrell has, since Easter, visited some priests in Staffordshire; some of them, I suppose, informed him that Bishop Thomas Talbot had received several scurrilous letters, without any signature, but one they are pretty sure is of Mr Thomas from Stella. Do you think it true? I never wrote a letter in all my life without signing my name, nor would I ever advise anyone to do it. But, as for the two Talbots, Bishop Walmesley, as his late Lordship told me last December 13th, called upon them to rise in defence of their religion, and was much incensed at their not circulating the Encyclical Letter. Their conduct is indeed mysterious, at least to me; I cannot account for it.

Have the 15 in Staffordshire who declared for the new oath, and addressed the Declaration to their prelate, who had, a few months before, declared it unlawful with his colleagues, ever received any check or reprimand?[2] They might indeed answer: our prelate never signified to us his disapprobation or synodical condemnation of the oath, for he never transmitted to us any encylical letter.

It really appears from hence to be too true what Charles Berington said to our late bishop at London, viz., that Bishop Thomas Talbot was of a different opinion but was at Hammersmith induced by our bishop to sign the contradictory. Now, had Charles Berington done so, i.e., dissembled his principles, and not signed the schismatical letter, he might have jumped into the dainty fare at London. But, 'tis probable he may not have all the craft of the old serpent.

Now, if you cannot satisfy the queries I have proposed, my busy visitor will be urgent for a meeting, but you may assure yourself that I shall neither write to, nor speak to, Mr Chadwick about the matter. If he invites me to give him and others the meeting (which will be ad graecas calendas, I suppose) I may go, not otherwise, and this my conduct will displease my visitor. I never forget the saying of old Bishop Petre: that he would never give his counsel or advice where it was not asked. Bishop Challoner provided him two coadjutors, 1. Mr Maire[3] of Durham, 2. Mr Walton, without so much as consulting him if I be not greatly mistaken. This I think is a sufficient model for me to forbear intermeddling in the choice of Bishop Matthew's successor unless I be expressly called upon. These

Ember Days put us in mind to pray for true and zealous pastors; this is the duty both of us and of all the faithful.

It is well I did not go to Douai College, but Mr Varley writes to my neighbour Mr Wilson that he pressed Mr William [Gibson], when he was at London on his way to Douai, to give up his charge. Perhaps the death of his brother may induce him to do it, and perhaps it may fix him in a resolution to stay.

I pray you answer this as soon as you can, which will oblige your most affectionate Uncle, R. Banister.

P.S. I pray you to say 6 Masses for me: viz., for Alice, James, William, Mary, Dorothy, Jacobus.

1. Missioner at Cottam.
2. On 25 January the Staffordshire Fifteen wrote an Address to Bishop Thomas Talbot expressing their acceptance of the term Protesting Catholic Dissenters as well as the new oath, the orthodoxy of which had been guaranteed by Bishop Berington and the Rev. Wilkes. They also gave Wilkes their support in his dispute with Bishop Walmesley. The Address was to cause dissension for some ten years and the matter was never resolved to everyone's satisfaction. The Fifteen were: Anthony Clough, VG, Thomas Flynn, George Beeston, George Maire, William Hartley, Joseph Berington, Thomas Stone, John Perry, John Carter, John Corne, Thomas Southworth (President of Sedgley Park school), Edward Eyre, John Wright, John Roe, John Kirk. [Ward, *Dawn*, I 208]
3. William Maire (1704–69) was always in poor health and died at his family home in Lartington scarcely a year after being consecrated Bishop of Cinna ipi by Bishop Challoner.

71. Banister to Rutter — Mowbreck, 7th June 1790

My dear Sir,

By this post I have dispatched to Mr Eyre the conclusion of my Memorial. It will occupy you a good time to write it out. I have told Mr Eyre that I am of opinion that nothing of it is to be suppressed, but the whole to be sent off as soon as possible to Hilton and to the Nuncio at Brussels if he be there. I mentioned too the Nuncio at Paris. Mr William Gibson may remit copies to them both. And if there be a doubt whether Mr Smelt will deliver it to Antonelli whole and entire, it will be the safest way to enclose it to Mr William Gibson, and desire him to dispatch it to Antonelli. And it would do well if he put it to his signature, for signatures it must have, as I have told Mr Eyre, or otherwise it will appear no better than a libel.

Mr Eyre tells me that Bishop Talbot will first fully understand the sense and desire of those over whom a future prelate is to preside, and then he and Bishop Walmesley will recommend to Hilton, by which he seems resolved to pay no regard to our late bishop's choice. I have said to Mr Eyre that a canvass of the whole District will probably produce confusion and that there will probably be many artful snares laid to turn the more general vote on one who either has [been], or will be, very complying with the wishes and designs of Committeemen and their abettors. Although the choice of our late prelate be suppressed, yet if the Brethren be informed that he named the person whom he wished to be his successor, they will certainly desire to know him, after which they may either accede to his sentiment or choose another.

I have informed Mr Joseph Orrell that our late prelate named one to be his successor, but suppressed the other part of your information, viz., that he confided the business to Bishop Thomas Talbot. I doubt not but Mr Joseph has sent this news to Blackbrook.[1] It will soon spread. I wish I could fly to Rome, for I would, if I might be heard, strenuously advise His Holiness to send two learned and pious Italian priests to be his Vicars Apostolic in this and the London District. For there is not, I believe, one amongst us all, either of the old or new clergy who will not be objected to by various parties. I look upon it an impossible thing that, in this nation of liberty and freedom of writing and speaking, a majority of votes of all priests in this large District, and of the gentry too (who undoubtedly will think that they have a right to vote) can centre on one. But His Holiness is not bound to stand to the election or votes of us priests, as was signified to the Londoners by a cardinal. Our bishop is then to be chosen and elected by votes as the members of parliament. The priests will then be his constituents and, from time to time, assemble and by the President give him instructions how he is to act, what new modes of discipline will be proper, what Briefs and Rescripts are to be rejected or admitted from Hilton, &c. Doubt not of seeing these things, or very similar ones, if Committeemen and their favourers are not opposed by some means or other.

Last Friday I received a copy of printed verses, directed to me, as I think, by Mr Coghlan. At first sight I apprehended them to be a lampoon upon our late prelate, which grieved me exceedingly. But I find them an ingenious satire on Geddes:

When G .... had ceased on his Bible to work,
Because it would suit neither Chapel nor Kirk

Had fretted his gizzard because all his printers
Declared not a copy would sell in ten winters, &c.

I hope you have seen them. I hope his translation will serve for nothing but to wrap up pepper and spices, or become offerings to Cloacina.

I am more and more grieved at heart for the loss of our bishop. He surely prayed as St Augustine did, viz., that God would either deliver his city Hippo and flock from the impending evils which threatened, or take him out of the world to himself, that he might not live and be a witness of them. St Augustine died whilst Hippo was closely beseiged by the barbarous Huns, and Bishop Gibson dies whilst Committeemen and their abettors are beseiging Rome and the Holy See to triumph over Paul V and all his Briefs, by indicting Charles Berington into the Vicariate of London. See the Memorial.

When you have received this you will hasten to Stella and do all you can for Mr Eyre, you have much more time to spare than he. The bishop had but just received the watch. I have told Mr Tarleton that it it is to be returned I can possibly get a hand to take it. See what Mr Eyre says. I remain, my dear Sir, your most affectionate Uncle, R. Banister.

P.S. My aunt's in good health and still fond of a toast,
Pray don't fail to write by the very next post.

This is the postscript of the foregoing copy of verses, or Letter of Simkin to his Dear Brother Simon in Wales.[2]

1. Blackbrook House, Parr, Prescot, home of the Orrell family and where John Orrell was chaplain.
2. Untraced.

72. Rutter to Banister — Minsteracres, 27th June 1790

Dear Uncle,

I received your two favours in due time. The last required no immediate answer, and the first, in which you wished to be informed concerning the particulars of his Lordship's death and whether he had nominated any successor, was sufficiently answered by a letter which you received from me about the same time. However, I should certainly have written to you before now, had I not known that you communicated with the fountain head and received from Mr Eyre every information he could give you concerning the present situation of affairs.

Moreover, I was no inconsiderable time in writing out the Memorial, as I write but slowly, especially when I wish to be accurate and distinct, as in the present case. I carried it to Stella on Thursday and it was sent off the day after, with your corrections, to Mr [Thomas] Smith to be forwarded to Cardinal Antonelli as soon as possible. Mr William Gibson, who arrived at Stella the Monday before, enclosed a letter to Antonelli expressive of his approbation, so that I have little doubt of its being favourably received at Hilton and fully answering the purpose for which it is intended, provided it gets there time enough. As the Nuncio at Paris has applied to Mr Gibson to give him some information concerning the present state of affairs in England, I am going to write another copy to be dispatched to his Eminence without delay. I like your Memorial upon the whole very well, but think that it might have pleased more if some few expressions had been softened, and, as a scribe, I wish sometimes it had been less copious and diffuse.

As to Mr President Gibson, he has not as yet given up his charge, but perhaps a mitre might tempt him to do it, for inter nos I think he looks that way. Whatever mean opinion I may entertain of his abilities I am averse to his resigning at present unless he can ensure a proper successor in his place. Travelling seems to have agreed with him for he says that he is better in his health than when he left Stella. He owns there has been sad confusion at Douai, and at the college too, for the undisciplined soldiers went there and did as they thought fit with the students, drinking and dancing with them for 2 or 3 days together. However, things were quiet at this departure and it was thought would continue so.[1]

Mr [Thomas] Hussey,[2] I suppose, is the person who wrote to Rome in favour of Charles Berington and who engaged the Spanish Ambassador in his interest. It is said that he had received an answer from Antonelli, not quite to his satisfaction, in which Berington is accused laxitatis. But the most authentic intelligence is from Mr Smelt who, in a letter received (I think) on Monday last, says that Antonelli was very desirous of laying the business before the Congregation, and had even fixed the day, but that he had altered his mind in hopes of receiving still more information from England. "He has", says Mr Smelt,

> caused enquiries to be made in England by different people, but after all is not able to make up his mind on the subject . . . Great dissentions prevail between the clergy and laity. Therefore they wish for a person in whom both parties may have confidence sufficient to reconcile them together, hence they prefer Mr Berington to Douglass, whom they say is a stranger little known at London. The cardinal does not

> wish to name a person disagreeable to the nobility and gentry who press so hard on behalf of their favourite candidate. But the affair of the oath is a stumbling block which he cannot well get over.

But the Memorial, I hope, will effectually turn the scale against him, and determine the Sacred Congregation to exclude him for ever from any episcopal jurisdiction in this country.

Mr Chadwick has written to Mr Lonsdale to proceed immediately to an election and to collect the votes of the north for that purpose; is he doing the same in your parts? Perhaps he has desisted from such an imprudent step upon hearing from Mr Lonsdale that you and Mr Thomas were recommended by our late bishop. I wish it may be so. But I can hardly believe that you are to be our bishop, I foresee so much opposition will be raised against you by Committee men and others. A certain gentleman has had the impudence to write to some of our senior clergy in these parts in favour of a young Paris Doctor, but without effect.

Have you seen a pamphlet just published: A Letter Addressed to the Catholic Clergy of England on the Appointment of Bishops [by A Layman]? The author[3] attempts to prove that "the election of bishops by the clergy and laity is a rule of the Church, that the existence of titular bishops is an abuse which ought to be removed, and that the oath taken by bishops at their consecration is a violation of the freedom of the Church and of the duty they owe to society". I must put down two quotations: St Celestine, 428 a.d., "A bishop should not be chosen who is disagreeable to the flock committed to him; it is necessary to have the consent of the clergy, the people and magistrates". Conc. Rome, 465 a.d., "Bishops are strictly prohibited from naming their successors because thereby lawful elections are prevented". Mr Talbot, I suppose, is for having this primitive discipline re-established.[4] But it is now late at night and can only add that I am your dutiful Nephew, H. Rutter.

P.S. The bishop's watch will be returned if you or Mr Tarleton can dispose of it.

1. The first effects of the French Revolution on Douai College.
2. Thomas Hussey FRS (1745–1803), an Irish Carthusian, chaplain at the Spanish embassy and afterwards President of Maynooth College and Bishop of Waterford. Boswell mentions him as a friend of Johnson; Charles Butler thought him 'a man of great genius, of enlightened piety, with manners at once imposing and elegant and of enchanting conversation'. [Ward, *Dawn* I 27.] Hussey had accompanied Richard Cumberland on a diplomatic mission to Spain in 1780 on behalf of the British government and again in 1786 he

healed an Anglo-Spanish diplomatic rupture, for which Pitt gave him a pension [Buschkill 30; see also No 94n].

3. Sir John Throckmorton V (1753–1819) of Buckland, Berkshire, a Whig and a leading member of the Catholic Committee.
4. Bishop Talbot had sent the late Bishop Gibson's recommendation as to a successor to Rome but he also invited the clergy of the Northern District to make their own preference known. Chadwick had already set an election in motion.

---

73. Banister to Rutter — Mowbreck, 3rd July 1790

My dear Sir,

Yesterday I received yours dated the 27th of June. I also received one from Mr President Gibson. I am now persuaded in my own mind that I and Mr Eyre were but intended to be two props to lift up Mr William Gibson—I assure you that I am much better in mind and corporal health on this very account. I exceedingly disapprove, however, of the mode of election which Bishop Talbot has now ordered and which is carrying on in great bustle here in this county.

Doubt not of my receiving the Letter Addressed to the Catholic Clergy on the Appointment of Bishops—it came gratis, and is sent to all, I dare say. I have translated a part of it into Latin and added an account of the present state of our affairs in this District, and composed another Memorial to his Eminence Antonelli. I sent the first part to Mr Eyre on Wednesday the last of June. and all the rest yesterday. You must therefore repair to Stella and transcribe it as speedily as possible that it may fly over the Alps. It is not half as long as the first, and as to softness, I know not what you would have. Have the oathites spoken softly of Pope Paul V; did Charles Berington speak softly when he told our late bishop that Bishop Walmesley doated [i.e., was in his dotage]; Bishop James [Talbot] was non compos; does Mr Joseph Berington write softly of the saints, and of the Catholics of old, when he says that the milder virtues of Christianity were but little known to them?

In this second Memorial I speak out concerning Bishop Thomas Talbot and affirm that he is not displeased with the doctrine of the letter-writer since he is executing it—in a District, too, not belonging to him, and where he has not even a delegated commission. I show him to be a favourer of the oathites; he never published the Encyclical; his coadjutor's testimony to Bishop Gibson affirmed him to be an approver of the oath; he is connected with the oathites and with the great philosopher Joseph Berington. I do not wish one particle to be changed or softened, but to be transmitted as it is to Cardinal Antonelli that he may have a better knowledge of our irregular, uncanonical doings, &c.

The conventus cauponarius may perhaps move the Cardinal both to laughter and pity: John Rigby is named second, John Douglass first, Henry Dennet[1] third. No-one, said Mr Joseph Orrell to me, when he gave me an account of their meeting, thought of or mentioned your name. I do not know but that the person whom I and Mr Eyre ought to have proposed will be opposed even more than us two. Yet is it not very fit that he should preside over the alumni whom he has sent us these last ten years?

Mr Finch came a very unexpected, yet most welcome, guest yesterday. but set off again this morning to say Mass at Four Lane Ends tomorrow. He will come again, he says, and stay a week.

Antonelli wants one to reconcile nobility, gentry and clergy—he must send us an angel from heaven. The oathites, he may assure himself, will never bend or recede; they will much more easily corrupt and draw to them the sound, but flexible, minds of others. If the person who expected to be propped up by us has no way of mounting but by Bishop Thomas Talbot, and must therefore be at one with him, then he will probably be unwilling that my second Memorial should go to the cardinal. But certainly the cardinal is too wise and discreet a man to let it be known by whom he receives good intelligence, although unfavourable to the Vicars Apostolic. They do not, I suppose, think them impeccable, the blameable conduct of Bishop Thomas Talbot is too public and notorious. Bishop Walmesley, as our late master informed me 13th December, 1789, was much incensed at the Adelphi not circulating the Encyclical Letter, and called upon them to rise in defence of their religion. Had they done like him, fifteen would not probably have signed a public and solemn approbation of an oath which the Vicar Apostolic had declared illicit and forbade their people to take.

Dear Sir, take good heed of what is said in the end of the new Memorial. If we prayed more and canvassed and talked less, and exterminated out of heart and mind and intention every human respect and every regard to self, either proxime or remote, our affairs would be in a better train. But, now it is quot. capita, tot sententiae. And almost every one thinks himself not worthy or fit to be a bishop indeed, but a competent judge of who is fit or unfit. Now, as a true critic ought to possess the fire and spirit of Homer in order to judge of his beauties and perfections, so, I believe, they who elect bishops ought to have most of the good qualities of a truly worthy prelate, at least a very great apprehension of cooperating or concurring to an unworthy choice. But, it is evident to me that all oathites at least, or their favourers, or connivers and gentlemen of the stage and coffee-house, card-table and bowling-green, &c., should have no votes.[2] I remain your most affectionate Uncle, R. Banister

1. Chaplain to the Andertons at Birchley Hall, Billinge, Wigan.
2. On 5 February Banister had written to James Haydock at Douai warning him against those 'liberal sentiments' which were imbibed by 'frequenting the theatres, the tables of people of quality, the assemblies of beaux and belles, &c . . . take a few times the tempting bait of a good dinner and good wine and you will insensibly slide into common opinions . . .' [*UM* vol. 14 (1904), 129]

---

74. Rutter to Banister — Minsteracres, 29th July 1790

Dear Uncle,

I received yours dated 3rd of July on the ninth and it being the end of the week, could not go down to Stella till the Thursday following. I brought back your second Memorial and wrote it out immediately that same week, but I find it is not as yet sent off. Mr Gibson and Mr Eyre dined here this week and, as far as I can judge, the former repents that he set his name to the first Memorial. For he was the first on the list which Bishop Walmesley sent to Rome and therefore he is afraid lest his intermeddling and writing against Charles Berington or others should be imputed to ambition and selfish views. Though this seems plausible, I am inclined to think there is another reason why he does not dispatch this second Memorial and that is because it tends to corroborate very forcibly the written instructions of our late bishop to the exclusion of himself and all other ambitious candidates. However, he does not positively say that he will not send it, but only that he will consider of it. For my part, I would have it go by all means and wish you could find out some other way of conveying it to Rome without passing through his hands. I suppose you would not have your own name affixed to it, and mine is too insignificant, otherwise it should be at your service.

I can see no foundation for your thinking that you were designed only as a prop to support Mr President. If Comana had intended this, why did he not give some intimation of it to Mr Eyre? This he never did, but only directed him to the drawer where he would find his will and other necessary instructions. Mr Thomas has communicated to you the intelligence he received from Mr Richard Gibson. It is curious indeed, but I am very sorry he has communicated the same to Smelt, for to what purpose except to perplex and embarrass Antonelli and to lessen the weight of the written instruction. However, Mr Thomas does all for the best. I am willing to think the same of Mr President Gibson, but I cannot approve of his ambitious views and would not have you depend much upon him. Mr Thomas has received a letter from Smelt which mentions that Bishop Walmesley had recommended Mr William Gibson as the successor of Mr Talbot; 2nd, Mr Robert Banister; 3rd, Mr Southworth. Mr Gibson, when he left the college, wrote to Mr Stonor signifying his resignation of the Presidentship in consequence of bad health, but, finding his hopes of a mitre not so certain as he had imagined, he now retracts. But keep this to yourself.

Our Vicar General, in writing to Mr Lonsdale and Mr Lodge, puffs off Dr Rigby as eminently qualified for the episcopal charge. But how does he and the Lancashire Brethren reconcile this with the address which they presented against the oath, since it is wellknown that Dr Rigby is a warm advocate for it. Mr Lonsdale does not approve of Mr Chadwick's mode of election and has therefore paid no regard to his request of collecting the votes of the Yorkshire clergy. The post is going off and I remain your dutiful Nephew, H. Rutter

---

75. Banister to Rutter — Mowbreck, 5th August 1790

My dear Sir,

I received yesterday your letter dated 29th of last month. The principal, or rather only, end and intention of the second Memorial is, first, to inform Cardinal Antonelli of the schismatical proceedings amongst our laymen, noble and gentle, and too many of the brethren, their obsequious dependents. Secondly, to show what a dangerous and uncanonical novelty is introduced under the direction and countenance of Bishop Talbot who, if we can believe his coadjutor, is no enemy to the new formula, and is connected with his brethren oathites. Thirdly, to show how irregularly and even scandalously the said usurped election is carried on, begun in a paltry alehouse, and then letters despatched on every side to the Brethren to send, with the utmost expedition, three names sealed up, which the rural deans were to transmit to the Vicar General, and he to Bishop Talbot, who will take care of the rest. And indeed, the expedition must have been great from these parts, for Mr John Lund sent this notice to the Brethren dated on the 28th and 29th of June. And on the 7th of July following, the Vicar wrote to Mr Lonsdale that Dr John Rigby had a decided majority.

Admitting that the brethren have a lawful elective voice (which certainly they have not, and no one can give it them but the Holy See, the fountain of spiritual jurisdiction) yet it is both inconsistent with prudence and with the wisest regulations of canons to call for the utmost expedition in a matter which requires the most mature deliberation and is of the highest importance. Is it not to be justly feared that in a hasty and precipitate election (supposing still that it is not usurped), many will unwittingly (yet not inculpably) burden their consciences with a grievous sin in voting: 1. rashly; 2. for human affection; 3. for friendship's sake; 4. influenced by faction; 5. by suggestions from Committeemen and oathites, as in the London election; 6. in view of some commodity, and if of nothing else, at least of more liberty to live free and unrestrained by a scrupulous pastor.

For my part, I have learned that electors of pastors of a parish become guilty of all the mischiefs that flow from their electing a less worthy and passing by the more worthy. What, think you, will Bishop Talbot have to answer to God for choosing an advocate of schism to be his successor? But he was not one when he chose him, yet he was so disposed both by his Parisian education and connection with his cousin.

But to return to the Memorial in question. It informs the cardinal that 9 voices in [the tavern conclave] voted 2 loco Dr John Rigby, a warm abettor of the new formula, and spectator [and applauder of theatrical spectacles]. Now, though I deem it an usurpation to pretend to give an elective voice, yet the interests of faith and religion will, I hope, justify me in endeavouring to hinder the promotion of a man who is positively unworthy. It is therefore very proper, and even necessary, that the cardinal be informed of Dr Rigby's principles, either from the second Memorial, or by a letter from Mr Eyre to Mr Smelt. If Mr Eyre does not choose to sign the Memorial, at least beg of him to write to Mr Smelt without delay and give him an account as above of this usurped, precipitate, scandalous election of an oathite.

Now, as to Mr William Gibson; if he can make his cause good at Rome I shall be very glad. Truly, the office of a President of Douai College, and of Spain and Lisbon, is more important than that of Vicar Apostolic in this island. For our presidents abroad furnish our bishops with a good or bad clergy according to the good or bad choice of alumni, according to the principles, spirit and manners in which they are trained up, &c. So, although Mr William Gibson has not been applauded everywhere for his administration of Douai College, he may have more success in an episcopal character.

May God be merciful to the soul of Bishop James Talbot but, if what Mr Richard Gibson says be true, viz., that he urged our late prelate to choose Mr William for his coadjutor, I cannot but fear he had nothing else in view but to draw him by promotion to the prelacy out of Douai College.

My dear Sir, I learn from St Thomas and other ecclesiastical writers that one may very easily, yet almost imperceptibly, fall into grievous sins in this affair of electing, accepting, advancing to, seeking for, begging recommendations, &c., to any prelacy with the cure of souls. And what can any one expect but a greater damnation, a more dreadful judgement, if he enter not by the door into the sheepfold, i.e., with a pure intention, without soliciting, entreating, submitting, fawning, or promising, &c.

But now, if I had power and leave to choose a Vicar Apostolic in this present crisis, I would forthwith nominate Mr John Cotes, for I think his virtue and wisdom are maturated to a great degree by a life spent in much retirement and prayer and study. But I must add that it was signified to some of our Lancashire electors that they were to vote for persons not above 50 years old. One would imagine that our Vicar General had received some very special instructions from the Holy See, but you may well surmise the cause of the intimation.

Yesterday I received a letter from Mr William Hull at Hatherop near Fairford, Gloucestershire, who says, "a report prevails that Mr Smelt will probably be sent back from Rome as Apostolic Vicar for the London District". I sincerely wish it; the Committee and oathites will, I hope, be thereby entirely disconcerted. Although you know that I am a very objectionable person, yet I apprehend Mr William Gibson will be as much or more, in this county at least.

Mr Wilson my neighbour has penned an address to his Brethren here showing that we have no power to elect, and that the presentation of names to the Apostolic See has, above a century past, been made by the Apostolic Vicars; that our late bishop was named by his predecessor on his death bed; that as the election has been begun and carried on, there appears to be unfair dealing, &c., that therefore we have nothing else to do but to abide by our late bishop's recommendation, &c. He is for putting this to the press, and distributing it before our meeting on the 31st of this month. I at first assented, at least did not gainsay, but, on very good consideration I must beg of him to forbear, at least if he wishes to be my good friend: 1. Because I think it quite unnecessary in order to set aside Dr Rigby; 2.

It will be known that he is the author and, as he is connected with me, I shall pass too for an author of it. Hence will arise a confirmed opinion of my aiming at a prelacy which, if miraculously I attain, will not be forgotten; and if I do not, it may be cast in my teeth.

Mr Eyre knows better than I do the principles of Dr Rigby and his close attachment with the oathites; therefore press him to try every method to hinder his promotion. I beg my kindest compliments to him, and remain your most affectionate Uncle, R. Banister.

P.S. As you ultimately wish and desire my salvation let that be your prayer, not that I may have to work it, with the greatest fear and trembling, in the episcopal character.

---

76. Banister to Rutter Mowbreck, 8th September 1790

My dear Sir,

Tibi soli. Yesterday I received a letter from Mr William Gibson, now at London, in which he says that he has unexpectedly received a letter from the Propaganda in which, after many compliments, they have fixed on him to be our bishop and Vicar Apostolic, and exhort him to support traditions and the authority of His Holiness which, they say, some of ours [nefariously and most impudently try to destroy]. He desires this may not be published as yet for some reasons which he does not communicate to me. He adds, "I have reason to tell you that this is a first step to get one fixed here who thinks right". Do not publish this, but if your vote is asked give it for Mr William Gibson, or you may, if occasion happens, say that you think voting is needless and that no regard will be paid to our election at Rome.

I am truly glad of his nomination. First, because the hopes of the Midland oathites are hereby frustrated; secondly, the Weldbank plot is vanished in a puff; and thirdly, the blooming, fat Parisian Abbe may continue to go to the theatre with less scandal. The Ravenhead election will, I hope, be recorded in some future Dodd; at least it cannot but be a standing jest in this present generation.[1] I was told at Mr Wilson's, last week but one, that when Sir John Lawson heard that there was talk about Mr William Gibson being appointed, he wrote to Dr Dunn and ordered him to take, at his cost and charge, post-horses, post-chaises and ride God knows whither to prevent it.

Last week our meeting was held at Preston; not a word of the election but an address to Bishop Talbot in the name of the Vicar General and of the Lancashire clergy was signed. The first article of which was that before they give any succour to the college, the President Gibson shall abdicate his office. I left the meeting before this and so I signed nothing. I had drawn up a statement of the college affairs and given it to the Vicar and some few others to read, but it was not read publicly. Our Vicar General, like old Kitchin of Llandaff, will now be obliged to veer about again.[2] As for me, you see I must now die Confessor non Pontifex.

I am in haste to send this in time to the post and so must conclude that I am truly your most affectionate Uncle, R. Banister.

1. C. Dodd, *Church History of England* (3 vols. 1737–42). Weldbank, near Chorley, was where John Chadwick was missioner.
2. Anthony Kitchin of Llandaff OSB, (1477–1563). In 1534 he renounced papal supremacy, became a chaplain to the King and, in 1545, a bishop. He recanted under Mary but again apostatised under Elizabeth. He declined, however, to participate in the consecration of Matthew Parker as Archbishop of Canterbury.

---

77. Rutter to Banister [Minsteracres, End of Sept.] 1790

Dear Uncle,

Your two favours came to hand in due time. The first regarded the mode of election which was then carrying on in your parts. The latter brought me the first news of Mr Gibson's exaltation, which two or three days after was generally known in these parts, and our family received the account of it from himself the Sunday following. Instead of being sorry on your account, I sincerely congratulate you that you are eased of a burden [fearful on angelic shoulders], for whatever charms the episcopal dignity may have in the eyes of some ambitious and aspiring churchmen, I am persuaded it has none in yours and that, with the Saints and Servants of God, you have always viewed it with fear and trembling.

With regard to Mr Gibson, considering how deficient he is in learning and theology, I am still bold to say that he would never have been the object of my choice. However, I sincerely believe that he is much indebted to you for his promotion inasmuch as your Memorial must have made a great impression on Antonelli and given the casting die, but I suppose our new bishop has too great an idea of his own merits to make such an acknowledgment. What say the brethren in your parts to his election?

A letter from Yorkshire says that some of the clergy think themselves very ill-used in being called upon to give their votes without any regard afterwards paid to them, and that they talk of drawing up a petition in order to have some other person put over them more agreeable to their inclinations; but I doubt the truth of suchlike reports. Mr Plowden[1] writes from the south that it is the wish of many to have Mr Gibson appointed to the London District.

There are some Kitchins of Llandaff in these parts as well as in yours, and it is amusing to hear the praises they now give Mr Gibson whom before they condemned as the most unfit person in the world. I own I am so far glad of his election that it sets aside oathites and Committeemen. All their schemes and plans must now fall to the ground, especially as they are likely to meet with opposition from another quarter, I mean from several respectable gentlemen. Mr Silvertop, I believe, has been very active in this business; for, when in the south, he waited upon Lord Arundel,[2] Mr [Thomas] Weld[3], &c., and they agreed to draw up a Remonstrance to the Committee begging that they will not take any further steps unless with the approbation of the Vicars Apostolic and the Holy See. This, I think, cannot fail of having a very good effect as it will be seconded by other gentlemen of fortune and respectability.[4]

The same post that brought me your last favour brought me likewise one from Mr Lodge, in which he says that my "vote was to be given concerning a new bishop". I answered him that as the Apostolic See had hitherto left the presentation of names to the Vicars Apostolic, I did not wish to deviate from this established custom and therefore begged to be excused. However, I find that most of the brethren in these parts complied with his request and gave their votes for Mr Douglass, whose nomination, it was said, was expected at Rome.

As to the written instructions of our late bishop, Mr Smelt writes that they were not regarded at Hilton as not having been officially communicated during his lifetime. I saw Mr Thomas [Eyre] a few days ago but he gave me no kind of information. He seems to be heartily glad that the business is brought to a conclusion, and is considered by many to have had the principal hand in it. It is not known here where the bishop fixes his see; I think not at Stella but rather at York. Mrs Silvertop received a letter from him on the 8th, he was then at Douai; the episcopalia have been sent to London to be ready for him at his return. He writes that the Heads of the monks are gone to seek an establishment at Ghent, the friars at Bruges.

You will have probably heard of Mr Strickland's removal from Liege; he is no longer President there. I am sorry to find that dissensions prevail amongst them as well as us, and that this is likewise the case at Valladolid College.

My friend and neighbour Mr Johnson has been long in a very poor state of health; we apprehended a decay but I begin now to entertain hopes of his recovery. I am. my dear Uncle, your most dutiful Nephew, H. Rutter.

P.S. In reading over my letter I find I have been too severe on our new bishop, but still I must say that I am dissatisfied with his conduct in the late business, but this I mention only to you and Mr Thomas. Pray, who will succeed him at Douai?

1. Probably Charles Plowden, SJ, missioner at Lulworth Castle; his brother Robert, also a Jesuit, was missioner at Bristol.
2. Lord Henry Arundell (VIII) (1740–1808); he was educated in France and Italy and succeeded his father at the age of sixteen. He married Mary Conquest of Irnham, Lincs., a wealthy heiress, and rebuilt his ancestral home, Wardour Castle, (1770–6 by James Paine and enlarged by John Soane), which he furnished and decorated sumptuously, over-reaching even his wife's ample resources.
3. Thomas Weld of Lulworth Castle, Dorset, known as the handsomest small man in England; he was certainly one of the richest English Catholics of his day. He entertained King George III and Queen Charlotte at Lulworth four times between 1789 and 1792. His eldest son became a cardinal.
4. The introduction of the Relief Bill was postponed because parliament was dissolved in June. A general election gave Pitt an increased majority and the Catholic Committee decided to present the bill in the next session.

78. Rutter to Banister — Minsteracres, 30th January 1791

Dear Uncle,

I had written half a letter to you a month ago to enquire after your health and to assure you of my best wishes at the beginning of the new year. However, as you were in my debt, I thought it better to wait a little, expecting every post would bring me the favour I looked for of a few lines from you.

You will have heard long ago of the death of poor Mr Johnson, my friend and neighbour. He is much regretted by his congregation and not without reason, for he was a zealous labourer in Christ's vineyard, who both by word and example edified the flock committed to his care. After lingering for a long time he seemed to be getting strength again, and gave us great hopes of his recovery, but nature was quite spent owing, perhaps, to intemperate study and the charge of a very laborious mission. His congregation, which is about 160 communicants, is now destitute of assistance, and I fear will remain so for some time, besides another congregation at Shields which he attended.

I am glad to hear of the consecration of our two bishops[1]. I shall say no more against one of them because he is now my superior, and as such I will endeavour to show him all respect and submission. I wish he may find the same dispositions in all the Lancashire brethren, for I hear there is great opposition against him. I hope you will assist him with your advice, and that he will open himself to you in a proper confidential manner, and not by halves. His brother, our late bishop, made a confidante of no one and, as far as I can judge, this seems to be the disposition of his successor.

I was greatly afraid lest affairs should go wrong when I heard that Mr Douglass was to be ordained at Longbirch, but as this plan was altered, and he was consecrated at Lulworth, I am willing to think that he has a better insight into matters and has been put on his guard against oathites.

The three persons named for Douai are Messrs. [Edward] Kitchen, Thos. Eyre and [John] Daniel. The first, who I think is by far the most proper person, is very averse, and it will be only conscience that can make him submit to the heavy charge. If the two bishops therefore jointly enforce the nomination and press the matter to him in a proper manner, I am persuaded he will yield at last and not otherwise.

Mr Charles Cordell died at Newcastle on the 26th Inst. in the 71st year of his age. But he carried his oddities, it seems, to the grave, leaving it in his will to be buried in his garden, which, however, was not complied with. His death will not be so severely felt at Newcastle as he had been for some time past unable to do any duty. As Newcastle is one of the most important places in these northern parts, I hope it will be supplied by some able person who, by virtue and learning, may shine forth on this candlestick to the edification of this neighbourhood.

I wish to know your sentiments on some of the pamphlets which have lately made their appearance; which are solid and worth reading and which are otherwise. Likewise on the following questions. Whether there be an obligation of saying Mass for those who are put down by Mr Silvertop in the family obituary to be prayed for as his aunts, &c. Secondly, whether a missioner can gain the Indulgence without going to confession at the appointed time. Pray remember me to all friends, and believe me your most dutiful Nephew, H. Rutter.

1. Three bishops were consecrated in Thomas Weld's new (1786) chapel at Lulworth in 1790: John Carroll, Bishop of Baltimore, on 15 August; William Gibson, Bishop of Acanthos, ipi, and Vicar Apostolic Northern District, on 5 December; John Douglass, Bishop of Centuria, ipi, and Vicar Apostolic London District, on 19 December.

---

79. Banister to Rutter Mowbreck, 12th February 1791

My dear Sir,

I have received your last two letters in due time. Since our bishop returned from Douai, and especially since he came up from Lulworth Castle to London, I have been in a continual correspondence with him. You may probably think it very confidential, but I know not whether it is not very similar to that which Horace speaks of between himself and Maecenas: ['Is the Thracian hen a match for the Arab and other topics which can be confided to an open ear'. Satires II, 6]. Like his predecessor he either begins or ends in the utmost haste or hurry, or has a multiplicity of letters to write, &c. But now, in confidence, I say that anyone with a tolerable pen and very little consideration might write a hundred such in a day. Mr Barrow of Claughton, when he heard of his promotion, complimented him with a letter in which he enumerated all his faults, amongst others his letter-writing; to which, I hear, he answered that he certainly knew how to write letters, having had so long and such continual practice.

I have pressed him to reside in this county in order to gain and to conciliate his opponents by his obliging behaviour and kind hospitality, which will have great power and influence over their minds: com: beef and port and turtle prevail more than their argumentation. But in answer to me he writes that he has several things to settle at Stella, and that he has some obligation of his late brother to discharge for Sunderland chapel, and that his finances at first setting off will be rather too low to furnish a house with necessary utensils, unless he can find some place where such things are remaining. We attribute this to pusillanimity, inasmuch as he dare not face his opponents.

Mr Chadwick and Dr William Dunn went up to London in October or November to try to oust him. They understood that Mr Hussey (the Envoy to Spain for our Ministry) was to go to Hilton for the Committee; so they thought that they could hedge in their errand and procure, I suppose, Dr John Rigby to be named bishop and Vicar Apostolic for this District. But their journey and labour proved abortive, although Dunn wore out 4 pairs of breeches in his assiduous perambulations through the town to promote the good design.

Acanthos thinks that Mr Chadwick, for his opposition, can not expect to be employed any more as Vicar General, [even] if one were otherwise disposed to employ him. I have signified to him other reasons and motives for his dismission. He has written to Acanthos to desire an interview either at Manchester or, if he can not come thither, at York. I have likewise desired an interview at Preston together with Mr Barrow and Mr Wilson.

Acanthos says that he wishes to have my consent to be his Vicar General, but I have told him again and again that I shall do him more good being out than being in office. Indeed, I have had information enough of his ways at the college; he never scrupled to sacrifice anyone to his own ease and honour or convenience. I have recommended to him Mr Marmaduke Wilson of Appleton, a Yorkshireman, telling him that we Lancashire-folk are apt to be envious if we see one of our own countrymen raised above us. And I added that he would make his opponents glad, and conciliate their favour, by not choosing me to be his Vicar General.

So, you think my Memorial gave the casting dye. Then I may apply to myself the famous verses of Virgil:

Hos ego versiculos feci, tulit alter honores
Sic vos non vobis fertia aratra boves
Sic vos non vobis vellera fertis oves
Sic vos non vobis nidificatis aves
Sic vos non vobis mellificatis apes.
[I composed the verses, another reaped the honours
Thus you oxen pull the ploughs not for yourselves
Thus you sheep bear the fleece not for yourselves
Thus you birds build your nests not for yourselves
Thus you bees make honey not for yourselves.]

But you allege no reason for your assertion. In his first letter to me to inform me of his promotion, he tells me "that he unexpectedly received a letter from the Propaganda in which, after many compliments, they have fixed on me and exhort me to support traditions and the authority of His Holiness which, they say, some of our nefarie et impudentissime labefactare conantur". This letter was dated by him the 4th of last September. It may therefore seem that they were well pleased with the Memorial, which he signed and sent as his own production. I could mention to you some others who have received compliments from Cardinal Antonelli, mea solius opera.

In my letters to Acanthos I have constantly, either explicitly or implicitly, wished him and his colleagues to exert vigour, intrepidity and resolution. I have said it is perfectly nugatory to condemn texts and propositions and still suffer their clergy to canvass the matter as doubtful, nay, to assert the contradictory both in word and writing and printing. Old Guy, the renowned Bishop of Arras, whensoever he condemned a book or proposition, extracted from it (which he often was obliged to do to preserve the depositum of faith and purity of morals), would never have suffered either doctor or divine to gainsay his decisions without a condign censure.

Last week but one, Acanthos sent me a parcel of encyclical letters, dated the 19th of last month, to be circulated to our brethren and gentlemen. Item, a printed Address to the Catholic Committee, but no signatures. In his last letter to me, dated 26th January, he says, "I would have you by all means encourage the signature of it, if we desire it, which shall probably determine on Monday at the latest". In my answer I call it a timid address, and infinitely prefer that which some gentlemen drew up in the Western District. I tell him that they might, with as much hope of success, send an address to the French National Assembly, for the temper, genius and spirit of the Committee is entirely congenial with that assembly. "They, the Committee, (says Acanthos, ibid) will not admit a new oath or an altered one, so those schemes are all to no purpose, nor would they before that I could find".

I told him that I conceived Mr Weld would be a proper person to convey a petition to his Majesty, and humbly request him to send to his Minister to stop the introduction of the bill in to the house. But Mr Weld is abroad, he tells me, but has given him power to sign the address in his name. What pusillanimity! To fly from the heat of the battle! I suggested to him that a bank bill of a thousand, or even of one half, politely dropped in foveam would do more than all the addresses they can invent.[1]

In my last letter but one, I signified that I would procure some subscriptions of the Address, but I corrected myself in my last and said:

On due consideration I find that I must not run before you, nor attempt anything without your special commission and in writing too. Besides, I pray you to give me leave to say that I do not think it proper to you, who are now constituted in authority, to send about to your clergy to beg, as it were, their subscriptions. You have published your Encyclical Letter, is it not with an injunction to all, as well regular as secular, to receive it and adhere to it? I would know whether all or only some of them abide by your determinations? In order to be informed of this write to every one of the missioners in your District as follows:

> Dear Sir, As we have in conjunction with our Venerable Brethren, Bishops Walmesley and Douglass, published another Encyclical Letter (which we hope you have received) dated at London Jan. 19 of this present year 1791, We expect to receive from you a full and explicit declaration of your unfeigned acquiescence and submission to the contents thereof by a letter within 3 or 4 days after you receive this our notification. With our blessing on you and on all your pious functions, We remain your servant in Christ
>
> + Acanthos, Vicar Apostolic.

I added that I never knew or read of bishops condemning doctrinal texts or propositions and then sending to their clergy to beg their subscription and approbation. I, moreover, said that when he has received a majority of voices adhering to and acquiescing to his judgement, he may signify (if it be proper and useful) to the Committee, that his clergy unite with him in proscribing and rejecting the oath, and all oaths which he hath not first approved. I sent this letter the 6th Inst., but have received no answer since. I assure you that I am every day more glad that I was not promoted.

You may read Mr Charles Plowden's productions with pleasure and advantage, but have you seen his discourse at the consecration of Bishop John Centuria? He extols the consecrator Acanthos, page 12, for his long labours in the government of our principal seminary. "His Holiness (says he) had counted the ministers of the word whom he there had formed by word and example to tread in the steps of hundreds who have issued from that same seminary to seal their faith with their blood". And our Lancashire Brethren, 30th August, 1790, voted him unworthy of his charge, and Mr Richard Southworth seriously declared that as long as he ruled there, the ecclesiastical spirit would gradually decay, unless by a miracle he should change his conduct. How different are the judgements of men. But have you not seen and read the like in the Lives of the Saints and in ecclesiastical history? You may read Pilling's works[2] and Mr John Milner's[3].

As for offering up Masses singula pro singulis in the family obituary, I know of no obligation you can have unless it be a condition annexed to your annual salary, as Mr Robert Westby[4] here requires about 23 in a year. I think a missioner may gain an indulgence when he goes out of time, as well as others, when an inevitable necessity was an impediment to his going in the time.

Several reasons hinder me from petitioning for Newcastle besides my doubt whether I should have any easier subsistence there than here; for Mr Cordell seemed to me to complain of Mr Cotes for depriving him of a part of an income which ought to have been his. Pray mention this to no one. Read Mr [Edmund] Burke; he highly condemns the confiscation of clergy property and the reduction of clergymen to a stipendiary allowance.[5] Yet [what] if it is our condition: I am forced to write to Vincent Eyre, Esquire, with as much humility (inwardly indignation) and obsequiousness as if he gave me his own. And I am forced to write twice, after waiting a long interval, before I venture to write the second time. But all this is good for us and to teach us to be poor in spirit.

I desire you to say 3 Masses for my intention. I remain ever yours most truly, R. Banister.

1. Bishops Gibson and Douglass had met in London in the middle of January to compose a letter reiterating episcopal condemnation of the new oath. It was read from the pulpits of London on Sunday 24 January [the text is given at Ward *Dawn* I 242]. The Committee was horrified and addressed a protest to Bishop Douglass on 2 February, as a result of which a meeting was arranged for 6 February. The conference was acrimonious and matters remained unresolved. The Committee decided to appeal to Rome and to publish an open *Manifesto and Appeal* to the bishops. All but two of the Committee signed the document, including Bishop Berington and the Rev. Wilkes. Bishop Walmesley promptly suspended Wilkes *a divinis*. The bill for the Relief of Catholic Protesting Dissenters was advertised for introduction into the Commons on 21 February and the bishops got Mr Weld to write to Pitt on 18 February asking him to drop the bill or to permit an alteration to the oath; Pitt promised that nothing would be done in a hurry.
2. William Pilling, OFM, a missioner in London: 'A Letter to the Rev. Mr Joseph Reeve on his view of the Oath . . .' (1790). Reeve, a Jesuit, was chaplain to Lord Clifford at Ugbrooke and had defended the oath). 'A Dialogue between a Protesting Catholic Dissenter and a Catholic . . .' (1790) (in reply to Sir John Throckmorton, et al)
3. John Milner (1752–1826), secular missioner at Winchester from 1779 to 1803 when he was consecrated Bishop of Castabala, ipi, and appointed Vicar Apostolic Midland District. He was the chief ultramontane protagonist in the controversies of the 1790s; most of his seventy publications are works of controversy.
4. Of Mowbreck who died in 1762.
5. Edmund Burke, *Reflections on the French Revolution* (1790).

---

80. Rutter to Banister Minsteracres, 12th April 1791

Dear Uncle,

Your kind letter dated 12th February, came to hand in due time. I suppose you have been lately very busy in collecting signatures against the Protestant Dissenters bill, and Mr Thomas Eyre was here on the same errand, but a letter from Acanthos, which Mr Silvertop received the same day, prevented him from going on with it. For his Lordship there says that the three Vicars Apostolic had already presented a petition to Parliament on behalf of themselves and the far greater number of Catholics, a copy of which petition he enclosed in the same letter. He, moreover, adds that it was the advice of the Solicitor General not to collect any other signatures as their own were abundantly sufficient. In consequence of this official information it was judged needless to proceed any farther, especially as there did not appear to be sufficient time for it. One cannot indeed help regretting that all things seem to be done in such haste and precipitation by both parties, and that his Lordship's letters are so short and inexpressive of their operations. At least, those which I have seen were just in the same style that you mentioned in spite of all Mr Barrow's admonitions.

Messrs. Maire, Silvertop and Messenger had already sent a letter to Mr Pitt similar to that which you wished to promote, and had likewise an interview with Counsellor [William] Lee and engaged him to write to his friend Mr Fox in our favour. It would have been fortunate if Sir John Lawson had been equally active against the oath with his brother Mr Maire, for he has the greatest influence, in my opinion, of any gentleman in the north of England, but we regret to see his name in the list of Committeemen.

What think you of the oath proposed by the 3 bishops? I can not believe it meets with your approbation, and hope it will never be tendered to us. Acanthos writes to Mr Thomas Eyre that they had drawn up this oath with a view to prevent a schism and that it was not to be taken but in the greatest necessity. But, if they must form a new oath, why not a proper one and such as might be taken as well as any other oath of allegiance.

Mr Maire's last letter to Mr Silvertop gives us an account of what passed in the House of Commons on the 1st of April relative to our bill. Mr Fox, with a liberality of sentiment which truly surprises one, acknowledges that the name of Protesting Catholic Dissenters is not applicable to us Catholics since we did not dissent from the Protestants, but they from us. He was likewise agreed that the infallibility of the Pope, and the clause concerning the forgiveness of sin, had nothing to do in an oath of civil allegiance, and these objectionable parts were accordingly expunged. It seems therefore pretty evident from these amendments, which the house so easily adopted, that our noble Committee have the sole merit of framing the oath as well as of defending it with so much obstinacy. I am informed that they have printed off 1,500 more copies of the second Blue Book to be presented to each Member of Parliament, which is another proof of the purity of their intentions to serve the public cause.

I am sorry to hear of poor Finch's misfortune. Is it true that on his return to Louvain he was frightened out of his senses and is now confined to a madhouse? I wish you had kept him with you in Lancashire and made him as good a missioner as he was a Carthusian.

In your letter to me you make objections to Newcastle; perhaps York would please you better, and indeed it seems probable that you will have an offer of it. For Mr Thomas has been there lately to transact business with Mr Lonsdale and the bishop, if he had come down, and he learns that Mr [John] Jones, who is at present supplying there, is not to stay, although much liked by the congregation, and that you were mentioned to the bishop as a proper person to be his vicar and to manage the clergy affairs in place of Mr Lonsdale, who means to retire to Dodding Green. In this case you will have a polite congregation indeed, but, I am told, rather difficult to be pleased.

I observe that some gentlemen, in consequence of receiving the tithes, are obliged to pay a certain sum to the [Anglican] curate for doing duty, likewise to repair the church and furnish wine at Easter. Now, I wish to know your sentiments on this point, and whether it is advisable to leave them in this particular to their bona fides? We hear the one Lord Southwell[1] is settled in Lancashire and our Lady wishes to know some particulars about him if you can send me any.

This day's paper disappointed us not a little, for we expected to see last Friday's debates on the oath, but it only states that amendments were made in it without specifying what they are. The Committee have given out that Mr Milner is mad, &c.

The last letters from Douai mention that things were in the greatest confusion there and that two had been barbarously murdered in cold blood. We have heard since that tranquillity is restored, but that great difficulties are apprehended by the colleges in consequence of the new election of bishops. A venerable old bishop has very lately made his escape in a smack to London to avoid the fury of the populace who sought his death. He brought with him only his breviary, and lodges next to Mr Thomas Lawson[2], but he has been visited by several of our Protestant nobility, who offered their assistance and begged he would draw on them for any sum he wanted.

Our bishop, I hear, is on his way to York. He must not expect to take up his habitation at Stella. I have said your Masses and remain, dear Uncle, your most dutiful Nephew, Hen. Rutter.

P.S. I could wish you would be so kind as to send me after Easter such of my books as you have no occasion for, especially if you go to York.

1. Lord Thomas Arthur Southwell (1742–1796) married Sophia Walsh in France.
2. The Civil Constitution of the Clergy (1790) imposed a gallican oath on the French clergy; those who scrupled against taking it were forced to flee the country and many came to England. Rutter refers to Bishop J. F. de la Marche, Bishop of St Pol de Leon, aged sixty-two [A Bellenger, *The French Exiled Clergy* (Bath, 1986) 100]. Lawson was a Jesuit missioner in London.

81. Banister to Rutter — Mowbreck, 22nd April 1791

My dear Sir,

I think you must leave gentlemen in their bona fides. And to reconcile you better to it, you must take it by another ansa or handle, viz., that they have not possession of, or property in, all the tithes, but only of that share or portion which accrues after deductions are made to the curate, repairs of the church and furnishing wine at Easter. So every yeoman and farmer has no power to withhold the tithes of his land; they must go, and are taken for the use and support of false prophets. So Our Lord paid the didrachma for himself and Peter, although our Saviour replied to Peter: "Then the children are free, but that we may not scandalize them, &c." Matt. 17, v.25, 26.

Mr Joseph Orrell (to whom almost the whole conduct and proceedings of Acanthos are objectionable and ill-concerted), made this prophecy on 24th March when I dined at his house, viz., that "Mr William Gibson will approve the Committee's oath as it is now altered, or will be altered, when the act passes. Or he will approve of the oath on which the act will be founded". I have received from him two letters, 13th and 14th April, in which he gives me an account of the alterations made by the house and one by the Marquis of Buckingham, viz.,

> And I do also in my conscience declare and solemnly swear that I acknowledge no infallibility, right, power or authority in the Pope, or in any general Council of the Church, save in matters of ecclesiastical doctrine and discipline only; and that no foreign church, &c.

He adds that this pleases Mr Douglass. But I object to it because (if I understand him right) the whole clause of the Committee's oath is subjoined to it as follows:

> And that no foreign church, prelate or priest, or assembly of prelates or priests, or ecclesiastical power whatsoever, hath, or ought to have, any jurisdiction or authority whatsoever within this realm, that can directly or indirectly affect or interfere with the independence, sovereignty, laws, constitution, or government thereof, or the rights liberties, persons or properties of the people of the said realm, or any of them.

I say I object to it because this Committee clause is subjoined, which seems to annihilate the clause going before it. See the first purple book, page 5 line 30, where the learned Committee show you that "the words any and whatsoever are surely tantamount to the words any jurisdiction spiritual or temporal." I therefore tell Acanthos that at Rome it will appear to be at least captious and ensnaring and therefore censurable.

I desire you here to observe once for all that I reckon 9 clauses in the first edition of the Committee-oath in the first blue book [are objectionable]. The first begins at line 9: hath any right or title whatsoever. The second in line 21: being Protestants. The third in line 22: as impious and heretical that damnable doctrine. The fourth in line 26: that neither the Pope, nor any General Council, &c. can absolve the subjects of this realm . . . from their allegiance to his Majesty. The fifth in line 29: or any spiritual authority, power, or jurisdiction whatsoever within this realm, &c. The sixth at line 33: no person can be absolved from any sin, &c. The seventh at line 39: and that no breach of faith with, or injury to, or hostility against, &c. The eighth at line 39: or of any oath, or of any compact whatsoever. &c. The ninth at line 40: I acknowledge no infallibility in the Pope.

Now I gather from the 5th clause, and from Master Throckmorton's publication on the appointment of bishops[1], and from the final clause in the solemn protest of the second blue book, viz., "we do hereby appeal . . . to the first of Catholic Churches, the Apostolical See, rightly informed". That the Committeemen are perfectly d'accord avec l'Assemblie Nationale de la France, viz., to style the Pope the first bishop, and the chief visible

Pastor, but without any power or jurisdiction. As King George is styled King of France, and the Archbishop of York as Primus Angliae. I have received from Douai five or six mandates and pastoral instructions of the Gallican bishops, viz., of Boulogne, Soissons, Langres, Chalons &c., which highly edify me, for they are truly episcopal and apostolical, and demonstrate the schismatical and heretical proceedings and decrees of the National Assembly.

Acanthos sent me immediately the formula which he and Ramatensis[2] and Centuriensis presented in manuscript, and even interlined, to Mr Pitt in the house. I objected to it, and I think it was a dangerous step, for from it the Minister might, I think, very naturally conclude that our bishops are but wax or reeds easily shaken by the wind. Yet Acanthos says in the letter which he sent me with his own formula on 3rd March:

> the Ministers, King, &c., know well we Catholics are determined not to give up anything spiritual, so no scandal can be given to them by any expression that may appear in a different light from what one would have expressed it in if it had been left entirely to ourselves.

But this does not appear to me very accurate; for oaths, like professions of faith, ought to be expressed in terms clear and unequivocal, not in Burnet's fashion, who says that they be made in such manner that they may admit of different literal and grammatical senses, even when the senses given are plainly contrary to one another. Yet both may subscribe the article with a good conscience and without equivocation. [It is not permitted to us who cultivate stricter laws to be so lax]: a parody of Martial.

Hence I wrote in my last to Acanthos that I could not see how the universal negative "that neither the Pope . . . can dispense with or absolve me from the obligations of this oath, or of any other oath, contract, promise, engagement or compact whatsoever, &c." [could be reconciled] with the doctrine of all divines and of the church that there is in the church and the chief pastors of the church, a power of dispensing in oaths ex cathedra [justly and legitimately]. The oath says: [no hostility can be just against heretics and infidels as such]. It is pretty evident to me, from the practice and conduct of Christian kings and princes, whom the church never disapproved on that account, that [some hostility is just against heretics and infidels as such, otherwise there should be no hostility unless arms have been brandished, war declared, battles fought], &c. I suppose, however, that all the hostilities of protests against a species of men, whom they generally reckon idolaters, are entirely justifiable as well as their sanguinary statutes, prisons, oppressions, sequestrations, &c. Now, although Mr Burke told Acanthos that in regard of the succession clause, we were merely passive and did not assent to anything that implied exclusion for anyone for thinking, as we did, if ever a change in regard of religion should take place, our oath falls of itself in that regard. The Attorney General says the same.

What does he say, think you? for the sentence seems to me very obscure. But I cannot but surmise that something is meant by inserting in the oath the Act of Settlement in the descendants of Sophia, being Protestants. Acanthos says Burke and others will not hear of an alteration.[3]

It is come into my mind that the Committee first inserted it through envy to Mrs Fitzherbert. For cannot you easily conceive that Lord Petre and the other Committeemen think themselves as high and noble as Walter Smith, and their daughters as beautiful as Wat's daughter, who has captivated so high a personage? You remember what jealousies were moved and what restraints were made when the regency was to be delegated to one who was supposed to have formed a matrimonial connection with Mrs Fitzherbert. But I believe in such cases, 'tis not religion that really actuates mens' counsels, but envy and spite against fellow-born subjects, lest they rise above their equals and superiors by the favour and grace of the Prince.

Acanthos has not made the least insinuation to me about going to York. Let it be divulged in York that I am to be appointed there and a deputation will immediately come to the bishop to deprecate the appointment. I wish for your satisfaction that this rumour were spread abroad in the city. On the contrary, however, I am of opinion that many here would regret my quitting them. Will York maintain me and a man and maid and horse? I have all here, nay, I have had two maids near two years. We are, with three boys, seven in family, and Jesus Christ makes the eighth in the person of an orphan girl who has no home nor harbour but with me.

I have not yet heard of Lord Southwell. Long ago, viz., 1774, I heard of the son and heir of Lord Southwell being at our college of St. Omers and becoming there a Catholic. A happy Easter to you. I am your most affectionate Uncle, R. Banister.

P.S. I am, however, with this family a little pinched, but Mr [Thomas] Penswick[4] has left £25 and a young man in Kirkham £20 this month.

1. Sir John Throckmorton (V) (1753–1819). A Whig and a close friend of Charles James Fox. He was a leading member of the Committee and published 'A Letter Addressed to the Catholic Clergy of England on the Appointment of Bishops, by a Layman' (1790) and a 'Second Letter . . . in which the objections to the first Letter are answered' (1791). A second edition of the original Letter with 'further considerations' was issued in 1792.
2. Charles Walmesley's see ipi.

3. The bishops had mobilised their lay supporters to fight the Relief Bill during its passage through the Commons and they obtained changes to the oath and the deletion of the term Protesting Catholic Dissenters. The bill went to the House of Lords substantially as the bishops wanted it.
4. Died while missioner at Wycliffe on 7 April 1791.

---

82. Rutter to Banister — Minsteracres, 30th April 1791

Dear Uncle,

I received yesterday your kind favour and hope to answer it personally at Mowbreck in a few days. Some business calls Mr Silvertop to Preston, and he has asked me to accompany him. We set out, please God, next Saturday, that is, on the 7th of May, and make Lartington our first station. On the Monday we expect to get to Preston, where I leave Mr Silvertop to proceed to Ormskirk on the Tuesday in the mail-coach, and return to Preston again on the Wednesday. On the Thursday I hope to have the pleasure of seeing you at Mowbreck, unless you are disposed to the meeting at Preston. On Friday we return back by the same route we came so as to get home on the Saturday. Perhaps you will leave a line for me at the George Inn if you can suggest any better mode of conveyance from Preston to Ormskirk, or inform me when the mails set out.

Mr Kitchen's appointment is come from Rome, but serious apprehensions are entertained that Alma Mater will be obliged to remove once more from Douai in the present distracted state of France.[1]

I remain, dear Uncle, your ever dutiful Nephew, Hen. Rutter

1. Kitchen was appointed President despite his reservations and probably because he expected the college to be suppressed by the intruded Bishop of Arras. He did, however, travel to Douai in July but only to find that the college was under threat from the mob. One attack was deflected when three students (John Gillow, William Riddell and George Silvertop) had the presence of mind to charge out of the building shouting pro-revolutionary slogans thus carrying the mob with them.

---

83. Rutter to Banister Minsteracres, 10th August 1791

Dear Uncle,

I am well, God be praised, and hope you are so likewise. The purport of this is to ask your advice concerning the oath, which in these parts has lately been taken almost universally both by clergy and laity. But for my part, who have never yet taken any oath of allegiance, I could wish to be excused this humiliating ceremony. Besides, I am unwilling to decide so positively concerning the Pope's spiritual power as if it could never interfere indirectly in temporal matters. That Christ only left him a spiritual power I am ready to grant, but I do not well conceive how this spiritual power can be exercised in its plenitude with regard to spirituals without its having an indirect influence on temporals. Even the appointment of a holiday or a fast, though objectively spiritual, seems remote to affect the civil concerns of life. I wish therefore to know what you have done and what I must do likewise, for you have studied these matters and can place them to me in a proper light. I therefore pray you to write by the return of post. For Mr Silvertop, who is just returned from the Low Countries, means to take the oath at Newcastle Assizes, which begin next week, and it will be expected that I should do the same if I wish to continue his chaplain.[1]

I have sometimes applications for holy water from persons who imagine themselves or others wronged or bewitched. Now what must I do on such occasions? Complying with their requests seems, in my opinion, to confirm them in their vain imaginations. There is in my neighbourhood an Irishwoman who pretends to cure by touching all persons that have been venomed. Pray is this not superstitious?

Mr Silvertop brings little news from France. Everything seems to be a most deplorable situation and he has in consequence removed his two sons to Louvain to be under a private preceptor. I am pleased to hear that cousin Finch is much better and that he is allowed to say Mass. I suppose our bishop is still amonst you conciliating matters as well as he can. Who is his vicar?

We have Lawyer Plowden's[2] book against the Committee, which is soon to be answered by Sir Henry Englefield.[3] Pray remember me to all friends and believe me, dear Uncle, your ever dutiful Nephew, Hen. Rutter.

P.S. I am told that the Pope's Nuncio interests himself in favour of Wilkes.

1. The second Catholic Relief Act received Royal Assent on 10 June and came into effect two weeks later. It gave almost complete religious freedom but still denied Catholics the franchise. Catholics began subscribing to the new oath at the subsequent meeting of the local assize court.
2. Rutter confuses Francis Peter ('Lawyer') Plowden (1749–1829) with his brother Charles Plowden SJ (1743–1821). The former was a staunch Whig and published 'The Case Stated . . .' supporting the Committee's view of Catholic relief. The latter served at Lulworth and wrote five pamphlets against the Catholic Committee; Here Rutter refers to 'An Answer to the Second Blue Book . . .' (1791)
3. Sir Henry Englefield (VII) (1752–1822), FRS, FSA. He wrote widely on scientific and literary topics. His baronetcy became extinct when he died a bachelor. He was an active cisalpine on the Committee and in 1790 he issued a *Letter* in support of the concept of Protesting Catholic Dissenters. The work anticipated by Rutter does not seem to have been published.

84. Banister to Rutter — Mowbreck, 17th August 1791

My dear Sir,

I received your letter dated the 10th on the 15th, too late to answer by return of post, and yesterday no post coming to or returning from Kirkham, I could not write before this day.

You have at least extrinsic motives and arguments to satisfy your mind that the oath (I mean the Irish oath with the additional clause of the Act of Settlement) may be lawfully taken, viz., the authority of our own bishop, of the Bishops Walmesley and Douglass, and of the Irish and Scotch prelates. The only demur I ever heard against it was the additional clause. But that difficulty was explained and cleared up in the House of Lords and the Bishop of St David's[1] affirmed to Bishop Douglass, Mr [James]Barnard[2] and Mr Milner that it is no part of the oath, but a mere recital of the Act of Settlement, and does not decide anything about the lawfulness or unlawfulness of the revolution. He said the same was the sense of the House of Lords, and gave them free leave to use his name as occasion should require.

Now, as to your difficulty, it arises from a misapprehension of spiritual and temporal power. Properly speaking the spiritual power (which Jesus

Christ gave to Peter and to his successors) never interferes with the civil or temporal power of kings and princes, but the civil power too often encroaches on the spiritual or impedes it. In which case he who is invested with spiritual power must maintain, support and defend it, not by a temporal power (which he has not), not by armies and fleets, but by exertions of the same spiritual power.

According to Suarez, with whom [Roger] Widdrington[3] agrees, and all must agree that are Christians, all temporal power is subordinate to the spiritual. "We grant", says Widdrington,

> with Pope Boniface VIII, that the temporal sword is under the spiritual, and that the temporal power is under the ecclesiastical, not only in nobility, nor yet of its own nature, as Cardinal Bellarmine and Becanus do well affirm, but only accidentally in regard of the sin which princes, when they abuse their temporal power, do commit. Which in very deed is nothing else than that a temporal prince in spiritual matters is subject to the spiritual powers of the church . . . Kings and princes in spirituals or in temporals (as in regard of the sin annexed (which is spiritual) they are made spiritual) are subject to the spiritual direction, command, chastising and government of the ecclesiastical power.

So far Widdrington. And again, ibid, he writes:

> we do willingly admit that Christ hath left in his church sufficient power to keep kings and princes in good order at the least by using the spiritual sword.

The Committeemen, in their first blue book, page 6, say, "if the constitution of a state" (I suppose they mean a Christian state) "were essentially wicked," (we need not seek long to find one such) "if the government of a state were to be tyrannical and unjust," (was it not so lately in Brabant, and is it not so in France at this present time?) "are not these as much sins in the eyes of God as they are crimes in the eyes of man; as such, are they not subject to the spiritual power of the church?"

Now, as the clause in the oath (about which you make a difficulty) is couched in these words: "And I do declare that I do not believe the Pope of Rome . . . hath or ought to have any temporal or civil jurisdiction, power, superiority or preeminence, directly or indirectly, within this realm", it leaves untouched his spiritual power. St Thomas of Aquinas says: cui committitur finis, committuntur illi media ad finem. Now, the salvation of the faithful is the end which is entrusted by Jesus Christ to Peter and to his successors: pasce agnos meos, pasce oves meas. Therefore the means to arrive at eternal felicity are entrusted to Peter and to his successors.

The observance of holydays to celebrate the mysteries of our redemption and the martyrdom of the saints &c., if not absolutely necessary, is at least a most advantageous means of salvation. The church may therefore, by her spiritual power, ordain and command the keeping of them. If any temporal power resists without a just reason, its resistance is impious and sacrilegious. The keeping of the evangelical counsels is not absolutely necessary to salvation yet a most excellent means. Therefore the church, by her spiritual power, may forbid any temporal prince to impede the keeping of them. If some individuals, as Luther, Carlostadius, Zwingli, &c., begin to broach new and heretical doctrines, the spiritual power cannot vi sua imprison them, or roast them, but it may order the temporal power to put an effectual check to their new gospel. So, if you become a fessarius to one of the 12 judges, you may vi clavium order him to reverse an unjust sentence he shall have given, or to condemn a criminal whose punishment justice demands. It would be a perverse order of things, says Suarez, if temporals were not subject to and subordinate to spirituals. As the body, says St. Gregory Nazianen, is subordinate to the soul, so is the temporal power to the spiritual. When, in fine, we declare that the Pope has no temporal or civil jurisdiction, directly or indirectly, within this realm, 'tis the same thing as declaring that temporal power is not spiritual, nor spiritual temporal, that the soul is not the body, nor body the soul.

If people ask for holy water in order to use it by way of a charm or counter-spell, you must not give it until you have explained to them that it is neither this nor that, but that its virtue and efficacy consists in being blessed by a priest with prayer and invocation of Jesus Christ and in being applied with faith and devotion. Read how St Francis Xavier sent the catechists with his cross, beads and reliquary to the sick or dying heathens. He bid them ask an infirm person if he believed in Jesus Christ &c, and if the man or woman answered that they firmly believed, the catechist touched them with the cross or beads and they were cured. At least make them understand that it is no charm or counter-spell, and that if it does them good it is to let them see that our crosses, blessings, and invocation of the saints are not superstitious but pleasing to God, since by them he operates cures on bodies either afflicted with distemper or bewitched.

If your Irishwoman be a sincere Catholic and uses no superstitious rites, but the sign of the cross with humble prayer and supplication and, above all things, exacts no pecuniary reward, or any temporal interest, she may, for aught I know, have what St Paul calls gratia opitulationum. But indeed such creatures are to be suspected for cheats and impostors.

Is Sir Henry Englefield a consummate sophister? For sophistry will be the only answer to Francis Plowden, unless there be some small inaccuracies in which the lawyer fails. I think there is wanting in some places clarity and perspicuity but lawyers have generally a stiff and obscure style.

I think I must have perfectly satisfied your dubia after having read this long letter. Make my respects and compliments agreeable to Mr and Mrs Silvertop, and to Mr Eyre when you see him. Our bishop was here a whole week; I hear no change of the vicar. I remain your most affectionate good friend, R. Banister

1. Dr. Samuel Horsley, FRS. He swung the debate in the Lords on the 1791 Relief Bill in favour of an oath closely modelled on that of 1778.
2. Vicar General, London District.
3. A Benedictine priest who died in the Clink in 1640. A controversy over the oath of allegiance raged in his day and he contributed a number of works to it, including one in response to the Rev. Francois Suarez SJ.

---

85. Rutter to Banister Minsteracres, 19th December 1791

Dear Uncle,

When I look at the date of your last favour to me I feel conscious of some neglect in not acknowledging it before now. After reading it over with attention I began to think more favourably of the oath, but other difficulties started up which still made me doubt whether to take it or not. At last, however, I was induced by the extrinsic motives which you mention to follow the example of so many others who were certainly better enabled to judge of it than myself and so, in October, took it with Mr and Mrs Silvertop at Alnwick, but not so willingly and with so good a heart as others seemed to do.

Since that, our bishop has favoured us with his company for about three weeks and seems to be in tolerable good health and spirits. He mentioned the difficulties he had gone through in regard of the oath and how much he had been abused by the Committee, but the congratulatory address from the brethren in Lancashire seemed to afford him no small pleasure and satisfaction. I take it for granted that you drew it up in that elegant style in which it is penned, though he did not mention this circumstance. You cannot easily conceive my surprise at seeing the names of some of the subscribers, especially the two Parisian doctors. I cannot account for it. From the favourable reception his Lordship met with from the brethren in Lancashire, it seems that their sentiments in his regard are very different from what they were formerly. I likewise resolved with myself, when I sat down to write, to imitate your example and not to say one word against his Lordship, though somewhat inclined to it from past impression.

Mr Silvertop has given £50 not to the Committee but to the bishop, and it is probable some other gentlemen will do the same. His Lordship would inform you of the letter which he received from Antonelli to compliment him on the zeal and firmness he displayed in the business of the oath. I have seen a printed one to the same effect directed to Mr Barnard in favour of Mr Douglass. I have not as yet heard what comments the Committee have put upon it, nor how they mean to proceed with Bishop Walmesley for suspending Mr Wilkes a second time.[1] Mr Charles Butler waited on Bishop Douglass and with a very long face entreated him to employ his mediation and so prevent the dreadful consequences which he apprehended from Bishop Walmesley's censure. But Mr Douglass prudently declined interfering. Our bishop writes that Wilkes is obliged to leave the Western District after leaving a scandalous remonstrance with his bishop, and that he has made application to Mr [Michael] Lacon[2] the monk to get him introduced into these parts, but Mr Gibson will not admit him.

I am sorry that Mr Kitchen's health would not allow him to stay at Douai, as his conduct seems to have given general satisfaction to the Seniors. Mr [Joseph] Hodgson, one of them, wrote to me that he was the man for them, firm and resolute in maintaining discipline. I have not heard for certain who is to succeed, but Mr Daniel most probably, as the bishop told me he was chosen by Bishop Douglass and Mr Kitchen.[3]

I have often heard it regretted that there is no proper index to Mr Butler's Lives of the Saints, a work so full of various matter and learning. Godescard, the French translator, has added one, but in my opinion not sufficiently copious. I am therefore at present employed in improving it, not without hopes of seeing it hereafter printed. What think you of it? There is likewise in the French a chronological index of all the saints, which enables one to read their lives in the order of time in which they lived, but this index is very different from one which I have seen made from the last edition of Mr Butler. Indeed, I easily conceive that there are many false dates in Mr Butler which the French editor pretends to have rectified but with what success I know not. The question therefore is, which chronology you think ought to be adopted. A certain Lady has written to Mr Thomas Eyre expressing a wish that he would print some few saints' lives out of Mr Butler for the sake of the poor. He wishes therefore to have your sentiments on this matter. I mentioned to him the plan which you formerly gave me to this purpose but I know of none to execute it except yourself.

Pray how must I proceed with a priest who comes to confession and who I know has no scruple of going to plays and that he has formerly gone to them? I wish you a happy Christmas and many such and remain, dear Uncle, your dutiful Nephew, H. Rutter

1. Wilkes promised canonical obedience to Bishop Walmesley in a letter of 10 Sep 1791 and his suspension was lifted. But the Committee became annoyed that it was being put about that he had retracted his opinion. On 28 September Wilkes therefore published a manifesto, in the form of a letter to Thomas Clifford, in which he explained away his submission as an expedient. Bishop Walmesley immediately reimposed the suspension and invited the Benedictine President General to recall Wilkes to his monastery. Wilkes's own congregation at Bath backed him but the bishop excommunicated six of their leaders when they decided to give their financial support to Wilkes rather than the chapel. Wilkes, however, had no option but to leave, and he went to Coughton in Warwickshire.
2. Benedictine missioner at Brandsby, Yorks. (See also N° 100 n4).
3. Disturbances had continued at Douai and Kitchen returned to England in October 1791 in ill-health to resign. John Daniel, Vice President and Professor of Divinity was appointed in his place; Hodgson succeeded to Daniel's offices.

---

86. Banister to Rutter — Mowbreck, 29th January

My dear Sir,

Your last letter to me is dated the 19th of December 1791, the anniversary day on which I was ordained priest 41 years ago by Bishop Dunn of Ossory (I think), at Beverage, a seminary belonging to the Archbishop of Cambrai, near Valenciennes.

Our bishop sent me £9 some time before Christmas with leave to call for more whensoever I want. Why should I either speak or write anything about him but what is honourable? In my correspondence with him by letters I am free enough in declaring my sentiments, for which he always thanks me, although he does not follow them in all. Anthony Lund[1] started the business of addressing him with a congratulatory speech and desired me to draw it up in Latin that it might be sent to Rome. He transcribed it and opened the business, for I told him that it would not easily go forward if I appeared in it. Our bishop in his last letter to me writes, "I have received a letter from Cardinal Antonelli full of thanks &c., after the finishing of the affair, [he asks fervently] that I would ask for some favour [confidently and by my right]. But whether the cardinal means a temporal or a spiritual favour, or one partaking of both, I know not.

I think you are well employed in improving Godescard's index. As chronology is, I may say, one eye of history and biography, as geography is the other, so I think a chronological index of all the saints' lives, made as accurately as possible, will be of infinite advantage in reading the Lives of the Saints and make the work a regular ecclesiastical history, far easier for the memory. You ask me which chronology is to be adopted? I cannot give you any answer but this: that which appears most probable, and to judge of the greater or lesser probability, I suppose you will be obliged to consult the original sources, or some eminent long-winded, patient chronologist. I remember Mr Butler making mention of one (I have forgot his name) whom he followed, I suppose, for he commended him as clear and accurate.

In this age of mine and occupation of the mission I cannot undertake any work for the public, yet I vehemently wish to see a proper collection of the saints' lives calculated for the reading and intellects of common people. I am sure Mr Butler's Lives are far above their capacity. So I would not, in my mind, advise Mr Eyre or any other to extract any of his [exactly as written] for the information and instruction of the vulgar. I would infinitely prefer the publication of the book of holy Toby, either [complete], or as it is abridged in the [Stories Selected from the Old Testament]. You say that you gave Mr Eyre a plan which I formerly mentioned to you. I believe I gave it only [verbally] but you shall now have it [also in writing] for a memorandum to you. But first I must premise that I would have the lives and deaths of some sinners inserted in my collection as rocks and shelves to be avoided by mariners. You see the word of God contains not a few examples of that sort.

Let me now suppose the title of the work to be as follows: The Life of Our Lord Jesus Christ collected from the New Testament; also the Lives of some Saints and Martyrs who lived before and since the birth of Our Blessed Saviour, collected and published for the use and devotion of the unlearned in one volume; price 4 shillings bound, Newcastle upon Tyne. The Preface to this work is to set forth the end and design of it, which is to make reading the lives of saints easy to the unlearned by a plain and simple style fitted to their understanding and capacity. And to gain this end the better, we shall endeavour to make the style of the holy gospels, which contain the life of our Blessed Saviour, our model or pattern. The life of holy Toby, writ by an inspired writer, and though very simple, yet very moving, is also a copy which we wish to imitate. It is not to be conceived, but from experience, how slow and dull the understanding of the rude and unlearned is. Words derived from Greek, Latin and French, although easy and familiar to scholars, are unintelligble to them. And when they find a book hard to be understood, they will soon be tired of it. The agents of the devil publish their little histories, romances, songs and novels in so easy and familiar a language that they are bought, and read and retained, with great eagerness. Comedies are written in as plain language as possible. The Beggar's Opera by Mr Gay hit the taste and understanding of all, both learned and unlearned, and was therefore represented oftener than any play that ever came on the English stage.

We shall, moreover, faithfully relate many wonderful miracles where we find them recorded by eye-witnesses and by persons of undoubted credit. For this reason, because the reading of miracles of any saint cannot but fill the reader with a great confidence of obtaining some assistance in his necessities through the prayers and powerful intercession of the same saint in case he will devoutly apply to him. What made all the multitude (as we read in St Luke c.6, v.19) seek to touch Jesus with so great pressing and thronging? Because a virtue went out from him and healed all. A virtue goes out also from his saints and servants, but unless the faithful be informed of this, and their faith, hope and confidence raised by reading their admirable miracles, they will not seek to touch them, that is, to address their fervent and devout prayers full of a lively faith and confidence without which (as St James says, c.1, v.7), let not a man think that shall received anything.

After the Preface there must follow in the first place the life of our Blessed Saviour, not too long nor yet too short. 2. the life of our Blessed Lady, beginning with her Immaculate Conception, to be proved in few and clear terms, and especially from the firm and constant persuasion of the faithful, adding also how advantageous a thing it is to honour it. For this, Boudon may consulted and St Teresa of Avila. To the life of our Blessed Lady you must subjoin some illustrious miracles and conversions worked by her, which you may collect from various authentic histories. Look over St Teresa's works. 3. the life of St Joseph and the great gain those receive who are devoted to him, and the miracles obtained by his intercession; read again St Teresa. 4. St John the Baptist. 5. St Peter. 6 St Paul and their miracles recorded in the word of God. 7. a short life of all the saints whose names are inserted in the long litanies and in the same order; yet some of them may be more prolix.

But in writing these lives of saints for the vulgar faithful, I think there is no need, nay it seems improper, to relate their actions in high life, as one may say, that is, their transactions with kings and princes and other grandees of the world. It will edify the poor faithful much better to read how they conversed with the lowest and meanest people, assisted them with both spiritual and corporal alms, worked miracles like our Lord himself, for the relief of their wants, by turning water into wine, and multiplying bread, &c. Above all I wish you could find the life of some holy woman, or women, married to an idle husband having 7 or 8 shirtless children, herself too almost naked, neither servant maid to assist her, nor anyone to comfort her, &c. St Monica had a bad husband but his fortune was much above low life. St Elizabeth too, the Queen of Portugal, was tied to an adulterous king, but then she had maids and pages, &c. You must find a saint in all the distress and poverty above mentioned with a husband both idle and a drunkard. St Gomar had a haughty, proud, self-conceited wife, but then he had a plentiful fortune and no children. But find a poor holy man tied to an errant vixen. St Maura had a bad father and at last converted him. St Zita's life deserves a most minute detail in order to teach servant maids how to behave themselves in service. And Homobonus's too, to teach tradesmen and shopkeepers how to unite true devotion with their worldly calling. St Mary, 1st November, was a slave and deserves a place in your collection. And also St Potamiona. In short I wish to see the lives of those saints who, living in a laical state, or in marriage, have by those virtues which, as St Francis of Sales says, grow at the foot of the cross, made their way safe and secure to eternal glory. But no more at present on this subject.

I have written this letter, as you will see by my dates, with many interruptions; a plain proof that I am unable to undertake any long lucubration.

The life of Holy Toby will not surely be omitted. The history of Susanna is an excellent instruction to teach young women how to resist both open and undermining solicitations. I have parted with Mary and keep her sister Margaret. I can do with one and a charity girl.

In answer to your last quere I say, if the priest will not promise you never to go more to any play whether comedy or tragedy, beseech him to excuse you from hearing his confession—[the rules of this District strictly prohibit priests from attending theatrical performances]. I remain your most affectionate Uncle, R.B. [Finished 5th February] 1792

1. Missioner at Ladywell, Fernyhalgh.

---

87. Banister to Rutter Mowbreck, 25th February 1792

My dear Sir,

I wrote to you lately a very long letter, but this may perhaps be a short one. It is to inform you that looking into a drawer in a dark closet the other day I found a surplice which, upon a slight inspection, I perceived evidently could be only your property. And I recollected that at your last coming hither from abroad you brought it with you, and at your departure enquired for it, but Mary my housekeeper denied that she knew anything of it. On the 30th of last December I paid to her in full her wages and discharged her, but she wept so bitterly that in pity I received her again. This passed in privacy, no one knew it. But on the 21st of January I gave her a public warning to quit and she left me the day following.

My reasons were, firstly, because I had no need of her. Secondly, because I perceived too much familiarity between her and my young man, although she be a full score older than he. Thirdly, she was rather a lumber than useful. Fourthly, my man told me that there was no living with her unless one courted her, i.e., kissed and clipped, i.e., clasped and entwined her in arms, which you will not allow, adds he. Indeed, in the time of my other man I had no small vexation to keep them on a fair balance. It was either peevishness or kissing to be friends. She and this man often stayed of late time behind me at the fire by night, to be sure, to say their prayers, and talk of celestial things, as sweethearts are wont to do when the devil pleases.

I look upon it as certain that she has done much harm to my young man, for he is far from being tractable to me; he is more properly my master than servant. He goes without leave and stays as long as he pleases and I must not ask him where he has been, or what he has been doing, or with whom he kept company. He is no bad gardener and keeps my cattle and mare in good order, and, I dare say, is honest, but he loves a book as much as your squire my neighbour, and generally keeps Thursday marketday and any afternoon he pleases. I dare not give him warning to go lest he go and marry, like like a madlikin, the long-toothed vixen. For, although both of them deny to me and to some others that there is any courtship between them, yet their behaviour is as yet to me a riddle. If he marry her I know no other advantage he can get but to work daily work to maintain a lazy woman, sick every fortnight or three weeks of hysterical flatulence, who must have tea twice a day, and wine when sick, and well too, if it may be gotten. So I say of this young man, he pays me well for all the disobedience I have been guilty of to my superiors and especially to our Lord, and he treats me infinitely better than the devils will do in hell. But though that thought be a very cogent motive to bear every slight and every contempt, yet I cannot always retain it so fresh in my mind as to be influenced by it. Yesterday he rode out 6 or 7 miles on my mare, but I can scarcely believe but that he would rather have gone his journey on foot than have said to me: If you please, I will take your mare to ride on. But enough of this.

Yet, I will add that if Mr Silvertop wants a man to be his groom, or to be underbutler. and the wages be tempting, you may make mention of my man. I suppose the squire and his lady and you take mighty great care to hinder all kissing, &c., but when you go into the kitchen, take good notice of the chairs whether they be not broken by carrying double. [Dirty vessels are difficult to handle]: there is no preserving them from damage or cracks without singular vigilance and care. I pray you to forbear too harsh judgement of the persons I have signified herein to have had too much familiarity; it was indiscreet, and so I have endeavoured to break it.

If you observe in the Lives of Saints by Butler, he describes them, almost all, in the continual exercise and practice of eminent, heroic good works, and especially of prayer. Now I do not find that the divine pen-men do so. Sara, whom St Peter proposes as a pattern to all women (1 Pet. c.3), laughed behind the door, and when the angel charged her with it, she denied it flatly. When Rachel said to her husband Jacob: give me children, he was angry and said: am I God, &c. David's lapses are rehearsed again and again. Samson's going in to harlots is also eternalised by the word of God. Ann, the wife of the elder Toby, was in a violent passion at her husband and upbraided him grievously, and put the good man into such sorrow that he prayed for death. Nor have the old writers of saints' lives concealed the frailties and lapses of God's servants, but related them as well as their repentance and other good works. All the evangelists have mentioned the fall of Peter together with his cursing and swearing which last circumstance Alban Butler would have suppressed I suppose; nay, perhaps with Baronius (if I well remember) would have excused him from mortal sin. And does not St Paul tell us that he was reprehensible, and that therefore he resisted him to his face. I therefore conclude that whilst a good writer of saints' lives exposes their piety, love of God and of their neighbour, practice of prayer and good works, he may, after the example of the inspired writers and others, expose their sins and frailties and show us that they were men, flesh and blood, and might say with St Paul, ch.7 v. 15: I do not that good which I will, but the evil which I hate, that I do.

Next month your surplice shall be washed and bleached and smoothed and plated a la mode du college, put into a box and directed to you at Minsteracres to be left at Mr Adam's office, Newcastle, unless you otherwise order.

On the other side I have copied a letter which I received from our bishop the second week in February. It is very curious indeed; the Committeemen are for making him to confess his secret thoughts and sentiments to them. They have published blue books which speak as plain a language as is possible, yet the world must believe that they never intended to injure religion, and that they are pure and orthodox in every point of religion. So Jansenius wrote plain heresy and the Jansenists would persuade the world that he wrote apostolical doctrine. His and the Committee's mental intention is known to God, but their sense and meaning expressed and printed are most injurious to religion. I remain your most affectionate Uncle, R. Banister

Copy of a letter from our bishop:

Dear Sir,

This morning I received a letter signed by four of the old Committee: Lord Petre, Sir Henry Englefield, Sir John Throckmorton and Mr Thomas Hornyhold[1]: "We conceive," say they,

that we should be wanting both to ourselves and to the part of clergy reflected on in it, (Mr Charles Plowden's answer to the blue book) if we did not endeavour to know how far Mr Plowden speaks your Lordship's sentiment. My Lord, we apply in the most solemn manner to you. We are charged with crimes of a very serious nature. You owe to us as Christians either to undeceive the public with regard to the opinion they must conceive your Lordships form of us, and leave to Mr Plowden the shame of having thus abused your Lordship's respectable authority; or candidly to say that such are your sentiments in our regard. We shall then endeavour to vindicate ourselves from the accusation brought by your Lordship against our moral as well as civil character. We are, &c. Lincoln's Inn, 2nd February, 1792.

A copy is sent by them to all the other Vicars Apostolic.

Mr Charles Butler is preparing (our bishop tells me) a history of facts, i.e., a history of lies, imudent assertions, misrepresentations, equivocations, &c. I believe the petty-fogger to be the author or writer of the letter above; it seems to be in his style.

1. Of Blackmore, Worcestershire; he represented the London District on the Committee.

88. Rutter to Banister — Minsteracres, 12th March 1792

Dear Uncle,

I have to acknowledge the pleasure of two favours lately received from you which came to hand in due time.

As to the surplice which is come to light, if you will use it yourself it is at your service; but if you have no occasion for it, you may send it me in the manner you mention. Poor Mary, who I am sorry for, forgot it at the time, I suppose, and I can easily account for the mistake for, if you recollect, she was then in love to a certain widower, whom I have forgotten. However, I hoped you had cured her of love long ago, but this disorder, it seems, is not so easily mastered.

Your first letter which you call a long one, appeared to me very short. Your plan of saints' lives pleases me exceedingly, and I shall be still better pleased to hear in your next that you are preparing to put it in execution. For unless you undertake it, it will either be ill-done or not done at all. I hope you will at least make a beginning by writing the life of our Blessed Saviour in that easy familiar style which you are master of. I once asked you what author you read for the purpose of forming a style, but you did not satisfy me. But, upon dipping into Swift's works lately, I am persuaded he has been your model. Is it not so?

A propos on the subject of authors, do you think it would be blameable in me to read occasionally such as Pope, Shakespeare, &c., by way of amusement and to quicken my stupidity? I find Bishop [William] Warburton[1], almost on a similar occasion, brings the example of St Chrysostom who, he says, is known to have been so fond of Aristophanes as to wake with him at his studies, and to sleep with him under his pillow. He does not say on what authority this assertion is founded, but he brings it in his own vindication for publishing an edition of Shakespeare. But the question in my regard is how far you think it advisable to read profane writers such as I have mentioned. Whatever you may say on authors of this description you will, I am sure, approve of one whom I purchased last year, and this is St Francis de Sales works in 2 volumes, folio, and a good edition. You will accuse me of bibliomania, and I own I cannot entirely clear myself of the charge, but I promise to amend.

I have a person in my congregation who keeps a stick with great care, reported to be brought from Ireland, in order to cure venom and poison. I thought to expect such an effect from an old dry stick was folly and superstition but this week I accidentally ment with a passage in Venerable Bede in support of this notion, which surprised me not a little. It is as follows:

We have seen that when some persons have been bit by serpents, the scrapings of leaves of oaks that were brought out of Ireland, being put into water and given them to drink, the same immediately expelled the spreading poison and assuaged the swelling. A note on this, if you please.

The index for Mr Butler's saints' lives which I mentioned in my last will, I suppose, go on, but I hope without my having anything more to do with it.

I can say nothing about your servant man because the family is from home, but shall hereafter inform you in case they have occasion for him. Mr Silvertop has been in London. The object of his journey was to get an Act of Parliament for a new road beginning at West Auckland over the moors by Minsteracres, Corbridge, &c., into Scotland, which will be a great opening to this country, and the nearest way from London to the north. The business was long talked of, and would certainly have been dropped had it not been for the perseverance and exertions of Mr Silvertop, which, I am happy to find by a letter, have been crowned with success.[2]

Mr Nicholas Clavering is going to leave Callaly, as his nephew is now capable of managing the estate himself, but where he goes I have not learned. Mrs Silvertop writes to me from Lartington that Mr Kitchen's health is in a very precarious state, and that Mr Billington is incapax and so quits Cliffe. She adds that a letter from Bruges mentions the poor monks at La Trappe were turned out with the rest, and that a house unfurnished had been offered them in Switzerland, where they now are, and that although almost in a starving condition, their novices refuse to leave them. But it is past 12 o'clock at night and I can only add that I am, with all respect and affection, yours, H. Rutter.

1. (1698–1779), Bishop of Gloucester: *Alliance between Church and State* (1736 and ten editions by 1846).
2. The modern A68 road.

89. Rutter to Banister — Minsteracres, 16th May 1792

Dear Uncle,

For some time past I have been flattering myself with the pleasure of seeing you at Mowbreck on the 19th of this month, and had got everything ready for my journey, but am unexpectedly prevented by a sick person who, this day, has desired my assistance. I should have accompanied Mr Silvertop as far as Preston, for he is going to Bristol where his son John has been drinking the waters for the recovery of his health. The accounts hitherto transmitted to us from Mrs Silvertop are very unfavourable and make us apprehensive that he is in a consumption. Mr Silvertop will meet likewise at Bristol his other two sons George and Henry, who are just come from the college in consequence of the commotions and disturbances in those parts.

I have now to congratulate with you on the happy issue of our Committee affairs, which rejoices me the more as I had entertained the most serious apprehensions for religion in consequence of Mr Plowden's gloomy prognostics. For he was firmly persuaded that the Committee would set up a schismatical bishop or two to oppose the Vicars Apostolic, and this conviction, he says, has been growing upon him for these two years past. He therefore wished the bishops to draw up an instruction setting forth in the most ample manner the dangers and consequences of schism. Mr Milner he proposed as both able and willing to ease the Vicars of the trouble of writing such a mandate. But, as matters have turned out, the business, it seems, will be between Mr Plowden himself and Joseph Berington, the leader of the Staffordian faction. Pray, have you seen Mr Plowden's animadversions on Joseph's works, for I hear they are printed and signed by several clergymen of the Western District?[1]

Sir John Throckmorton's late publication has not reached us. Mr Plowden calls it a scandalous attack on the See of Rome and the Catholics of the last and present age. You would, perhaps, observe this gentleman's name in the list of those who compose the Reforming Club. Mr Wilkes, I hear, is going abroad after finishing the 3rd blue book; Bishop Walmesley's obstinacy is much talked of at Bath in not admitting the Protesters to their Easter Communion.[2] I suppose our bishop did not observe the same firmness in these parts. His Lordship went from London with George and Henry Silvertop to drink the waters at Bristol for a week or two.

You would hear of the death of Mr Eyre at Nice, occasioned, it seems, by the mismanagement of his physicians. Mr Vincent Eyre is the chief of his executors. Do you hear anything of Mr [Ralph] Standish who succeeds to Stella Hall, or whether any of his connections are likely to come and live there?[3]

I shall expect from you soon a long letter and remain, dear Uncle, your dutiful Nephew, H. Rutter.

1. The Catholic Committee was dissolved at the beginning of May 1792 since its raison d'etre lapsed with the Relief Act. Many members, however, formed a 'Cisalpine Club' (called by Rutter the 'Reforming Club') to keep its principles alive. Many of the disputes between the lay and clerical leadership of the Church also lapsed and an attempt at reconciliation on outstanding issues was made by an independent group of lay 'Mediators'. One of these matters was a quarrel between Joseph Berington and Charles Plowden caused by the latter's *Remarks on the Writings of the Rev. Joseph Berington (1792).*
2. Wilkes continued to be a problem. He refused to submit to his bishop or to return to his monastery. Instead, he went on an extended tour of the continent with Sir John Throckmorton of Buckland, who had come into his inheritance at the death of his grandfather, Sir Robert, in December 1791.
3. Thomas Eyre was for 'many years afflicted with violent fits of the gout . . . and at last died of it at Nice, whither he was gone for the benefit of his health, March 26, 1792, without issue'. The estates at Stella now moved out of the family; Mary Widdrington (b. 1713) had married Rowland Eyre of Hassop; her brother Henry Francis died without issue in 1774 leaving the estates to her issue, with remainder to his other in-laws, the Towneley and Standish families.

---

90. Banister to Rutter — Mowbreck, 8th October 1792

My dear Sir,

To the best of my remembrance the last letter I have received from you only informed me that you were on the point of taking a trip into this your native county but that a person of your congregation fell dangerously ill which obliged you to stay at home to attend.

On the 12th of last August I was very ill at my stomach and much worse on the 15th about, 2 hours in the evening. The day following I received a letter from our Bishop calling me to meet him at Manchester and go up with him to the Metropolis, admitting no excuse nor delay, for the business was of importance and could not be discussed or settled by a communication of letters but only in a meeting. This put me to great distress, fearing to be ill whilst abroad. I therefore on Thursday evening tried whether riding to Mr Wilson would agree with my health and consulted him what I should do. He said I must necessarily go and bid me eat and drink heartily and allowed me to eat flesh-meat on days of abstinence, which I did only twice.

On Friday therefore in the morning, August 17th, I rode to Preston on my mare, Richard walked on foot. At Preston we took a whiskey to Bolton, 22 miles, but as no post-chaise could be had there, he took me forward to Manchester, 12 miles more of bad road, where I arrived at an inn much tired and over-done. I only saw the Bishop that night at Mr [Roland] Broomhead's[1] and returned immediately to the inn, and to bed, and by lying long in the morning, was pretty well.

On Saturday night I lodged at Mr Broomhead's in his own bedchamber and he went to Mr Reynolds's[2]. On Sunday at 5 o'clock p.m. we left Manchester and went only 14 miles to Disley. On Monday 66 miles, but on Tuesday from Leicester 98 miles to London and 2 more to No. 34 Great Ormond Street, Mr Varley's, where we found at 7½ o'clock Bishops Walmesley and Douglass, the Revd. Messrs. Robert[3] and Charles Plowden, Barnard, Pilling and Milner. The day following after Mr Barnard had celebrated a Missa de Spiritu Sancto and Bishop Walmesley the hymn Veni Creator Spiritus, we 9 conferred together upon the business, which had brought us to London so far from home, from about 10 o'clock a.m. to near 3 p.m. seven days successively. Mr Robert Plowden indeed left us on Saturday 26th and his brother on the 29th. At 3 o'clock we all dined together at Mr Varley's and in the evening walked out.

On Sunday 26th August I went with the Rt. Rev. Prelates Acanthos and Centuriae to the Spanish Ambassador's chapel, Manchester Square, to hear the High Mass and the famous Mr Hussey preach, to whom they give primum locum, Archer only secundum. He read the Gospel of the 14th Sunday post Pentecost, which was Matt. 6: A man cannot be the slave of two masters &c. One of the best to expatiate upon, and to be instructive, but I never heard a Gospel so murdered, never anything so improper to it. He might as well have taken his text from Ps. 82: May their princes fare as Oreb and Zeb, and Zebee and Salmana. A great head, a small body, and little tail. You may be sure I was asked how I liked his sermon. I without hestiation declared my sentiments and once, somewhere, said I did not care if my opinion were carried to him.

One evening Mr [John] Earl[4] came to No. 34 and there I inveighed before him against Hussey's sermon and against the theatrical tones and inflections of voice used by preachers and particularly against their studied language, eloquent periods &c., and against reading Protestant sermons, as dry insipid things which afford no milk of devotion &c. But Earl mentioned one Protestant author, I have forgot his name and do not regret it, whom he praised much and read and will read, I fear. Against all such reading I think the authority of the church ought to deter our youngsters for it forbids [reading religious works written by heretics even if they do not contain heresy]. I hope you do not read, nor ever will read, such unhallowed productions, but as for your reading for some relaxation &c., a Protestant poet or Ovid or Virgil or such like, I believe there is no harm in so doing.

We left London the 10th of September and arrived at York the 12th. I stayed there in Little Blake Street till Wednesday 26th and arrived home on Saturday 29th about 8 o'clock p.m. safe and well during all my journies and stay both at London and York, thanks be to God, and pray you to thank him too, and better than I can. Our Bishop told me that Mr Silvertop had invited him to come and stay a month with him at Minsteracres, and I think he will, though he did not say so. You will therefore, if he comes, probably hear from his own mouth some intelligence of the business for which we met at London. Bishop Talbot was politely invited to come but he answered that he did not see any good that could come from meeting more now than last May; that he expected some guests; and that his harvest was at hand. This rainy season has probably done it great damage.

You certainly have seen Mr Charles Plowden's letter to all the Catholics of England.[5] Pincerna's letter is the most curious part in it; you see there the accomplished hypocrite, the double-tongued, the devout rebel to lawful authority. Pincerna's theological career: who never went beyond Ovid and Virgil at the College.

Sed haec hactenus: I have been obliged to postpone many Masses during my absence from home. I therefore desire you to celebrate for the following faithful departed, viz., one Mass for each, in all, ten Masses which I hope you will say in 5 or 6 weeks: Dorothy, William, Richard, Ann, James, Elizabeth, John, William, Richard, Ann. I hear nothing from Ormskirk so I reckon that they are all well there. I remain your most affectionate dear Uncle, R. Banister

P.S. Richard fetched me from York in a Whiskey. I arrived at Lord Southwell's near Clitheroe on Friday for dinner, stayed all night and was most kindly and hospitably received and entertained. He is a very good Catholic Christian. His title is Viscount. I saw the Bishop of S. Pol de Leon, he dined with our Synodicals. Item. I saw at No. 34 and conversed with the Bishop of Limoges, aged 70, but of the vivacity and action of 40. He arrived at London the 7 or 8 of September in great trouble about his brother Bishop of Seez who was, he said sous le Coutae at Paris.

1. Missioner at St Chad's, Rook St., Manchester.
2. Not a priest; possibly a hotel.
3. Ex-Jesuit Missioner in Bristol.
4. Chaplain at Spanish Place.
5. *Address to English Catholics* (1792).

---

91. Rutter to Banister Minsteracres, 30th November 1792

Dear Uncle

I received your favour in due time and was extremely glad to hear of your safe return to Mowbreck, for which I have more than once returned thanks to Almighty God. I hope you will entertain me on some future occasion with a more particular account of your journey.

By seeing Messrs. Milner, Plowden, &c., you would probably obtain a greater insight into the proceedings of our Committee. For my part I hear nothing of this kind since Mr Eyre's departure from Stella. I suppose you know that he has left these parts to go and live with Mrs Silvertop near Wooler. I cannot indeed well justify this step in my friend in leaving an old and numerous congregation to bury himself in a desert country where there is nothing to do. There are now three considerable congregations adjoining to mine which appear to me not to be sufficiently provided for. Mr Ashmal at Newhouse, who is 97 years of age at least, has been unable to do duty for a long time. No priest has been fixed at Pontop since Mr Johnson's death. Nor is Stella, as I hear, yet provided with a Pastor. For the present indeed Mr [Thomas] Story from Hexham says prayers there and Mr [John] Worswick[1] at Pontop, but many things, I fear are omitted when priests are not fixed and supply only for a time.

I have heard that Dr [John] Rigby has published a new catechism for the Catholics at Lancaster and that it is very clear and concise.[2] Pray, have you adopted it in your part?

What you mention concerning Mr Hussey's method of preaching is amusing and very contrary to the idea I had formed of him. I think you would have liked Mr Archer better, for, however inferior he may be to Mr Hussey in point of delivery, it is generally allowed that his composition is much superior. Many admire his printed sermons and read them to their country congregations, but they are not entirely to my taste, for you have taught me to prefer a more simple natural style and not to mind fine language and ink-horn phrases. However, I doubt our sentiments in this respect are contrary to the general practice and that S. Ignatius himself thought very differently. For in his life written by Bohours it is said that he made it his business to speak Italian very correctly and for this end he ordered young Ribadeneira, who was perfect in the tongue, to note all the faults he should commit in speaking, and he was so exact herein that he would write down with his own hand the improper words and expressions which were observed to come from him. And in the Constitutions, speaking of the religous who were to be trained to preach, he says for this purpose 'they should endeavour to be perfect in the vulgar tongue'. Hence it follows (says the writer of his life) that the Jesuit who neglects to speak correctly neglects his Rule,' &c. What would you say to the authority of so great a man?

Mr Silvertop's 2 eldest sons are at home. John is somewhat better than he has been so that his parents have hopes that his lungs are not ulcerated as the Bristol doctor imagined. George is about 19 and is seemingly a good tempered young man. His father endeavours to make the country as agreeable as he can and with this in view he has got him a pack of hounds, which I follow sometimes, but very cautiously.

At Stella, all has been sold off for the benefit of the place. Mr Eyre and the attorney employed on the occasion thought proper to sell a parcel of old books that had been laying in the garret for years, thinking they were of little value and would probably be destroyed by the servants in lighting the fires. These books I have bought bona fide without knowing what they were. But Mr Eyre (who is far more conversant in books than I am) had a catalogue of them in his own handwriting showing the year they were printed in. However, since they have come into my possession, amidst rubbish I find 3 or 4 volumes which, though of no intrinsic value, will sell very well to some of the present typographical virtuosi, and it has cost me a good deal of time and pains to know this. Now, I wish to be informed whether I can keep to myself all the profits which may possibly arise from them?[3]

I have said all the Masses which you desired me and remain Dear Uncle your dutiful Nephew, Hen. Rutter

1. Missioner at Lartington; brother of James, missioner at Newcastle 1795–1843.
2. Missioner at Lancaster 1784–1818. Gillow gives no date for Rigby's catechism but remarks that Matthew Gibson when a bishop preferred the Douai Catechism to it, hence it must have been published before 1790.
3. For an account of the disposal of this library see A I Doyle, 'The Library of Sir Thomas Tempest: Its origins and dispersal', *Studies in Seventeenth-Century English Literature, History and Bibliography* NS Vol. 46 (Amsterdam 1984).

---

92. Banister to Rutter Mowbreck, 3rd March 1793

My dear Sir

Mr William Hull, who was two schools above you at Douai College, will either bring or send you this. Tomorrow he sets out from Weeton to Preston and Manchester. From thence to York, from York to Bedale to his uncle Mr [William] Danson, living at Askew, and from Askew to Stella, his appointed residence. Our Bishop has wished me to write to you to give him the meeting there. I do not well know what service you may be able to do him but, however, as he is coming to be your neighbour I think you will do as you would wish him to do to you if you can hit on a day to meet him. He has been near 12 years on the Mission and so is no novice; and in point of urbanity and conversation the Captain's sarcasm upon parsons in Dean Swift cannot apply to him:

A Parson, when just from the College broke loose,
Can hardly tell how to cry Bishop to a goose, &c.

So I wish him to be introduced to the acquaintance of your family and I am of opinion that you yourself will be glad to see him often. For I believe his tongue and his heart grow together; he knows not how to speak sophistically. [The crafty man is hateful] says the wise man.[1] Therefore, he who speaks candidly and unfeignedly must be amiable.

I imagine you have received by this time the Pastoral Instruction in which Sir John Throckmorton's propositions are proscribed and condemned in globo. Now therefore I need not tell you my errand to London the last August. In the meeting, which was continued 4 or 5 hours p. diem, during a week or more, several of the foresaid propositions were unanimously judged to be heretical, but, however, it was thought better to omit that qualification.[2]

I have seen and read the Rigbean catechism. For your own consideration I will transcribe two questions and the answers:

> Lesson XV. Q. What then must we say of those who are out of the communion of the Church?
>
> A. We must hope that God will excuse their error and that they may belong in spirit to the Church.
>
> Q. But how can they belong in spirit to the Church if they be out of her communion?
>
> A. By their baptism if they be sincerely desirous of knowing the truth and willing to embrace it.

Read Dr [Edward] Hawarden's Charity and Truth [1728 vol.] 2 3d, page 17 and see Bishop Hay's, where he treats at full length the case of invincible ignorance.

One Mr [James] Haydock is just arrived from Douai College. It does not appear from his talk that they are in any great apprehension of being sent away. He says the Municipality of St. Omers has published a declaration that all the English, whether families or individuals, are to be protected provided they observe the laws. He came with a pass-port from Douai, which was signed at Calais, and crossed the Channel in a French vessel, with several Frenchmen, to Dover.[3]

If my respects and good wishes may be agreeable to Mr and Mrs Silvertop, please make them in my name and accept my poor heart for a small token of love from your affectionate uncle, R. Banister

1. Proverbs 14, 17.
2. A joint Pastoral Letter by Bishops Douglass, Gibson and Walmesley, issued on 26 December 1792, condemned 12 statements in Throckmorton's book on the election of bishops. (Bishop Talbot declined to sign the letter because he wanted to bring the bickerings to an end.)
3. The college was seized a week later. Many students had already returned to England, like Haydock, and in the months that followed about twenty managed to escape and get back to England, but a group of forty-seven staff and students were held in a prison in Doullens for over a year.

93. Rutter to Banister 1st August 1793

My Dear Uncle,

I was sorry to leave you indisposed but I hope it was only some slight cold which had no bad consequences. However, I should be glad to hear from you that this was the case. I will now give you an account of my journey from Mowbreck.

I did not stop long at Preston, but saw Messrs. Dunn and Morgan and their magnificent new chapel which, I understand, will not add to their popularity with the congregation, as many of them dislike the change. At Mr Dunn's we talked of Panzani's Memoirs by Berington and, from an extract of a letter which he read me from one of his brethren, it appears that the Philosopher will give great offence to the ex-Jesuits if not to all the Regulars.[1]

I arrived at Ormskirk in good time and was extremely glad to find both my father and mother in great good health and spirits. My father, who is now 77, carries his age surprisingly well and is without complaint. But I was still better pleased to learn that he is so much reformed and that for a considerable time he had been very punctual and regular in all spiritual duties. This, you may imagine, gives me greater pleasure and satisfaction than I can express and I pray God to confirm more and more what he has begun. My father was very good company all the time I stayed and kindly enquired after you. I acquainted him with your intention of sending him some more of your clothes, which make him appear very decent and save him an expence which, in his present circumstances, he can but ill afford.

On the Thursday I went to Liverpool where nothing was talked of but the alarming stagnation of trade and this was still more the topic at Manchester. On the Friday I went to Wigan and lodged at my sister's, who has a very decent house with every suitable accommodation. Her husband seems to be a very civil and obliging man, and my only objection to him is on the score of religion. He does not, however, molest my sister in the practice of her religious duties and Richard told me that she is now more exact in them than formerly before marriage.

On Saturday I met again with my old pedagogue Thomas Southworth at Manchester and disputed with him the same ground over again but to no purpose except to bring on myself a violent headache. Mr Broomhead and Mr [Edward] Kenyon[2] were likewise against him and so were most of the priests in Lancashire, as he acknowledged, insinuating, however, at the same time that he had met with some of more enlightened minds. After saying Mass on Sunday I proceeded in the afternoon to Rochdale and slept that night at Elan near Halifax. The day after, I got to Leeds and agreed with Mr Binns[3] concerning my books which he said he would purchase after he had seen them. Accordingly I sent them to him and have just received an answer that he is not willing to buy them so I must send them to London to get what I can for them. I sent off at the same time a box of old books for you which I think ought to reach you about this time. To the best of my recollection they were to be left at the George Inn.

On Tuesday I arrived at York and lodged in Little Blake Street but nothing corresponded there to my expectations except the cathedral which surpassed them. I was glad to get home on Friday and to find all my congregation as well as I had left them.

We have lately had our meeting at Newcastle. Mr [James] Mather was there and sung with all the glee imaginable a loyal song to King George. He came afterwards to Minsteracres and says he is so happy in his present situation at Yarm that he would not return again to France to be Archbishop of Paris. He narrowly escaped with his life and seems to have little hope of religion being restored in that distracted country.[4]

According to your advice I will think no more of changing my situation for the present. However, my nerves may advise to the contrary. Is it your practice to marry Catholics with Protestants? Or to baptise the children of those nominal Catholics who know nothing of religion and never come to the chapel? Or to church those heathenish ignorant mothers who never come near you at any other time? I remain, dear Uncle, your ever dutiful Nephew, Hen. Rutter

1. J Berington, *The Memoirs of Gregorio Panzani* &c. (1793). In the 1630s Panzani had tried to reconcile the Jesuits and seculars in controversies which had arisen over: the oath of allegiance; Jesuit involvement in the Gunpowder Plot; and the continued presence of the Society in England. Berington's translation was therefore topical but his Introduction was partial and gave offence to the ex-Jesuits; Charles Plowden issued *Remarks* on it in 1794.
2. With Broomehead at St Chad's, Manchester.
3. Presumably a secondhand bookseller.
4. Mather had been taken abroad by his Jacobite uncle and aunt, George and Mary Flint, and educated for the priesthood in Paris where he served in a parish. He now felt able to renounce his Jacobite upbringing. See L. Gooch, *The Desperate Faction?* (1995), ch. 8.

94. Banister to Rutter Mowbreck, 19th December 1793

My dear Sir

On this day I was ordained Priest in 1750, so I want 6 years to my jubilate, that is, to its beginning. Four others out of Douai College were ordained with me, viz: school-fellows Phil. Butler, William Daniel and George Gibson, the late Bishop James Talbot, then Master of Philosophy, was the fourth.[1] We were two nights at Valenciennes, now rendered famous, two miles from Beverage, a seminary belonging to the Archbishop of Cambrai, where we received ordination from Bishop Dunn of Ossory in Ireland.

Our Bishop first ordered our young refugees to Old Hall Green; presently after he countermanded them to York. He has now assembled in a house contiguous to Mr Gillow's Messieurs John Woodcock, James Worswick, John Lancaster, Thomas Gillow, Thomas Penswick, George Haydock (although the two last, obeying the first order, were gone off to Old Hall Green), perhaps [John] Bell and [John] Rickaby. Mr [John] Gillow[2] is their Master. Our Bishop wishes me to teach them but says nothing more. He desires me to come to York to consult about this new establishment and other important matters. To be asked to teach these or any other theologians gives me immediate pain of mind. I find myself extremely attached to my present situation, and yet, keeping house is so changeable, and my farm with the burdens annexed to it so dear, and so many infirm to vist ad indulgences, that I sometimes resolve to petition for another place, when one becomes vacant, that may fit me.

I cannot tell why any proposal of my teaching Divinity is so apt to raise in me a strong impression of mind. Is it from heaven or from the implacable enemy of mankind, or from nature? Sure it is (I hope) that if I could be morally certain that it is the will of God, my repugnance would be easily conquered. At all events, you may assure yourself that I shall not undertake it without the most mature consideration. And perhaps the Bishop has no real intention, at least not a steady one, to engage me in it. I could never agree to it unless the ancient college mode be adopted with unabated assiduity, of dictating and writing the whole body of Divinity, so that all may be [of one way of speech and one language[3]], not like a Babel divided into various tongues by reading and studying different Divines.

Mr Robert Blacoe arrived at Mr Varley's, London, on the 10th Inst., in the evening, much indisposed. So he only wrote a very short letter and could not relate the circumstances of his escape from that country of Monsters and Atheists. He prays me to give him the finishing stroke by teaching him his last year of Divinity rather than that he be sent to Old Hall Green. I have consented to his request and expect him this week. Whensoever the rest can escape, the Masters and Professors, now at Doullens or the confines of Picardy, may resume their functions in Little Blake Street. When I went from Douai to Rouen, we dined at Doullens, about 5 leagues from Amiens. I have little idea of it, only that it is a small town not larger than Henin Lictard.

I long since received the box of books which you sent me. St. Basil is admirable in his translation although not very clear in several places but embarrassed. But I do not read much these short days and none at all (except a chapter in the New Testament) at night. For unless I go to bed at 10 or soon after and lie till 8 next morning, I am not very well.

The Bishop informs me that the Club of Cisalpines are going without delay to establish a Cisalpine College. John Carter of Wolverhampton and Thomas Wright, a Sorbonnist, are to be Masters. He supposes that it is to be in the Middle District. 'Tis well known that the first mentioned is an admirer and friend of Joseph Berington; whether he is to teach all or most of his theological notions, I do not know. I can hardly doubt but some of the most capital will be the subject of a theological treatise. Ex gratia, that the Pope is head of the Church in discipline by ecclesiastical institution; that he has his prerogative and we (nous autres) have our privileges; and that he has a limited superintendency allowed him by the community for the sake of good order; that governing by Vicars Apostolic is abusive, in itself an evil and productive of evils. 1. It is dependent on the Pope. 2. It is arbitrary. 3. Without subordination having no metropolitan head. 4. The Vicars are not elected by the clergy. See these assertions in his Memoirs of Panzani in calce. Send me your refutation of them; show their futility, &c.

Which way, do you think, is our Bishop to procure revenues to maintain and support a school or college of 40 or 50? The greatest part of our Douai College funds are for ever lost in France.[4] I know of no recourse but to rich, devout Catholic widows and to gentlemen and rich merchants who have no children or families. The greatest part of the money which built in your time Douai College was obtained by the late Mr Richard Kendall; he made a tour through this nation, but then only to clergy families (the Jesuits were not suppressed), and by an admirable address accompanied by sweetness, simplicity, candour and modesty (which were (as it were) natural to him) procured great contributions. I suppose that the last building of the college did not cost less than 4 or 5 thousand pounds. Our Lancashire clergy appear to be quite averse to contribute anything out of the General Fund which, however, would be the easiest and most speedy way, and the least felt by individuals, and do the greatest service. For £200 taken out of the capital of our General Fund would but lessen each individual's annual dividend 4s., and £200 would purchase bedding and necessaries in ready money for not a few.

Do you know that in their meeting of August 1790 they drew up a pompous, flattering address to Lord Thomas of Acone [Bishop Thomas Talbot] praying him to use his best endeavour to get Mr William Gibson President of Douai College to be ejected, esteeming him a dilapidator &c. I apprehend this prejudice against him relative to his economical manouevres is still deeply fixed in the minds of some people. For my part I think we ought to resume the simplicity, humility and assiduity in prayer and studies of [Cardinal] Allen and his times. Mr Wilson my neighbour observes that they come and have come these late days from Douai College like petit Maitres.

[The year 1768 was the jubilee, viz. the two hundredth of Douai College. The festal day was in June and the abbot, prior and the enclosed with the whole company was called to the feast. The Rhetoricians and the Poets recited their poems; among others I composed one which was entitled 'To the College, that its strength and courtly customs may never be cut off'. It was published under the name of my pupil George Witham. Another, which I wrote under the pseudonym of Joseph Leon, had the title, 'To the College: educated boys ought to be more severely disciplined following the example of the ancestors'. But I was singing to the deaf. The renovation of the College preceded the regeneration of the Kingdom of France—you see ruin on all sides. Yet I do not blame President G ... n alone as some do for it was almost completed before his accession. Now I greatly fear that (if a new College is eventually established in this District) a regimen will be followed quite unlike the primitive times under Allen:]

Tunc mensa parea, et caena onena brevis fuit
Vilis spaellex, curtaque res domi.
Benigna sed tum vena fluxit
Ingenii. Sutiisque Pubes
Nutrita, faustis sub Penetralibus
Acerevit, et Nessem attulit auream,
Virosque foecundos bonorum, et
Martyris facilies perire.
His to juventam ritibus erudi, et

Glorere cernes ingenia aemula.
Musaeque notos et Minervae,
Eloquii dociles et artis

ex Josepho Leon[5]

The Hilton envoy is, I hear, mighty thick with Lord Petre and Sir John Throckmorton; Wilkes recommended him to the latter; his name is Erskine, a subdeacon and canon of St. Peter's.[6] I began this on Thursday 19th and finish today 21st. May God keep you in his special custody is the prayer of your most affectionate uncle, R.B.

1. Banister's contemporaries were all dead: Butler and Daniel had died in 1777; Gibson in 1778 and Talbot in 1790.
2. Genesis 11, 1.
3. Now begins the search for a new college; it will be successful ultimately, but Bishop Gibson's indecisiveness in the matter will test everyone's patience to the limit. Gillow was missioner in York; he had been a professor at Douai until 1791.
4. Banister composed an Address imploring the Pope to restore the Holy See's donation to Douai College to which the ex-Jesuits laid claim. He sent the draft to Bishop Douglass on 12 September. [WAA/XLV/206, 207]
5. It is not known where Banister published his verses; he may have meant only that they were recited publicly. It is not altogether clear why Banister preferred anonymity or if Witham was pleased to be his mouthpiece. At any rate, a literal translation of the poem under the name of Leon follows: 'The food was sparing, and the meal was short, The furniture was cheap and the household expenditure modest. The force of native wit was used sympathetically. Youth was nourished and grew under favourable patronage, And raised a golden harvest, and good men ready to die as martyrs. Instruct youth on these lines and you will see souls rivalling to win glory And men familiar with the Muse and Minerva, well-trained in eloquence and the arts'.
6. Monsignor Charles Erskine was of Scottish and Italian descent (with strong Jacobite connections) and was educated in the Scots College, Rome, for the law. In 1782, when aged forty-three, he broke off an engagement to marry on being appointed Devil's Advocate by the Pope and became a subdeacon. Erskine was sent to convey the formal thanks of the Pope to the British government for its protection of the Papal States; he also had private instructions to sound out the possibility of establishing diplomatic relations between the Holy See and the Court of St James's. The Spanish government had suggested these negotiations would be best handled by Thomas Hussey, and Bishop Douglass was also nominated, but Sir John Cox Hippisley, who represented British interests in Rome 1792–6, ensured that his friend Erskine was appointed. Erskine spent several years in London but he was treated with

great reserve by the Vicars Apostolic, who thought his presence inopportune, and great caution by the government. Though Erskine was presented at court, the King was more interested in talking about his Roman job than the purpose of his mission in England.

95. Banister to Rutter Mowbreck, 16th January 1794

My dear Sir,

I sent you a letter some weeks ago and although I intended to send you some intentions and request your aid in fulfilling them, yet such matter came into my mind to write to you that I entirely forgot them. Therefore I will begin with them, the number is ten: Richard; Ann; William; Richard; Catharine; Ann; James; Margaret; Oliver; Dorothy. For each of these I received a shilling to which you will have a just title and will receive either while I live or when I am dead if I die worth anything, in which last case you will forgive me I hope.

There are now at Old Hall Green Academy number 12, viz. Mr [William] Beauchamp, [John] Law, [John] Bowland, [Edward] Peach, [John] Devereux, [Thomas] Gillow, [Edward] Monk, [Thomas] Penswick, [Thomas] Potts, [William] Fryer, a priest from Rome who desires a little time to prepare himself better for the Mission (when I read this I cannot help the rising of a certain resentment), [?] Cook (said to have been formerly a Methodist, and a preacher, too, I think) now constituted Master of the little boys (21 in all), and George Haydock, my correspondent and informer, whom you may possibly remember and have seen here a little boy. He says that Mr [William] Coombes is their Master, formerly Professor of Rhetoric

> and is now doing all in his power to further our progress in all learning, especially in the English language, which is greatly recommended by his Lordship Bishop Douglass in order to evade the reproach cast out (perhaps with justice) against our negligence in that particular at Douai College. Tuesday is assigned to that study, only we are allowed to take a walk out in the afternoon as we are every day during the hours of recreation . . . Thursday is what we call a whole play day, entirely free from study . . . At 6 p.m. Church Music, to which particular attention is recommended as necessary in our future state . . .

> The Divinity we make use of at present is Collet, which will be adapted by the Master to the Thomistical as we proceed.

His letter is very long and that you may have a fuller specimen of his genius and of his epistolary phraseology, I will transcribe a few more extracts. He begins:

> Long have I been kept in suspense whether or no a letter from me would meet with your kind acception. But shame at length has broken asunder the bands of doubt and freed me, at all hazards, to satisfy the obligations which beneficence seems to require and exact from my ungrateful hands. For when I remember that you are the primary cause of all I know, of all I am, of all perhaps I ever shall be, what black ingratitude could prompt the neglectful suspense which now reddens my brow with the scarlet colour of guilt.

Then, after another complimentary preface, but not so pompous, he writes of the proceedings at Old Hall Green:

> I am afraid they will give you less reason for pleasure than poor Douai has done of late. The world appears in far more brilliant colours than it did at that unhappy place which, alas!, must still ever remain dear to my afflicted breast . . . There we overflowed in innocent delights, there we enjoyed all that the heart could desire, all that the soul could wish for. No accommodation for pleasure, study or prayer was there wanting &c. But here alas! we are restrained within a thousand little ceremonious customs, here we are bound down by the chains of a worldly dress, better adapted for the followers of pride than for the humble (as they ought to be) servants of the Gospel. Little does this place suit for the intended purpose.

He says again: 'if we are permitted to wander in the meanderings of a proud licentiousness such as Old Hall Green affords', it will be hard to be restrained in the enjoyment of liberty. Then he goes on:

> the silk stockings of Douai College are here verified. Most of our new Academicians are all arrayed in grandeur. Every day sees them exulting in the pomps of the world. Instead of the decent neatness of poor Douai, a resplendent worldly magnificence. Instead of powdering on Sundays, we here perfume and powder on every day of the week. No one scarce is here to be found but who can ornament himself in pumps tied with silk ribands, or strings, or in fine with grand silver buckles or looking-glasses, who cannot appear in silk

> stockings &c., and (which indeed savours of a ridiculous pretence to modesty) only one who cannot strut in the robes of mourning made in all the elegance of fashion. I need not after this inform you of ruffled shirts &c. you may easily judge of the other decorations from what has been said . . . I dare not add anything more to this horrid description . . . But I must inform you, to take off the aspersion which I may be judged unjustly to have laid upon it, that our present constitution is only suffered till a more proper can be devised. Our good Bishops knew very well the extent of the Douai liberties and accordingly have, with a clemency and condescension agreeable to many, allowed what I have mentioned. They must wean us like infants by slow degrees. Divines, notwithstanding the divine laws and precepts in Divinity occurring at every page, I might almost say at every line, to condemn the vain practices of the world, are still infected with a worldly spirit in many things. They must therefore be brought to a more perfect spirit by the milk of a mild and tender clemency.

This young man, as you may observe, although he laments the loss of Douai College and bestows upon it great encomiums, yet plainly owns that a worldly spirit prevailed in it, that the students has great liberties and learned a fondness, and even a passion, for dress and show. I have for a long time perceived this, and what I resented still more was the irregularity with which their studies in every class were conducted and carried on. Syntaxians made themes like Figuricians, nay, not so true as a High-Figurician formerly. The study of Latin and Greek in the old canonical classics was postponed to French. Philosophy consisted of Locke's ideas and Newton's attraction and a waste of time in the Experimental Room. Scarcely one in 20 had his 4 years of theological studies, and writing dictates was out of fashion. In short, that zeal for true erudition, that slow but solid progress which the Chaplain (i.e., Dodd)[1] says he observed in Douai College in 1710 has been decaying there these late years past. If the gentlemen at Old Hall Green had all remained in Doullens College with a small well-chosen collection of books, paper, pens and ink, and with very little better accommodations of bread, meat and drink, they would, if their Masters were zealous, and not pains-sparing men, become far better accomplished for the duties of Missionaries.

Our Bishop has not sent me a letter this month or more, so I do not know what scheme he is pursuing. In one letter, dated 17th December, he writes: 'if we stay till they (the young Theologians) have finished, there will be neither pedagogues or any students in Divinity for others to model after'. If the description given above by Mr George Haydock be worthy of credit, it will be better to have no model at all than that of Old Hall Green. He is, I believe, very desirous of founding a college in the North and, to be sure, on the plan of Douai College, but I cannot wish it to be so. I wish for one in which none can be received that are not absolutely designed for an ecclesiastical state. Let merchants' sons and such like found a college for themselves and according to their own ever-varying ideas and whimsical notions. There is Tudhoe and Old Hall Green and several other schools that may serve their purpose. They aim at no degree of true erudition and learning; reading, writing, speaking French, dancing and talking fluently are the grand accomplishments.

But I cannot miss this post and therefore am obliged to leave a little white without a scrawl. You will now, I hope, send me your nouvelles in a little time, which will be always agreeable to your most affectionate Uncle, R. Banister

1. In *The History of the English College at Douai from 1568 . . .* by R.C., Chaplain to an English Regiment (1713). The author was Hugh Tootell, alias Dodd (1671–1743), priest and prolific historian and controversialist; Gillow attributes sixty works to him, the best known of which is *The Church History of England 1500–1688* (3 vols. 1737). (See also N° 98).

96. Rutter to Banister — Minsteracres, 3rd February 1794

Dear Uncle,

Your favour of 21st ult. I duly received and return you many thanks for it. I am glad to find by it that you are still in the Bishop's favour and one of his Privy Council. I have heard little of his designs since he left Minsteracres. He then talked much of a new college which he wished to be established in the north. He had pitched upon Flass [Hall] (a gentleman's house about 5 miles from Durham and 15 from Minsteracres) as a proper place to receive the refugee students pro tempore, and had nearly agreed for it in my presence, when an unexpected letter arrived from Bishop Douglass to signify that he had changed his mind in favour of Old Hall Green, though before he had decidedly given the preference to the north. It seems that his Lordship, upon more mature deliberation, is not willing to entrust our Bishop with the direction and management of so important an undertaking, and that the London clergy do not entertain a more favourable idea of his economy than they do in

Lancashire. And I am not surprised at it when I consider all his proceedings at Douai College.

If the two bishops cannot agree about the situation of this new college or the plan of studies to be followed, I suppose they will each have their separate school, one for the north and the other for the south. In point of cheapness, however, the former is far preferable. Mr Silvertop assures me that in a large house the single article of coals will make the difference of £100 p.a. they are so much cheaper in the north than in the south. There is likewise a very great difference in the price of provisions in general in so much that gentlemen here keep as good a house for £2,000 p.a. as they do in the south for £3,000. I fear our Bishop will find it somewhat difficult to procure revenues to his college as Mr Douglass, I understand, is in possession of the greatest part of the funds belonging to Douai. However, I trust our gentry will see the necessity of lending their assistance on this occasion, not by prescribing a plan of education, which they seem ready enough to do, but by opening their purses. Last Summer Sir John Lawson, when here at Minsteracres, seemed to interest himself much in procuring for the Bishop at York a more comfortable dwelling place. He proposed it to several gentlemen who were desirous of seconding his design. Mr Silvertop offered £100 on that occasion. I have heard no more of it since that time, but surely they would be willing to apply their subscription money to the far more necessary work of erecting a new college.

If, in compliance with the Bishop's request, you should resume a lecture on theology, I hope it will be only to a few at Mowbreck whom you may form and fashion as you please, for should you go again to another Douai College, I fear it would not be much to your own satisfaction of mind, as I am fully sensible that your sentiments on education are very different from those of our Bishop.

I am glad to hear from Mr Warrilow that Joseph Berington's works are about to be condemned at Rome, in which case I need not undertake their refutation. Indeed, I have not as yet seen the work which you refer me to, I mean his Memoirs of Panzani, and hope in your next you will give me a fuller account of it. At present I have another object in view which of late has often been in my thoughts and that is to write the life of Christ. For this purpose I wish to know your opinion on the following particulars: 1. Which is the best plan to be followed? 2. which authors I must chiefly have recourse to? 3. Which version of the New Testament I must follow, Mr Witham's[1] or Bishop Challoner's? What I propose at present is to give the life of our Blessed Redeemer in the very words of the Evangelists arranged according to the most esteemed concord, which I presume to be that of Jans. of Ghent, which was afterwards improved and completed by a Paris Doctor and printed in 1654 as Mauduit mentions, who likewise follows it in his analyse with very few trifling exceptions, which I shall examine, by Calmet and others.

It is now some weeks since I began this answer to your first letter, since which I have received another dated 18th January. As to the intentions which you mention, you may depend on my fulfilling them in a very short time. The accounts you give from your correspondent's letter at Old Hall Green are curious enough, but I hope somewhat exaggerated for he seems to paint in very glowing colours.

The reason of my not finishing this letter sooner was that I expected our family home from Yorkshire in hopes of sending you some nouvelles, but they bring nothing very interesting. Mr Silvertop had some conversation with the Bishop concerning the new college and, as far as I can learn, the gentlemen are willing to subscribe to it, but, I believe, on condition of being themselves the trustees for it, which I would never submit to. The Cisalpines &c. it seems have got the start of us for we clergy are always slow and dilatory. It is surely high time to do something. I have not yet seen the proposals for the Cisalpine school; they were not sent here or to Lartington, but only to Committee Gentlemen and, amongst the rest, to Sir John Lawson who did not, however, answer the latter, it being his determination, as Mr Silvertop assures me, to act with the bishops.

This last post brings me a letter from Mr Eyre in which he says that the Bishop is desirous of knowing the sentiments of the Brethren 'on the most eligible mode of founding a college in England. Where the best situation. Who to be the Administrators and Trustees. How far any Lay-Gentleman to have concern in it &c.' His Lordship therefore urges Mr Thomas Eyre to repair to York next week to consult on these and other important matters and, if I go with him, as he proposes, it will be in part to have the pleasure of seeing you there.

I find some gentlemen are very averse to your plan of having a distinct college in which none are to be admitted but such as designed for the ecclesiastical state, what they want is another Douai in which their children may receive a solid education and be formed to virtue as much by example as by precept, and the Bishop expressed himself to the same effect when here. I am informed that in opposition to the Cisalpines, Lord Arundel, Mr Weld, &c., are to patronise a school in the south which, I suppose, will be Liege transplanted to England. At least this is talked of.

Mr Silvertop's two youngest sons have been at home this winter for want of a proper place to send them to and are under the tuition of Mr

Bell, a sedate young man who, though from Douai, has nothing about him of the frippery of a modern Beau. I remain, Dear Uncle, your ever dutiful Nephew, Hen. Rutter

1. Robert Witham (1667–1738). President of Douai College from 1715 to his death. In 1727 he translated the New Testament and three years later he issued two volumes of annotations on it.

97. Rutter to Banister — Minsteracres, 5th May 1794

Dear Uncle,

Our good Bishop is here on a vist and talks much of a new college. He expected Bishop Douglass would have given him the meeting in order to agree on some plan for its establishment, but business prevented him from coming so far north. Our Bishop's design is, as far as I can learn, to take some convenient house in the vicinity of Durham to receive the emigrant students for the present and afterwards to build a great college as soon as circumstances will permit. Centuriensis in his last letter says that he approves of its being in the north and that he will send his subjects to it as soon as it is ready to receive them, but he will contribute nothing towards the expense of such an undertaking.

Mr Eyre from Wooler met with the Bishop and Mr Silvertop on the 3rd inst. to look at a place called Crook [Hall] which is about 11 miles from Newcastle and the same distance from Durham and Minsteracres; a very retired situation and which I believe might be had at a very low rent. According to their report it is more eligible than Flass and would easily contain 40 students; coals at hand and extremely cheap. Today the abovementioned gentlemen set out for Lartington over the moors in order to wait on Sir John Lawson who is there and who is considered as the properest person to set on foot a subscription among the gentlemen which may enable the Bishop to carry his design into execution.

But why was not all this done long ago as might reasonably have been expected? The Bishop will say because he was not seconded and supported by others and was in want of money. But some there are who will throw the whole blame upon his Lordship and ascribe it to his slow, ambiguous and irresolute way of acting. Indeed I never thought him to be a man of business, although he has been President of Douai College and is now honoured with a mitre. However, in the present case I am glad to find that his Lordship does not build so much on gentlemen but on his own bottom, and therefore, when Tudhoe was proposed to him as a proper place for a college, he declined the offer unless the premises were first made over to him by Sir John Lawson. And here, in my opinion, lies the grand difficulty to be adjusted between the Baronet and His Lordship, for, if Sir John, as a leading man here in the north, espouses the present cause and interests himself (as is expected) for a subscription among the gentlemen at the Spring meeting at York, a considerable sum of money may easily be raised, and this, I hope, to be afterwards deposited in the hands of the bishops. But if this is to remain in the hands of the Baronet to be dealt out to their Lordships at his discretion, according as he in his great wisdom shall think fit, in this case the Bishop will not accept his offers and we must go a begging ourselves or remain just as we are at present.

The Bishop, if I am rightly informed, thinks it advisable, in case of necessity, to appropriate some part of our Fund-money to his favourite scheme of a college and, as I am one of the 3 in whose names the money is placed, I wish to know your sentiments on the propriety of such a measure.[1]

I will fill up the remaining space with a short abstract of Antonelli's last letter to the Vicars Apostolic dated 1st February. After congratulating with them on the late Relief shown to the Catholics of this kingdom, in consequence of which they have nothing to apprehend from external enemies, he is sorry to find that the contest now is with the domestic ones: [Like Micah it is necessary to make oneself secure from sons and to attend especially to one's servants]. I suppose he alludes to Cisalpines and Beringtonians. And Bishop Douglass, in his last letter to Acanthos, says it is the opinion of Mr Barnard and [John] Lindow[2] that the Staffordshire priests will soon be schismatics.

The Cardinal then touches on the French Revolution which he deplores as a [calamity than which none greater or more pernicious has ever taken place], on account of that democratic fury, [the criminal conspiracies of the people through which the Catholic religion is blasphemed, morals corrupted and the ecclesiastical order exiled, and what further purposes we do not know]. And as Douai College is no more, he strongly recommends the erecting of others in this kingdom. He mentions likewise the desolate condition of the missions in Asia. [The mission in Asia, which was sustained by the seminaries of Paris, is now destitute and begs help]. And therefore the Holy See can never think of leaving [so many Christians on the aforesaid mission bereft of pastors], though indeed the Roman treasury is ill able to provide for all these pressing necessities. I am, dear Uncle, your ever dutiful Nephew, Hen. Rutter.

1. The Northern Brethren's Fund was managed by three officials: a First Superior (Henry Cotes 1739–94), a Second Superior and a Treasurer cum Secretary (Thomas Eyre, 1787–1808). Rutter was elected Second Superior in 1793 in succession to Nicholas Clavering, and First Superior in 1808 in succession to Arthur Storey.
2. Missioner in London.

98. Banister to Rutter — Mowbreck, 12th May 1794

My dear Sir,

I received your last dated 5th inst. last Saturday 10th. The Bishop, you say, thinks it advisable, in case of necessity, to appropriate some part of your Fund-money to his favourite scheme of a college. Last September I mentioned the very same scheme to him of a contribution of £200 out of our Fund, and then, as the stocks were very high, that sum might have been raised with no greater a loss p.a. than £8, that is, about 4s. diminution in each individual Fund-member's annual dividend. Whereas if a voluntary contribution be proposed by subscription, scarce £40 would be raised amongst all the members of our Fund, for we most of us are poor and house-keeping is become excessive dear. I told the two Wilsons, Marmaduke and Robert, and Mr John Lund of this scheme, and the last-named in particular greatly approved of it. Mr Joseph Orrell was not forward for it but Mr John Barrow of Claughton answered me in a letter dated 21st September 1793 as follows:

> I heartily approve of your method regarding the Funds. Something, undoubtedly, ought to be done immediately and effectually. But I fear the rising college will be put into the hands of Gillow and suchlike creatures of Acanthos. If this should be the case, I will oppose with all my might, zeal and fire, everything done in favour of such. Let the discipline of the college be brought back to its ancient footing. Let no one be concerned with its morals and finances who have had so great a share in the destruction of both at Douai. On these terms I freely consent not only to £200 but to double that sum if necessary, but on no other. You must recollect that Douai, before these disturbances took place, was ruined in its finances, its discipline much decayed, its morals corrupted beyond any former period of time. And you and I and every

other person know at whose door these crimes out to be and are laid. Be cautious therefore how you vote away money before it be secured for its proper purposes. There is more reason for a rigid discipline in England than abroad for obvious reasons.

So far Mr Barrow.

I wrote to Messrs. Dennet and John Orrell about the same time and upon the same subject. The first answered nothing at all in favour of my scheme, but rather impertinently, of which I informed the Bishop. Mr John Orrell wrote to Acanthos himself and told him plainly that he was quite against applying £200 capital of our Fund to the new college, though willing to subscribe, if it will prevent the Beringtonians from establishing a school. To which the Bishop answered in his letter to me dated 3rd October 1793 from Minsteracres:

> How can I tell whether it will certainly defeat any scheme they may have or not. From the above you see plainly that Mr John Orrell will oppose your scheme about the £200. Such opposition will cause a noise and this noise do more harm by far than the £200 will do good. Therefore I wish you to drop that plan about selling the £200. I desire, at least, you will not mention my name in this afair of the £200. I am much inclined to think it will be best to say little or nothing to our Brethren in Lancashire about contributing money towards it, for I have always found this has caused confusion and much talk and done no good at all, but harm, and made almost everyone think he had a right to direct everything, and so many ifs and directions always prevent [impede or embarrass—RB] all undertakings of importance. For whatever is done there still will be many difficulties to surmount and the £200 will not go very far. I only wish you to get them to consent to encourage such an establishment as they can conveniently, and to approve of it that we may not have opposition to the thing itself.

So far our Bishop to me. But he adds in a short postscript: 'Best to leave gifts in Lancashire to everyone's private generosity I believe'.

The last letter that I have received from Monseigneur Acanthen is dated 20th March, with a copy of Cardinal Antonelli's letter enclosed. He wishes to know my opinion, or rather should be glad to see me. As to my opinion, I have long since put him in mind to act as Bishops Challoner and James Talbot did in 1769 and 1770. A large subscription was obtained for building Douai College by Mr Richard Kendall, to whom the bishops above-named gave credentials. 14th December 1793 I wrote as follows:

> as to laymen, I can recollect several, each of whom have riches enough

> to found and furnish a school or college of 20 or 30 . . . but your rich and devout widows are the most to be depended on, and I vehemently exhort you to apply all your rhetoric to their understandings and hearts. When the late Mr Richard Kendall[1] went through the kingdom a begging for the building of Douai College he succeeded to a miracle. Procure one of his temper and address and send him on your important errand and doubt not of great success.

Thus I wrote My Lord Acanthen. I refrained from naming the person whom I could think the fittest to be the Bishop's agent or quester. If Mr Morgan of Preston were one of ours, I can think of no one more proper. If you were not so nearly allied to me, I might probably think you very able to undertake the agency, except that you want a little more intrepidity perhaps. And yet Mr Kendall assured Mr Joseph Bolton that as often as he knocked at the doors of great men, his heart was in trepidation.

I think that what I have written is a sufficient answer to your query. [Judge for yourself], but let not the refusal hinge on you. It seems from what Acanthen writes to me that he is sensible of the prejudices of our Lancashire Brethren against him. And indeed those that voted his ejectment from Douai College on 27th August 1790 on account of his dilapidations, either real or thought so, will not easily vote money into his hands for a new college.

Now, as to the building of a new college in the north. First, the ideas of the Bishop and mine are, I believe, widely different. I should wish for a very plain building, with bare necessaries but he, I suppose, thinks of a far more magnificent edifice. There must be a dormitory and chambers for the noblesse, and a dormitory and chambers for plebeians; a grand refectory; a fine parlour and drawing-room. In short, an elegant superb edifice to which all the gentry and nobility in England of all descriptions will turn out of their way to see and visit, and one or two of the masters or professors will be frequently called on to show the house, the curiosity room, the library, church, refectory, dormitory and chambers of the nobility, &c. For all this was the modern mode at Douai College since its degeneration, which preceded that of France. Then, as to studies and [torn], I should strenuously vote for that which Chaplain in his History of Douay College, 1710, describes as follows:

> I had not an opportunity to be an eye-witness to the order of their studies and the economy of the house, but by the relation I had. Their way of living appeared very edifying and the order of their schools very methodical . . . The progress they make is slow and gradual, and by consequence, must be solid . . . They are obliged to about an hour's devotion every morning and every day in like manner is finished by public prayer.

> Their hours of rising and going to bed are 5 and 9. This college entertains no foreigners yet there are a mixture of English in it; some designed for the church, other persons of figure and plentiful fortunes in their country; some of mean parentage, others of the prime nobility, and yet the discipline of the college runs so that there is not the least distinction observable either in dress, diet or apartment. If there is any preference or partiality, 'tis only when a singular progress in their studies recommends them.
>
> So far the Protestant Chaplain.[2]

In short, I wish us to return to Cardinal Allen's primitive simplicity and poverty. But when I consider these modern times, the mighty tide of riches and wealth which perpetually flows into this nation, the improvements made in all arts, liberal and mechanic, the fashionable mode of education, the run of taste, &c., I am not so ready to condemn our Bishop's ideas and schemes of a new Douai College in the wilds of Northumberland.

I may possibly write to you again in a short time. I remain, Your most affectionate Uncle R. Banister

1. A missioner in London and Dean of the Chapter. In his will of 1780 he left to his bishop 'a plan of my dear Alma Mater [which is] to be kept in view'.
2. See No. 95n; Banister misdates the book.

99. Rutter to Banister — Minsteracres, 31st May 1794

Dear Uncle

I return you many thanks for the favour of your letter dated 12th May which I received in due time. In my last I mentioned the Bishop's journey to Lartington; I shall now proceed to inform you of the result of that meeting.

After some shuffling on the part of the Bishop, it was agreed to draw up a short Memorial stating to the public the necessity of entering into a liberal subscription in order to found a new college here in England in consequence of our foreign ones being destroyed in France. And this college was to be not solely for ecclesiastics but on a plan similar to that at Douai, and to be under the 3 bishops, Walmesley, Gibson and Douglass, and in the Bishopric of Durham. A copy of this Memorial was accordingly sent to the 2 bishops for their approbation in order afterwards to be printed. But Bishop Douglass, as I am informed, objected to Mr Walmesley interfering in it and wished for a little time in order to deliberate on an affair of so great importance. When Acanthos last heard from him he had not come to any determination and, it seemed to me from the general tenor of his letter, that he did not enter cordially into the views of our Prelate. He speaks in favour of Old Hall Green, which he wishes to become a classical school and to have the approbation of the bishops, though at the same time he pretends that it is not to clash with the general college. How the business will be finally settled between the 2 bishops I know not.

The great disadvantage our Bishop laboured under was in having no fixed place of his own to recommend, but Providence has now provided him with one, contrary to my expectation. The place I mean is Tudhoe School, which Sir John Lawson has made over to the clergy, and which happened very unexpectedly in the following manner. Mr Eyre and I accompanied the Bishop from Minsteracres to Durham, and there being informed that Sir John was to dine at Tudhoe the day following, we agreed to wait upon him having previously prepared the business with Mr Storey. We went accordingly in a chaise the next day, although the Bishop was a good deal indisposed. After dinner, Sir John, in a very handsome manner, informed his Lordship that he was now willing to make over the place to him in conjunction with Mr Thomas Eyre and Arthur Storey, and that he might from that day look upon the school as his own. You may easily imagine how rejoiced the Bishop was at this unexpected presentation, which he had long wished for and which sets him on a level with Mr Douglass, if not above him. For I believe Tudhoe School to be superior to that at Old Hall Green, and that with the additions made to it both in land and building since you were there, it may become a complete little college if put under proper regulations.

Now, as for a general college on the plan of Douai, his Lordship seems to think our farm a very eligible situation, which lies about a mile and a half from Durham on the Great North Road as you go to Tudhoe. But others think it too much exposed to public view as likewise too near the town. There is another farm adjoining to our premises which is now to be disposed of and which, being less public, appears to me less objectionable, and it is now in contemplation to purchase it with a view of building there in case the clergy should approve the situation for a new Douai College. In the interim it is the Bishop's design (at least it was so when I left him on the 23rd inst.) to assemble the refugee students at Tudhoe and to bring an architect with him from York to see what alterations can be made for that purpose. The misfortune of it is that they cannot so properly add to the present building unless old [William] Salvin[1] would part with a small field adjoining to it which he will not hear of. But this favour would easily be obtained of the son [William Thomas] if it were in his power. However, I cannot but regret that Crook Hall is abandoned and that the Douatians instead of being assembled there are to be crowded together at Tudhoe School which at present is far too small to receive them. Besides, as it was merely calculated for little boys, it must either undergo a total regeneration or there will be a strange mixture and confusion. I hope, therefore, the Bishop, upon more mature deliberation, will adopt a better plan such as you may suggest to him by taking Crook or some other place for the present.

He set off from Durham last Monday with Mr Eyre to go to York as Sir John Lawson had desired, it being the Spring Meeting there. But I do not find for certain that any immediate subscription is to be entered upon amongst the gentry, but only that Sir John is to prepare the way for it amongst his acquaintance such as Riddell, Clifton, &c. and afterwards, I suppose, an Address is to be sent to them as well as to every priest and congregation. But previously to this, I wish there had been a meeting of the bishops and the heads of the clergy such as you, Messrs. Lonsdale, Eyre, &c. at London, and that a regular plan had been agreed upon concerning this new college and 1. whether we are to have one or wait till the fate of Douai College be ultimately determined on. 2. In case you judged a new college expedient, which is the most eligible situation. 3. On what plan it is to be erected and what persons to inspect the building. 4. What the pension is to be. 5. What the discipline and method of studies &c. In this case, the want of confidence would have been removed, which at present the Brethren in Lancashire and elsewhere entertain in regard of Acanthos, and we should all, both clergy and laity, have been hearty in the cause, each one contributing his mite according to his ability.

I once heard you mention Mr [George] Chamberlayne[2] as a proper person to be President at Douai; he certainly should have my vote as to this new college because I know of none more likely to reconcile all parties. As to the pension, it appears to me that £30 p.a. will not be too much if clothes be included, as certainly they ought to be in order to preserve uniformity. For the experiences of other schools such as Old Hall Green and Tudhoe amount to more, as I am well informed. Indeed, the original pension at Douai College, I believe, was £5 p.a. at a time when the price of provisions was twice as low as at present. Pray excuse my inpertinence in writing my sentiments so freely.

The last letter from Hilton solely regards the Roman College where the bishops wished to place an English President.[3] But this their request was not acceded to and the reasons alleged are somewhat curious, one of which

I recollect is the great expense of travelling in case the Italian climate should disagree with his health. I am, dear Uncle, your obliged and ever dutiful Nephew, Hen. Rutter

1. Of Croxdale Hall, Durham.
2. Son of an Anglican rector in Norfolk; educated at Eton College and at King's College Cambridge where he became a Fellow. He converted to Catholicism in 1778, was ordained at Douai College three years later and appointed chaplain to the Jerningham family at Costessy in Norfolk. His sister married Benjamin Kennicott, canon of Christ Church, Oxford. Dr Johnson was much impressed by Chamberlayne's renunciation of an assured career in the established church. In 1786 James Woodforde dined with Chamberlayne (on fish and rice pudding, it being a Friday) and remarked on his giving up a living of £800 a year. As it was, Chamberlayne left some £5,000 at his death in 1815.
3. See N°. 55 n2.

---

100. Rutter to Banister Minsteracres, 30th September 1794

Dear Uncle

The Bishop has been long and is still in these parts, but I am sorry to say it has been to little purpose, I mean in regard of the establishment of a school. Since my last letter to you on this subject you will have been informed that his Lordship went to London to adjust matters with Bishop Douglass. He travelled in company with Bishop Hay, by whom he was introduced to his former scholar Mr Erskine, the Roman Envoy, whom, he says, he convinced of the propriety of their Lordships' conduct in regard of Committee affairs. From a printed paper addressed to the public you will have learned that the three bishops agreed upon a plan for a general college which was immediately to commence at Tudhoe. Our Bishop accordingly came down again highly pleased, no doubt, that his favourite scheme of a general college in his District was at last brought to bear and expecting, I suppose, that money would flow in upon him from all sides to enable him to put it in execution. But no such thing.

And after being at Tudhoe for some time he became sensible that it would be too small for the reception of 20 or 30 more students, being already nearly full of little boys. The consequence of this was that Bishop Douglass declared off and resolved to keep his own subjects at Old Hall Green according to his first intention. Thus the bishop's plan for a general college falls to the ground a second time. What therefore remains for him to do but still to take a house, which I wish he had done long ago, in order to assemble his own subjects and get forward as well as he can. When I waited upon his Lordship at Tudhoe, I did all I could to push him on to something of this kind in spite of his imaginary difficulties, and we went to examine different places such as Hylton Castle, a noble edifice about 3 miles from Sunderland; to Bishop Middleham and to St Helen's Auckland. This last place, Sir John Lawson actually agreed for with the proprietor, Mr [Ralph] Milbanke,[1] but the Bishop was still irresolute and undetermined what to do, which so disgusted Sir John that he made a tender of the house to the Lierre nuns,[2] who were glad to accept of it and are now established there to their great satisfaction. The Bishop, having put himself out of every other, Crook only remained for him which, at last, though reluctantly, he has been pleased to accede to. Accordingly it is now taken and preparations are making with all speed to open the school as soon as possible, which I suppose will be about the 4th of October. [Let him be proud insofar as he is happy].

I have not heard who is to be President of this establishment. The Gentlemen from Liege, it seems, have not been so long about this business, being already, as I understand, settled at Stonyhurst, which place the Clergy might have had a year ago when the Liegeois had no thought of coming over.[3] But on what footing are or ought these Gentlemen to be? I mean in regard of the Bishop's control. The National Assembly in their Civil Constitution of the Clergy allowed bishops to choose the superiors of seminaries but it was to be in conjunction with their Vicars and by plurality of suffrage. But the ex-Jesuits, I suppose, will not allow our Bishop any influence at all in the choice of superior at Stonyhurst, which, no doubt, partakes of the nature of a seminary because it is to be for young ecclesiastics as well as for others.

The French bishops in answer to this part of the Constitution expressly reject it and say that the bishop himself is to choose the directors of seminaries: [How can he answer to himself for the vigilance and capacity of those he has not chosen? It is an essential part of the jurisdiction]. And the present Pope, in his Brief to the French bishops, is equally strong and express: [Is it not incontestable], says he, [that the bishop is the chief and the first superior of a seminary?][4]. And then he proves it from the Council of Trent, Sep. 23 de Refor. c.18. It is clear, therefore, to me that a bishop may, de jure, inspect and nominate superiors in these houses that are destined for the education of clergymen. But this right inherent in the episcopacy will not be admitted by the Gentlemen of Stonyhurst, nor by many others amongst the gentry and clergy who side with them. One of this number is Milner, which I am much surprised at after all that he has written in favour of bishops. But allowing this right, a second question arises how far it may be expedient to exercise it. Bishop Douglass, in his last letter, is of opinion that at the present juncture they must be left to themselves to pursue their own plans because supported by so powerful a party. But, at any rate, I would have the bishops in England, after the example of those in France, vindicate their right however they may be disposed to forego the exercise of it for the sake of peace and union.

The monks too, in my opinion, have been acting a strange part at their last meeting in choosing one for their Provincial who was lately disordered in his head and another for their Vice President who has distinguished himself so much against the bishops.[5] The friars, I hear, are going to settle at Esh, about 6 miles from Durham and Crook, where there is a large old house belonging to Sir Edward Smith.[6]

I am very desirous of knowing your sentiments on the present state of affairs that I may be better enabled to judge of them myself as well as to advise with others. The Bishop is pleased to ask my opinion sometimes and I give it him as freely. I wish he had you to consult with and to write his letters that he might not expose himself as he does. It seems he has profited little of Mr Barrow's advice on the epistolary style for I believe he is the worst letter-writer in the kingdom.[7]

I am of opinion that the bishops have not yet finally determined on what is to be done and whether each is to have his own respective college or not. The Western Bishop strongly recommends only one general college, and Bishop Douglass wishes to have all the divines at Old Hall Green. Nothing has been subscribed in the south towards this great and necessary undertaking. I am, dear Uncle, your ever dutiful Nephew, H Rutter

1. Not a Catholic.
2. A community of Discalced Carmelite nuns with their chaplain the Rev. James Roby.
3. The ex-Jesuit Liege Academy was given Stonyhurst by Thomas Weld; he also gave a house in Winchester to a community of Franciscan nuns of Bruges and established a community of Cistercian monks on a farm at East Lulworth.
4. Translations in this paragraph are from the French.
5. At the Chapter of 1794 Cuthbert Wilkes was elected Vice President. Bishop Gibson told Bishop Walmesley that he took Wilkes's elevation as 'a direct condemnation of our proceedings' (Clifton Archives, 1794, No. 59). The Provincial of the North elected that year was Richard Lacon. He found being a gentry-chaplain was beginning 'to affect his spirits very much' and left

Brandsby. After a period with his brother at Linley, Shropshire, he was reported to have recovered and was back on the mission at Aberford. (Ibid, 1793, No. 71)

6. Smythe had loaned Acton Burnell Hall in Shropshire to refugee English Benedictines from Douai and Dieulouard but no community took up the offer of Esh Hall.
7. William Gibson's epistolary style was but one problem, for his letters were often illegible and he refused to take a secretary; the clergy spent hours with each other trying to decypher his handwriting. He would live for a further twenty-seven years and, although he eventually accepted the necessity for an assistant, and took Thomas Smith as coadjutor in 1810, the latter was never allowed to help with the administration of the vicariate except to carry out the arduous confirmation tours.

---

101. Banister to Rutter Mowbreck, 26th October 1794

My dear Sir

You write to me very entertaining, pleasant letters, for which I am greatly obliged to you. Mr Melling brought to me half a dozen circular letters signed by the 3 active bishops at London 20th June of this year. Some of our Brethren think our Bishop ought to have followed it, and, with a proper address to the feelings of humanity (to use an expression now almost canonised), made it efficacious and productive. It is at present nothing but a dead letter, yet far more modest than the puff of Mr [William] Cowley[1] at Vernon Hall, a mile from Liverpool, and without the Oscott[2] boast of teaching <u>the most enlightened piety</u>.

Mr Wilson my neighbour thinks that our Bishop did not accept of St. Helen's Auckland because Sir John had hired it, and consequently would have a power or dominion over the school or college in which Acanthos intends to have no partner or competitor. You cannot disapprove his conduct in this. The gentry, the Ex's, the nigri Fratres, &c, all seem to be eager, if not for a total independence, at least for an equal authority and jurisdiction with the bishops and the Vicars Apostolic. I therefore think our bishops are bound to defend and maintain the jus divinum of bishops without regard to any who may be displeased at the exertion of authority. What God has given to bishops he will certainly not suffer to be annulled or made void unless in his wrath he abandon a nation or people like France to apostacy.

The German emperors for several centuries usurped a jurisdiction not belonging to them of giving the investiture of bishoprics, abbeys, &c. by the crosier and cross and ring, notwithstanding the prohibitions and excommunications of many successive popes, yet at length their obstinacy was overcome. Whenever a bishop has a clear and evident right and neglects to maintain it, he is guilty before God of a great and important omission. Whence it follows that our Bishop ought to negative at least the election of superiors and masters of schools and colleges within his District when there appears to him a just cause for doing it. Thus the Bishop of Paris put his negative on Dr Joseph Strickland[3] and permitted him not to be President of St Gregory's. Thus Monseigneur Conzie, Bishop of Arras, did not suffer Joseph Berington to publish and preside over his Physical Studies, by which prohibition he was effectively discarded from his professorship. I mention these because well known to me but there are undoubtedly a thousand instances of the same kind.

I sent our Bishop a letter yesterday and told him in short that if he does not restrain the nigri Fratres (and the monks) to their ancient and undisputed places, but permit them to extend their pales, they will become his co-partners and rivals in his Apostolic Vicariate. Their zeal [would be pure] if it stood only in readiness to fly to work when it is called for, but when it is for seizing new lands without call, I apprehend that there is some alloy mixed with it.

You ask me how you are to comport yourself in the present circumstances. As from the past take an observation to the present and future. If your counsels have been attended to and followed even in one minute circumstance, you may then, when asked, presume to give more. But if not even one single particle of your wise counsels, as you certainly judge them to be, hath been embraced and executed, you must then believe that God has not chosen you to suggest wisdom and prudence to the wise and prudent, but that he enlightens and directs them by some other means and ways.

It is a year or more since Monseigneur Acanthos wished me to come to York to deliberate and consult about founding a college. I made my excuses by alleging the season &c but my real motive was because I could say no more at York than what I wrote in my letters. My journey to York would have operated as much as his late journey to London, viz. a zero. He writes too long letters and in too great haste, by consequence they cannot be accurate. I believe they likewise very much resemble his public conduct like being ambiguous and dubious and embarrassed. Mr John Barrow of Claughton has many times said the same of the conduct and letters of his predecessor. There may also be in some of them a finesse purposely affected which, although it may serve men of politics, yet it seems to me unworthy of a prelate. St Francis of Sales never used such worldly arts, either in discourse or letters; he was too much in love with honest candour and simplicity.

I have just received a letter from Mr Barrow of Claughton in which he says: 'I have been informed that the Bishop has altered his plan, place and discipline of it, viz. the college, so often, no one will contribute a farthing to help him while he is at the helm'. And my neighbour Mr Wilson tells me that his brother Marmaduke of Appleton is quite averse to give or contribute anything, because he observes how he connives at the loss or at least at the danger of loss of some monies which we know to have been bequeathed to pious uses. But his brother did so before him. I do not think that any of our Brethren are guilty of embezzlement or alienation of monies, but I think that I may confidently affirm that the clergy in general very unwisely and heedlessly expose their monies to be lost irretrievably and in effect many sums have been lost. You remember too that at one meeting in August 1790, the Brethren with Mr Chadwick, Vicar General, at their head, signed a petition to Bishop Acone [Thomas Talbot] to pray him to procure for Douai College a fit president and to get Mr William Gibson excluded.

All these circumstances, when I reflect on them, grieve me extremely and I am quite puzzled how to answer or alleviate these objections, especially as I know that his ideas of education and mine are not in unison. To assist him, however, I have given information of some Lancashire Funds which are not shipwrecked at Paris: One from Finch Mill estate, near Wrightington Hall. Half a fund of old Mr [William] Winkley, who baptized me at Hesketh Bank in October 1725. £800 of one Ralph Gerard. £500 of Mr [William] Husband, in the hands of Js. Taylor, Deputy Clerk of the Peace at Leigh, and 2 funds of old Mr [John] Elston in the trust of Miles Stapleton, Esqr. There are at least 2 funds in the Bishopric, of which Mr Cotes has the trust; the Withams were upon them at Douai College if I mistake not.[4] A considerable legacy at Rome was on the tapis two years ago: whether it should go to the Old Clergy or to the Liegeois, who strenuously pursued it on a hot scent, for that family, I believe, never hunted coldly. Most of the Propaganda were for the Old Clergy, and if our two bishops Acanthos and Centurien have gained it, so much the better. But as to the old college pension first given by Gregory XIII, I find by a letter of Antonelli to our Bishop, of which he sent me a copy, that we must not look for it any longer. The burden of eastern missions &c. are so great and so numerous, and the revenues of His Holiness are so much diminished, that it is impossible to supply us with remittances from Rome.

Mr Shepherd has at last obtained his dismission from Tudhoe. Our

Bishop first, and soon after Mr Storey, wrote to me to engage Mr Blacoe[5] to succeed him. I answered his Lordship that:

> Mr Blacoe out of pure submission and obedience to you, will go to Tudhoe, but he desires me to make known to your Lordship one request, viz., that when you have ordained him priest (he is only a subdeacon) you will not enjoin him to do missionary duties, either at Newhouse or elsewhere, whilst he is teaching and attending boys at Tudhoe, for he well observes that a young missioner ought to apply himself 6 days in the week in preparing to acquit himself on the Lord's Day, and he is sensible of his inability to do both, viz., of teaching and attending boys and of preparing himself for the functions of the ministry. I was extremely well pleased at his putting me in mind to express to your Lordship this condition on which he is willing to take a trial and to do his best at Tudhoe.

The Bishop in his letter to me writes thus: 'I hope you will give Mr Blacoe some instructions on the great art of teaching young boys'. To which I replied as follows:

> As to to my showing him any way or method or art in teaching boys, I believe he must fortify himself with what I want, viz., an invincible calmness of mind and patience to suffer and endure the inattention, indolence, obstinacy of rude, impertinent, fearless and undaunted patrician boys. I am very much of the opinion of a gallant captain in Dean Swift:
>
> To give a young gentleman right education,
> The Army's the only good school in the nation
>
> especially in time of war. But I apprehend that many who are fearless and undaunted in Umbra Scholae are mere poltroons in praelis. You see the French plebeians fight like heroes in an impious cause and their patricians and nobles are fled like cowardly ignoble peasants.

So far to Acanthos. I can not always bridle although my pen has generally been under due command.

On the 18th of this month a meeting of 23 gentlemen, Mr Fr. Houghton being Chairman and Lord Grey next him, was held to consult on the necessity and propriety of raising a Regiment of Lancashiremen for the defence and safety of the county against both foreign and domestic enemies, but of the latter sort there are not many, 'tis hoped. Near £7,000 was subscribed, your ancient scholar and ward subscribed £300 and is to be a captain. Js. Taylor has sent a circular letter by the high constables of the county to all the clergymen of both communions, Catholic and Protestant, to invite their respective congregations to contribute their pittances for he says

> that it is not the magnitude of the sum subscribed that illustrates the affection of the inhabitants of Lancashire to their king and country but the unanimity of opinion that prevails among all ranks of them, and that the subscription spared from the hands of honest industry, however small, is equal to and will be esteemed as well as those of the largest amount and will equally serve to convince the enemies of this kingdom that the country is united in one heart and one hand in support and defence of the laws and constitution.

It was resolved in the meeting just mentioned that the clergy of the county be requested to allow a subscription paper to be opened in the vestries of their respective churches, chapels and places of public worship. Js. Taylor, the Secretary, therefore has printed and published the foresaid circular letter. The Earl of Derby, though he be Lord Lieutenant of the county, takes no part in this business, nor subscribes a penny as far as I have heard. I have contributed my wig, i.e., a guinea, and therefore must be content to wear the old ones another year.

Times are so hard and every article so dear and taxes and poor rates so great, I am sinking every year and am often in straights. For you must know that I have a long annual rent to pay and an old hall to keep in tenantable repair. I have several times been thinking that if I outlive Mr Lodge I will petition our Bishop to permit me to succeed him. But can you inform me what income there is, whether the house be rent-free, and whether a part of his mission lies in the country or is only in town? I believe I may venture to follow Mr Lodge in the administration of the Soc. of Pen. I am persuaded that he is not of that kind of prophet mentioned by Ezekiel: qui consuunt putrillos sub oi cubits mannii (Ez. c. 13 v. 18).[6]

I am entirely of opinion that your style will be more natural, more clear and perspicacious, more easy and uniform in writing your own conceptions than in translating those of another. Therefore, I advise you to lay aside that translation of which you showed me a specimen, and pursue the life of Jesus Christ forming one, plain, simple and well connected narrative out of the 4 evangelists. Choose for yourself and follow the best harmony or concord of the gospels, but do not break the continuity of your narrative by critical discussions; these ought to be in notes or at the end of a chapter.

I hope they are all well at Ormskirk for I hear nothing to the contrary. Your father, though 7 or 8 years older, is more robust and firm in constitution than I am. This my letter will certainly tire you, I therefore only add that I remain your most affectionate and dear Uncle, R. Banister

1. President General of the English Benedictine Congregation 1794–9.
2. St Mary's College, Oscott, near Birmingham, the seminary for the Midland District, just as Old Hall Green, Ware, served the London District.
3. After taking his doctorate in 1752, he accompanied Thomas Stonor as travelling-tutor on the Grand Tour and became chaplain at Stonor Park in Oxfordshire until his death in 1790.
4. Established for the education of priests; those named here were priests.
5. Robert Blacoe and Joseph Shepherd were Arthur Storey's first assistants at Tudhoe School. Charles Waterton thought Blacoe 'a holy and benevolent priest' and Shepherd 'a very correct disciplinarian'. Shepherd once provoked Waterton into biting him on the calf during a birching. Waterton knew when he was in for it because he noted that Storey always wore an unpowdered flaxen wig to administer the rod. [P. Gosse, *The Squire of Walton Hall* (1940), p.5.]
6. Ronald Knox in his translation of the Old Testament observes that this text in Ezekiel 'remains hopelessly obscure'. Banister does not help to clarify it; he may, of course, have given the wrong reference. Similarly, it is unclear what he means by 'Soc. of Pen.' unless he means pensioners. John Lodge had moved to the secular mission in Durham in 1786 and was now seventy-two years old. Banister was aged sixty-nine but still thinking of moving to another job.

---

102. Rutter to Banister Minsteracres, 18th February 1795

Dear Uncle,

I return to you many thanks for your favour dated 26th October which I ought to have acknowledged before now. If you are desirous of changing your situation and are fond of a town, I most sincerely wish you success at Durham as soon as a vacancy offers there. It is certainly the best place we Clergy have in these two counties and is even double to most of them. According to Mr Cotes' statement it is as follows: In government security £65; from Mr [Basil] Forcer's legacy £25; interest of £250 from William Salvin Esqr., £10; the field opposite the house; the furniture belongs to the house. And the congregation, which is chiefly in the town.[1]

As to Crook, it was opened on St. Teresa, 15th October, Mr Thomas Eyre being appointed President pro tempore. Everything as far as possible according to the Douai plan. The pension 25 guineas exclusive of clothes. The Bishop came from York to give orders at Christmas when the following gentlemen were ordained: Robert Blacoe and John Bell, priests; James Worswick and John Lingard, deacons; Charles Saul, Edward Monks, Thomas Gillow, Richard Thompson, Thomas Penswick, subdeacons. The 4 last had not taken the college oath and the Bishop was at a loss what kind of oath to propose to them. That which they took was merely to serve the mission without any restraining clause to this particular District. But without such a clause, is it not in the power of any priest so ordained after modestly soliciting the bishop's leave to go and serve in another District even though his own bishop refuses him permission? Was not this the very case in regard of Bishop Walton upon his coming on the mission?[2]

I have not heard that anything is agreed upon between the Bishop and the Gentlemen of Stonyhurst. They say little themselves to the Bishop on this head, but (as their method has always been) say a great deal to gentlemen whom they interest in their favour by means, I fear not always justifiable. I have seen Mr [Marmaduke] Stone's[3] letter to the Bishop desiring him to approve of his establishment at Stonyhurst and the Bishop's answer which I will transcribe because it has been, I find, a good deal misrepresented. The Bishop, after giving Mr Stone &c. faculties (though not so extensive as was desired) concludes his letter with a compliment and then adds a p.s. as long as the letter itself, as follows:

> As to your desiring me to approve of your establishment at Stonyhurst: as I do not know the rules of it, nor on what footing you wish to have it, I shall defer saying anything on that head till another time, or till I have the pleasure of seeing you. I shall only observe to you that I most sincerely wish that all may be fixed on the most firm basis of peace and union which I have reason to hope for from your good dispositions and those of the other gentlemen with you and that the rules of ecclesiastical discipline may be our guide in an affair of such importance both in relation to those who preside over such an establishment and the studies pursued in it.

I have transcribed this because it has been strangely misrepresented as if the Bishop had thrown out some suspicions on the doctine of Exes, and in this light it was represented to Sir John Lawson as Mr Nicholas Clavering assured me.

Mr Mather, alias Flint, alias Makepeace, left Yarm some time ago and took refuge at Minsteracres. He was very kind to Mr Silvertop when on his travels, who therefore now keeps him at Stella until the Bishop is pleased to employ him. Why the Bishop has not employed him since his leaving Mr Meynell though after repeated solicitations, I know not, but I am very sure that this has preyed more on the old man than when he was obliged to leave Mesnil le roi[4] and to fly for his life from his persecutors. He may probably succeed Mr Thomas Story at Hexham who was taken off very suddenly at midnight on the 2nd inst. after supping with Sir John Lawson at Newcastle.[5] He had just repaired his house and finished a handsome, elegant chapel, and were I to consult my own ease and convenience I should certainly wish to succeed to him, although the fund is not above £45 p.a., but I have not applied to the Bishop for it because I am pretty certain he would not grant my request.

I am Mr Story's executor and I wish to know whether after all his debts &c are discharged I am entitled to any recompense in consideration of any trouble and labour? For nothing of this kind is mentioned in his will. He wills that '£26 be given for Masses to be said as soon as can be' for his intentions. I ask whether this is sufficiently complied with if Mr Story's successor at Hexham undertakes to say these Masses, or rather will it not be necessary to sell off his effects in order to raise the said money immediately and so distribute it as soon as possible amongst the Brethren. In which case the house will be stripped naked of all furniture, but the testator will sooner enjoy the benefit of prayers.

In regard of Crook, a considerable debt has been incurred, I believe to the amount at least of £400, and when the Bishop was here there was no prospect of its being discharged, especially as his Lordship was unwilling to urge the business of subscription any further either with gentlemen or the public at large. In this distressed situation of Crook, Mr Silvertop and Sir John Lawson came forward to its assistance and not only liberally subscribed themselves but earnestly and effectually recommended the same to all their numerous acquaintance. In short the business was going on prosperously as follows: Sir John, £100; Mr Silvertop, do.; Mr [Henry] Maire, do.; Mr [Henry] Errington do.; Mr [Ralph] Riddell, do. When behold! a cold, ambiguous letter is sent by his Lordship to Mr Silvertop and Sir John, evidently calculated to undo all that had been done, or that was likely to be done, for the new college.

The case appears to be this: the Bishop wishes (though he does not plainly say it) that all subscription money should be placed immediately in his own hands, while everybody else, both clergy and laity, wish to have two other respectable clergymen concerned along with him. Mr Silvertop, who has lately seen Sir John on this business, assures me that it is not Sir John's aim to have the disposal of this money himself, but only that the Bishop should not have the sole and entire direction of it without the concurrence of 2 other clergymen. And one of his reasons is because he finds that this is the general sentiment of all in Lancashire. If the Bishop will accede to this (and what can be more reasonable) the subscription may still go on, but if he is resolved to have all the money solely in his own name, I am fully persuaded there will be an end of the business and that he will never get forward in his undertaking. I am really sorry that the Bishop should disoblige by his way of acting [towards] some of his best friends and stop the current of public liberality when it had just begun to flow. I mean to send by next post a long letter to his Lordship to inform him of the real state of the business as far as I am acquainted with it, and wish you would do the same so what you write will have great weight.

I began this letter a long time ago and must now finish it by subscribing myself your ever dutiful and affectionate Nephew, Hen. Rutter

1. Basil Forcer of Harberhouse, Durham, died in 1782 the last of his family; William Salvin of Croxdale, still alive.
2. An oath was taken by all clerical alumni of Douai College which bound them to obey the college rules; not to join any religious order; and to repair to the English mission when required to do so. (Harris 144)
3. President of Liege Academy 1790–4 and then of Stonyhurst College 1794–1817.
4. Mather's dismissal from the mission at Yarm may not be unconnected with his lapse from Jacobitism (see N$^{o.}$ 93) and Meynell's continued attachment to the cause.
5. Story had been so scared at being accosted by some ladies of the night that he dropped dead on reaching his lodgings.

---

103. Banister to Rutter — Mowbreck, 13th March 1795

My dearest Sir

I received your letter last Sunday; it came 3 or 4 days later than it ought because you put in the superscription Preston instead of Kirkham; remember this.

Mr Lodge is not more than 3 years older than myself, so if he die of old age I shall have a very just reason to say with Holy Job: [daily I look for my deliverance. Job 14, 14]. At Candlemas 1800 my lease of this farm expires. I give £16 16s. to the proprietors p.a. for it. The poor taxes and high constable taxes amount yearly to £2.13.6d; the highway tax to 19s.6d;

window money £3.2s; repairs uncertain but at least 18s; land tax &c 10s: total £24.19.0d. Per contra, the money I have raised from this farm the last year is about £5; then it supplies us with butter, milk, cheese, and all sorts of vegetables from the garden which, if bought in from the market, would probably amount to £10 a year as my family consists of a housekeeper, and a man and maidservant, and a guest from time to time, as lately I took into my house near 3 weeks a man, able indeed to walk, but entirely disabled either to feed or dress himself.

To support all these expensive burdens and to keep pace with the continual increase of the price of all commodities: malt, wine, butcher's meat, flour, salt, candles, soap, &c., would be impossible to me if I had not received in the year 1793 about 11 or 12 guineas extraordinary; and in the last year a legacy of 9 guineas and from our Bishop 6 guineas before Christmas from Bishop Petre's legacy, as I imagine, though he did not make the least mention of the source from whence he drew his beneficence.

After reading this you will perhaps begin to think that quitting Minsteracres for Hexham and £45 p.a. will not be consulting your own ease and convenience. I do not think that you have as yet learned with St Paul: abundere et egere. For there seems to be no indigence at Minsteracres. Pray stay where you are until I want you, either here or when I am translated to Durham. If God is pleased to take me out of this life after a short illness, I shall not need your succour, you will only have the trouble of collecting the remnants of a small fortune. But if I should be like Mr [Adam Francis] Cliffe[1] or like Mr Ashmall, you will be in God my only staff of old age and infirmity.

You will be entitled to a full indemnification of all costs and charges sustained by you in the execution of Mr Story's will, but nothing more unless it be bequeathed to you in his last will or in some writing signed by him. He wills that '£26 be given for Masses to be said as soon as can be for his intentions'; it is very possible from those words <u>for his intentions</u> that, in his scrupulous apprehension, he imagined he was in debt for many omissions of Masses. You ask me 'will it not rather be necessary to sell off his effects in order to raise the said money immediately and to distribute it as soon as possible among the Brethren. In which case, the house will be stripped of all furniture'. From which words I conclude that he has left little or no ready money, or bills equivalent to cash, for if he had, there would be no need of stripping the house. Wherefore I think your best method will be to defer a little while until the Bishop has appointed a successor. If the successor chooses to take the furniture at a just valuation, let him take it, but for ready money, and if he chooses to say ten or twenty

Masses at half a crown each, you may indulge him in that, for if he say 5 a week then he will acquit them in one month. £26 is equal to 208 half crowns; if you are certain that the furniture and whatever else he has left will both pay all debts and all your necessary expenses, and completely and fully yield 208 half crowns, then in that case I would write to such priests in my neighbourhood in Bishopric and Northumberland, whom I know are punctual and not overdone with intentions, and desire them to say as soon as possible 20 Masses at half a crown each and which you will remit to them as soon as money can be raised from Mr Thomas Story's effects. But see that you do not over-run your mark. You may perhaps very safely venture to send to 4 and be yourself a 5th. Thus one hundred will be presently discharged. I leave the rest to your own discretion or you may consult the Bishop.

I am indeed convinced in my mind that our Bishop's cold, ambiguous letter to Mr Silvertop and Sir John proceeded, as you surmise, from his wishes and desire that all the subscription money should be placed uncontrollably in his own hands. It was his wish at Douai College, and Mr Varley with a deal of ado, as he told me at London in September 1792, procured it to be vested in 3, of which the Bishop is one, John Daniel another, the 3rd I remember not. At the time just specified, Mr Varley produced the securities which our Bishop signed and I also as witness thereof. I believe Sir John has expressed the true sentiments of all our Brethren in this county, I mean of the prudent and intelligent; as to our giddy, gay gentlemen, I make no account of them. I have begun again to propose to some of our Brethren a tender to our Bishop of £200 out of our General Fund for the establishment of his new college, but doubtless they will agree to give nothing if the Bishop is to be the sole economist and steward of it: they too well remember the economy of Douai College.

You wish me to write to him on the subject, but I choose rather to leave that task to others. I have two or three other topics to discuss and lay before him, not indeed with any hope of success, but merely that I may bear witness of my own sentiments and of some others of the Brethren: 1. Concerning the discipline of the house. 2. That it ought to be a seminary for none but those who intend or are designed to be ecclesiastics. 3. To eliminate all French doctrines, and the French language, too, it being a key to all their impious errors.

I am almost sick in reading at the end of the new Directory[2] the puffs that are so copiously announced from every school or academy by the undertakers. They very much resemble the Greeks at Rome in the time of Juvenal boasting to teach every art and science: grammar, rhetoric, painting, wrestling, fortune-telling, magic, &c. Juvenal Sat. 3 v 76. What will you think if I make a puff in Coghlan's next directory, not in the usual style but as follows:

Mowbreck Hall, near Kirkham, Lancashire.

> The Rev. Mr Robert Banister will undertake the education of four boys, only twelve years old or under, to teach them to be ignorantly learned and learnedly ignorant. His plan is also to learn himself whilst he teaches others to be tractable and docile, dutiful and obedient, to be firm in Catholic faith and to live according to its holy precepts and maxims. To learn every day by heart some sentences out of the Holy Gospels, or out of the books of wisdom, to become a fruitful seed in the hearts of young boys. He will not suffer them to read any sort of magazine or other profane works as plays, novels, romances and the like, but the Holy Scriptures, Instructions of Youth, Saints' Lives and the like only. 15 guineas per annum; 6 to be advanced at their coming, the rest in the 11th or 12th month.

You ask me whether those who have taken an oath to serve the mission without any restraining clause to this particular District may not, after modestly soliciting the Bishop's leave, go and serve in another District, even though his own bishop refuses him permission? Reply: affirmative. How can the bishop refuse to give his consent unless he be in extreme want of labourers? Consult some canonist on this subject; you will find that priests ordained ex gratia by the Bishop of Arras or Paris or Rouen passing from their respective dioceses into others without censure or blame. Observe how the ancient Irish saints left both their dioceses and their native country; in our times, how many ordained priests from the plough or the anvil and sent to begin their latin grammar, have remained in France, become curates, vicars, chaplains, etc. We sold our liberty at Douai College for a very small consideration by living a few years on the Pope's pension. I even disapprove of the oath they have taken at Crook Hall. The promise they make in the hands of the bishop at their ordination—[Do you promise reverence and obedience to me?]. Promise is abundantly sufficient if they be taught, as they ought to be, the true interior spirit of an ecclesiastic.

Our Bishop's postscript to Mr Stone, which you have transcribed and sent me, is in a style very superior to his ordinary letters. He signified to me before Christmas that it was rumoured about that he disapproved of their doctrine. Undoubtedly he disapproves of their doctrine in all those points in which they differ from our Douai College dictates, but not as to think of or meditate any condemnation or censure of them unless they revive their old condemned propositions taught by their Fathers Gobat, Tanburning [?] and many others. He will not suffer them, I hope, to put into their catechism as they did at St. Omers, the absolute sufficiency of attrition.

I heard last night that Daniel and his professors and scholars landed in England.[3] I wish they would continue their Doullens discipline, rigour and confinement at Crook Hall, but such wishes are in vain. Liberty and Equality, says Mr Wilson my neighbour, universally persuade all minds and hearts in the same manner as the genial warmth as Spring excites and animates all nature both animal and vegetable on earth, sea and heaven.

I have been lately pleasing myself with a conceit to get my picture drawn and in such a manner as to express very emphatically my sentiments and marked disapprobation of the doctrine and errors so lately diffused amongst us. I may perhaps send you my scheme, but rudely designed. Your affectionate uncle, R. Banister

1. Cliffe was aged seventy-one when he died in 1799 at Great Singleton, one of Banister's neighbours. Ashmall would die in 1798 aged ninety-eight, assisted at Newhouse, Esh, in his last three years by John Yates, his successor.
2. James Peter Coghlan, publisher, probably a native of Preston, set up as a printer and publisher in London around 1760. He took over James Marmaduke's *The Laity's Directory*, and issued it annually from 1773 to his death in 1800.
3. Despite their privations the imprisoned students had continued their studies in Doullens and after their return to the town of Douai in November 1794 they resumed something of an academic life in the ruined Irish College. Dr G. Stapleton negotiated the release of the Omerian students and the Douatians, and on 2 March 1795 a group of almost one hundred landed at Dover.

104. Rutter to Banister — Minsteracres, 28th June 1795

My dear Uncle,

I arrived here last night safe and sound, thank God, after a journey of between 3 and 400 miles. I have this day been visiting my old blind man, who is about to make a much longer journey, I mean to the other world, which I pray he may be fit for. It is well I did not take York in my way home, as I should have found neither the Bishop or Mr Daniel there; for, behold, they are both in these parts, but nothing is yet finally settled in regard of the general college, the 2 bishops still pulling different ways and striving to have it in their respective Districts.

Thorp Arch[1] being rejected in the north, Mr Gregory Stapleton went back to find a suitable place in the south, but no such place could be found. Upon this it was resolved to begin at least a grammar school at Old Hall Green under the direction of Mr Stapleton. But soon after, at a meeting at the Castle, Bishop Douglass, Barnard, Milner &c., being present, it was determined that instead of a grammar school the general college should be established there, the bishop being willing to give up the premises for that purpose and, moreover, engaging that in case they returned to Douai, he would refund one half of the expense they would now be at in making suitable additions and accommodations.

Mr Daniel, however, who is decidedly in favour of the north, thought that Tudhoe (which is now given up by Sir John into the hands of the clergy) and Crook joined together might perhaps be an equivalent to the proposals of Mr Douglass and, in company with our Bishop, came to examine them. Nay, he had formally accepted of the presidentship at Crook, Mr Eyre resigning it into his hands, as he understood it to be Mr Daniel's wish. But this was scarcely agreed upon when, behold, Mr Gregory Stapleton comes posting down from London with a bullying letter from Bishop Douglass to Mr Daniel stating that while Bishop Gibson and some of his clergy were for the north, Bishop Walmesley and his clergy, Bishop Berington and his clergy, Bishop Douglass and his clergy, were for the south, besides Monsr. Erskine who had urged the matter very strenuously and, I conjecture, at the solicitation of Lord Petre or Bishop Berington or, perhaps, Gregory Stapleton himself.

Mr Daniel, in consequence of the above letter, the contents of which he discovers only to one or two, desires now to be considered no longer as President of Crook but only as a stranger, and proposes, I believe, to set out for London in a day or two. I called upon him yesterday in my return home but could get little from him except that nothing was as yet agreed upon and that as to himself he wished it to be in the north. The above intelligence I received from Mr [Thomas] Smith who is intimate with both parties. Upon the whole it is a curious piece of business. But I wish to know what Erskine has to do in this affair, as I have heard he was not to meddle with anything of an ecclesiastical nature.

As to the objections brought against the north, I have heard of none except that some of our very refined Douatians are afraid of children spoiling their accent in these parts. This is a weighty objection, to be sure, but I should hope it might be got over if they considered that housekeeping is at least one fifth in the north and that the proximity of Old Hall Green to the metropolis must render it a very improper situation for a great general college where young men are prepared for the ministry.

Bishop Berington, it is said, will not consent to unite with the bishops if the general college be fixed in the north, but if in the south he will then use his interest with the gentry in its favour and make over to it the money already subscribed for Oscott, which is between 4 and 500 pounds p.a. for 4 years. Mr Daniel, as President of Douai College, supposes that wherever he is, Douai College will follow him, but I understand that he is threatened with a dismissal unless he accedes to the above southern plan and that he will have nothing to do with the pensions.

Mr Fletcher is fixed at Hexham, Mr [James] Worswick at Newcastle and Yates at Newhouse, so that all places are full.

I found my father and mother and all my relations in good health and spirits. My father enquired very kindly after you and wishes to be on better terms with you in the eye of the world and that either you would go to see him, or he you. I sincerely wish my brother Thomas may succeed in his courtship, as the young woman whom he pays his addresses to has been well educated, is a good Catholic and has a decent fortune.

At Swinnerton I met with a person whom I had long wished to be acquainted with on account of her singular piety and charity, I mean Mrs Heneage, but the Esqr. was not at home, being gone to Buxton for his health. I called upon him there in company with his chaplain Mr [John] Howell, who conducted me as far as Sheffield. I must needs likewise stay a night at Harrogate to see the fashion of the place and drink its stinking waters. I accidentally met with Miles Stapleton at Catterick [torn] who is much recovered of his late indisposition and kindly enquired after you. I passed [torn] in his return from Crook, but did not know it till after.

Please excuse this hasty letter and believe me with all affection and respect, your ever dutiful Nephew, Hen. Rutter

1. Near Wetherby where there was a disused mansion.
2. He was the secular missioner in Newcastle for forty-eight years and worked ceaselessly along both banks of the Tyne singlehandedly for much of that time. The street in which St Andrew's stands was named after him.

105. Rutter to Banister Minsteracres, 16th July 1795

My dear Uncle,

I wrote to you on my return home to give you some information how affairs were going on in these parts. I believe my information was accurate and from it you will have learned that the business of the college is still undecided. All agree that an establishment of this kind, on which the good of so many souls depends, is an object of the first importance and necessity; but where to fix it is the point. The three Apostolical Vicars in their address to the Catholic body last year recommended the County of Durham as an 'eligible situation for such an undertaking for cheapness of fuel and provisions, healthiness of climate and other considerations'. And these reasons weigh equally with Mr Daniel for preferring the north to the south. But Bishop Berington, Mr Gregory Stapleton and Erskine have, it seems, adopted a different plan and Old Hall Green must be the place without assigning any reason of preference.

I am aware that some object to the north merely on account of Bishop Gibson, but such persons would do well to consider that the college is not to be under his control but solely under that of the President and the Propaganda as at Douai. Besides, Bishop Gibson is not to live for ever. But how much does pique and passion blind people! For my part the more I consider the business without any regard to party or prejudice, the stronger is my conviction in favour of the north. For: 1. The cheapness of house-keeping in these parts will be found upon calculation to make the difference of at least £5 p.a. to each individual. 2. There is a greater number of priests from this District than from the south. 3. The proximity of Old Hall to London must occasion endless visiting and dissipation &c. 4. The ex-Jesuits, the Friars and the Monks have established themselves in the north, a certain proof that they consider it an eligible situation.

Bishop Douglass indeed says that the major part of the clergy, even in the north, are decidedly in favour of the south and on this he lays great stress. But I believe the contrary is the truth and I wish to make it appear, by signing an Address for this purpose, in favour of this District, which perhaps may have some weight with Erskine himself. Wherefore it is my intention to call a meeting of the Brethren here with the view of choosing a First Superior,[1] but principally to obtain their signatures to an Address of this nature, which I trust you will draw up for me and send me as soon as possible. A strong remonstrance might perhaps prevent many from being duped by Mr Gregory's finesse or frightened by Erskine's pretended power, and might open the eyes of others who vote for the south without considering why or wherefore except that it is in opposition to Bishop Gibson.

I think I told you in my last that Douai College was transplanted to Crook for the present with the hearty consent and approbation of Mr Daniel, who had taken possession. But, in consequence of Mr Gregory's manouevres, he decamped a few days afterwards and is now in the south. I should not be surprised if Mr Gregory, before his return there, pays a visit to some of the Brethren in Lancashire to reconcile them to his measures.

Since I began this letter I find it reported that the above two gentlemen are jointly proclaimed Head-Superiors at Old Hall Green. If you think proper to proceed with the above mentioned Address or Remonstrance, it might be signed by the Brethren in these parts and Yorkshire first, and afterwards sent back into Lancashire for the same purpose. But if you think all opposition fruitless, I shall immediately desist and content myself with praying to the Lord that he may build the house wherever he pleases that it should be built.

I beg you will authorise me in your next letter to ask Mr Eyre for the manuscripts which you sent to him relative to the oath. Dear Uncle, your ever dutiful Nephew, Hen. Rutter

1. Of the Northern Brethren's Fund consequent on the death of John Cotes in 1794 and that of his successor Thomas Story within the year.

---

106. Banister to Rutter — Mowbreck, 23rd July 1795

My dear Sir,

I received your two letters, one dated 28th June, the other dated 16th July, last Monday 20th July. I hope the enclosed[1] will be time enough to answer your design. I lay a great stress on the number of Catholics in this District; the great number of Clergy, ex-Jesuits, Monks and Friars, all born in this District and now spread over the kingdom. Colleges would be almost destitute without recruits from this county alone. I own that before your last roused my attention, I never viewed the propriety and necessity of a college in the north in the same light. I am now intuitively convinced, as far as intuition can go in congentibus, that we ought to have a college in our own centre. And I do not entertain a doubt of its flourishing, unless our Bishop, by his sublimity and ideas of grandeur, deranged it. I really surmise that in his notion a college without Lords and Squires is a very mean sordid business, for which reason I put in the second resolve, but limited by a proviso, as you will see.

In the year 1792 or 1793, I am not absolutely certain, I wrote a Latin letter to Cardinal Antonelli for the two Vicars, Gibson and Douglass, in which they declare their full and firm resolve to form a college in the north and specify Durham city. Do not disclose this, nor utter a word of the last resolve, if you fear any consequence to my prejudice, for I am designing to visit his Lordship, as is his wish, the beginning of next month. But I know not how to proceed either in advising or advancing anything material.

Please to present to Mr Thomas Eyre my most affectionate love and service and tell him that I desire he will be so good as to deliver to you for me all those writings which I sent to our late Bishop and to him concerning the Committee-oath; and also that Memoir which was sent to Cardinal Antonelli after the death of our late Bishop in which there is the character of Charles Berington and some propositions extracted from Joseph Berington. Tell him, moreover, that when I heard that he had resigned his office of President, I was much grieved and displeased. Say that I hope he has resumed it and will not resign it again. I have signified to our Bishop that, without making comparisons, which are often odious, Mr Eyre, our ancient missioner, is the fittest and best qualified to superintend a college. I know him to be a lover of discipline. But how do the mimicks of muchness glorify themselves interiorly and condemn disciplinarians of rigorism and intolerable severity.

My mare is hurt and lame of a leg; if it be not cured I must send for yours. Mine is 17 years old and I was in hopes that he might last my time. But for your part you must live (please God to grant it 'tis my hearty prayer) to bury half a dozen mares or geldings.

If I go to York, I shall not set out before Sunday 2nd of August. Your most affectionate Uncle, R Banister

1. Draft Address—missing. See endorsement at the end of No. 107.

---

107. Rutter to Banister Minsteracres, 21st August 1795

My dear Uncle

I have deferred writing to you not knowing whether you are at Mowbreck or York. This is only to acknowledge the favour of yours dated 23rd July and to thank you for the Address which was enclosed with it. At our meeting on the 12th inst., it was read, approved and signed by all that were present but some of the Brethren, I am sorry to say, did not attend. I then delivered it into Mr Eyre's hands to be forwarded to Lancashire for the same purpose. For Mr Daniel, when at Crook, seemed to approve of our design and is willing to second it at his return into Lancashire. But Mr Eyre did not inform Mr Orrel who was the author of the Address, nor was your signature or those of Mr Wilson and Mr Lund affixed to it. I am told that Messrs. Rigby and Horrabin have been in your parts and reported to their Brethren at London that the Lancashire Clergy were for the south, but I hope it will soon appear that this is not the case.

The young divines at Crook are said to have defended much better than was expected, for it was their first exhibition and the [conditions?] there not the most easy. As you have Mr Daniel and the Bishop with you, I need say no more but remain, dear Uncle, your ever dutiful Nephew, Hen. Rutter

P.S. Mr Eyre has not delivered to me those writings which you sent to him concerning the Committee-oath, nor does he seem inclined so to do. He says you need not be apprehensive of their falling into improper hands.

[Endorsed by Banister: 21st August 1795. The Address to Bishop Gibson for a college in the north signed at a meeting of the Clergy Priests of Northumberland and Bishopric.]

108. Banister to Rutter Mowbreck, 11th September 1795

My dear Sir,

Concerning the Address, the Bishop writes to me from York as follows:

26th August 1795

I was glad, and shall be glad, to receive signatures expressing a wish or opinion that it should be in the north, but I must own I do not like that letter and shall not be pleased to find it has been circulated as it is worded. I do not approve of the manner in which it speaks of the indecision and fluctuation &c. of the bishops, particularly in regard of myself. You and they know well that more than 3 years ago, in consequence of letters from Rome, I proposed to establish a college. No-one seconded it. I afterwards got the consent of the other bishops to begin at Tudhoe on supposition that it was to be signed over to us and scarce one person moved a finger to assist me. All this confusion would have been avoided had they concurred with me. Who, then, was undecided and who fluctuated, not the bishops?

Besides, it has the appearance of an introduction to their taking on themselves, in consequence of the neglect of the bishops, the right of establishing a seminary for the education of ecclesiastics, which seems to be the spirit of the letter. The last resolve or Address to the Bishop to persevere in the sentiments expressed in the letter of 20th June 1794 supposes, when joined to the beginning of the letter, a change of opinion. Now Mr Eyre and Mr Rutter know well that both I and the other bishops expected Tudhoe to be signed over to me and that it was a condio sine qua &c. This is not done yet.

When you wrote some time ago to me about a seminary where the founder or laymen might present a President to the bishops, I seemed to perceive clearly that your nephew had been speaking to you on that subject and wanted to have your opinion to back some notion conceived of such a thing. I hope you did not send such opinion to him or Mr Eyre. I may possibly be mistaken in regard of his having spoken to you, but I have some reason to think it may have been so as much has been said by some concerning these matters. If this be consented to, the Bishop of the District will not have any command over even one student in any college in the whole District &c. Does anyone think that a bishop, for the sake of a few hundred pounds, can agree to place all the foundations, monies, &c. for the education of ecclesiastics through the diocese in such a situation?

In their letters to me no place is mentioned as proper to begin in and go on at. This is the very point that has caused most delays. I suppose they will send the same letter to you and Mr Orrell. I do not wish to see it signed as it is. After having said so much to them, I wonder they would draw it up in that manner. I have told you, and repeat it, Crook is too small for me ever to mention as a place for a college, and Tudhoe is not in my hands.

So far verbatim Episcopus Acanthos. He adds: 'They have begun to build at Old Hall Green and Bishop Douglass has appointed Mr Gregory Stapleton, President'. I answered Bishop Acanthos as follows:

5th September, 1795

My dear good Lord,

I think you should rather attend to the design or intention of the Brethren who sent you an Address from Northumberland and Bishopric than to the mode and manner in which they expressed it. At least I wish you would rather suppress the resentment it seems to have raised than offer your objection to it. A particular meeting was held at Preston on the 25th ult. consisting of about 11 or 12 Brethren, but I was not one of the number. They signed an Address and vote, drawn up in haste by one of them who pompously takes the lead on all occasions, which possibly somebody will send you.

But now I see everything in a very different light, by the information of Mr President Daniel. By his return to England, he is so far from being put out of the power and authority of a President of Douai College that he is rather confirmed in it, and the administration of Pope Gregory XIII's pension is still committed to him. I therefore look upon it as undeniable that Douai College comes over in and with him; that the admission of scholars, the putting them on funds (where he has the nomination) belong to him; that receiving them to the college oath belongs to him; and presenting the alumni to Holy Orders, by virtue of His Holiness's diploma, is still vested in him. You may either examine the ordinandi, as of late years Conzie the Bishop of Arras did, or confide on what the President usually inserted in the presentation: [exonerating your conscience whilst however burdening our own Most Reverend of Douai, we present our alumnus to holy orders] as Monsigr Baglion de la Salle, Bonguize and other bishops actually did.

St Omers College is also, if you will, come over from Artois with Mr Gregory Stapleton but in a very different form, for Gregory Stapleton has not the least power or authority of a President in England in virtue of the Royal Institution. For no power in France either has or can constitute him a president in this notion in all respects like Mr Daniel; and not the least mite of revenue follows him. Bishop Douglass is his sole constituent. But will he, or Mr Gregory, or both together, contend for the Roman pension, or half a moiety, or any moiety of it? It will be, in my thinking, as absurd and frivolous as if Mr Gregory still abiding at St Omers had made a claim of a part of it.

I now can see but one object before you, that is to assist Mr Daniel in buying or farming a spacious house in which he may establish Douai College with its professors, masters, alumni and scholars, under its ancient discipline and the rules of Alexander VII. If His Holiness and the Cardinals of the Propaganda be but duly informed of this sole and single motive of President Daniel's choice of the north: because His Holiness's pension will maintain at least one third more alumni in the north than in any county near London, it will be enough to gain a full approbation of his conduct and choice. But he may justly add that the principal source of secular clergy and catholicity is in these northern counties.

Mr Rutter only stayed with me one night in June last; I read to him part of a letter which I had sent you and in which I spoke of the jus-patronatus of laymen: of colleges and monasteries founded by princes, noblemen, laymen and women, and in consequence thereof, that they sometimes retained a power of interfering in the choice of curates, abbots, presidents, &c. The French kings presented to all bishoprics and royal monasteries and abbeys. A marshal's daughter of St Flines had only one vote of the community, and the king, Louis XV, named her abbess. If a community had permission to choose a regular abbot, they presented 3 to the king who usually, I suppose, named the first.

I am still of the same sentiment, that if 3 or 4 generous laymen should found and endow a college and reserve to themselves a power of nominating one for its President out of 3 presented by the bishop, or by the senior fellows, with authority to visit and see that there are no dilapidations or alienations of revenue, no ill sequel could arise from thence, nor encroachment on episcopal or spiritual authority. I am verily persuaded that if all our Clergy affairs, funds, pensions, &c. had been in the trust of honest laymen, we could not have succeeded worse and might have been far better.

But now, if Douai College, i.e., the Pope's college properly so called, be established in the north, or in the south, east or west, the Pope alone will name and appoint a president of it [2 words illeg.] with the same rights and privileges as he had at Douai, and you or Bishop Douglass will have just the same jurisdiction over him and it (and no more I think) as the Bishop of Arras had and assumed, whilst it existed at Douai. When it was translated to Rheims it was still and was called Douai College, i.e., it had the same government, privileges and rights. The present case is an exact parallel, except that it has not yet found a suitable harbour in its exile; and I see no way of procuring one unless some munificent laymen step forward and purchase and repair an old hall for the occupation of Mr Daniel, his scholars, alumni, masters and professors.

All the Brethren in this county, as far as I can learn from good information, will be ready and willing, as far as their ability and influence extends, to concur to and promote Douai College, i.e., the college of His Holiness, under its own President, having the same power, authority and administration and as independent as formerly at Douai. And although they contend for the northern situation, it is not because they wish to exclude the boys in the south, or elsewhere, from partaking of the Pope's pension nor to make this District paramount to the other 3. Whilst the college remained at Douai, any of the Vicars Apostolic, as well as Bishop Challoner, might have sent us a chapter upon our junketings, feasting, drinking, riding post round the country and other like extravagances, [not authorised but through the venality of the brethren].

[A true copy of the letter to Bishop Gibson].

I have thus sent you two confidential letters. Acanthos, perhaps, has before this time chastised your presumption in charging him and his colleagues with 'fluctuating, indecisive conduct', and for assuming to yourselves a right to establish a seminary, Episcopus negligentibus. He draws a curious sequel from the hypothesis that a layman appoints a President of a college founded and endowed by himself.

Never let my intelligence transpire, for that will do no good and may [hurt?] me much. I am grieved to the heart in seeing so much useless debate, but it has [torn] a mischievous demon haunting the clergy and our small remnants of orthodoxy.

I read my answer to Messrs. Marmaduke and Robert Wilson last Tuesday; they approved of it very much, and the former asserted again and again that all the Brethren in his neighbourhood would be ready to concur in the establishment of Douai College, i.e., as I describe it, independent of either Acanthos or Centuriensis or Hierocaesarea.[1] The ten years government of Douai College under Acanthos will never be forgotten; 'tis that which hurts him as much as anything. As to their being undecided and not knowing what to do, I scarce need to mention that the scholars were sent to Old Hall Green and down again, here and there, to their great and useless expense. Crook is too small; why was it preferred to St Helen's Auckland? [But enough of this].

I desire you to ask Mr Eyre no more for those papers. If he pleases to keep them he is entitled to them from me in gratitude for his bounty to me and to you too. Thank him in my name for the Thesis he has sent me. I have just received it and have not perused it through, but I have seen nothing in it but old orthodox Douai College divinity and principles: [may they live forever and flourish in the minds of all our alumni].

Mr President Daniel says that, in his last conference with Erskine, he seemed to acquiesce to his reasons for fixing Douai College in the north and bid him wait until he heard from him again. Wherefore Mr Daniel returned immediately to Lancashire and is now, and will stay, with his brother the time-maker at Kirkham till Erskine writes.

Mr John Serjeant of Scorton departed this life 31st ult., octogenarian and 50 years a missioner. The Propaganda, with the authority of the Holy See, has directed Bishop Berington to retract publicly his past subscriptions and adherence to the Blue Books &c. and to promise other things. Item. The Blue Books and Oath are condemned, ita Acanthos in his letter of 26th August. Wilkes, says he, is virtually condemned, but I think so notorious an assertor of schismatical writings ought to be proscribed nomination. You will without my leave communicate my answer to Mr Eyre; indeed, I wish to know his sentiments.

I now clearly see that our Saviour's promise to St Clare (I will always protect you) is magnificently verified. Sit nomen ejus benedictum in aeternum.

This moment, 5th September, I received a letter from Mary Hodskinson the nun. She came over with the last 13 to Portsmouth with the baggage of all the community, and arrived in London on 21st inst., where Bishop Douglass received them like a tender father. Two houses near London are in question and they expect daily a final answer. They are in all 39. The

Rouen-clergy would not consent to their coming over for a long time, but their English friends pressed them and the clergy yielded with great regret.

1. Berington's see ipi.

---

109. Rutter to Banister n.d. [November 1795]

My dear Uncle

Yesterday's post brought me intelligence of Mr Lodge's death but, as I was just going to begin Mass, I could not write by the same post to inform you of it. He had been failing for some time past but was expected to have held out a few weeks longer. He departed this life on the 3rd and is now, I trust, in a happier state enjoying the reward of his past labours. For, as far as I knew him either personally or by hearsay, he was a worthy clergyman and most edifyingly exact in the discharge of all pastoral duties.

Now, if you are disposed to quit dear Lancashire and to come and live among our canons at Durham, I hope you will make immediate application to succeed him, unless you have done it already. Our Bishop will doubtless be glad that he has now an opportunity of testifying his regard for you and of rewarding, in some measure, your past services. But I think no time should be lost. I know only of one difficulty in the way and that is the Bishop himself who, tired of his lodgings at York, has been long looking out for some more eligible situation and therefore many are of the opinion that he will go to Durham himself and keep a chaplain to serve the congregation. Sir John Lawson, who is patron of the place, wrote not long ago to Mr Eyre in favour of Mr Nicholas Clavering, the former incumbent, but you will certainly have the preference in case you are willing to come amongst us.

I believe, indeed, that our northern Address if known to be your composition would not be any great recommendation in your favour to his Lordship. His letter to me on that subject was indeed a castigation I did not expect. He tells me there are 'many things' in it which he did not like and that it 'seemed as if we wanted to make a public apology for ourselves by throwing the blame on the bishops'. He then adds: 'I wonder your conscience did not reproach you when you signed it'. I assured him that the object of our Address was solely to support his Lordship and Mr Daniel in favour of an establishment in the north and that I was at a loss to comprehend his meaning. It is, as yet, a perfect secret in these parts who drew up this objectionable Address, and I hope it is so in yours.

His Lordship has been lately confirming both in Yorkshire and Bishopric. I saw him about a week ago at Crook, when he had little to say against our Address, but a good deal against that of the Brethren in Lancashire. The grand business of the college is still in status quo but must soon, I apprehend, be finally settled some way or other, in consequence of the intelligence received lately from Rome through the medium of Erskine, which is that there is only to be one college and that its situation is to be determined by the majority of bishops. In which case I fear we shall not carry our point in favour of the north. The Bishop was at Durham last week and sets off today for London. Mr Eyre at Crook desires his respects to you but, being taken up with his present employment, declines writing because he has nothing to say or propose in this uncertain state of things.

Pray, is it your opinion that the French priests who are employed upon the mission should be admitted into the number of the funded Brethren? Are they admitted [end of page; remainder of letter is missing]

---

110. Banister to Rutter — Mowbreck, 31st January 1796

My dear Sir,

I long since received your letter in which you seem to invite me to Durham; but on consideration I judge it better to stay amongst my old acquaintance than to seek new. The Bishop was here two nights, viz., 16th and 17th of last month and, although he made mention both of Durham and Hornby, he did not offer either to me nor appear to be inclined to take either for himself.[1] As to Hornby, he said it is too little a house for him and another and that he could not take upon himself the care of the congregation in either place. And, as he made no offer to me, I made no motion to him, not so much as by any innuendo. He rather by an innuendo fixed me where I am, telling me that I lived in a palace. But this palace costs me above £20 p.a. so that now, as times go, I am sinking every year and if I live some years I shall bequeath you nothing except woe.

Our Bishop, when he was here, seemed reserved and close with regard to what was said at London in his conferences with Bishop Douglass and the Vatican Sub-deacon. Erskine, however, he told us, acknowledged that he might have a college or a seminary according to the canons and the

Council of Trent for his own District. Upon which he several times said, and with vehemence, that if we had but an acre of land our own, we could build upon it. He rehearsed at large the shuffling tergiversation [and] infraction of promises of Sir John Lawson, on hearing which I did not forbear to call a spade a spade, that is, to call a man by his proper name, the name that he acquires by his behaviour and conduct . . . What can ennoble cowards? Alas not all the blood of all the Howards.

He went from Mowbreck to Mr Brockholes at Claughton, and there Mr Barrow Senior made him a most munificent and regal offer of 5 acres (equal to 10 of statute measure) besides an estate called Buthill of 85 acres. On the first he might begin to build in a most agreeable and healthy situation, and feed and graze cattle on the other for his college, with the charge of keeping a priest for Claughton congregation. Mr Barrow himself sent me in a letter a true and succinct statement of his offer but added this question: Has he resolution enough to do anything? What could I answer, think you? He has written to Mr Daniel and again to me that Bishop Douglass presses him to send a positive and definitive answer whether he will or will not join him in forming a general college, for the building at Old Hall Green is to be made less or more capacious according to his answer. Moreover, our Bishop desires Mr Daniel to collect the sentiments of the Brethren. This is acta agere, for the general opinion of the Brethren in this District is for a college in the north and has been made known sufficiently by Address to him.[2]

Three Douatians arrived at Crook Hall the last week, viz, Thomas and George Haydock, brothers, and Robert Gradwell. I hope the first at least, if not the second, will soon return. If Douai College had continued the first would not have been received by Mr Daniel as he (Mr Daniel) assures me. Mr Fryer soon sent him back from Lisbon. Mr John Lund (who has, I believe, washed them white to our Bishop) long ago told me that the foresaid Haydocks were chiefly in quest of an easy genteel life. With what face or conscience he can recommend them I know not. Perhaps he will assure me when I see him that he has had no hand in promoting them to Crook. Tell Mr Eyre that he must use the most dexterous stratagems to dive into them. But winking, conniving and seeming neither to see, hear or understand the least impertinence or pride or vanity or idleness in them may entice those finesses to come forth more boldly. A pretty white goose would be [taken as a wise magician]. I have sent our Bishop word that the fame of Thomas Haydock is gone out through all this part of the county. What, think you, a monk told me the other day? That Prior [William] Sharrock, now coadjutor,[3] said when asked: why do you take in such? We are like to have some. Is Crook then to be garnished with Anythingarians? You see that one such has left it, [such are these painstaking times!]. Our Bishop had perhaps done better if he had presented to him [a chalice with hemlock] than [a defiled chalice and paten].

Mr Charles Plowden has proved to a demonstration that the Protestation deposited in the Museum is a changeling, not the authentic original. The 4 reporting lawmen look very little.

Four youths are returned from Lisbon College [in the middle or having almost completed the course]. What the cause of their dismission may be I do not know. Perhaps the prevailing spirit of insubordination. Perhaps the discourse and conversation of Tom Haydock may have cast in a leaven. [A little is enough to corrupt the whole]. They are all Lancashire born and bred, viz., [James] Wilkinson, [James] Greenough, [William] Walton and [Anthony] Sparrow.[4]

I do not admire the President of Lisbon College [William Fryer] nor [his] manner of educating and training up workmen for the mission. He sent off Mr Henry Parkinson as soon as he was ordained priest at the age of 23 and one month. At my request our Bishop fixed him with Mr Cliffe, who is unable to do any functions. I procured him admission when he was a boy into the college and am now chosen by himself to be his counsellor and director. He is indeed of a most happy temper, patient and meek, two qualities highly requisite in his situation.

I am so offended at my two young ones, brother and sister, my man and maid, that I sometimes seriously think of giving up housekeeping, but then I cool again and resign myself to endure.

Mr Daniel has just been telling me that a little wine or any other inebriating liquor flushes Tom Haydock instantly and puts him off his guard. And he attributes this to the weakness of his head not to the malice of his heart. Good and simple men invent, I believe, many glosses and excuses for cloaks to hide vice and deformity. If a young Telephus sits by Sappho and gives her frequent sweet kisses, must not a good man judge that it is all holy love and charity, for fear of rash judgement?[5]

I was thinking to ask our Bishop to give you Hornby. 'Tis a house well-furnished, with a garden and croft and good salary. I hear he has placed a Frenchman therein, I presume for an interim only. If Durham is not disposed of, I would have you petition for it for yourself.

Not one of all your family has crossed Ribble this Christmas to come and see me. Indeed I am not very able to entertain guests or to go abroad. I must go to bed soon and lie long. I have had a very teazing cough. I remain your most affectionate uncle, R Banister

1. Hornby was vacant by the death of Thomas Butler, missioner since 1763. John Worswick took over when the French priest (referred to later in the letter) left in 1798.
2. Despite all the talk of an English Douai, Banister had told the bishop on 16 November 1795: '. . . there is no need of coming to any fixed resolution concerning the site of a general college. When peace is made (and that epoch may not be too distant) we can scarcely doubt but the French will agree to restore to British subjects the property which they had and enjoyed in France before the war commenced. In which case Douai College will return to its ancient walls and recover its Paris actions and rents and the arrears too ('tis to be hoped) of interest which at this present date amounts to £7,000 . . . I think it very precipitate to talk of making a general fixed college either here or there, or anywhere in this nation. My neighbour Mr Wilson is constantly of one mind that Douai College will return to its old site.' [Milburn, 53.] Banister never said this to anyone else and it is another example in this correspondence of his wanting to ride every horse in the race. At any rate, if Bishop Gibson was taking into account advice such as this, his temporising over a new college is more easily explained.
3. To Charles Walmesley in the Western District; Telmessus was his see ipi.
4. See M Sharratt *Lisbon College Register 1628–1813* (CRS Vol. 72, 1991).
5. Banister told Eyre on 27 Apr 1797 that he was 'mentally glad' that Thomas Haydock had left Crook Hall.

---

111. Rutter to Banister — Minsteracres, 9th March 1796

Dear Uncle,

I did not receive your favour of 3rd January till 9th February. However I may regret your not coming to Durham on my own account, yet I certainly do not on yours, and believe I should have acted the same as you have done had I been of your age and in your situation. However, if I had experienced the difficulties of housekeeping as you have done, perhaps I might have been of a different opinion and I was willing to think that this consideration might have preponderated with you to leave your present poor place and come to Durham which is so much better. Here you would have been abundantly supplied not only with the necessaries but likewise the comforts of life:

> . . . good food and generous wine.
> These are the rights of age and should be thine.

I thought at least the Bishop might have made you an offer of the place if he did not intend to go there himself. Mr Smith serves Durham for the present, but whether he is to continue there I know not. I think it is probable he will unless wanted by Mr Daniel because he is a great favourite with his Lordship.

As to myself, I frankly own that I am not a proper person for a place of such importance and should form indeed a very striking contrast to the other priest who is there, I mean Mr [Edward] Walsh[1]. He has travelled much and passes for a very agreeable companion; is great with all the prebendaries and constantly one of their parties. In return for which he gives a grand rout once a year to which all the Gentlemen and Ladies are invited, and at his last was honoured with above 90 persons of the first rank and gentility in the neighbourhood.

If Hornby was vacant and offered to me I should prefer it to Durham as far as I can judge at present. But I see not the most distant prospect of either place or of any other because I apprehend the Bishop will not consent to remove me as long as I suit this family, whether it suits me or not. About 2 or 3 years ago I had a mind to change my situation, and as Thropton was about to be vacant, I petitioned for it though a poor place. But the Bishop refused my request and afterwards would not allow Mr Himsworth to change his place in order to keep me more effectually out of it. When Hexham became vacant I signified to his Lordship that I was willing to go there if he thought me a proper person, but he took no notice at all of it. And therefore I gave up all thoughts of a change, especially as I understood from His Lordship that you likewise were averse to it. But if the Bishop was not inclined to consult my inclinations at that time when I flattered myself with enjoying a share in his favour, I have little to expect from him now when I have some reason to think him displeased at my conduct.

In consequence of some houses being disposed of in the Bishopric without his consent and approbation, he wrote me a letter just before he set off for London expressing his disapprobation at what had been done, and this chiefly directed to me as having been, as he thought, 'particularly urgent to have them sold'. He thus goes on:

> I was not consulted nor previously acquainted. You cannot but know that Mr Eyre can only act in quality of agent appointed by the Bishop. Do agents sell houses or lands or deliver up deeds concerning such matters without acquainting those who appoint them? . . . Is not the Bishop bound to look after these matters? I wish you to consider

> what may be the consequence . . . The priests' houses and chapels may be sold, it seems, by the same right. What a precedent? &c.

I did not write an answer to his Lordship till after his return to York. After expressing my sorrow to find him so much displeased at the sale of the said houses, and that the blame should be chiefly thrown on me, I proceed thus:

> But, my Lord, it may be truly said that whatever I might think of the propriety of disposing of these houses, I had as little to do in the business and was as little consulted as your Lordship. The truth is that these houses were long ago to have been sold by order of Mr Cotes and the other Superiors before I came into office and therefore all the blame must rest with them, if there is blame at all. But, my Lord, I am decidedly of opinion that they were perfectly right in wishing to dispose of them and I only regret that they did not then meet with a proper person to purchase them, and for this obvious reason, because old houses are the worst property we can have as bringing in very little and constantly wanting repairs.
>
> Wherefore I see no very great reason for your Lordship lying under any apprehensions lest 'the priests' houses and chapels are going to be sold by the same right'. No, my Lord, I am as little disposed to trench upon your episcopal rights as I am to give up my own. But surely your Lordship will allow the Superiors of the Fund-general to manage their affairs as they may think proper as your predecessors have always done . . . Even the very next house adjoining to Mr Lodge's house and chapel belongs to the Fund, as I can show your Lordship in Mr Cotes' own handwriting . . . However, I should be sorry to do anything in opposition to your Lordship &c.

You will easily see that I was not in the best humour when I wrote the above to his Lordship, and if you think it too harsh, I am willing to soften and apologise for it in my next. I certainly admit that he has a right to look after monies belonging to the mission and wish he had exercised his zeal a little more this way by calling some to account in Lancashire instead of interfering in our Fund-concerns in this part. However, I am ready to allow that his Lordship meant very well in all this and hope that both sides will be satisfied when things are properly explained.

But this is not the first time when he has wrongfully imputed blame to me as one principally concerned when, in fact, I scarce knew what was going on. I have not forgotten his letter to you last August in which he taxes us with the design of

> taking upon ourselves in consequence of the neglect of the bishops the right of establishing a seminary for the education of ecclesiastics and that I wanted to have your opinion to back some notion conceived of such a thing.

What a pretty construction is this on our letter and on our endeavours to serve his cause in the north!

Having said so much in my own defence I must say a word or two in that of Sir John's. For truly I think much may be said *pro* as well as *cont.* I really believe he had a great desire of promoting the public good and that he would have been very serviceable to the Bishop in the execution of his designs if he had been resolute enough to form any and candid enough to explain them. But his Lordship's distrustful and indecisive conduct was sufficient to disgust anyone. But let us come to facts.

Sir John certainly interested himself not a little in finding out a suitable place to receive the students from Doullens. He proposed St Helen's Auckland and afterwards, when Crook was pitched upon, he made application to Mr [George] Baker[2] for it and succeeded. As to Tudhoe, I allow that the Baronet, after promising to make it over to the clergy, delayed some time before he executed his promise by a formal and legal surrender of it. But then, he considered his given word as sufficient until he had made the place a little more complete. For he had not, I believe, quite finished the purchase of some land which was to be added to it. Besides, I recollect that the bishop's new plans of pulling down what had just been built and of making a new wing did not altogether please him at the time.

However, the business is now completely finished, every thing having been signed, sealed and delivered by Sir John to Mr Eyre on the 2nd of this month at Newcastle. Wherefore it is now clergy-property to all intents and purposes, to wit, a good, new, well-furnished house with all conveniences; between 11 and 12 acres of land; pensions for 3 masters at 20 guineas p.a., besides a little fund for taxes, cesses and repairs. After this, let us be grateful for such a present and endeavour to make a proper use of it for God's honour and glory. However, I still doubt whether the Bishop will be satisfied because the deeds were not delivered into his own hands. I hope you and a few more will consult with his Lordship how to put it on a proper footing. I must not forget Sir John's subscription of £100 for the relief of Crook in its greatest distress and, besides, promoting the same amongst his friends.

I am well assured that the Bishop has applied to Rome in order that the

Gentlemen of Stonyhurst may be obliged to study their Divinity in his seminary. This I find is much talked of and reprobated by the Gentlemen.

I remain, dear Uncle, your ever dutiful Nephew, Hen. Rutter

1. The ex-Jesuit missioner in the city.
2. A sympathetic Anglican gentleman of Elemore, Co. Durham.

---

112. Rutter to Banister — Tynemouth, 6th June 1796

Dear Uncle,

I arrived at Tynemouth on Thursday last and am to stay here about 3 weeks. Our family came to this place for a change of air and have allowed me to be of their party, as our chapel at Minsteracres is undergoing some repairs and embellishments, as well as the house. As to my health, it is much the same it was last year when I had the pleasure of seeing you, but I hope bathing will improve it, as I believe it is much recommended in nervous disorders, which are now so generally prevalent. Tynemouth puts me in mind of our old nature spot Hesketh Bank and commands a fine view of all the ships to and from Shields. There are, likewise, the remains of a rich old monastery where Mr Silvertop goes every morning to say his prayers.[1]

Nothing, I believe, has yet been done by the Bishop, nor do I find that anything is likely to be done by him. He leaves to Mr Eyre the labouring oar and does nothing but find fault with all that he can do or say. Indeed, if I had been in Mr Eyre's place, I should have given up my charge long ago, and this, I apprehend, is what his Lordship wished for if we may judge from his letters and his way of acting towards him. Mr Eyre has certainly been long in a most disagreeable situation. Bills come in from all sides and no money to pay them, the Bishop seemingly insensible of his distress, and withholding the small relief that he had in his power to send him, and forbidding him to make application elsewhere for it. 'I do not agree', says he in one of his letters, 'that you should apply to the public to enable you to establish or carry on a college or seminary at Crook or Tudhoe; I never had a thought of giving you any such power'.

As to Tudhoe, I was in hopes, in consequence of its being made over to his Lordship and two other clergymen, that he would have taken it under his protection and patronage and place it on a more respectable footing. I went to York since Easter to try whether I could prevail with his Lordship to do anything of this kind, for I conceived that, whatever plan his Lordship had in view for an ecclesiastical establishment, whether at Douai or in England, that Tudhoe might be made introductory to it, and of public use for the education of youth. But all that I could say signified nothing. The Bishop replied that Tudhoe only 'increased our difficulties', which appears strange to me and utterly inconsistent with all his former declarations. Mr Eyre and Mr Storey wrote a joint letter last week to his Lordship in which they humbly request that he will be pleased to give some directions concerning Tudhoe, assuring him that on their side, they are most ready to second his Lordship in his undertakings. Mr Storey is willing even to give up the presidentship of it, if his Lordship thinks proper, and to confine himself merely to his missionary labours.

As to Crook, the Bishop gives Mr Eyre to understand that it will very shortly be broken up and that then he may go back to Wooler. He gives him hopes, likewise, that the debts at Crook will be paid. The Haydocks are still there and, as I am informed, behave very well. From the character you gave me of them it is well they do not impose on Mr Eyre, for he, like many good men, is, in my humble opinion, liable to imposition.

The Bishop did not appear to be offended at what I had written to him. I said not a word concerning Durham or Hornby, either for you or myself. Mr Smith is fixed at the former place.

Mr George Silvertop[2] is just returned from the Metropolis, but I hear little news. The Cisalpines, I understand, have still their meetings and are not a little sore that Bishop Berington is not confirmed as Vicar Apostolic; he cannot therefore give Holy Orders, &c. I do not find that Erskine is much liked by them for they conceive he has acted a double part. His first object, I believe, in coming over here was of a political nature and, though he has never been formally acknowledged as the Pope's envoy, yet I find he is considered as such by the Corps Diplomatique.

I sometimes hear of my cousin at Haggerston but I do not correspond with her.[3] It is, I am well informed, a most eligible situation in regard of fish and cheapness of provisions. I propose, Deo volente, to make her a visit next year. Pray what is become of your mare which in a former letter you told me was lame? Mine was so at the same time insomuch that I was obliged to part with her and have now got another which I hope will prove equally serviceable. I had almost forgot to tell you that I am lodged here in the same house with His Royal Highness, Prince William of Gloucester, only that we have the better part of the house. I remain, dear Uncle, your ever dutiful Nephew, Hen. Rutter.

1. St Mary's Priory (founded c. 625 AD).
2. John Silvertop's eldest son and heir.
3. Sister Mary Agnes (Hodskinson) of a community of Poor Clares. Sir Carnaby Haggerston loaned them Haggerston Castle as a temporary residence on their expulsion from France and subsequent inability to find a home in the south of England.

---

113. Rutter to Banister Minsteracres, 7th November 1796

Dear Uncle,

Your birthday is just past but not without my often thinking of you and wishing you many returns of it. It is an age since I heard from you and I am at a loss to account for this long silence.

I have enjoyed better health this summer than usual, which I attribute to my bathing at Tynemouth. I did not quit that place without first paying a visit to Jarrow, sanctified by the presence of Venerable Bede. Little remains of the monastery, but they show you Bede's chair in the vestry which bears marks of great antiquity. And likewise his well, about a mile to the west of Jarrow where children that are troubled with any infirmity are frequently dipped.[1]

Since our return home we have never been without some company or other, and amongst other visitors was our good Bishop to give confirmation. He has been here since and in the neighbourhood for about 2 months. As to his plan of buying a piece of land and building a new college (in the present uncertain state of things) it does not seem likely to take place, though he is still perpetually recommending it. I do not know one single person that coincides with him on this subject.

It seems his Lordship had not resolution enough to dismiss Mr Eyre from Crook, though I had reason to believe it from his letters. His strange behaviour to him, as well as his disagreement with Sir John, have produced a coolness in this family, so that Madam and he do not correspond now as formerly. In short, his Lordship, as far as I know, whilst he appears diffident of all, seems to have lost the confidence of all, though none, I believe, are more desirous of promoting the public good. When I consider his present forlorn situation I cannot but ask what is become of his knowledge of the world and of all the maxims of politeness by which he expected to carry the world before him, whereas never Bishop had less influence in enforcing or executing any public undertaking than Acanthos. However, do not imagine from what I have written, either here or in a former letter, that I am one of his opponents, ever ready to carp at and criticise his proceedings as, however exceptionable they may appear, I take no notice of them but profess the greatest respect both for his person and character.

He left Crook last week to go to Durham in order to have an opportunity of seeing young Trevelyan of Netherwitton who, it is said, is going to become a Catholic to the great vexation of his father who, during his stay with him this summer, has had 2 clergymen in his house to dissuade the young man from such a resolution.[2]

Some time ago I had a letter from Sister Mary Agnes at Haggerston to thank me for a pound of tea which I had sent her. I understand she has had but poor health for these 5 or 6 years past, but she was then considerably better and, I hope, will continue so. They cannot, I believe, be in a more plentiful situation than at Haggerston and therefore they have reason to pray for the life of their benefactor, Sir Carnaby, for, should anything happen to him, I am well assured that his brother Mr Thomas Haggerston (who is at present our neighbour) would soon remove there to take up his habitation in the old castle, to which, I believe, he is much attached.

Pray be so kind as to send me the best account you can of the origin of our family of the Banisters. I am no genealogist, but dipping, the other day, into Collin's English Baronetage I found that Richard Hoghton Kt. married Sybil, daughter and heir to Henry de Lea who had great possessions and were owners of the manor of Molington Banister in the county of Chester. He came into possession of this manor in right of Clementina, daughter of Robert Banaster, Baron of Monaton, and wife of William de Lea, who received the same from her father. I found likewise that a daughter of Adam de Hoghton married Sir Thomas, son of Sir Adam Banister Kt. The names Robert and Adam Banaster which are our family names, made me conjecture that possibly we might be descended from that family.

The elder [James] Haydock was to leave Crook on last Saturday to go first to Manchester[3] where his brother was to meet him. He is just returned from a tour into Scotland.

Have you seen Joseph Berington's observations on the late miracles that are said to have been wrought at Ancona. He pays not the least regard to them, nor would he, as he himself declares, if he had been an eyewitness of what is recorded to have happened, and though all his senses should have testified the same, because [it would be] repugnant to the Deity thus to authorise superstition. He announces to the public his grand work on the Rise, Progress and Decline of the Papal Power, to be comprised in 5 vols. quarto. The 2 first almost ready for the press.[4] I am expecting the publication of another history in your parts of a much more useful nature. I mean Mr Daniel's History of England[5], setting forth the falsehoods of Hume and other Protestant historians. Such a work has been long wanted and therefore I hope you encourage him in the undertaking.

We are at present over-run with French priests. 180 landed in this neighbourhood: ten of them are settled within 3 miles of Minsteracres, 20 are to live at Pontop new chapel as soon as it can be got ready for them. They are all of the diocese of Coutance in Normandy. I am for the present their interpreter and do what lies in my power to make them comfortable. The corporation in Newcastle has set on foot a subscription for their relief, but little has yet or is likely to be subscribed.

In a large party, where improper toasts are given, I mean of double meaning, is it a mortal sin to pass them to your next neighbour when at the same time you have no bad intentions or design in so doing? I remain, dear Uncle with all respect, Your ever dutiful Nephew, Hen. Rutter

1. St Paul's (est. 685 AD). The well was near Monkton and, in addition to the practice of individual dipping, a 'large concourse of people . . . used to resort to it on Midsummer Eve, with bonfires, music, dancing and other rural sports . . .' (W. Parson & W White, *History, Directory and Gazeteer of Durham and Northumberland &c.* vol. II (1828).
2. The ancient Catholic estate of Netherwitton was divided between Margaret and Mary, daughters of James Thornton who died in 1745. Margaret married Walter Trevelyan, a staunch Methodist; he required John Cotes, the chaplain, to remove himself and his chapel out of Netherwitton Hall and into an old tower-house at Witton Shields. The conversion of young Trevelyan did not take place; he became instead 'a red-hot Methodistical preacher', and shortly afterwards he closed the chapel altogeher.
3. To become chaplain to John Trafford of Trafford Park.
4. *An Examination of Events termed Miraculous as reported in Letters from Italy* (1796). Bishop Douglass extracted thirteen propositions from Berington's works and invited the author to explain them, which he did in a printed Letter of 25 February 1797. Douglass accepted the letter and told Berington: 'I deem your faith pure and orthodox'. To avoid prejudicing his new credentials, Berington decided not to issue his history of the papacy, and forbade its publication ever.
5. This was eventually published in 1815 as *Ecclesiastical History of the Britons and Saxons.*

114. Banister to Rutter Mowbreck, 23rd November 1796

My dear Sir,

Your affectionate letter dated the 7th I received on Sunday the 13th. I have been a long time in your debt for your letters which I pray you to forgive, my memory has often suggested to me my debt. But either some other letter, writing or other avocation has hindered me and, to tell you the real truth, a little business now is to me a great one. I no longer sit up till 11 or 12 o'clock, nor rise at 5 or 6, and a visit to a sick person is a whole morning's or afternoon's work.

I do not remember so long an interval of mutual letters between the Bishop and myself as these last 3 or 4 months. In fact there is nothing that I can recollect which requires at present any frequent correspondence of letters. In the last but one, dated, or rather sent without date, the beginning of this summer, he writes as follows:

I have not yet settled either Hornby or Durham for certain on account of the uncertain state of our affairs. There are two places to serve at Hornby, viz. Clafton. I fear it would not suit you to go to different places if you should like it. If we should have a college in Lancashire I have had some vague thoughts that it might be a residence for me with another; but in such uncertainties what can be determined on? All stands still because the power of moving is in different persons.

In my answer I neither accepted or refused Hornby, but in very explicit words desired him to send you thither. And as I had, in a foregoing part of my letter, signified to him my strong suspicion of a finesse in one of the Exj's, I said that to free him from the trouble of surmising a finesse in my request, I would candidly declare its end and object, which is that, wishing to retire from missionary duties and to prepare myself for eternity, I could do it with you at Hornby. I presume he has not given you the least hint of this either by letter or during his stay at Mr Silvertop's. I believe it may be best to make no mention of it.

You wish, I suppose, to be emancipated because while you live in a family you seem to yourself to carry a chain. But on the other hand, reflect that you have nothing to do with house-keeping, no rents to pay, no servants' wages to find, nor a thousand other articles to distract you. If company and visitors do not fill your head too much with unprofitable narratives and rumours, you may retire to your garret and shut out all distractions, perplexities and anxieties and solicitudes, and pursue your meditations and studies without interruption. In a former letter I told you that old friendships and acquaintances are preferable to new. I know none at Hornby, nor do they know me. I should there never see Mr Wilson, and he is my very old friend with whom I should most unwillingly part. And as for quitting missionary functions, I believe it best to refer that to the entire disposal and will and pleasure of our Blessed Saviour.

You do exceedingly well and wisely to take no notice of our Bishop's proceedings. If you happen to hear them made the topic of any conversation, I doubt not but you observe the same prudent caution and reserve. I think I transcribed to you (or perhaps to Mr Eyre) part of a letter which he sent me last year containing his apology and defence and casting the blame on his clergy. By which it seems very probable that he is not aware that he has lost the confidence of all, or at least, that he would act in any other manner than he has done if all things were, or could be, brought as far back as 1791. His strange behaviour to Mr Eyre and unfriendly letters (of which Mr Eyre gave me some information) appear inconsistent with that grateful sense which he ought to have for him if he knows and remembers that Mr Eyre in 1790 was <u>considered by many to have had the principal hand</u> in effecting his promotion. What you see underlined is taken from your letter of September 1790 after you had heard that Mr William Gibson was named Bishop and Vicar Apostolic by the Propaganda.

Young Trevelyan is [a rare bird at present]. The knowledge of the world and the language of business and the maxims of politeness cannot be better understood nor translated more intelligbly than by S. Gregory: [to cover with trickery, to veil the ideas of the city, to show what is false to be true and vice versa &c']. Have you not often observed in reading the lives of the saints and ecclesiastical history the inverse difference between the nobles and gentry of these later ages and those of the 7th, 8th and 9th in England, and of the 10th and 11th too (the times of cimmerian darkness, if you will believe Joseph Berington). The language of business was unknown in those days and the finesses that now pervade almost all transactions between man and man. What innumerable foundations of religious houses, what number of nobility and gentry left the world and all the fair prospects it offered them of riches and honours. Thirty young gentlemen accompanied S. Bernard to the primitive [a word illeg.] institute of Citeaux. And though many in those ages were eminently wicked, yet, by retaining a sincere faith, many of the worst of them became eminent converts. Witness William, Count of Toulouse, Sorgius, the father of S. Romuald &c. At these times the heavens drop no dew, no stillicedia gratiae, few or no vocations to a life of rigorous and exemplary penance. The number of conforming monks was great in France, as Barvel testifies: a certain mark that they either entered in to monasteries for worldly views or were corrupted by example.

However, when I recollect the great number of chapels and dwelling-houses raised from their first foundations in this county within the space of little more than 20 years, I cannot but think well of my countrymen and believe that there are many who honour and promote the worship of the Deity in the church of Jesus Christ: at Manchester two; Weldbank one; Liverpool one; Appleton one; Blackbrook one; at Scolls one; at St. Helens one; at Gorsewood one just finished; at Formby one just finished; at Culceth one; at Blackburn one; at Ribchester one very elegant, by Mr William Fisher; at Preston one; at Cottam one; at Fernyhalgh one, cathedral-like; at Claughton one; at Hornby one with an excellent house, by Mrs Fenwick; at Brown Edge one with a very good house by [Oswald] Faves the monk; . another near Chorley by Mr [George] Clarkson, an Exj; another at Brindle with a house, by [Joseph] Hadley the monk. Now, if I ask you whether all these chapels and houses were so successfully begun and finished, because the power of moving was not in different persons but in one only, can you give me satisfactory answer or solution?

Mr Daniel, President, is still at Kirkham, extremely tender in health. He communicates nothing to me of any History of England; he is, I think, out of the proper sphere for composing a work of that nature. There is no learning in Kirkham but that of adding more and more: 'get money, money still, And then let Virtue follow if she will', Alexander Pope. 'Tis the maxim and motto of all the world.

I received a letter from J.P. Coghlan the 9th inst. in which he desires me to send him Mr Joseph Berington's thesis, for which he was outed from Douai College by the Bishop of Arras in 1771. He says that Mr Milner wants it, and Mr [William] Pilling junior, and also Mr Charles Plowden. So I inclosed it and sent it. Coghlan tells me that he will print it and perhaps set forth a translation of it, which latter, I told him, could be of no service, in my opinion, to religion. When I was at London in 1792 I one day asked who was Coghlan's ghostly father because if absolution ought not to be given to the subscribers of Blue Books, neither ought it to be granted to the printer. This, I dare say, was carried to Coghlan, so he writes:

> I was advised to print the Blue Books as the only means to defeat the horrid plans which have appeared since. Rome never would have known had I not carefully sent all thither. And I have now by me a

silver medal which His Holiness sent me and my wife permission (now mark the Irishism) to enter the Poor Clares during her life at Aire, (not after her death) which house you know is the Pope's own enclosure. Monsigr. Braxadere, now Secretary of the Propaganda, received my packets and forwarded them to Cardinal Antonelli and made good use of the time. But when Sir John Throckmorton and his company went to Rome they found me out and now [Thomas] Booker,[1] not my shop, is the place of rendezvous. As this is over it is best said little about, and attend to present business which has become important. And I tell you honestly what application this Thesis will have: to defeat a system of irreligion and phrenzy . . . By letters 6th October from Aire, the Abbess again asserts the English, Scots and Irish houses of Douai and Cambrai are sold. Mr Taaffe[2] of Cambrai says the same. Mr [Thomas] Parker's account therefore (he has been very lately in my neighbourhood to see his two aunts, viz. Betty Cottam and Peggy Moss, and seemed resolved to return to Paris) of restoring the English College must be defective, or those who live so near must be deceived.

So far J.P. Coghlan.

Gregory Stapleton wrote about two months ago to Mr Daniel informing him that Douai College and St. Omers were exempted from sale and put into the hands of one Mr Depords, a great friend of Mr Daniel, to whom he gave a Letter of Attorney, empowering him to act in his name. Stapleton's letter brightened Mr Daniel's hopes which I, being unwilling to give any check to, have concealed Coghlan's statement. If Brabant and all Flanders, both Austrian and French, be ceded to the Emperor and exchanged for Bavaria, whose Duke will in this hypothesis become Duke of Brabant and Count of Flanders (a thing long ago talked about, as Mr Daniel tells me), then Douai College may possibly be redeemed.

Have you seen and read Coghlan's Directory for next year? From the short statement he gives of China, Tonquin, Cochin China, the Christian Catholic faith spreads its rays on all sides, amidst the temporary persecutions it sustains with a primitive constancy and magnanimity. I am exceeding affected with the narrative, it is such an amazing contrast between the Catholics of those countries and of our own, who although they be instructed in the Catholic faith from their infancy and upwards to 14 or 15 years of age, yet often either abandon it totally, or much oftener live the lives of pagans. Were not the French generally such before the revolution? 'Tis highly probable because the hatred, animosity, outcry and persecution of religious, priests and others were so universal. 'The kingdom of God will be taken away from you and given to a people which yields the revenues that belong to it'. (Matt. 21 v. 43) To the Chinese, Tonquinese, &c.

Several French priests say Mass every day at Coghlan's. I advised him, in a long letter which I wrote to enclose the Thesis, to permit none of them to celebrate in his house unless he would candidly and explicitly, and with sincerity of mind, receive the Brief of Pius VI condemning and censuring the Synod of Pistoia in Tuscany, and especially the 17th page in which he again rejects and annuls, as his predecessors Innocent XI and Alexander VIII did, the Gallican Declaration of 1682, which I constantly hold to be the primary cause of the downfall and ruin and utter extirpation of the Catholic Church in France. If you have not the Brief above mentioned, fail not to procure it and read it with great attention. In the propositions that are extracted and censured you will, I think, without much difficulty find a remarkable similarity of expression between the authors of that Synod and Joseph Berington: ambiguity, doubting, questioning, not plain asserting or denying, yet every where insinuating error, falsehood and impiety. Mr Daniel, when he returned from London about the end of last May, told me that the French priests muttered their dislike of the 17th page of the Brief. I compare them to Jews who to this day cannot be persuaded that their dispersion is owing to their rejecting of Jesus. And French priests will not open their eyes to see and understand that their grand monarch with Bossuet and 36 other time-serving bishops in opposing Innocent XI and setting up that golden calf, their infamous Declaration, with the same very pious intention, as Luther had, ad in commedandum papatui, were the original cause of their bigotted and attached to gallican liberties and to the Declaration of 1682. I should, I believe have been less inclined to assist them, yet not have refused it because even Jews in distress are objects of compassion and call for our superflua stators at least.[3]

Query: Is it a mortal sin to pass improper toasts, for example, of double meaning, to your next neighbour, when at the same time you have no bad intention or design in so doing? For an answer to this read the Introduction to a Devout Life, part III chapter 27. Intention cannot excuse that which is per se evil. To pass it to your next neighbour means, I suppose, to repeat the double meaning toast to him. There are divines, I believe, very easy and lax in exculpating double meanings, but I think it better to abide by the advice which a gentleman gives his son just arrived from Paris (in Newberry's Collection of Letters, ed. 1767, the last letter) in which he cites Lord Roscommon: 'immodest words admit of no defence, for want of decency is want of sense'.

You will send me a letter at Christmas. Pray for me, I am middling well, thanks be to God. Every kind wish to Mr Eyre. I remain most affectionately yours, R. Banister.

P.S. I have entirely forgotten (what a pity!) to satisfy your enquiry about our family but will not fail to do it (please God) another time when you have sent a more intelligble extract from Collins. Is Molington and Monaton the same? Banastre and Banister are undoubtedly synonymous. What arms or escutcheon doth Collins give of the Banisters, what crest?

If you can pick up at Durham Mr [John] Smith's[4] folio volume containing all the Opera Historica of Ven. Bede, do so for me. Mr Smith at Durham knows it well for he has seen it in Douai College library. I have little money to buy books now, provisions, taxes &c., are now so chargeable; notwithstanding, I wish for the foresaid work.

1. Catholic bookseller of New Bond Street, London.
2. Unidentified; not a priest.
3. Banister to Eyre, 26 Apr 1798: 'The French priests behave very well in all places, but notwithstanding their moral character, I believe many of them are bigotted to gallican liberty, to their infamous gallican declaration of 1682; witness their muttering against its last and late proscription by Pius VI in the General Synod of Pistoia'.
4. A prebendary of Durham who published Bede's works in 1722.

115. Banister to Rutter Mowbreck, 28th January 1797

My dear Sir,

I sent you a letter some time before Christmas which I hope you have received long ago. I received a letter from Mr William Croskell, successor to Mr Lonsdale both at Linton and as Agent of the Clergy, dated 23rd December, in which he mentions a new edition of Alban Butler's Lives of the Saints to be published in numbers by John Moir at Edinburgh. He adds that Bishop Hay, Bishop Douglass, Mr Horrabin, Mr Coghlan, &c., are unanimous in giving the printer their support in carrying on his undertaking. He likewise sent me a specimen of the type and paper with the conditions. I was about to subscribe for 6 or 7 sets when I received a prospectus of an edition of the same work by Mr Francis Coates. Both Moir and Coates promise to give the whole work to subscribers in 42 numbers, one shilling each number, to be paid on delivery. I am in great doubt whether to choose Moir or Coates. You see, the type of Moir is larger than that of Coates, but I am dissatisfied with Moir's Old Testament of which I subscribed for 50 copies. Mr Wilson took one half off my hands and sent them to Preston to be stitched up in blue paper. And there turns out only 24 sets and two incomplete sets and some supernumerary sheets.

I cannot comprehend what Coates means by setting forth an edition of the Lives of the Saints in opposition to Moir, telling us that Moir is a Protestant. I am sorry for it; nevertheless, he may possibly be as honest as Coates; and Coates, though not a Protestant may possibly be a Catholic like several in Preston and some in Kirkham whose catholicity consists in putting on their Sunday's apparel and appearing in a Catholic chapel. It resembles Hudibras, writing of which the ludicrous poet[1] says:

We grant although he has much wit
He was very shy in using it,
And therefore bore it not about,
As being loath to wear it out
Unless on Holydays or so,
As men their best apparel do.

Bishop Hay (for Moir, I suppose) first promised to give the New Testament in sheets at 20d. He writes again that, by reason of the dearness of paper and printing, the subscribers cannot have it for less than 2s.2d. in sheets. I wrote to Croskell that I subscribed for 25 at 20d. each; since he informed me of the advanced price I have returned no answer. You must know that the 25 sets of the Old Testament, including carriage from Edinburgh to York and from York to Preston, have cost me £7.4s. which has exhausted all the money in my hands (given me to buy books for the poorer sort) except 14s.8d. £7.4s. divided by 25 sets makes every set (i.e. 4 tomes) come to 5s.9d. and the binding of 4 tomes will amount to 5s. So each set bound in 4 tomes will be 10s.9d. I thought to have gained one shilling at least by each set, but I despair of gaining anything.

A thought has come into my mind that this Francis Coates is connected with Committee men and that he is set on and encouraged by some of them, for he tells me that subscriptions will be taken in by T. Booker (at whose shop Committee men and friends now assemble, as Coghlan informed me 6th of last November. If it be so, I do not think it fitting to encourage him. In his conditions he mentions a Centenary that will be given. Have you given him your written Centenary? Also 'an alphabetical index of all the lives in the work, which in all former editions has been entirely omitted'. This is not true for I have one in my copy.

After all, I must refer to you to choose either Moir or Coates, but whichsoever you choose, order two months to be stitched up together and covered in blue paper and to be sent to you that you may immediately inspect them and see that nothing is wanting, and if anything be wanting, advertise the printer of the defect that he, without delay, may repair it. Eight sets are what I want: of which 5 are for 5 persons at San Albano, one for a Richard Billington, one for the Rev. Mr Henry Parkinson at Great Eccleston in the Fylde, and one for myself, or some other perhaps. 8 sets at £2.2s. per set make £16.16s. I will send you one half at or about Easter.

I could wish to see the first and genuine edition to be printed in the type which is given in the prospectus and all the additamenta in a smaller type, for I apprehend that both French, Irish and English have given, or will give, several things for Mr Butler's that are not his, or if his, which he never designed to see light. If the little secretary[2] is at the bottom of Coates, depend upon it that he will introduce something that may patronise gallican notions concerning the papal power &c.

In my last to our Right Revd. Prelate, I called him the perpetuum mobile in the business of erecting a college. He answered as usual that nobody seconded him. I also said that considering that above 20 chapels (and some great and magnificent ones) have been built in Lancashire, and several with a good messuage or dwelling-house, within these 20 years or a little more, I was grieved that one college could not yet be erected. He gives me a smart rebuke upon it, and still smarter upon my having said that Crook college was not so very improper for students, it being so solitary and not easy of access and did as much as Lisbon and San Albano put together. I intend to make a very short reply, viz. that I cannot but blame those who advised his Lordship to send his students thither. The king, you know, can do no wrong; his advisers and ministers bear all the blame. It must be so in our case.[3]

I hope you are well; I am in good health, thanks be to God. I remain your most affectionate uncle, R. Banister

1. Samuel Butler (1612–80). *Hudibras* is a mock-heroic satirical poem (modelled on Don Quixote) which ridicules the hypocrisy and self-seeking of the Presbyterians and Independents.
2. Charles Butler.
3. On 24 Apr 1797 Banister wrote to Eyre: 'Mr Blacoe informed me last February that you went with our Bp. and Mr Storey to take a view of Gainford: 168 acres, but no house fit for a college. Our Bp. often laments that there will soon be a scarcity of missionary priests in this District because we have no college. In one of my letters I represented to him that on the one hand there are not near so many Catholics in the kingdom in this era as there were in

the beginning of Queen Bess's reign, and on the other hand we are not without clergy seminaries, viz. at Rome, Lisbon and Valladolid. Then there is Crook College which may furnish as many missioners as all the other three at the rate they go on. But in the year 1778 there was not one college, seminary or convent of men to train up missioners for the faithful in this kingdom. The Bp. answers me as if I had thought or wrote that Crook is a proper place for a seminary. I well remember that I commended it for its retired situation and for being difficult of access to strangers. And mighty well and happy it would have been if Douai College had been of as hard and difficult an approach; many expenses in dinners and wine would have been saved and fewer play-days granted to the importunities of noble and simple guests. Then Divines and Philosophers might have written their dictates and not hunted up those that were written by their assiduous predecessors. He says "that one of the most effectual means to prevent amnything being done, is to support Crook". And again: "The point now is either to fix on a place and buy it and build by degrees or to give up the affair as such a place as the present continued will prevent more good than than it will do good". I hear the situation at Gainford is very beautiful, why is it not bought? Money, I presume is wanting. St Cuthbert and others founded in the 7th and 8th century many monasteries in your northern valleys and mountains and woods; but of what kind think you? I believe this hated Crook Hall would have been to the best of them as Blenheim House to an ordinary farmhouse.'

---

116. Rutter to Banister — Minsteracres, 12th May 1797

My dear Uncle,

You will think me very long in answering your last letter which I received on 1st February last, especially as it was upon business, I mean, that of procuring you the Saints' Lives. But the reason of my not answering you sooner was because I did not know how to execute this commission. Knowing that Coates had previously intended to publish Mr Butler's Saints' Lives, I was inclined to patronise him preferably to the Scotchman (whose publication of the Old Testament did not please me any more than it did you). But Coates is, and has been, at a loss to know how to proceed as he has not met with that support which he expected. I went down last week to Newcastle to know his final determination and to agree with him accordingly if his terms should appear as fair as those of Moir. But he seems inclined to drop the undertaking as his competition has got the start of him and is supported by Charles Butler, Coghlan, &c.

Hence I have done with Coates and have bespoke for you, through the medium of Mr Eyre, 8 copies of Moir's Saints' Lives which I shall order to be sent to you and left for you at the George Inn, Preston. As to their being first sent to me at Minsteracres to be examined and inspected, I think it both unnecessary and expensive, for it is a clear point with me that if they be found imperfect, as was the case with the Old Testament, the publisher is responsible and obliged to make good the deficiency and therefore, in the case you mentioned, you should in my opinion, have advertised Mr Croskell of the mistake that he might have rectified it if made by himself, or written to Moir if originating with him. In your next be pleased to let me know whether you will have the Saints' Lives bound, stitched or in sheets.

Our Bishop, I believe, is going to publish his translation of Mahis's Verite de la Religion Catholique, but I hope it will be first revised either by you or some other person capable of such a task. For though his Lordship has published an English grammar, I question much whether his translation will be very good English and in a style to please the generality of his readers if we may by allowed to judge from his epistolary style.[1]

You probably have heard that Joseph Berington has made his retraction; the particulars I have not learned but wish it may be such as to satisfy you and others. However, it has appeared satisfactory to Bishop Douglass who has therefore granted him faculties.[2]

As to the new college, it remains in status quo. Gainford, though seemingly very eligible, was not purchased for want of money and chiefly because Mr Daniel &c seemed unwilling to cooperate with his Lordship and still looked back to Douai. I may safely assign a third cause, and that is the Bishop's own irresolution in these matters. The method proposed for raising the purchase money (which I think was about £6,000, was by taking out of the funds a certain sum of money belonging to the mission. For this part we will suppose £600, a greater sum for Yorkshire, Lancashire and the episcopal revenue; the rest was to be raised among friends and by applying to the several congregations of the District. I went to Durham on this occasion with Mr Eyre and was induced to consent, from the necessity of the case, that the above sum standing in per cents should be sold out for the purpose just now mentioned. For, though I thought formerly and still think that Crook and Tudhoe, if properly regulated, might do for a while, yet as the Bishop will hear of no such thing and as there seems no prospect of ever returning back to Douai, the sooner we set about making a permanent establishment the better.

This is what the Scotch bishops have lately done; for despairing of recovering their foreign establishments, they have found out a proper place for their purpose and have taken a lease of 107 years on terms very favourable to them, trusting, as they say, to kind Providence and good friends for help to accomplish their designs. But you probably have seen their printed letter to the faithful on this subject composed by Bishop Geddes.[3]

When at Durham (it was 24th February, the feast of St. Matthias) I spoke my mind freely to the Bishop and he seemed to take it in very good part. I insinuated to him the necessity of placing a little more confidence in his clergy and this by the example of St Peter addressing the rest of the apostles and disciples and consulting with them on the occasion of the election of St Matthias. And as I did not like the Bishop's appearance (which I thought indicated something paralytic) I put it to his Lordship whether all public functionaries as we are, should not have all public monies properly secured and in the hands of clergy executors, glancing at the same time at the neglect of Bishop Talbot in this particular in not legalising his will, the consequence of which might have been the loss of many thousands to the mission. I next advised his Lordship to choose a coadjutor who might be of great assistance to him in his present undertakings and might likewise prevent any of that confusion which took place at his brother's death. He gave me to understand that I need not be under any apprehension on this score, and he had settled the last point with Bishop Douglass in case of any sudden emergency.

This day's post brings us the Pastoral Address of Mr Hussey, now Bishop of Waterford and Lismore, to his clergy, in which he very properly censures the unwarrantable proceeding of those in Ireland who drive the Catholic military to Protestant places of worship after the most solemn promises to the contrary. Things there are, I am well informed, in the utmost confusion and I cannot but blame the strange conduct of Ministers as the cause of it, in preferring the private interest of individuals to the general sense and the public good of the nation at large.

I have just heard that Joseph Berington promises to repair, as far as he is able, the public scandal that he has given and to desist from the publication of his intended work on the rise and fall of the papal power. We all cry shame here on Sir John Webb for leaving his immense fortune to his bastards.

Sometime in February last Mr Stone sent one of his young men (I do not recollect his name) to Durham with a letter to the Bishop desiring he might be ordained priest, for that he meant to send him to a place in the south then vacant, although this person proves to be a native of Lancashire and consequently immediately subject to the Bishop here. Now what right has the President of Stonyhurst to send one of this District to another, without the bishop's leave and permission? Is not this a manifest infraction of the general discipline of the church? Does it not properly belong to a Bishop to place and dispose of his Clergy? I should have no doubts on this head only that it appears to me that you have some and that I have heard you say a missioner may go after first asking his Bishop's leave, from one District to another without censure. I wish to know whether you think the Ex-jesuits justifiable in sending from Stonyhurst young clergymen to their several places jus patronis and why [we] may not do the same?

I am sorry to find that my cousin has very indifferent health. She has sent me a crucifix which she brought from France together with some relics and registers. We have agreed mutually to pray for one another and therefore in my mementoes she comes immediately after you.

I have enquired but in vain for Smith's edition of Ven. Bede's historical works but think you might easily procure it from London. I have your Louvain edition of his Church History set forth, I presume, by Dr Stapleton the year after he had published the translation of it, and this is at your service.

Mr [James] Orrel left his son at Crook on Wednesday to return to Lancashire. 4 new priests were ordained there in Lent, all promising young men and now studying hard for universals, if the Bishop will allow them, for he threatens to send them all on the mission by Whitsundtide unless something is done for a new college.

I am sorry to hear such scandalous accounts of certain priests at London and Liverpool. O tempora o mores.

Be pleased to remember me in your prayers and believe me, dear Uncle, to remain your ever dutiful nephew, Hen. Rutter

1. *The Truth of the Catholic Religion proved from the Holy Scriptures* (1799). Gillow ascribes a French but not an English, grammar to Gibson.
2. On consideration, Douglass thought Berington's statement was inadequate and the suspension was again imposed until a formal and comprehensive retraction was made.
3. In October 1796 Bishop Hay took a ninety-nine-year lease of a farm at Aquhorties (near Inverurie in Aberdeenshire). The only major outlay was on the rebuilding of the house.

117. Rutter to Banister   Minsteracres, 5th September 1797

Dear Uncle,

I ought long since to have informed you of my safe return and to have thanked you for your kindness when at Mowbreck. I had the pleasure of finding my parents and all relations well and was particularly pleased at the reception I met with from my brother at Liverpool. He seems indeed to have made a most excellent choice in regard of his wife, though I did not see her to advantage, she being in deep affliction for the loss of her mother just dead.

I returned home by Crossbrook, Wigan, Blackburn, Stonyhurst, Broughton, Layton and Brough. I did not write to you concerning Mr [Edward] Barret's[1] intentions because he himself was just setting out to pay you a visit at Mowbreck and I shall be glad to know how he settled matters with Mr Blacoe. When I saw the situation at Stonyhurst, and so large a house, I could not help regretting that our Bishop had refused Mr Weld's kind offer. I dined there and was treated with great civility. At Brough I met for the first time with Mr [James] Barrow[2] of Ness, an old schoolfellow of yours who enquired kindly after you, as did many others.

I received the Bishop's answer a few days ago as follows:

> Dear Sir,
>
> I received your letter in due time. As I could not give such an answer as you seemed to desire, I did not answer it so soon as you might have expected or as I should have done otherwise. Both the objects you mentioned were then out of the question. I hope you will think it better they were so as I have a great regard for you and wish to see you of the same sentiments in this respect.

So far his Lordship. This is the last push I shall make and as it has proved unsuccessful I conclude it to be the will of God that I remain at Minsteracres. In my answer to the Bishop I shall repeat my wishes and inclinations and then leave the matter to his Lordship's decision. I could likewise wish that you would write to him on the subject either pro or con. In the above letter the Bishop says of himself:

> Dr Lawson the other day advised me in <u>very serious manner</u> to go to Bath for 6 weeks or two months and begged I would think of it

in earnest and go soon. I dare say his advice is very good but I do not see how I can follow it. It is a long way off.

Hence I conclude that his Lordship's health is in a most precarious state and therefore would advise him to choose a coadjutor as soon as possible in order to prevent the disagreeable consequences that took place at the death of his late brother Matthew. I hope you and others will urge the matter to him. I have been thinking in my own mind of some proper person to succeed him but am perfectly at a loss to find one duly qualified for so arduous and exalted a station unless your age would allow you to undertake it.[3]

I am sorry to hear Bishop Walmesley is dying, but his vigour and firmness he retains to the last. Perhaps you have not seen his last Pastoral Instruction and therefore I shall copy it out for you, for I understand it makes a great noise:

Charles, Bishop of Rama, Vicar Apostolic to the Clergy of the Western District

Dear Brethren, St Paul, by his words attendite vobis &c., admonishes bishops of the duty they owe to themselves and their flock in the government of Christ's church. Strict attention is to be given by them to prevent scandals and erroneous doctrines taking place among the faithful under their care. But notwithstanding our efforts to prevent, with deep sorrow we have seen these evils happen and though we have waited a considerable time in expectation that the guilty would renounce their errors, hitherto our hopes have been for the most part vain. Therefore after serious reflection we have thought it necessary in discharge of our pastoral duty to send you the following orders. If any of those persons

1. Who signed their names to the noted Protest and Appeal (2nd Blue Book, pp. 30, 31) against our condemnation of the oath

2. Who assented to, or allowed their manes to be affixed to, the heterodox proposition restrictive of the spiritual powers of the Church (3rd Blue Book, p. 46)

3. Who signed their names to what is generally called the Staffordshire Creed containing various errors and heretical doctrine set forth in an Appeal to the Catholics of England p.22

come into the Western District, we require you if laics not to admit them to the participation of the sacraments, if clergymen to the exercise of any ecclesiastical functions, until they have explicitly and publicly disavowed or withdrawn their signatures from those scandalous and erroneous acts.

> In the article of death, if any of the above persons call for your assistance with a truly penitent heart, we require of you, before you administer any sacrament to them, that you exact and, if possible receive in the presence of 2 or more respectable Catholic witnesses, the retraction of the said acts and duly inform us of the same.
>
> This measure we trust will be a means to induce those gentlemen to adopt orthodox sentiments and preserve the faithful in our District free from error and scandalous novelties. Loquere quae decent samam doctrinam, &c.
>
> Bath, 3rd June, 1791. + Charles, Bishop of Rama, V.A.

Then follows a list of the names he refer to, which you may find in the Blue Books and amongst the rest, Charles Berington, Bishop Hussey, Mr O'Leary, Mr Strickland &c. I do not recollect what heterodox proposition was maintained by those the Bishop alludes to in No. 2 as restrictive of the power of the church. I understand Bishop Douglass gave great offence to Bishop Walmesley by admitting Joseph Berington's sham retractation and this was one reason, according to Mr Robert Plowden, that called forth the above mandate.

I shall now begin in good earnest with the Life of Christ and beg you will repeat the good hints you gave me on this subject when at Mowbreck and which have unluckily escaped me. I remain, dear Uncle, your very dutiful nephew, Hen. Rutter

1. Missioner in Wigan.
2. Older brother of John.
3. Bishop Gibson was, however, able to complete a confirmation tour in Lancashire in September. Banister wrote to Eyre on 30 September giving an outline of the tour, which included 'the solemn benediction of Mrs Hesketh, the Lady Abbess of the Benedictine Nuns now of Preston, late of Ghent'. He also noted his discussions with the bishop about a new college which both agreed should be 'a permanent independent college subject to no control of Laics, so large and spacious as to entertain 80 or 100 scholars'. But that was as far as it went, for Gibson could not be brought to a decision about its location.

---

118. Rutter to Banister Minsteracres, 16th May 1798

Dear Uncle,

I have said 6 Masses agreeably to your intentions which were signified to me by Mr Hull, and shall be happy to say any other Masses for you that you desire me. I flatter myself that your health is no worse than it was last summer when I had the pleasure of seeing you at Mowbreck, otherwise I hope you would have informed me.

Nothing has occurred in my regard worth communicating to you and this is not the time for putting you to a useless expence, but perhaps you will think that for this reason the present letter might have been spared. Whatever judgement however you pass on it, I can assure you it proceeds from a good motive which is not only that of enquiring after your health and of testifying my duty and respects, but likewise of sending you the following advertisement: Durham, 10th April, 1798.

> To be sold by Auction on Saturday the 5th day of May next a Beautiful Residence called Shincliffe Hall, within 2 miles of the City of Durham, consisting of a genteel modern-built mansion house, containing a Dining Room and Drawing Room, each 36 feet in length; Breakfast Room, Servant's Hall, kitchen, etc. 5 bedchambers and garrets, with stables, coach house, menservants' rooms and other detached offices; together with upwards of 40 acres of rich land and a house and garth in the village of Shincliffe. The premises are all freehold and tithe free elegantly bounded by Shincliffe Woods and the River Wear. May be entered upon at pleasure. Part of the package money may remain on mortgage and the purchaser be accommodated with part of the furniture on an apprisement. For particulars apply to Mr Thos Hopper, Durham.
>
> Hutchinson, in his History of Durham, speaking of this place, says it is 'a delightful retirement, commanding a solemn view of the sequestered vale with its hanging woods, which form a beautiful amphitheatre; a scene excellently adapted to study and contemplation'.

I wrote the above some time ago in a great hurry in order that you might engage the Bishop (whom I supposed in Lancashire) in favour of Shincliffe, which I considered as a most eligible situation for a college in every respect but that of water. However, as the Bishop had been informed of it I thought it better to meddle no more in things of this kind, especially as there appeared so little prospect of success. The Bishop did write to Mr Smith a few days before the sale, but in such a manner that it was difficult to guess his meaning.

I have nothing particular to say about Crook, everything going on in the usual way and Mr Eyre in great want of money, till Mr Daniel relieved him. The road to the house, which was almost impassable, is now much improved and will soon be made very good.

You probably have seen Mr [John] Bell's prospectus for an abridgement of Mr Butler's Saints Lives[1] in order to accommodate those who are unable to purchase the whole work. He is very sanguine in his expectations of success and means to apply the profits towards a new college.

As to my work in the Life of Christ, I am far advanced in it and hope to finish it in the course of another month or two, not with a view to its publication but to my own amusement and advantage, for I am not adequate to such an undertaking. However, I might say of such a work as much as Martial allows to be said of any other: [there are good things, there are some mediocre things, but there are more bad things. Reader, do not expect too much!]. The benefit would be the 4 Evangelists incorporated into one according to an approved harmony, together with a good deal of Maudit's Analysis to illustrate and explain the text. To this is added whatever has been handed down by tradition from primitive writers, which seems more agreeable to the present taste than the pious conceptions and representations of St. Bonaventure and other mystical writers. I should be very glad, if not too troublesome to you, to submit my performance to your corrections and emendations before I transcribe it de nous, or perhaps you might prevail on your neighbour Mr Daniel to revise it.

A military rage has seized all in these parts and everyone is entering into some Association or other to defend his King and Country. Mr Silvertop is raising a troop of horse and his son George another to secure peace and quiet at home in case of foreign invasion. Such a measure indeed seems to be particularly proper in these parts to overawe the unruly pitmen and keel men who in the best of times are ever ready for mischief.

What must I say to a young woman who hires herself to a neighbouring parson? I had a letter in not long ago from my cousin at Haggerston in which she says that you are become a bad correspondent. She invites me very pressingly to go and see her this summer and I probably shall do myself that pleasure. I was very sorry to hear of the sudden death of your friend Mr Wilson. Pray, who is his successor?[2]

In regard of deeds and papers belonging to foundations in Lancashire, Yorkshire, and Bishopric, it seems most proper that they should remain, as has been the usual practice, in the hands of the Vicar [General], or some other prudent person whom the Bishop can depend on, that so recourse may be had to them as occasion requires, which would not be the case if removed at a distance. However, the Bishop seems desirous of getting them all into his own hands and I wish to know what you and others think of such a measure. I remain, dear Uncle, your very dutiful Nephew, Hen. Rutter

1. A professor at Crook Hall. His abridgement in three octavo volumes was published in Newcastle in 1799.
2. Wilson died on 14 January 1798 at Salwick Hall, but, being aware that John Clifton intended to terminate the chaplaincy, he had made arrangements for the altar plate and vestments to be delivered into the hands of John Gradwell for a new chapel in Lea Hall; Clifton objected but failed in his law-suit for their restitution. (See also N$^{o.}$ 137).

119. Banister to Rutter — Mowbreck, 2nd July 1798

My dear Harry,

I received your last in due time for which I return you grateful thanks and for satisfying the 6 obligations.

I am glad to hear that you have nearly brought your own work ad metam [to an end]. If you wish me to revise it, bring it hither yourself, and if you be not in haste to commit it to the press I shall keep it all the next winter and read it to mine and my neighbour's family after evening prayers. If my country-hearers are pleased with it you may be sure it is good. You know, I presume, that Moliere read his comedies to his servant maid and from her feelings or emotions rightly judged what would please and affect his audience on the stage. [Sometimes even the vulgar] (says Horace) [recognise the truth].

Our Bishop came hither 5th of last month and stayed with me 3 weeks and a day. Many topics were treated in conversation: 1st, and before we heard of the death of Bishop Berington, whether his ordinary and extraordinary faculties were to be delivered to him, because on the 9th of last May he wrote to our Bishop with some degree of acrimony because he proposed to the surviving Staffordshire priests who subscribed the appeal, commonly called their creed, a formula of retraction, and said that there is nothing reprehensible in it except an inaccuracy of expression, whereas Bishop Walmesley declares that it contains various errors and heretical doctrines. He also had written a letter to Mr Cowley, an extract of which he sent to our Bishop and which I read with surprise and grief because Hierocaesariensis in strong terms declared himself advocate of Wilkes.

He died on the 8th June in his way to Longbirch from Sedgeley Park with Mr [John] Kirke,[1] between Wolverhampton and Longbirch. In the relation sent to Bishop Douglass by Dr Bew, his horse startled and he dismounted (in Mr Appleton's letter to our Bishop his horse ran away with him which put him into a greater commotion. However, he stopped it and dismounted and sat down). Accidentally Dr Morison came by and took him into his arms (Mr Kirke hastened to fetch a surgeon but long before either Mr Kirke or the surgeon came) he expired immediately. His death ended all further deliberation about delivering to him his faculties. Acanthos had written to Bishop Douglass in the strongest manner against the delivery of them until the Propaganda were informed how Hierocaesariensis stood affected in regard of Wilkes and the Staffordshire Appellants.

You do not know, I presume, how anxious and how busy these important appellants are to procure a successor who may be agreeable to the general wish of the District. Dr Bew, in the letter which announced to Bishop Douglass the death of Bishop Berington, tells him that Dr Rigby of Lancaster or Mr James Corne of Shrewsbury would be acceptable to the District. Mr Richard Gibson of Mawley transcribed and sent to our Bishop, when he was here, a copy of two letters, both of which were written to him on the same page. The first was from Dr Bew in which he tells him that the votes of the Brethren were collecting; that he had written to Mr [Edward] Beaumont of Norwich and Mr Robert Beeston, two Vicars General,[2] to gather votes; that Bishop Douglass approved of the measures; in fine, that Dr Rigby and Mr Corne were thought on as likely to please. The second letter (written underneath the first) was from Mr Kirke. In it he tells Mr Richard Gibson that he cannot but add Dr Bew himself as a person well qualified and most agreeable to the general wish; that he is well assured that if Bishop Berington had lived he would have chosen him to be his coadjutor.

Our Bishop wrote without delay to Bishop Douglass believing that he had approved the measure, i.e., the collecting votes, for Dr Bew positively wrote so to Mr Richard Gibson. But our Bishop has just informed me from Fernyhalgh that Bishop Douglass has written to him and assures him that he never gave his approbation to collect votes; that he has written to 5 priests of the Midland District who had written to him on the same supposition, viz., that he had approved the mode of collecting suffrages. Bishop Douglass is much displeased with Dr Bew. You see how appellants, innovators in faith and discipline, and all such like never hesitate to commit to writing or printing any falsehood, misrepresentation, equivocation, &c.

Monsignor Erskine, on hearing of Bishop Berington's death, told Bishop Douglass that the Vicars Apostolic might apply to him that he would forward their dispatches and let the Propaganda know the character and fitness of the person, or persons, proposed for the Midland District. In reading this I told our Bishop that I would lay a wager with him that Erskine himself would be named Vicar Apostolic.

John Corne,[3] the brother of James, has written to Mr Richard Gibson that it is now the time to break the knot or junto of Longbirch. He is, then, no longer of that junto, yet I never heard that he has retracted his signature to the appeal. His brother never subscribed any address or appeal. John therefore may wish to forward him to the mitre and thus tacitly renounces his connection with the junto. Our Bishop has more than once said to me that Bishop Douglass's approbation of Joseph Berington's pure and orthodox faith has made him in a great measure lose all his authority and to be deemed a favourer of the Staffordshire faction.

Pray tell me what were the houses and the little land near Durham sold for and why you and Mr Eyre sold them expressly against the wish of your Bishop, which he, both in letters to me and tete a tete, calls a disobedience? He calls it land unalienable without the express consent of the Bishop; he says the person who held the title deeds gave them up contrary to his order and command. Another thing much displeases our Bishop, viz., the vesting of Tudhoe in 3 names. If it had been solely vested in him he would be able to convert it to the great and important design of buying Gainford and erecting a college thereon. But surely Mr Eyre and Mr Storey will not obstruct so laudable and so necessary a thing as a college for the maintaining a succession of missionaries. 'Tis evident to me that Tudhoe is no fit place. Sir John (whose generous acts you once extolled to me in a letter) built something at Tudhoe and after all 'tis nothing but a most inconvenient house, scarce able to hold 20 scholars, with masters and servants, and there is no water fit for culinary uses, but at a great distance. Sir John has given a bond for an annuity for ever of £73 and bought 10 or 11 statute acres and made them the property of Tudhoe.

When I had written thus far, 4th July, I received a letter from our Bishop desiring my attendance with some others of our Brethren at Fernyhalgh, 10th July, as there will be business of great importance to be transacted. This business is to find ways and means to purchase Gainford and our

Bishop supposes that there will be wanting for the said purchase six thousand pounds. The interest on Sir John's bond will pay interest of £1460 at 5% Those 11 acres may be sold for £400. Our Lancashire General Fund (though burdened with £102 p.a.) will be able to pay the interest of one thousand at 5% An estate in Lancashire may be sold for two thousand pounds at least; now sum up all

Impr. Sir John's bond answers for	£1460
item the sale of 11 acres	400
item our G.F. answers for interest of	1000
item the sale of an estate	2000
	4860

But to make up six thousand there is wanting £1140. I hope the Yorkshire Brethren and you and your Brethren in Northumberland Bishopric will answer for the interest of £1140.

But what if Messrs. Eyre and Storey will not consent to turn Tudhoe and Sir John's bond into this channel (although you long since told me that Sir John said to them they might do whatever they pleased with it) their dissenting will be a great embarrassment, and if the motive of dissent be not evidently just and reasonable, there can be no excuse for it. n.b. that I have written both to Mr Barrow and to our Bishop [about] these ways and means as suggested by my own consideration. Next Tuesday I hope to meet with some others, more prompt and adequate, [got together] by Mr John Barrow who is now most zealous for an episcopal college and I think he is in the right to be so. For, as for Douai College what hopes are there now of its being ever restored? If it be, will the university win the free and open exercise of the Catholic religion be ever restored? 'Tis not in appearance at all probable.

Last year a young whelp got into my Saints' Lives and tore out ten leaves in October from page 145 to page 194 inclusive; item eight leaves from page 333 to 349, all in the life of St Teresa; four leaves from page 361 to 368 inclusive and one leaf only page 663 & 664. You know that I have subscribed for 8 sets of Saints' Lives by Moir. He then will surely oblige me so far as to draw off the few leaves I want to repair the first edition. You may be almost certain that the leaves of his edition will not correspond with the leaves of the first edition. You must therefore be obliged to take on before and to proceed further than absolutely necessary. I shall be most willing to pay him for every leaf. It is but goodwill to do it, for I do not ask him to set the press but only to draw off the sheets. If you do not choose to write to Moir, perhaps Bishop Hay will procure it to be done for me for I hear that he inspects the printing. I am afraid little

Butler will foist on us, if he can, some stuff of his own. I said so to our Bishop and he said: shall I tell Bishop Hay to beware of any intrusion? I remain ever yours, R. Banister

1. President of Sedgeley Park school 1793–7 and successor to Charles Berington as missioner at Longbirch.
2. Beaumont was at Norwich, where he opened St John's chapel in 1790 and Beeston was missioner at Eastwell, Lincs.
3. Missioner at Stafford.

120. Rutter to Banister Minsteracres, 12th August 1798

Dear Uncle,

I return you many thanks for your kind and affectionate letter which came to hand in due time.

In announcing to me the Clergy-meeting at Fernyhalgh you gave me a glimpse of hope that something would be done for the establishment of an episcopal college that great object of all our wishes, but when Mr Eyre afterwards showed me the resolutions agreed upon on that occasion I experienced a joy and satisfaction not easily to be described because a fair prospect then opened itself of seeing these hopes realised. However, this pleasing view soon vanished, or at least was much darkened in consequence of the dismissal of Mr Barrow and the Bishop's disannulling the resolutions to which he had subscribed at Fernyhalgh. Both of them will doubtless have sent you their statement of this matter and perhaps much may depend on the judgment you form of it and the manner how you write to the Bishop. The great question is what you conceive to be the meaning of the resolutions then entered into? Was it that Messrs Eyre, Barrow, Gillow and Smith should be merely receivers of the money to be subscribed for a college or that they should form a committee jointly with the Bishop to transact the whole business till its final accomplishment?

It is clear that his Lordship is afraid of being under any check or control and that he wishes to carry on the business snugly to himself in virtue of his episcopal and supreme authority. His vicar, Mr Eyre, dares scarce open his mouth on the subject, but I tell his Lordship freely and frankly that if he does not allow the gentlemen to act as agreed upon at Fernyhalgh, he is not a jot nearer the desired object than he was 5 years ago. Whatever idea he may himself entertain of his own transcendent abilities, I fear little will be done if all is to be left to his management, especially considering his infirm state of health, which seems still declining. He is perpetually alleging the Council of Trent and the Brief of Pope Pius in his favour, but when an express article of the resolutions secures to him all his episcopal rights and authority in regard of a college, and when all are agreed in thinking Ushaw a most eligible situation, where can be there any real difficulty in allowing the committee to proceed?

However as I wish to state the case impartially to you, I must own that it appears to me that the Gentlemen at Durham were too hasty and a little too harsh in bringing forward certain articles for his Lordship to sign when there was no necessity for it. The first thing to be done is to purchase Ushaw farm in the vicinity of Durham which we all here conceive to be a most excellent situation and I am happy to inform you that the Bishop has received from Sir Edward Smith[1] a very favourable answer in which he expresses his readiness to dispose of the estate in question for the public good. Hence Mr Eyre is of opinion that Mr Barrow should not trouble Mr [Peter] Holford[2] or the Bishop any more on the subject till the purchase is made and conceives it would be highly improper that Mr Holford and Sir Edward should have the most distant suspicion of any disagreement having taken place among the Brethren. You will be pleased to notify this to Mr Barrow with Mr Eyre's compliments as soon as possible because he thinks it of great importance. I beg the favour of an answer that I may know in what sense to take the Fernyhalgh resolutions.[3] Likewise whether I am to throw any obstacle in the way of the Bishop in case he be determined to purchase only in his own name. Moreover I wish to know your thoughts in regard of the purchase. I mean in regard of the most proper mode of conveyance in order that it may be secured in the best manner possible.

The Bishop came here on the 8th but I have not heard what stay he makes with us. A mitre, I hear, has been offered to Mr Gregory Stapleton with the view, as it is supposed, of removing him from Old Hall Green. The disagreement between Mr Hussey and Bishop Douglass is likely to be be compromised.[4]

You desire to know why I and Mr Eyre sold the houses and the little land near Durham. I sent you formerly a copy of the letter which I wrote to the Bishop on that occasion in which I told his Lordship that I had no more to do in the business than he had, being really ignorant that Sir John the Trustee had sold them. It had long been in contemplation to dispose of these old houses as being a losing concern, and the little land had been offered to the Bishop during 3 months but he had not resolution to purchase it. His Lordship may call it land unalienable without his express consent but I maintain the contrary and that in what regards the Fund we are independent of him. I could say more on this subject if necessary but shall only add that it is no proof of the Bishop's candour to bring forward this old complaint against me when he knows or ought to know that I had no hand in the sale in question.

In regard of the Saints' Lives, the same accident befell the set which you let me have as befell yours and a young whelp tearing out some leaves. I therefore sent them with your leave and approbation to my father after first writing out what was wanting. Had you not better supply what is wanting in your copy from that which my father has, or exchange sets? For I have no connexion with Moir or Bishop Hay and am totally unknown to them. However, I will get somebody to write to one of them in case you desire it.

I am glad you will be so kind as to revise the Life of Christ which I will bring along with me when I come to Mowbreck, but I doubt it will not be this year. You need not apprehend that I am going to appear in print; if ever this is the case it shall be left to your judgement and others.

The Bishop sends off by this post another letter to Sir Edward. I remain, dear Uncle, your most dutiful Nephew Hen. Rutter

1. Of Acton Burnell; usually known as Smythe.
2. Smythe's agent in Durham.
3. See No. 121a.
4. In 1793 Dr Hussey obtained from Rome ecclesiastical jurisdiction over the Catholics, mostly Irish, in the British Army. In 1798 Hussey, now a bishop and chaplain at the Spanish Embassy, delegated the task to his assistant Thomas Fallon without consulting Bishop Douglass by whom Fallon had been suspended *a divinis* for misconduct. Douglass therefore suspended Hussey too. To avoid embarrassment to the Pope by the suspension of one bishop by another, the matter was compromised on the basis that a misunderstanding had occurred, but Fallon's appointment stood. [Ward *Dawn* II 198–200]

---

121. Banister to Rutter Mowbreck, 17th September 1798

My dear Hal,

Mr Barrow came hither on Thursday last (with Mr John Lund, and on his way called upon Mr Anthony Lund). All three combine in an opinion opposite to his Lordship. Mr Barrow stayed all night and only left me yesterday about 4 o'clock. Fortunately your letter came in the morning early after he had said Mass. I was vesting but could not forbear opening your letter and reading its contents. I sent immediately for our champion and gave it to him, which he has amply answered and desires you to communicate it to Mr Eyre.

I am writing a pretty long letter to his Lordship who, on the 1st and 7th inst. wrote to me but widely mis-stated the business; hear what he says in the latter letter:

> (Mr Barrow) would have me sign a paper that we all had equal powers in the business and that everything relating to purchase place &c. &c. was to be determined by a majority of votes . . . I then informed him, as indeed must be known to all, that I neither did nor ever intended to give such powers, and that if anyone imagined I did, as I even could not properly give away such at least from a successor as Bishop that I withdrew and disannulled anything of the kind. This was necessary that such pretensions might not hinder us from getting forward some way or other . . . This has afflicted me much and I may expect much talk but am not discouraged . . . Your advice may make him cautious about what he does that neither himself nor others be drawn into difficulties of conscience which may long make them uneasy. What right had he to draw up such things for me?

I write exactly his words and in their place—I mark the two &c. Is not all this a misstatement when compared with the 3 articles of Mr Barrow? The two &c. &c. are put in to make me believe that Mr Barrow is striving to divest him of all, or a great part, of his episcopal power and authority. There is no such meaning or intention in the 3 articles. The third expressly gives him the direction of the college (when built), which appears to me more than is his due by the Council of Trent; it orders the Bishop to choose 2 counsellors, ancient and grave Canons of his Chapter, I presume not to be cyphers or mutes but to be heard and attended to and, as Pope Benedict XIV speaking of Cardinals in the Consistory, reverenty yet with firmness and fortitude declaring their counsels and advices.

How the first article infringes or touches his episcopal jurisdiction I cannot conceive. The contributions are voluntary and not given to the Bishop personally but to the future purchase and future building and, because not things but persons are capable of being invested with a trust, therefore the Bishop and four others are chosen to be depositaries and trustees. I verily believe the good prelate was more nettled at that than anything else. Do not you think so too? So he never ceases to resent Tudhoe made over to him and 2 others, nor the old houses sold and disposed of without his consent and I presume, without catching a penny.

The second article appears at first view as contrary to the Council of Trent and if it be, ‘tis but in a matter very indifferent, viz. the choice of the place and of the plan for building. If our prelate had an episcopal palace and a cathedral contiguous to it, what an obstinate brother must he be who should refuse to concur with his Bishop if he desired a seminary or college near both? As this is not the case, I think a debate about the site by a great deal too trifling, provided it be healthy. Yet I am entirely of opinion that the building ought to be exceeding modest and frugal, not superb and grand in order to allure innumerable needless guests to come and see it and to be regaled with good dinners and various sorts of wine. Such comers and intruders did great mischief to Douai College, embezzling her revenue and making students and masters idle and lose half their precious time by getting them play-days.

This, with some other things, I hope to write to his Lordship next Monday with most earnest and humble entreaties to acquiesce in the 3 articles, and write to me or Mr Barrow a frank and candid assent. He may depend on this as certain, that if he will not, the Brethren will abandon him and not contribute a farthing. And then, as he has often done before, lay all blame on them. You cannot conceive how I was quite ground down during his 3 weeks stay here by hearing so often his scheme and his complaints against the Brethren.

I begin to fear my left leg will break into some ulcer: St. Camillus had 5 in his legs, which he called quinzy misericordias Dei. Pray for me, my dear heart, and believe me ever yours, R. Banister.

[Written on obverse of 121]

121a John Barrow to Rutter Mowbreck, 17th August 1798

Dear Sir

No sooner did your letter arrive at Mowbreck than Mr Banister brought it to my room to read and answer those parts which regard my conduct and that of the other gentlemen concerned with me. You say ‘it appears to you that the Gentlemen of Durham were too hasty and a little too harsh in bringing forward certain articles for his Lordship to sign when there was no necessity for it'. I can easily conceive that you may be misled by the Bishop if you do not hear both parties. The matter of fact is this (as Messrs. Gillow, Eyre and Smith will testify) that, when he continued to persist that we were merely counsellors and not delegates with equal powers with himself, we proposed by word of mouth the following propositions, to which he has appeared to give his assent, on which we put them down on paper for his signature which he refused to sanction. They were thus:-

In order to proceed with harmony and to remove all difficulties that may arise in the prosecution of our pious design of establishing a college for the education of the Catholic youth of this kingdom, we the undersigned have judged expedient, in consequence of the commission signed by the Bishop and his clergy at Fernyhalgh on 10th July 1798, to subscribe the following Resolutions:

1. That all the monies given for the above purpose shall be immediately lodged in the hands of a banker, appointed for that end, in the names of the Rt. Rev. William Gibson, the Revv. Thomas Eyre, John Gillow, John Barrow and Thomas Smith.
2. That the purchase of the lands, the situation of the college, the plan, buildings and everything relating to money matters (till the plan agreed upon be completed) shall be regulated by a majority of voices of the above five gentlemen.
3. That the undersigned bind themselves to sign an Instrument purporting that all lands, monies, &c. confided to their care for this purpose are held in trust, to be wholly and solely appropriated to the erection of an establishment which, when built, shall be under the direction of the Bishop of the Northern District for the time being, according to the decree of the Council of Trent in the 23rd Session 18th chapter, and as explained by Pope Pius VI in his Brief to the Archbishops and Bishops of France.

4th August, 1798.

This transaction took place on Saturday, 4th inst., and was again renewed the day following after dinner, when he formally dismissed Mr Gillow and myself with these remarkable words and angry countenance: 'You may go home as soon as you please, I never will sign it'. On which Mr Eyre immediately departed for Crook Hall and, at the earnest solicitation of Mr Gillow, I went to the inn and ordered a post chaise to take me away the next morning. Was this our behaviour too hasty or too harsh after his formal dismission and after having been with him at Durham from the 26th of last month?

But that you may form a proper judgement of our proceedings by the trust confided to us underneath, I send you the Resolutions of the meeting at Fernyhalgh on the 10th of last month.

At a meeting of the undersigned clergymen convened at the request of the Bishop at Fernyhalgh, 10th July, 1798, the following Resolutions were unanimously agreed to, viz.

1. It is expedient that a college should be established for the support of the mission.
2. That such college, in the opinion of the undersigned, should be established in the Northern District.
3. That some eligible place be purchased. Gainford on the banks of the Tees was mentioned by the Bishop and appeared a likely place.
4. That for the purpose of providing funds for so essential a purpose, the members of the meeting engage, with the consent of their Brethren, to pay the interest of £1,000, from various monies belonging to the said Fund. Mr Gillow hoped to engage the Brethren of Yorkshire to do the same, and Mr Storey trusted the Brethren of Durham and Northumberland would subscribe liberally.
5. That it appears to the meeting that an estate held by Mr James Orrell yielding about £80 p.a. may be sold for the above purpose.
6. That the establishment at Tudhoe vesting in the Rt. Rev. William Gibson, Thomas Eyre and Arthur Storey may hereafter, if found expedient, be applied to the forwarding of the said college.
7. That Mr Daniel, as President of the late College of Douai, engages to pay for the use of the said college such interest of monies in his hands as can be spared until the affairs of the college late of Douai be finally settled.
8. That the following gentlemen be appointed a Committee with full powers of transacting everything relating to the said establishment, viz. the Rt. Rev. William Gibson, the Revv. Thomas Eyre, John Gillow, John Barrow and Thomas Smith.
9. That the said gentlemen, whenever anyone of them shall die, or absent himself from the Northern District for the space of one year, do immediately elect another clergyman in his room, the Bishop of the District always being one.
10. That the above gentlemen do forthwith proceed to take the necessary steps for the purchase of Gainford or of any other lands that may be deemed more eligible and, as soon as may be, apply to every Catholic congregation in the kingdom for its support, printing and circulating for that purpose such a statement of the whole

of their proceedings and views as shall appear most conducive to the proposed end.

11. That notwithstanding the appointment of the said Committee, the meeting understands that the Bishop of the time being shall have that control and authority over the proposed establishment as is ordained by the Council of Trent and advertised by Pope Pius VI in his Brief to the Archbishops and Bishops of France.

[Signed:] Gul. Acan., V.A.; Rob. Banister; Marmaduke Wilson; Arthur Storey; John Orrell; John Gillow; John Lund; John Worswick; John Daniel; John Barrow; John Rigby; Ant. Lund.

Let all impartial readers of the above judge to whom the fault of disagreement is to be ascribed. Read the Council of Trent in the 18th chapter of the 23rd session, as also the extract of Pope Pius VI to the Archbishops and Bishops of France. Neither one or the other speak a syllable in his favour. The former evidently speaks of monies, lands, houses &c. under the control of the bishops, whereas the benefactions for a future college must come out of the pockets of each subscriber. The first is spiritual, the second is merely temporal and ad libitum.

Mr Gillow and I were well aware that he would throw the blame on one or both of us. Being well acquainted with his all-grasping power, I disposed myself particularly to receive exclusively the charge he makes against me. But, thank God, he has not the power of charging me with any one action in the business that was not the act and deed of the other three gentlemen.

With real regard and much esteem, I remain, dear Sir, Your obedient, humble servant, J. Barrow

122. Rutter to Banister Minsteracres, 5th January 1799

My dear Uncle

I was not a little concerned at first to hear of your bad leg but upon more consideration I was disposed to hope it might be advantageous to you as a drain in your old age, especially as it relieved your other complaint. I believe that my grandfather in his declining age had likewise a bad leg to exercise his patience and to increase his crown. I have heard my father say that he made a most edifying end. I thank God that my health is much as usual.

I was at Crook this week to procure some information for you concerning the college but I heard nothing new. My last letter to you on this subject was soon after the dismissal of Messrs. Barrow, Gillow &c. from Durham, and in your answer was enclosed an apology by Mr Barrow for himself & co. I easily admit what he says in his vindication, but his subsequent conduct seems to be far more objectionable and has given much greater offence to the Bishop.

You may remember that a little after the date of my last, his Lordship signed at Minsteracres certain articles which seemed equally strong as those which he had just before rejected at Durham which, I believe, was wholly owing to Mr Silvertop's influence with him. When this point was gained, I concluded that the main difficulty was got over and that things would go on prosperously, hoping at the same time that Mr Barrow would be quiet for a while till the purchase of Ushaw was made and completed in the manner agreed upon. But it seems that Mr Barrow soon after wished to adopt another plan and what it is I cannot make out unless it be to drop the purchase of Ushaw and to join them at Old Hall Green. If so, I attribute this change to Mr Horrabin's fine speeches on the subject which however made no impression on me when, about 2 years ago, I saw him at Crook together with Bishop Douglass. For I cannot easily be persuaded that Old Hall Green is a proper situation for the education of young missionaries, being so near to modern Babylon and so utterly unprovided of fish and fuel, &c. However, as I do not pretend to know the merits of the question between Mr Barrow and the Bishop, I shall say no more; certain it is that his Lordship is so displeased with his conduct that he has struck his name out and substituted that of Mr Lund.

As to the purchase of Ushaw, it is not yet completed, but I hope will be in a short time. Mr Holford who transacts business for Sir Edward mentioned some time ago that there was an estate in the south worth £3000 to be sold and proposed that we should buy it to be exchanged for its equivalent at Ushaw, which advice I could have wished the Bishop to have followed, considering our small resources. His Lordship however is for having the whole estate at Ushaw, though he is not disposed to sell out of the funds any of his episcopal monies and to place them on the purchase. For my own part I cannot but apprehend great difficulties without the hearty concurrence of the Lancashire Brethren. I suppose our Bishop will expect me to accede to whatever his Lordship and Mr Eyre shall think proper in regard of selling out of the funds the missionary monies that stand in our 3 names, but as to our Fund-money, I shall take the liberty of thinking for myself.

The Bishop has taken up his habitation at Durham and has therefore sent for all his books &c from York. His translation of Mahis's Controversy is actually in the press and will, I suppose, cost 3 or 4 hundred pounds which in my humble opinion might have been better applied to the new college.

I lately received a letter from my father and am glad to find that all your family is well. He mentions his journey to Mowbreck and the kind reception you gave him. About the same time I made likewise a little excursion as far as Haggerston to see my cousin Mary Hodkinson who was in better health and spirits than I expected to have found her. She received a letter from you while I was there and seems to be very happy, to want for nothing but a little tea which I shall take care to send her from time to time. I went to Haggerston by Callaly and Eglingham and came back by Wooler and Biddlestone, which last is the seat of Mr [Thomas] Selby, and met with great civilities wherever I came.

I have written to Mr Moir to supply your deficiency of the Saints' Lives but as yet have received no answer.

I have seen Mr Wilkes' apology, by which it appears that he has imposed on his Brethren, many of whom, however, I doubt not, perfectly coincide with his sentiments.

We have not yet heard for certain who is to be Bishop of the Midland District. Some say it is to be Mr Gregory Stapleton because Bishop Douglass wishes him to be removed from Old Hall Green.

Our Bishop is better in health and spirits than he was. Dr. Clarke, an eminent physician of Newcastle, tells him that his complaint is the gout. I urged him 3 or 4 times very pressingly to appoint a coadjutor, alleging the present critical situation of affairs both in Church and State but this, I am clear, will not be done.

I daily think of you at my prayers and hope you remember me likewise in yours. With best wishes, I remain your ever dutiful Nephew, Hen. Rutter

123. Banister to Rutter — Mowbreck, 13th April 1799

Dear Sir,

I received your letter dated 4th & 7th of this month [missing] yesterday. As you are one of the trustees for the money in the stocks, the interest whereof is for the maintenance of several priests, I cannot see how either you or any of your fellow trustees can justly and conscientiously deliver up your trust. A trustee of minors e.g. may justly meliorate the income of his charge, but not deteriorate it. If he sell out of the national funds those monies of his pupil which were placed there and lend them at a greater interest on good security, as he thinks, but it not proving to be so, he loses either all or a part, he will be compelled to make up all the deficiency, and very justly, for no security is to be reckoned equal to that of the Bank of Great Britain.

The case you state to me is much worse, for, by selling out and placing it on a purchase, you deteriorate it. Item, you may often wait two months or 3 or half a year before you receive the interest, which may be owing to hard times, or to the former's losses, or to his vices, &c. In the interim the priests must live on credit. Your own reflection will suggest some other reasons why you cannot, in conscience, comply with the other trustees in selling the monies placed in your names in the national funds &c. But you must not communicate your reasons too freely or even at all, because if you do so there will be endless altercation and debate. 'Tis sufficient to say that justice and your conscience forbid you to sell out even one farthing. If Acanthos can do it he will undoubtedly expel you from being a trustee: bene est, fiat, fiat. You will lose nothing, you have no hope or expectation of being made his coadjutor.

I see in all this affair a true image of Douai College under his administration. He told me at Claughton 3 years ago that the college received annually from Paris funds and actions 1800 gain[illeg.] before the revolution. I asked him: Why did you put so much on a French bottom? Because, he replied, the interest was better. But a wise farseeing man would have formed a judgement of the future from what had often passed before, viz. that French actions were very fluctuating and their securities upon a frail bottom. English stocks yielded not so great an interest but they afforded a solid security. And is not that to be preferred to a greater interest? I also remember Mr Ralph Platt's letter in which he informed the clergy of this county how that in order to pay the debts he had contracted he had it in contemplation to sell some funds which were destined to maintain students. You know he came over and met the two Talbots and his brother Matthew at London. Varley went back with him and went also to Paris. The affair was so well conducted that Mr Richard Southworth was sent off and Platt was represented as one who had written many falsehoods and turned upon the mission without ever going to the school of divinity, as he told me himself. He picked up a small pittance whilst he was writing-master. In short, there was a continual change at Douai College, for as soon as he found any professor, master or prefect opposite to his measures he discharged them.

Hence he was obliged to then take them from divinity at the end of one, two or 3 years and these not proving to be of his liking, he sent them a'packing too.

I believe it may be improper to say much, even to your most intimate, about the present debilitated state of his mind and body although that is a good reason for suspending all operations. I advise you to say nothing about his signature of articles at Minsteracres; he will not regard them unless they coincide with his principle view, and what is that? To be both Bishop and President, the sole controller of monies and funds, the purse-bearer and paymaster general. Say nothing of his episcopal monies; he ought not to alienate or deteriorate the income of himself and of his successor. In guarding his income he is, as you are, a trustee. As to your demanding of him an explicit statement of the ways and means which he hath in his power to make good all deficiency, 'tis needless, for he has no means but in his own idea. What, think you, did I hear him say one day? 'Oh! that we had but had a college some years back, we would have had thousands by this time'. I did not ask him how, it appeared to me so like a golden dream. He who administered Douai College 9 years whilst all its reserves and funds fructified and nevertheless saved not single mite. How would he have saved thousands in these days?

You tell me that he entertains not the least thought of a coadjutor. You surely have never heard from Mr Eyre what I informed him of the last year, viz. that he said once, and I believe twice, in my hearing, item, in Mr Eyre's hearing, item in the hearing of some others: 'that Bishop Walmesley had thoughts of making his brother Richard [Gibson] at Mawley bishop'. And in a letter to him of the last year I write thus:

I have been informed that Mr N., whom you mentioned as a person fitting to succeed Charles Berington, is of a family in very mean circumstances and that one or two of his sisters are insane. Mr N., to conceal his pedigree, passed for a Yorkshireman but he was born in this county. You also thought Mr Thomas Eyre too old and if that be an objection 'tis much more so against your brother Richard who is, as I am told, older than you. So, without alleging other reasons at present, his age must deter you from choosing him to be your coadjutor.

But Mr John Barrow gave Dick no quarter in a letter to his Lordship. He tells him that if he wants one to handle an ox or sheep and to inform him whether they be fit for slaughter, he may take his brother &c.[1] In the same letter he tells him that the new college must be pontifical and he shall claim no more interference or authority in it than what the Bishop of Arras did claim in Douai College, who never pretended to control the president in making alumni, in sending to orders, to the mission &c. He was, I presume, so stung with this that he turned Mr Barrow out of the Committee, but as he did not choose him in, so neither can he turn him out.

I doubt not of the reason of his leaving York. He neither can make Mr Gillow think as he doth nor shift him from York so he removes himself. When he was here 3 weeks and a day (Oh! how I was accablee) the last June, he often talked of selling out funds. I always replied that it could not be done without great loss, the stocks being so low. Mr Eyre appears to act inconsistently and imprudently; Acanthos neither made him nor you a trustee and therefore cannot take the trust from you. If the Brethren who are interested in this matter, and whose income in part at least is derived from the stocks, choose another in your place more compliant than you, the affair is settled. What if Acanthos ruin you in the good graces of Mr Silvertop? Then you must quit Minsteracres; to prevent that I think it will be proper to ask your Squire whether a trustee is not bound in justice and conscience to defend his trust and not suffer it to be deteriorated. Our Brethren would not consent to sell out, but agreed to pay the interest of a thousand at 5% until the purchased land and profits of the college shall be able to redeem the debt.

But we are, I believe, all unanimous to give nothing but to a pontifical college in the sense above specified, we are all so well apprised of his doings at Douai College the space of 9 years or more. And yet the good man was never heard, at least by me, to believe, say or acknowledge that he was imprudent in the steps which he took. I will now dismiss this subject, I think I have said enough to satisfy you.

[torn] in no concern if you publish my decision and even to Acanthos himself. He seems to desire to equal Stonyhurst, but he never will. He will surpass it by many degrees if he procures to have a well educated clergy, well taught, well disciplined, well matured by a very regular course of humanity, philosophy and divinity of 12 or 13 years, under aged and experienced masters. Here is [John] Rickaby at Garstang, a poor, scrupulous and ignorant man; Mr Barrow of Claughton has scarce patience to hear his absurd doubts. What learning had Himsworth acquired, tell me? Did the Bishop of Durham [not] tell him that he would never give him any living in his diocese? Undoubtedly he saw him to be an impure scoundrel, an anythingarian for Liber et Venus. Could no one at Douai College discover him to be such?[2]

My leg, thanks be to God, has been healed these two months, but to preserve my health I have an issue a little above knee on the inside of my thigh. Be sure to perform your promise and come hither in July.

I presume you have no tax to pay for your income. I give in an income of £88, the 55th part of which is £1.12.0d. Nevertheless I am not able to buy for myself as yet a suit of clothes. A present was lately made me of 26 yards of Irish cloth for shirts, which I was in extreme want of. As far as I can see you will inherit nothing of mine but books and pictures. A limner has drawn my picture, framed and glazed; it is thought by some to flatter me by making me look younger. It is, however, nearly as like to your father as to me. When you come you must get Thomas to draw it in oil contours together with my profession of faith, i.e., [burning coals fall upon them; thou wilt cast them down into the fire (Ps. 139, 11), viz., Gallican Articles 1682 defended by Bossuet]. The three Blue Books 1789, 1790, 1791 opera omnia Joseph Berington, opera Jo. Throckmorton, the letters of Wilkes, the Staffordshire clergy's creed and appeal. I remain ever your affectionate Uncle, Robert Banister

1. In a letter of 31 August [*UM* 24, 1914, p.177], Banister told Thomas Eyre that Richard Gibson had been sent to the mission in July 1763 after only 'a pittance' of three years Divinity. Nonetheless, Bishop Gibson had 'often said to different persons, and at different times, that Bishop Walmesley had thoughts' of making Richard a bishop; Banister, too, understood that Gibson had intended to nominate his brother to the London Vicariate. When the Lancashire Clergy met at Preston in August they unanimously agreed to recommend that a coadjutor be selected but while they thought it would be going too far to mention Richard as unfit and quite unendowed with episcopal abilities, nevertheless, their hints are pretty broad and must be easily understood if family connection and partiality do not blind him.

   Banister hoped the clergy on the eastern side of the Pennines would send a similar letter and he privately warned the bishop that 'if unfortunately either family connections or any undue partiality should so far prevail on your Lp. as to choose one to be your coadjutor whose little learning and inidoneity are well known to the brethren, they will leave no means untried to avert the disgrace and dishonour of the whole District.'

   Banister took the view that it would be better to have no coadjutor at all than to have Richard Gibson, and none was appointed until 10 years later.
2. Rickaby, like Himsworth (see No. 57 n2), died in an asylum. In the letter to Eyre referred to in n.1, Banister remarked: 'A certain priest, one of our ancients, once said to me, "I wonder what sort of confessors they have at Douai College?" Assure yourself that it is often the duty of a confessor to advise and press youths to return home as being unfit to proceed . . . A youth is lately returned from abroad in medio cursu quite deranged and so addicted to drinking that if it come in his sight he cannot refrain. They also return thence potatores, tabaci fumigatores and lowngers (for which I cannot find a latin word).'

124. Banister to Rutter — Mowbreck, 18th April 1799

My dear Nephew,

I sent off a letter to you last Saturday 13th inst. Yesterday I sent one to Mr Eyre in answer to his last dated 4th January which contained several queries. After having given an answer to each in order, I begged his leave to put a query to him, viz:

> whether a trustee of a major or minor can in justice and conscience deteriorate his trust. For example whether he can justly and conscientiously take a security for the capitals which are in his trust inferior to that in which they exist, and again whether he can in justice and conscience take an interest much lower than that which arises from the situation they are in. I asserted that the highest security in this nation is government security, for even mortgages on land are too often fraudulent and the interest not easy to be recovered, at least in its due time. If then the trustee has the trust-money in the public national funds and sells out and lends the money to another, how is he just in taking an inferior and weaker security? How is he just in taking a lower interest? If such a trustee loves changes and aims at some secret mark, he may say that the security which he accepts instead of government security is quite sufficient but this will not vindicate him from just reproach nor from the obligation of making full restitution if the security which he chooses instead of that of government proves faulty and insufficient. But if the major or minor agree to adopt an inferior security and a lower interest then the trustee may act as he pleases in that hypothesis which, however, is very absurd for who but idiots will ever agree to let their monies be taken out of the security in the nation and to be lent at a much lower interest. But my query concerns such persons as cannot assent to the changing of securities. If I have made my case intelligible to you, I think you will be of my sentiment.

So far to Mr Eyre. Adhere therefore to your resolution of keeping your monies in the public funds because neither justice nor conscience permit you to change your security, much less to sell out at a great loss whilst stocks are so low, whilst they that buy stock in the 3%s for example can get 6% but can at most have only 5% on land security or mortgage. In the American war Mr Vincent Eyre of Sheffield bought for me and my place £56 p.a. for £94.4s. in the 3%s. If Acanthos should propose to him to sell out and lend it to him to purchase Ushaw, do you think he would or could in conscience do it, not consulting me first? And as I am only tenant of the money for my life, could I in conscience change the best security for a weaker security, or would Mr Eyre persuade me to be such an idiot as to take a very low interest (which, from loss in selling out, would certainly happen) instead of a much higher? I think my case vis a vis to Mr Vincent Eyre similar to that of the priests vis a vis to you and your fellow-trustees. I dare venture to foretell that if the capitals in the stocks are sold out and sunk in the purchase of Ushaw, more complaints, murmurs, resentments and severe censures of the measure will ensue than would fill a volume.

I heard the other day that the nuns remaining at Paris are in one house, either at the Rue de la Fosses [Saint-Victor] or Rue S. Antoine, and that they have a numerous school of girls whom they teach and thereby get a very competent subsistence. Mr [Thomas] Shelley, a clergyman of Douai College is one of their Directors; Mr Henry Parker and Mr Robert Kellet, monks, are also their assistants.[1]

Mr John Lund of Cottam has been long laid up by a severe gout. Mr Daniel went on Monday in Holy Week to assist his congregation and is there as yet. Dr Charles Stapleton[2] died on Monday in Holy Week about 7 o'clock p.m. and was buried on Holy Saturday a.m. Mr Blacoe was present when he died. Mr Finch is at his brother's, viz. Thomas, but not very easy in mind because his brother is niggardly and unhospitable. I have tried but ineffectually to get him into a sinecure. You have so many French priests about you that you, I believe, cannot serve him. I remain your most affectionate Uncle, R. Banister

1. The English Augustinian convent in Paris was suppressed under the Directory but it was used to intern all the English nuns remaining in Paris. The nuns were freed under the Consulate; the Benedictine (or Black) and Franciscan (or Blue) nuns shortly came to England but the Augustinians remained. Shelley was chaplain to the Blue Nuns in Paris from 1778. He accompanied them in 1800 to Costessy, where Sir William Jerningham gave them a refuge, and then retired. Kellet and Parker were also interned but stayed in France after their release.
2. Nephew of Bishop Charles Stapleton.

125. Banister to Rutter Mowbreck, 23rd August 1799

My dear Sir,

I received on 18th inst. a letter from Mr Thomas Eyre dated 12th and I answered it on 19th. 'Immediately', says he,

> on his Lordship's receiving the second deed from my brother Vincent he sends me a letter to say that my brother had not made any alterations, whereas my brother certainly suggested that of its having the following words inserted, viz. "that the purchase had been made with the joint monies of William Gibson, Thomas Eyre and Thomas Smith".

Nevertheless, if I rightly recollect he submitted the insertion to Matthew Gibson, the bishop's nephew.[1] Moreover, as soon as he had received your letter he posted away his man to tell Mr Thomas Eyre that you consented to sell out, but took care to suppress the conditions on which you consent to sell out. Mr Eyre also writes ibid as follows:

> I vehemently suspect that his Lordship will not confine himself to the resolutions which were drawn up and signed at Minsteracres, but will be for requiring more obligations from Mr Smith and me, as the former informs me that he appears to have hinted more than once, but does not speak out for fear of being thwarted in the main object of his ambition and desire.

Then he asks me

> Who is to keep this second deed? Upon it certainly depends all. Mr Smith's right and title to Ushaw is also mine and if his Lordship should insist upon his keeping it in his own hands, any day he thinks proper, or any of his heirs, whether designedly or otherwise, may destroy it and then his heirs (e.g. Richard Gibson) will become absolute masters of the land. I cannot say I have much confidence in Matthew Gibson's transactions. There has been a bundle of letters between them which are cautiously kept from anyone's inspection. As his Lordship is to a great degree suspicious and jealous of me he will never allow me to keep the second deed, I shall propose Mr Rutter as an indifferent person, but this, I doubt much, his Lordship will never consent to. In short, what to do for the best and how to

act? I never was so much at a loss to know as I have been these 5 years and shall be happy in having your advice how to proceeed.

I answered him and inculcated the using of the most cautious steps and to trust to nothing that is not rigorously legitimate or according to strict law. I again repeated: [the snake hides in the grass. But do you believe that there is a snake in the grass? It seems to me an omen indeed that the lord and master of Ushaw Farm is Mr Richard Gibson, and thereby he obtains the coadjutorship instead of someone more worthy or more suited to that office. What can he know about building and adminstering a college when he is only familiar with rustic matters—pasturing, slaughtering, pots and pans, coaling and stone-picking?].

If this letter comes not too late before you have signed away all power, I do vehemently exhort you, let what will follow thereupon, that second deed is nothing else but a fallacious contrivance; you are by it said to purchase Ushaw for 10s. and divers other considerations. Whereas in the first deed William Gibson is said to purchase it for £4200 which may be esteemed a full or sufficient price. When at the death of the Bishop, his heir at law, or his heir by will, e.g. Richard Gibson, shall enter into a suit for Ushaw against Mr Eyre and Mr Smith and these latter, to maintain their right, produce the second deed in which 'tis said that they purchased it for 10s., but by the first deed William Gibson purchased it for £4200, what a contrast there will appear, what a strong suspicion of fraud in Messrs Eyre and Smith! And to corroborate the suspicion, it may justly be said that William Gibson when he conveyed away Ushaw for 10s. was not compos either in body or mind having had several paralytic strokes which almost totally debilitated his mental faculties. What a figure Messrs. Eyre and Smith will make in an open court of judicature. How they will wish they had never signed away their monies out of the stocks.

Therefore sign nothing, until a single deed be made conveying Ushaw to all three as joint-tenants and to the survivors and survivor of them, inserting also that the purcahse is with the monies of all three and a clause binding each not to break the joint-tenancy by writ of partition. For observe well by 31 Hen. 8 c1 and 32 Hen 8 c32 'one joint-tenant may compel his co-tenants by writ of partititon to divide the land'. This, I doubt not, will throw his Lordship into strong emotions and resentments, but fear nothing, only stick to your point. You may say as mildly as possible that you have the best reason and advice to act as you do but do not name your advisers.

I am thinking, if I can go to the meeting, to get, mediante tamen alis e.g. Dno Jo. Barrow, an unusual petition of all at the meeting to our Bishop to choose a coadjutor, in which also they must make exception to Richard

Gibson, not for want of religion and piety in him, but for want of sufficient learning (as all know) to qualify him for so high a station. If his Lordship's partiality, or any other consideration, moves him to choose his brother, the Brethren will unanimously present to the Propaganda his indoneity.

I remain your most affectionate Uncle, R. Banister

N.B. I desired Mr Eyre to communicate to you my last letter; you may also communicate to him a good part of this.

1. A lawyer in Hexham.

---

126. Rutter to Banister Minsteracres, 14th October 1799

My dear Uncle

It is high time to give an account of myself since I left Mowbreck. I took Durham in my way home and found matters arranged just as I had expected. The Bishop, in consequence of my letter to him which I sent from Mowbreck, had procured letters of attorney for banker [John] Wright and desired my signature to them. This I refused to give till I was well assured that Messrs. Eyre and Smith were to be joint-tenants with his Lordship. The second deed was not engrossed for this purpose and he refused to give me a written declaration by which he engaged to place Ushaw equally under their power. Consequently nothing was done. His Lordship, however, insisted on my taking with me the powers of attorney to save the expence and trouble of sending them after me.

On 19th August he wrote to me in a very peremptory style to send back immediately the declaration by which he had engaged himself to indemnify the clergy for any money he might borrow off us, together with the letters of attorney. But I only sent back the latter, assuring his Lordship that the said declaration should remain in my custody till the business of Ushaw was finally settled. He afterwards employed Mr Smith to write to me on the same business and then Mr Eyre, but to no purpose. Finally, I met the Bishop at Crook on 27th of last month and after some vague discussion I agreed to sell out to a certain amount, but not before he had signed a declaration by which he engages to make Messrs. Eyre and Smith joint-tenants to all intents and purposes and to execute the second deed for this purpose without delay and without any other alteration than such as had been suggested by Mr Vincent Eyre.

Thus you see the business is finished in my regard. But you will ask why I did not insist on a single deed being made to convey Ushaw to all three in the first instance. This is certainly what I could have wished to be done but I could not urge the necessity of it as the second deed had been approved of by the most eminent lawmen, such as Charles Butler, Vincent Eyre, &c. Mr Thomas Eyre wrote to his brother a second time stating his objections to the said deed but he received the same favourable answer that it was the most unexceptionable method of proceeding in the business:

> to take the conveyance from the family of Sir Edward Smythe to a real purchaser and that there was not the same reason for a blind in the conveyance from Mr Gibson whose heir at law could not make the same pretensions to the estate as might do the heir at law of Sir Edward Smythe.

I most sincerely hope that all will unite heart and hand in forwarding the great work of the college which I am confident will be the chief nursery for the mission to all England.

I presume you have now perused my Life of Christ and shall be glad to hear your judgment of it, as that of Mr Daniel, to whom I beg my respects. Without aspiring to the merit of authorship, I shall be content if it is found to be a useful compilation which exhibits the literal and spiritual sense of the Gospels, a solution of their principal difficulties, and approved harmony of their seeming discrepancies, together with such moral reflections as tend to nourish true piety and religion. Something of this kind is certainly a great desideratum to our English Catholics, and if you and Mr Daniel will be so kind as to favour me with your corrections and emendations I shall be happy to profit of them for the public good. But if you dislike the plan of the work, or the principal part of its execution, then I shall drop all further thoughts of publication, hoping that Our Lord will accept of my good will and raise up some other person better qualified for such an undertaking. What I intend this winter is to improve the preface and to add some controversial notes and pious reflections where you think they are wanted. Wherefore if you and Mr Daniel can finish your corrections and animadversions I shall be gald to have my manuscripts sent back together with my Dictionaire Historique in about 5 or 6 weeks time and I beg you will let me know by what waggon they are sent and when I may expect them.

Be pleased to give my respects to Mr Barrow when you see him. He received me very kindly and afforded me much entertainment. Tell him that The Psalms of David for the use of Parish Churches which he heard at Lartington, are published by Edward Miller, Bookseller, No. 5 Old Bond St., London, price 10s.6d.

Pray how is the affair of Salwick chapel settled?[1] I do not hear that the Bishop pays any attention to the petition of the Lancashire Brethren concerning a coadjutor. I am sorry that Dr [John] Brewer[2] has undertaken the cause of Wilkes.

We have been full of company since my return home. At present Mr Silvertop is confined by the gout. My cousin at Haggerston is still in the infirmary. I am, dear Uncle, your dutiful Nephew, Hen. Rutter

1. See Nos. 118 n.2 & 137.
2. Succeeded Cowley as President of the English Benedictines in 1798.

---

127. Rutter to Banister — Minsteracres, 17th January 1800

Dear Uncle,

It is now some time ago since I informed you of the purchase of Ushaw farm and on what conditions I had acceded to the Bishop's demand. I did not agree to sell out of the funds till he gave me a written declaration by which he engaged himself to make Messrs. Eyre and Smith joint-tenants with him, and this declaration he has now legally executed so as to vest the estate equally in the power of all three. Nothing more, I believe, has been done. The Bishop proposes to his colleagues to take the farm into their own hands immediately and is, I fear, rather too sanguine in reckoning on the profits they shall make. He has received various plans of a new college from different parts, but I do not hear that anyone in particular has been adopted.

The state of his Lordship's health is much the same as it has been except that he cannot walk so well. He gave deacons' orders before Christmas but not without some difficulty. I suppose that in consequence of my opposition to his Lordship's designs I have forfeited his good graces and I wish you may not have done the same by putting him in mind of a coadjutor. The affair of Wilkes, I hear, still gives him a good deal of concern as his apostolic powers are now acknowledged to extend to the Middle District.

The farmers here have had an exceeding bad harvest and had not finished it by Christmas Day. I hope your neighbour Robert Blacoe[1] has been more successful. The season seems equally adverse to health as to the harvest, for I am informed that 3 thousand persons are now sick at Newcastle. The gout has been particularly prevalent. Mr Silvertop and his butler have been severely attacked and are just now recovering. The chaplain, I fear, will have the next turn, for I already discover some symptoms of it and wish to know how I may counteract it.

You will probably have heard of the death of poor Mrs [Mary] Maire of Lartington which was quite unexpected. Her loss will be severely felt, not only by Mr [John] Maire but by all her indigent neighbours. It is not likely that Mr Maire will marry again, but in case this should happen and he have children, his family would be cut off from the Lartington estate. Mr Silvertop's second son, whose name is Henry, is at present considered as presumptive heir to it and is soon to be married to Miss Eliza Witham of Cliffe.[2]

I have been long expecting to hear what judgment you and Mr Daniel have formed of my little work which I left with you. I am willing to hope that the longer you keep it the more perfect you will make it by your corrections, additions &c. Be so kind, however, as to inform me how soon I may expect it back at Minsteracres and what are your most material objections to it, as likewise whether you think it may be useful to Christians of every denomination and as such deserving of encouragement. I am sensible indeed that it is little more than a compilation but, if it be a useful compilation and likely to promote the cause of virtue and religion, I am content and willing to be considered only as another Kath, mentioned in sacred history who, being poor, had recourse to a powerful rich man named Boaz and gleaned in his field the ears of corn after the reapers. For so I, in like manner, being conscious of my poverty and inability have gone into the fertile field of the Evangelists and have followed the steps of the holy fathers, the first reapers, and of other approved labourers, in order to gather a plentiful supply such as may not only suffice for my own spiritual nourishment but likewise for that of the faithful in general in all their several wants and necessities.

In my last I desired you to send me my Biographical Dictionary because it is useful to consult occasionally. But if you make much use of it yourself, you need not send it but some other work to fill up the box as the Lettres Critique or the Journey to the Holy Land written in Latin or any other that you can spare the best. I hope that Charles Butler made you a present of the Life of his uncle Alban for your trouble in supplying him with the best part of it. It will not, I think, add much to his literary fame, and is but little relished in these parts.

I have perused this winter another small work which I believe is much better entitled to your approbation than the Life of Alban Butler; it is Dissertation Historique sur les Libertes de L'Eglise Gallicane & l'Assemble du Clerge de France 1682, a Londres 1799. The author, who is supposed to be Monsr. L'Abbe La Pointe, asserts that the Gallican Declaration has more connection than is generally imagined with the present misfortunes of the Gallican Church, for that it gave a handle to the parliaments and secular magistrates to oppose and reject the Pope's rescripts and to arrogate to themselves all ecclesiastical causes as protectors of the gallican privileges. After they had thus combated the popes on the ground of supporting the bishops, they employed the inferior clergy against the bishops, meddled with the administration of the Sacraments, banished priests, burned episcopal mandates and, finally, introduced the greatest confusion both into Church and State. Some of the French emigrant priests condemn this performance but they will find it difficult to refute its arguments.

I beg your opinion on the following cases. Is a person who bespeaks a play, or who takes his children to the theatre, admissible to the Sacraments? What distance do you think will excuse a man or woman in health from coming to Mass on a Sunday in winter time and bad roads? The Massacre of the Huguenots in France in 1752 is universally condemned by Catholic as well as by Protestant writers. Pope Gregory XIII, however, highly approved of it and expressed his joy on the occasion in a public manner by having medals struck in commemoration of that event; on what ground would you undertake to defend him?

Cousin Hodskinson has been long expecting to hear from you. I hope your silence is not occasioned by bad health. With best wishes for the new year, I remain dear Uncle, Your dutiful Nephew, Hen. Rutter

1. A tenant-farmer at Mowbreck and father of the priest of that name.
2. See N° 133n.

---

128. Banister to Rutter

Mowbreck,
begun 23rd November 1799,
completed February 1800

My dear good Sir,

I received your last dated 14th October in due time. You may perhaps attribute my delay in answering you to sickness, but it is not strictly the case, for I have been in a very tolerable good health, thanks be to God. But I am very slow to execute anything of moment or importance; it is the character of old age, and if you live to my age you will very probably know it to be true by your own experience.

You give me six weeks and then I am to send you the long manuscript which you left in my hands; a hard task indeed to me who cannot now lucumbrate by a candle and small fire till the midnight knell. Moreover, as I perceive that you follow, or even translate your admired French paraphrase, I judge it necessary to consult my interpreter Maldonatus, in whom I find a collection of interpretations from the holy fathers and other ancients. For I think with him that new and modern interpretations of the Holy Scriptures are to be generally suspected or received with caution.

Your neighbour Mr Eyre, by following the sense which Abbe [Joseph] Hooke,[1] that frenchyfied Sorbonnist, has given to all the texts on which the ancient fathers and general councils grounded the full power of the Pope, the successor of St. Peter, to feed, rule and govern the universal Church of Christ, has strongly perverted, though under some kind of disguise, the obvious and universally received sense of the texts aforesaid. And to give one instance of his disguised Hookism: he defines the Church (These Ursali 1798, page 14) without the least mention or insinuation of the Roman Pontiff being the visible head of the church or its supreme pastor, supreme ruler, supreme governor, as the Council of Florence defines, saying

> [The Roman Pontiff is the successor of St Peter, Prince of the Apostles, and truly Christ's Vicar and head of the whole Church and Father of Christians who rules and governs the universal Church with the full power handed down by Our Lord Jesus Christ.]

He says that other definitions ['do not sufficiently consider episcopal rights'].

Mr Eyre in his definition therefore can have no other meaning than that the church is [under the government or full power of the episcopal college]. I defy Mr Eyre and Hooke to find either in the holy fathers or general or Pastoral Councils one single sentence parallel to this. But the Pope is named, says Hooke, in the definition just given [only as a bishop with surpassing power]. Our modern innovators and high flown gallicans deny not the Pope to be the first of the bishops, Hooke adds [with surpassing power], but in what can that consist since Hooke, page 331, asserts

> [the full power of Christ's church was not left only to the Supreme Pontiff with whom in others it was derived, but left to the college of the apostles and succeeds to the order of bishops].

But this will, I hope, suffice to make you very cautious both in reading and much more in following and imitating French writers.[2]

You say you are sensible that your work is little more than a compilation, but when I see you take Alban Butler word for word, I cannot but call it a plagiarism or a patchwork of which the said Alban remarks that compiling patchworks cramps genius and invention &c. Translating and quoting an ancient father is very laudable but pilfering scraps from moderns in the same language and without acknowledging the debt, is insufferable. Compare the lives of several English saints in Britannia Sancta,[3] and again by Alban, and you will find that the latter steals nothing from the former but casts a saint's life in a new and much superior mould. Certain it is that all the mysteries of Our Saviour's life and death are such copious themes that no eloquence of man can exhaust them. But if you cannot say more than Alban hath written, say nothing. Nevertheless, I believe that without far-fetching and without deviating into impertinences, much may be very aptly added by way of comment or instruction. Lewis de Puente is very copious on the circumcision of Our Lord and on the Magnificat &c. I wished you to take him with you and to borrow freely from him or rather to meditate, ruminate and masticate his excellent meditations and being filled with their odoriforous honey tangam apis argumentosa, pour it out on fine paper.

I cannot here omit a short anecdote. Two reverend priests, whom you knew when a boy, in my hearing whilst we were in the Vice President's room at our coffee after dinner, observed that Alban in his Lives of the Saints had, with his pencil admirably well designed a copy from an original, that is, a lady of high rank, known to all three. I never purposely looked for the said portraiture but accidentally hit on it in reading your plagiarism from Alban upon the Visitation, 2nd July. I have heard that Alban in her presence hardly spoke a word but let her go on in a volubility of tongue 'to pour out', as he words it, 'her embryos of half-formed conceptions', (she never had any other kind) 'and speak of the most noble subjects in an undress of thoughts'. This is a proof of the great command he had acquired over his passions, for although I speak so well of him in my little narrative (the best part of which Master Charles has not given) nevertheless I have known him irritated. It is also a proof that he was capable of writing a keen satire.

Whensoever you speak, preach or write of the adorable Trinity, you cannot be too cautious in your expressions. I totally disapprove of this (chap 2 1st page 6 'He (St John) represents the word as a cause or principle acting extraneously from himself upon the void space in order to give a being to all creatures'. There was no void space before the creation. But I presume you borrowed the expression from your paraphrast or some other gallican exotic.

I hold with Maldonatus that Our Blessed Lady, the most eminent pattern of true love and friendship, did not leave her cousin Elizabeth till she saw John both born and circumcised, swaddled and suckled, and his mother well recovered. Your French paraphast (if I mistake not) fancies that it would be indecent for the Holy Virgin to stay and assist her cousin in her travail. Wonderful nicety! But Benedict XIV seems doubtful whether Joseph or Our Blessed Lady circumcised Our Saviour; she undoubtedly was present and took care of the wound in order to its being healed. Our Blessed Lady by seeing the pains of child-bearing and her cousin, and observing what was wanting to swaddle an infant, learned two things. First, to praise and glorify God who exempted her from all pain in the birth of her son. Secondly, to see what she was to provide for the swaddling of her infant God and in what manner she was to swaddle him. Do you think that she learned all this by revelation? And if you do not, you must think that no time or place were more opportune than the birth of John and the Holy Family of Zachary. In these days not only young ladies of rank and fortune but even of the lowest class are quite ignorant of the duties of a mother when they are married and continue so in high life generally being too proud and too lazy to do maternal functions or occupied in both diurnal or nocturnal amusements.

In your letter dated 17th January you wish to know how you may counteract the gout. 1. By exercise moderately taken. 2. By not studying too long at a time. 3. by not studying in the night but rising in the morning to your studies. 4. By refraining from fat luscious food which is too nutritious and overloads the stomach.

The French emigrant priests who condemn or show dislike to the dissertation of Abbe de la Pointe deserve to be suspended a divinis and if the Bishop would hear my advice I should counsel him to make every one of them who reside in his District 1. To say the Roman Breviary only and follow our Directory or otherwise be forbidden to say Mass. 2. To take the Dogmatic Brief of Pius VI by which he condemns the Synod of Pistoia and rejects, annuls and declares void the infamous Declaration of 1682, otherwise to be suspended a divinis.

If a person bespeaks a harmless play and takes his children to it, I cannot deny but that he is admissible to the Sacraments. Alban did not condemn it in usta hypothesis. But how dangerous it is to allow even the smallest [sign of the Devil's pomps!] A distance of 8 miles may probably excuse a man who enjoys good health from coming every Sunday in bad seasons and rugged ways; women are not as able to come so far by much. My dear Sir, talk not of distances but enquire whether there is in persons living at a distance any good and sincere will. This St Paul calls charity in the Epistle of yesterday (Dom. 50ae) without which nothing can avail.

Did Pope Gregory XIII rejoice for the massacre precisely as such, or not rather for the good consequences which he believed would follow, viz. the suppression of rebellion, the extirpation of the seeds of rebellion, heresy and impiety. Grattan was a strenuous speaker against martial law in Ireland, nevertheless it was carried against him and all his rhetorical amplifications of its bloody cruelty. And I am glad it was for thereby many lives of innocent men were saved and a more speedy end was put to rebellion. You and Mr Eyre can muster up queries to me in abundance, and you cannot but know that my resources for just and adequate answers are very few in my small library and I cannot ride every week to Manchester to consult the best, I suppose, and most numerous in this county. What if all this tale of Pope Gregory's rejoicing for the Massacre of Huguenots be a French Huguenot's fiction, as the murder of French ambassadors returning from Rastade by Austrian Hussars is now known to be the fiction of French Jacobins. The motive of this latter was assuredly no other than to raze the stagnated spirits of poor gallic wretches to fight more battles against perfidious Austrians. And the motive of the former was to decry His Holiness, and the motives of those pious good bishops, with Bossuet at their head who coined the infamous Declaration of 1682, was to incommode Pope Innocent XI, as Luther would gladly have denied the real presence because he thought that nothing could incommode the pope so much.

After Easter I intend to send your manuscript with Lewis de Puente, but not the Dictionaire Historique, for meditating Puente and reading that Dictionary are almost as incompatible as inspirations from above and suggestions of Satan.

I am, thank God, pretty well. Brother Thomas was last Thursday here; at about 8 o'clock he was very ill in his stomach, but by camomile tea, gin and rum he was relieved and went to bed at 12. He went after dinner to Preston. I pray you pardon me for not writing. I remain your most affectionate uncle, R. Banister

1. Died 1774. A second edition of his *Religionis Naturalis* (1762) was issued by Dom J B Brewer, OSB, in 1774.
2. Banister is probably citing Eyre's translation of Charles Gobinet's *The Instruction of Youth* (1783).
3. By Richard Challoner, 2 vols., 1745

129. Rutter to Banister Minsteracres, 4th June 1800

Dear Uncle,

I return you many thanks for the favour of your letter and hope to profit of the good advice it contains. As you do not seem to approve of my Life of Christ, I shall for the present drop all thoughts of proceeding in it, hoping that somebody else may undertake the work and do justice to so noble a subject. A work of this kind, if properly executed, would, I think, be highly acceptable to the Catholics of this kingdom as well as to Christians of every denomination and would greatly serve the interests of piety and religion. As to my self, my first design in undertaking the work was chiefly to give a harmony of the 4 Evangelists with a few additional notes such as were necessary to explain difficult places and reconcile seeming contradictions. For a desire to know the words and actions of Our Blessed Redeemer in their proper series, and to see all that the Evangelists mention concerning him incorporated in to one narration appeared so just and natural that it was truly a matter of surprise why no such English harmony had ever yet been printed for the benefit of the Catholics of this country.

However, when I began to consider how few and scanty the notes were in Bishop Challoner's edition of the New Testament, I thought it advisable to enlarge my plan in the manner I have done by elucidating the sacred text more fully and suggesting such observations as tended to confirm our holy faith and promote solid piety. For this purpose I had recourse chiefly to the Analogie of Maudit which you recommended to me when abroad, and which, I believe, has ever been considered as a masterly performance. Hence in the new edition of the Introduction to the Sacred Scriptures the name of Maudit occurs in the list of the eminent ecclesiastical writers of the 18th century. My chief labour was in condensing, abridging and incorporating this analysis into the text, which was sometimes more difficult than perhaps you may imagine. However, I did not implicitly and blindly follow the above mentioned author, being aware of his gallican notions, but have all along compared him with others both ancient and modern, from whom I have extracted whatever seemed proper to illustrate the evangelical history. The controversial notes were chiefly taken from the accurate commentary of Dr. Witham and I was happy to borrow anything from Mr Butler or Bishop Challoner because you recommended them to me.

In short, my chief concern was to have good materials and never gave myself the trouble of translating from Sandinus or others what I found already done to my hand by Mr Alban &c. Thus what I have said of the instruments of Christ's Passion is chiefly transcribed from Alban, and it seems to be more in its place in a Life of Christ than when inserted in the lives of saints. However, I have not the most distant idea of assuming any honour to myself from the labours of others; if this had been my object I should not have had recourse to such authority as Mr Butler &c, but in order to avoid detectionm, would have preferred such as were more ancient and less known. The truth is, I was perfectly indifferent whose it was that I wrote down, provided it appeared useful and answered the end which I had in view. For what matters it to the public if the work be good who it was that composed it. If you had allowed this Life of Christ to go on I should not have affixed my name but should have pointed out in the preface the sources from whence it was compiled, and this, in my opinion, would have been sufficient to clear me from the charge of plagiarism. But, as you think otherwise, and as this is the principal charge you allege against me, you will excuse me if I add a few words in my own defence. I agree with you that in works of wit and genius to steal from others is inexcusable plagiarism, though I believe such plagiarism is common even among authors of some celebrity, at least Dr Burn say it is so, though he condemns the practice of it.

But if this long apology appear unsatisfactory, I have another question to propose to you, viz. what is your real opinion of the work when I divest it of all those scraps from Witham, Butler, &c. so as to consist only of the harmony, the analysis of Mauduit, the observations of Sandinus and what little I have added myself? In this state would it meet with your approbation or that of Mr Daniel, or could I easily cite the authority I take from? I hope soon to receive back my manuscript with your corrections. I thank you for that which you pointed out in your last concerning the void space which had escaped me. The omission of the 2 words will rectify the mistake.

You advise me to be very cautious in my expressions when I speak of the Trinity and I will endeavour to be so next Sunday when I explain that adorable mystery. I recollect that last summer, when I had the pleasure of seeing you at Mowbreck, you objected to an expression which I had made use of in speaking of this subect, viz. different persons, and it was my intention to correct it, the first opportunity. But I find the same expression made use of by an eminent divine of Douai College, viz. S[ylvester] Jenks, and that in his abstract of the Trent Catechism[1] where he ex professo treats of this sublime mystery. How shall I follow your advice?

Mr Silvertop has been at London with his son Henry who tomorrow is to be married to Miss Witham of Cliffe. They are to live at Hardwick [Hall], a place belonging to Mr Maire, about 11 miles from Durham. Mr George Silvertop writes to me from London that Gregory Stapleton and Mr [John] Nassau are set off for Rome to recover the English College there.[2] He adds that Joseph Berington is in town and that most people attach blame to both sides. Although the price of everything is in the extreme, yet he says that luxury was never at a higher pitch nor London ever more full. Our Bishop is much the same. Mr Orrel when in these parts approved much of the purchase of Ushaw but I hear of no plan or subscriptions. I am, dear Uncle, your dutiful Nephew, H. Rutter

1. *A Letter concerning the Council of Trent* (1686). Jenks was nominated Bishop of Callipolis ipi and Vicar Apostolic Northern District but died in December 1714 before his consecration.
2. Actually the two priests went to Rome to submit the question of the marriage of the Prince of Wales and Mrs Fitzherbert to the Holy See.

130. Rutter to Banister — Minsteracres, 10th June 1800

Dear Uncle,

I lately sent you a long letter by the post for I did not suppose that Mr Hull would have gone so soon into Lancashire. I dined with him yesterday at Stella and he was so good as to say that he would take with him and deliver to you the supplementary sheets which I lately received from Moir and which I hope will repair your first edition of Saints' Lives. I yesterday took my last farewell of poor Mr Mather who is much reduced and cannot in my opinion hold out above 2 or 3 days longer.

Our family are returned home. Mr Silvertop is a good deal indisposed. I hear no particular news except that Bonaparte has restored to the Austin nuns of Paris and to the Poor Clares of Aire all their property and I suppose Mr Daniel will lose no time in soliciting the restitution of all ours at Douai. Mr Gregory Stapleton expects to be reinstated at St. Omer. As he is gone to Rome and is no bad contriver I shall not be surprised to hear that he brings back a mitre.

As to my Life of Christ, though it may be useless to others it will amuse and instruct me. What think you of the chronology which I followed? I have preferred that of Sandinus to Usher's because, though the latter has been much in vogue, yet the former was most generally received in the church. The opinion that Christ died on 25th March and not on 3rd April prevailed, I believe, without dispute in the church till the end of the 13th century when it was attacked by Roger Bacon on the ground of its being contrary to astronomical calculations. On this account, according to Wading, he fell under some suspicion as to the soundness of his faith. Alfonsus Tostatus adopted his opinion in the beginning of the 14th century and having proposed, among other things, in a public thesis 'that Christ did not die on 25th March but on 3rd April, and in the beginning of the 33rd year'. This occasioned so great a sensation in the public mind that he was obliged by order of Pope Eugenius IV to undergo an examination before certain judges who condemned him. Enough, however, on this subject which is above my reach.

I lately received a letter from my sister Susan who lives now with Lord Clifford at Ugbrooke, Devon, a most beautiful situation as any in England. She says that Lord and Lady Clifford are very kind to her so that I hope she will find it to be a comfortable place.

I hear you are going to keep your Jubilee at the end of this month and I beg you will accept my most sincere congratulations on the occasion. You are now almost the eldest son of Alma Mater, and that you may long continue such is the wish of your ever dutiful Nephew, Hen. Rutter.

---

131. Banister to Rutter — Mowbreck, 7th July 1800

Most dear Sir,

I do highly approve of both your design and your work. Nevertheless, I believe it to be susceptible of improvement and that you are capable of giving it, provided you will take time and leisure. There are two kinds of borrowing in works of wit and learning: 1. By taking word for word and in the same language all before you. 2. By taking the thought, argument and proof from another but giving it a new stamp. I therefore can not but say that wheresoever you borrow from Mr Alban word for word it is properly plagiarism, but if he has handled the subject so well and so amply that nothing more or better can be said, I would touch that very lightly. I have sent you by Mr Hull this letter and one tome of Lewis de Ponte (whose canonisation has often been requested by his Catholic Majesty) from which you may cull abundant matter and excellent spirituality to nourish both your own and your reader's devotion to all the mysteries of Our Saviour's birth and life and mission. The 2nd tome contains all the mysteries of his Passion Death, Resurrection, Ascent and Descent of the Holy Ghost. Now, whatever you take from Lewis de Ponte, whether translated word for word or cast in a new mould, I shall not deem it a plagiarism. Probably Bishop Challoner did cull many thoughts and sentences from him but I think the copy very inferior to the original. I wish you to insert his comment on the Magnificat, at least abridged, and exhort your reader to learn the canticle by heart and to recite it daily thus joining with the universal voice of God's Church.

You follow, I presume, Venerable Bede in fixing the death of Our Lord on 25th March and you dissent from him in the number of years of the life of Our Saviour. It appears from Lancelotte's quotations of ancient fathers and writers that it was a current opinion that Our Lord lived in his mortal life 30 years only. St Augustine delivers himself upon this point with great reserve and nevertheless he seems to give to Our Saviour only 30 years. I wish you to speak with the reserve of St Augustine. It is, I think, needless to adopt with a tone of certitude and infallibility either your opinion or mine.

I write all this in too much haste. I am not as fluent as Milner or many others so consequently unfit to furnish a printing press: a dull inertness impedes my flight, I creep and languish when compelled to write.

Mr [William] Poynter[1] informs Mr Daniel the 30th of last month that Gregory and Nassau are arrived in Hamburg. I remain your most affectionate Uncle and good friend, R. Banister

1. Vice President, Old Hall Green.

132. Rutter to Banister — Minsteracres, 25th October 1800

Dear Uncle,

I received by Mr Hull your kind favour and the first volume of Lewis de Ponte. You do not mention your health but Mr Hull informed me that you were pretty well and I hope you still continue so.

In consequence of your encouragement, I propose this winter to take up again my pen in order to improve my little work in the manner you are pleased to direct. Wherefore I beg you will be so kind as to send it to me by carrier in a box directed to me at the office of A. Adams Esqr., Broad Chair, Newcastle upon Tyne, and that you will advertise me when I may expect it. If you have not entirely corrected my manuscript, I hope you have pointed out at least what places stand in need of correction, either as to the thought or expression, what additions are to be made and, in short, whatever you conceive may improve the work.

In regard to chronology, I must here beg leave to make a few observations in answer to your last. Thus in regard of the death of Christ, which I fix on 25th March, Benedict 14 affirms that it is an ancient and constant tradition. As to the moderns, Henry Philippe reckons up above 30 writers of note who maintain the same opinion, and many others might be added since his time. Among the rest, the learned Henschenius, whom I consulted in Mr Maire's library, refers to above 20 ancient martyrologies in support of the same which he had seen in different parts of Europe in manuscript. You say that I dissent from Venerable Bede in fixing the number of years of Our Saviour's life. But this, I apprehend, you will find to be a mistake if you consult my chronological table at the end, which I translated from Sandinus, and where I inteneded to write 33 and not 32. But enough of these learned critical niceties which have divided the most knowing chronologists and which therefore it is in vain to pretend to determine.

I will endeavour to cull out of de Ponte useful lessons of spirituality. His meditations, however, appear to be too diffusive to enter into my plan and perhaps it is more advisable that Christians should attach themselves to the words of the sacred text which are the word of God rather than to long commentaries which are the words of men. For this reason I frequently omitted any reflections at the end of chapters when the Gospel itself was sufficiently clear and supplied matter of meditation. I beg that you will point out what chapters are deficient and whether you would have me divide the work into different books, or leave it as it is &c.

I suppose you know that Mr Mather died on 30th of last month. I had last week a letter from my cousin at Haggerston and am glad to find that she enjoys much better health now than formerly. She complains much I did not go to see her this summer. I hear nothing of the Bishop. His farm has been exceedingly productive this year in consequence of the high price of hay which is now got to £9 or £10 a ton. I beg my respects to Mr Daniel. Your most dutiful Nephew, Hen. Rutter[1]

1. Rutter visited Banister in the interval of Nos. 132 and 133. During that period Banister and Thomas Eyre exchanged letters about the increasingly autocratic

behaviour of Bishop Gibson. On 8 April 1801 Banister urged Eyre 'not to 'flinch nor recede one inch from the college or your functions and offices 'until you have exposed to all the brethren of Northumberland, Bishopric, Yorkshire and Lancashire your case, and finally to the Propaganda itself, which ought to be be well informed of Acanthos's indisposition, that his mental faculties are impaired by a paralytic informity.' On 20 April Banister expressed his indignation that Eyre got no money from the bishop for the maintenance of Crook Hall and that his salary of twenty guineas a year was seven years overdue. Banister would acquaint John Barrow and the Lunds of the situation and told Eyre to inform other 'ancients and discreets' among the clergy. There was no doubt but that John Barrow would champion his cause with the bishop but, 'for fear least he do it with too much vehemence, so as to hurt the cause', Banister would write more temperately. He assured Eyre that if Gibson dismissed him, the brethren would remove the students from Crook Hall to Lisbon. Banister was also thinking about writing to Bishop G. Stapleton prompting him to inform Propaganda or Erskine of the infirm state and condition of Bishop Gibson.

133. Rutter to Banister — Minsteracres, 5th June 1801

My dear Uncle,

I write this to thank you for all the kindnesses and civilities which you showed me when at Mowbreck. I arrived safe at Minsteracres on the Saturday night. In my way I dined with Mr Lonsdale who seemed to be of the same opinion as yourself concerning the line of conduct which Mr Eyre had to adopt. The storm, however, seems now blown over for when they met at Ushaw all was peace and not the least notice was taken by the Bishop of any disagreement.

I saw Mr Eyre last week but he brings very little news from Sheffield. He and his sister in law are the only executors to his brother, and therefore a good deal of trouble will fall to his share. The Duke of Norfolk, who had placed an implicit confidence in Mr Vincent Eyre, declares himself perfectly satisfied with his conduct though it had been oftentimes represented to his Grace in the blackest colours. For the sake of the father the eldest son Vincent will succeed to a part of his stewardship.[1]

Our young Esquire, Mr George, is just arrived from the metropolis and is setting out again for Hamburg, Copenhagen, &c., not for pleasure but for the sake of his commercial concerns. He informs me that Bishop Stapleton has been extremely ill but that he is now recovered. Mr Poynter succeeds him as President of Old Hall Green. As Mr Gregory is acceptable to Mr [Thomas] Clifford and the Brethren of Staffordshire, they are ready to instal him at Longbirch, which I suppose would have been withheld from the new bishop had he not been to their liking. It appears that Seigneur Erskine is still at London but he does not seem to be a favourite either with clergy or laity.

To my great surprise Mr [Henry] Maire has brought back with him a wife. Her name is Miss [Catherine] Fermor of Worcester; she is said to be accomplished and to be about 32 years of age. This marriage can not be supposed to be very agreeable to our family; however, they carry it off extremely well.[2] Mr and Mrs Silvertop are gone to Hardwick where Mrs Henry [Witham] is daily expecting to be confined. The stagnation of the coal trade is a serious loss to this neighbourhood but we live in hopes that the Baltic will soon be opened to us.

I have not seen the Bishop since my return. Mrs Silvertop dined with him last week and says that he looks ill though enjoying good spirits. Not long before, his doctor apprehended a serious fit and recommended bleeding as absolutely necessary to which his Lordship consented.

In addition to the books which you were so kind as to lend me, I borrowed in my way home another volume of Mr [Thomas] Wilkinson at Kendal.[3] It is entitled Dilucidationes Selectorum S. Scrip. Quaestionum in Historiam & Concordium Evangelicum. The author is F. Martin Wouters, a Louvain divine who writes entirely in the scholastic form.

In regard of the Life of Christ, I have a query or 2 which I forgot when at Mowbreck: 1. Must I divide it into separate and distinct books or leave it as it is at present? 2. In case you recommend a division, how would you divide it? Would you divide it into 3 books? The first to comprise Christ's private life to the end of the 1st pasch; the 2nd, his public life; the 3rd to commence with the 4th pasch till his ascension into heaven? Vence divides his harmony into 6 parts. In case this work should ever go to the press, would you have that part of it which is incorporated with the sacred text to be printed in italics or only distinguished from it by inverted commas? Would you print any quotations from the fathers in Latin? If the work should be too large for 1 volume 8vo, would you have it to be in 2 volumes 8vo or 1 volume 4to? I again return you many thanks for your corrections and remarks on my manuscript and could wish you had kept it a little while longer to point out more fully its deficiencies and redundancies. To what particulars would you chiefly direct my attention in revising it?

As the post is waiting, I must conclude with assuring you, dear Uncle, that I remain your most dutiful Nephew, Hen. Rutter

1. On 20 April Banister sent Thomas Eyre condolences on the death of his brother Vincent, noting: 'All the monies bequeathed by Robert Westby late of Mowbreck for the maintenance of a priest here were in the trust of Mr George Wilmot, Mr Westby's executor, and then in the trust of your brother Vincent.' He hoped that the heir, also Vincent, who was twenty-five years old would succeed as the duke's steward in Sheffield.
2. See N$^{o.}$ 127. The significance of Maire's second marriage was that since he had inherited the estates of his uncle John Maire in 1771 and had changed his name from Lawson, his property would devolve on the children, if any, of the second marriage; but if there were none, and if Henry succeeded to the Lawson baronetcy, the Maire estates would pass to his younger sister Catherine, married to John Silvertop, and through her to Henry Silvertop, her second son. This is exactly what happened. At the death of his older brother Sir John in 1811, Henry resumed the name of Lawson to become the sixth baronet. Meanwhile, as we have seen, Henry Silvertop married Eliza Witham and had changed his name to inherit the Cliffe estate from his father in law Thomas Witham. Ultimately, then, three important Catholic estates came into his possession: Cliffe, Hardwick and Lartington, but he was thriftless and a gambler and squandered much of this inheritance. His second son, Monsignor Thomas Witham, put it well when he said 'that Harry Witham did not keep racehorses seems not to have prevented him losing large sums on the turf'. On one occasion Witham arranged a ball at Lartington to celebrate the anticipated win of *Doctor Syntax*, a wellknown horse owned by the Catholic Ralph Riddell of Felton Park. But the horse lost, the ball was cancelled and Witham fled to Scotland to escape his creditors and stayed away eight years. The Hardwick estate had to be sold and it went to the Earl of Darlington; since it lay over the east Durham coalfield, it shortly began to yield a fabulous profit. Then Cliffe had to be sold but his mother, fortunately, lived until 1832 thus preventing the dissolution of Lartington. Monsignor Witham, who inherited Lartington, observed ruefully that if it had not been for the extravagance of his father, he would have been the richest commoner in England. (He is said to have applied to Rome for a dispensation to marry so as to maintain his name but the Holy See, indifferent to the priorities of the English gentry, refused.) [Gooch, thesis]
3. Thomas Wilkinson (alias Livesey and Berington), assistant priest at Kendal.

---

134. Banister to Rutter Mowbreck, 27th July 1801

My dear Sir,

I think it will be more proper to make a division of your work, and that of Monsieur Vence appears to be a very clear and accurate division. I would rather call them parts than books, for the 4 Gospels are but one book or history of the birth, life, acts, works and miracles of Jesus Christ. As to those short interpolations in the text, they ought to be rather in italics, provided they be good and clear, and this ought to be noted in the preface. I would have you print only short Latin quotations of the fathers, where it may appear necessary, to support your assertion. If one 8vo be not sufficient make two, but do not make a 4to.

I do not remember in your manuscript any attempt to express the sorrows of Our Blessed Lady when she lost Jesus or when he was nailed to the cross and lived 3 hours upon it, she standing near to it. Mary kept all in her heart, pondering them not homilizing on them, nor uttering mournful exaggerations. For a short instruction or document to married persons you may observe that Mary and Joseph did not mutually blame or accuse one another for not taking care of the child Jesus; both were pierced with grief and set out without delay to seek him and ceased not to seek till they found him. I finally hold that Our Blessed Lady stayed with Elizabeth until John the Baptist was born and circumcised and was the chief one of those whom Gabriel foretold would rejoice in his birth. Moreover, the Blessed Virgin was advanced in her pregnancy more than 3 months, I believe 4 months or more, otherwise St Joseph, who had not the remotest suspicion of his spouse's infidelity, but admired her most chaste and most devout behaviour, would not have fallen into a thought of privately withdrawing himself from her unless his own eyes had informed him of her pregnancy. Instead of adopting Alban's harangue on idle visits and impertinent overbearing loquacity of women, make a short observation on Elizabeth's words to show the admirable power and efficacy of the Blessed Virgin Mary's salutation which could sanctify the child in its mother's womb.

It seems to me very proper to say something of the dolours of Mary. Why did Our Lord either command or wish or will his most loving mother to stand by him and see him suffer and die and bear all the blasphemies that were uttered against him, to look on while the soldiers divided his clothes and insulted him and gave him vinegar, &c. She, by humbly intereating him, obtained his consent to be partaker of his cross and, as St Bernard says, to die with him by compassion and to enter into the great mystery of the cross more deeply than all others.

I advise you to omit in totum the chapter that treats of the various opinions about the year and month of Our Lord's death. Your dissertation is too short to satisfy fully a curious enquiry and too long and unnecessary for a devout and pious reader.

I am very soon fatigued. Mr Storey was here last Monday 20th July. I exhorted him to stick to Tudhoe, to make his scholars read Catholic books only: the Old Testament; Fleury's Historical Catechism; England's Conversion and Reformation Compared; Saints' Lives; Instruction of Youth.[1] What a shame it is for us to be outdone by Mahometans who teach nothing but the Khoran and make it be learned by heart. And I fear not one, either in nunneries or schools, is ever made to learn by heart a simple verse of the Holy Gospels. I made R. Parker however to learn many, which I hope may be seed springing up. I wish Douai College had practised it.

Lingard and John Fletcher[2] made me a visit. I understood from the former what Mr Eyre had noticed to me, that Mr George Haydock is kept at college to mortify him, viz. poor Mr Eyre.

I am thinking to write to San Albano and proposing to one of my former scholars to come over and live with me and complete his studies here. He was ordained priest last October and his income with mine will keep us.

I am, thank God, well and very much and truly your most affectionate Uncle, Robt. Banister

1. Robert Manning, a Dutch-born, Douai-educated secular priest who died at Ingatestone in 1731 published *England's Conversion and Reformation Compared; or The Young Gentleman directed in the choice of his Religion* (Antwerp 1725). The *Saints' Lives* were Butler's and the *Instruction* was Eyre's.
2. Missioner at Hexham.

---

135. Rutter to Banister   Minsteracres, 24th November 1801

My dear Uncle,

I have been too dilatory in acknowledging your kind letter. I thank you for the hints you gave me concerning the Life of Christ and will pay due attention to them. I have been a good deal occupied in revising my work and fear it is still very unfit to make its appearance in public. I have made some corrections such as I think you will approve: The analyses at the beginning of each chapter appeared to you superfluous and accordingly I have suppressed several of them; the reflections at the end of some chapters I have sometimes curtailed as being too long; and some inaccuracies have been corrected which had escaped my observation. I must confess that my natural indolence and the apprehension of difficulties have frequently disposed me to relinquish my design but I take courage again and proceed, flattering myself that such is the will of God.

With all my retrenchments and erasements, I perceive that my work will be long and the printing of it expensive. I flattered myself with the hopes of receiving some pecuniary assistance from Mr Maire of Lartington but he answered me that he had no money to advance owing to his new change of life. I am now thinking of making application to my brother Thomas to lend me a sum of money for this purpose. I mean to take of 1,000 copies and the expense of such an impression will amount to above £200. However, if I can borrow half this sum, it will enable me to go to press. I cannot as yet ascertain the price of the work but think it cannot be under 8 or 9 shillings considering the advanced price of paper and printing.

I am sorry you did not read the whole of my manuscript and wish you would inform me which part you passed over, whether the beginning, the middle or the end. I have since showed it to one or two of my friends who encourage me to proceed, but one of them advises me to leave out the controversial notes which I am not inclined to comply with. What is your opinion? I expect to be ready for the press by the end of February.

Mr Silvertop for some time past has been in a declining state of health; he complains of shortness of breath as if he were asthmatical. The doctor tells him it may be the gout and is trying to produce a regular fit of it. A severe one might perhaps be of great benefit to him and restore him to his former vigour. I pray God to prolong his life for the sake of his family, for his death would, in my opinion, occasion a great change in it, not much to my satisfaction.[1] It is true his eldest son, George, is come to years of maturity and is considered in the world as a prudent sensible young man. But, in my estimation, there is something wanting to him, and that is the main thing of all—religion. He is, indeed, of a far more amiable disposition than his father, but he is a man that is less domestic, less inclined to the country. He is a man of fashion and pleasure, I do not mean in the vulgar acceptation of the word, as if he were a drunkard, a whoremaster and a profligate swearer and curser, but one who is of an Epicurean turn and tainted with the spirit of the world. The second son, Henry, is settled in marriage and will, I hope, do very well. The third son Charles, is destined for business at Newcastle, but he is giddy and thoughtless and little, it seems, disposed to second the intentions of his parents.[2]

I have but little news to communicate. Messrs. Lingard and Fletcher were much pleased at the kind reception which you gave them at Mowbreck. The former is, I think, a great support to them at Crook. Everything goes on there as usual. The Bishop, before he set off for London with Mr Smith, had an amicable interview with Mr Eyre and still talked of building at Ushaw.

I suppose you have lost your neighbour Mr Daniel who would doubtless be in great glee at the prospect of recovering Alma Mater. The Duke of Norfolk made Mr Eyre an offer of taking him to Paris and I wish he had accepted it in order to look after our clergy property. The Duke himself intended to apply to Bonaparte for the restoration of one of the English nunneries which was founded by one of the Howard family, I think it was the house at Brussells.[3] Bishop Hussey's residence in France has given offence to our government; he is gone to Bath for the sake of his health. I hear that he recovered for the Irish and Scotch the property which they had in the French funds. I hope that we may be equally fortunate.

Some of our French priests are gone and others are about to go. The mission in these parts will feel the want of them.[4] I learn from a letter lately received from France that there is still a great deal of religion there, but many, it seems, were not pleased at the Pope's requiring the resignation of the gallican bishops.

Have you got from Valladolid the student whom you mentioned in your last? You will stand more in need of him now Mr Daniel is gone, especially this winter time. Mr Hull is well, and that you may be so is the sincere wish of your most dutiful Nephew, Hen. Rutter

1. John Silvertop died on 26 December, aged fifty-one. In the last ten years of his life he had concentrated on completing the mansion at Minsteracres, incorporating such innovations as WCs and bathrooms. His annual income from his coal business had been about £8,000 but his expenditure was very heavy and he left debts of some £59,000. George his heir had to obtain a private act of parliament permitting him to sell entailed real estate to settle his father's affairs.
2. George Silvertop was a liberal and so Rutter did not like him; as we have seen (N° 133n), Henry was unreliable; Charles became known as Don Carlos having been commissioned colonel in the Spanish army.
3. Cardinal Philip Howard founded a convent of Dominican nuns at Vilvorde

in 1660 which moved to Brussels in 1669. The first English nun was Antonia, youngest daughter of Thomas Howard of Tursdale, Co. Durham.

4. The situation was different in the west of the District. Banister wrote to Thomas Eyre on 12 Oct 1800 about the numbers of spare priests: 'there are four, and not one place in this county or Westmoreland, Cheshire or Cumberland vacant. Mr Blundell indeed is ready to abandon Stockport, that he may not starve, and probably Mr Saul is as willing to quit Carlisle for the same reason . . . I hear of new places but I hear of no revenue. What necessity then is there of extruding young priests out of their colleges with little learning, less experience, and a scanty mother-wit? Mr Thomas Horrabin, whom I saw at Claughton the 24th of last July, told me that he immediately discovered R— to be deranged'. [*UM*, vol 24 (1914) 284/5]

136. Banister to Rutter — Mowbreck, 22nd June 1802

My dear Sir,

I received your letter dated the 18th [missing] yesterday. This will go off tomorrow the 23rd, for no post either comes or goes from Kirkham on a Tuesday.

I cannot understand for what reason you or any other is solicited to be administrator of St. Omer's College whilst it is so uncertain whether the site or buildings, and still more uncertain whether the ancient royal revenue of 6,000 livres p.a., will be restored. But, as you are invited and solicited without seeking or asking for the office on your part, I can see no reason for refusing it provided, however, that you incur no charge, no expenses for journies or maintenance. If you prosecute your work (which I hope you will) you will have no cash to lay out in journies seeking perhaps a phantom. Before Mr Daniel left Mowbreck he told me that he had saved £150 to bear his own and Mr Smith's expenses in their endeavours to regain Alma Mater. But hitherto I have heard nothing either from him or about him. He plays in obscure. To leave your place whilst your work is on the anvil or in the polishing engine will not be convenient to you, for if the Bishop send you to Pontop or Stockton or the late Himsworth's residence, you will be a mere novice in housekeeping and your mind will be more or less distracted than it hath ever been hitherto in your whole life. I could wish you to stay where you are whilst Mr William Gibson is living.[1]

He is now at York and wrote me a letter from thence, the better half of which I neither can read nor divine his meaning. He touches the old string, blaming the Brethren for their nonconcurrence with him in building him a college or seminary. He says, I think, that he is obliged to put an end to all this confusion &c. It was only last week when I held some palavering with the Rev. Joseph Orrell, then at Kirkham, that I formed an idea of his meaning, for Mr Orrell told me, as a secret not to be revealed, how that when our Bishop was at London, and the Rev. Thomas Eyre likewise there, that a Baronet offered him his house, which I saw in my return home from York and stayed one night with Mr James Melling [phrase illeg.] palatio Regis and as much land as he would choose to purchase. Bishop Douglass and Eyre &c pressed him to accept the offer, which he did at London but ran back at his return to Durham. I presume he is roused up again and is come to York to transact the business.[2] In his letter he says that he is not certain whether he shall come as far as Stonyhurst; I hope they will not ask him to give Holy Orders for by the accounts I hear he is not capable.

The person whom you call a friend for informing you that Mrs Silvertop thinks you will not suit her son in the capacity of chaplain is more probably your secret enemy and biassed by envy or some self interest.

Our Vicar General[3] is in a chronical distemper and will not probably overcome it. At present I am well, thanks be to God; Mr William Hull did hear that I was in danger of death. You see that when an answer is wanted I give it without delay. Pray write to your cousin Mary at Haggerston and tell her I am very well but have had no letter from Robert her brother this year.

On further consideration I think it proper to remind you of some things worth your attention. You lived some time at St. Omers College and was a witness of their bad discipline and of their illiterate masters and flimsy education of their scholars also of their council, sometimes a triumvirate or sometimes a quinquirate, and this latter was required by a royal institution. You must certainly recollect too how many went from Douai College to teach at St. Omers and were flirted away from there to the mission or, being disappointed of their expectation, went off spontaneously.

There is as much intrigue and jockeying in a college as in a court. Mr William Hull was one of the council when Wilkinson tried all means to get the council to vote for the admission of Joseph Berington, but Mr Hull resolutely opposed it and would not give consent. Whether this did not soon after hasten his dismission I cannot certainly say; I know that he was not long there. As to Gregory Stapleton, he jockeyed room Mr Daniel most egregiously getting him from Crook up to London. Mr John Gillow told me that he was to travel with a young gentleman (I do not recollect his name) but Gregory, by his intrigues, wriggled himself into the business. I do not know how he wrested in to St. Omers to be its Principal. What benefit has that college at St Omers ever done to the mission; it educated by half-Irish, Dutch, Spanish and Portugese and some English, chiefly Protestants. When they could get no masters from Douai College they took in Irish and laymen, viz. Philip Berington who became Sous-principal, if I am not mistaken. Mr Daniel told me that Gregory durst not show his face anymore, for Medin of Douai said of him: il est un homme dangereux.

Now suppose yourself to be at the Omerian college, nay, suppose yourself to be the Principal. The councilmen vote you out as it did Mr Wilkinson, or threatened to do, so he came to England and the college allowed him an annity of 400 livres. Again, I would have you balance in one scale old Posket's cottage on a [illeg.] moor with a small maintenance, with a fire of your own, with time to pray read and study. And in the other, the training of boys that want pocket money, the envious countenances you will meet as often as you dine or sup, the getting or paying of cash, the buying provisions and all kinds of necessaries. But, without a doubt you will possibly be as good a procurator as Mr Simon Strickland or Mr Frank Hinde, of whom Mr Robert Wilson told me wonders. I presume you will now think that I totally am averse to your accepting the office that is offered you. Indeed I am convinced that you will repent of it. I am your devoted and affectionate uncle, R. Banister.

1. The new chapel and presbytery at Pontop were given over to a group of fifteen French exiled priests between 1796 and 1802 and the mission was served from Crook Hall. On one occasion in 1807 Thomas Smith, the lay patron, took the priest to task for forbidding the congregation to stand by the fire in his parlour to warm themselves and discuss politics before Mass as they were wont to do: 'Nowhere else did such a thing happen'. (UCM *Smith Papers* OS/D3 Smith to John Bell). John Daniel (2) had died at Stockton in February and his place was not filled until December by the newly-ordained Thomas Storey (nephew of Arthur). Himsworth had lately vacated Thropton.
2. Sir Walter Vavasour of Hazlewood Castle offered Bishop Gibson his seat and sixty acres, on the Great North Road west of Tadcaster, which had been completely modernised in 1770; see No 139 n1 for the outcome. Melling was Vavasour's chaplain.
3. John Chadwick, at Weldbank, Chorley; he died in October 1802.

137. Banister to Rutter Mowbreck, 19th September 1802

My dear Hal,

I have subscribed for 10 sets, that is, 20 tomes or volumes of your Harmony, which will amount to six pounds. Unless my onions and cheese bring in a good sum, I know not how I shall pay you. I believe many have subscribed in this county and I am of opinion that both you and the Keatings will be gainers.[1]

Was not our Bishop most kind in coming to see me for I neither was able to go to the meeting (on 3rd August) at which he was present, nor after it to go out upon a journey? He came on the 12th of August and returned to Barton Lodge (from whence he came) near Mr [James] Mawdesley[2] on the 14th, to the dwelling of Mr Heatley, lately a Captain in the Lancashire Fencibles.

My illness was a bastard pleurisy, that is, in the right side. My doctor had a mind to take some blood from my arm but I would not agree to it, so he only put on a blister of constarides which answered well. I had read in Bayliri that anointing a pleuristic stitch with linseed oil is very beneficial. This was done to mine several times, which I believe did some good. On the 8th of August I was able to say Mass which I could not do on the 1st nor all the whole week.

Old Evan Wearden came hither to keep me company on Saturday 28th of August and stayed a full week out of the most thronging guild of Preston that anyone can remember. I also went to the George Inn on Monday 13th of September and stayed till the 17th. But went not to the Playhouse, which has been frequented every night (except Sundays) by a numerous company and honoured by the presence of Rev. Joseph Dunn, who was one night very near to Mrs Corry, olim Parker. He has 5 boys and one girl; she has one boy and one girl. He is a joiner, builder and a dealer in a cotton factory. He is happily a Catholic and of good repute. He has drawn a plan of a house and chapel which must not stand in Salwick but in Lee. He computes that the whole cost will amount to £520. I told him that I wish they had set it to him, I believe he would complete it much sooner than they can.

Now, you may conjecture from my journey and writing that I am in good health, for which I thank God and pray you to do likewise. You will oblige me very much by saying four Masses for Rev. Barlow, his family, the souls in purgatory and the conversion of England and Scotland. I was at Douai College 2 years on a partial fund for which I am obliged to say 6 Masses every year [for life]. It is called Gerart's Fund, so probably one Gerart bequeathed it, not Barlow, but make your intention to pray for the donor &c as above.[3]

I told the Bishop very plainly that I approved of the mode and manner of conveying Ushaw to three joint-tenants and to the survivor, and maintained that the purchase of Hazlewood ought to be settled in the same manner. We altercated very earnestly about it on the 1st night of his arrival. I cannot say that he absolutely intends to make the purchase in his own name and so keep it without any conveyance to joint-tenants. I reminded him of Bishop James Talbot dying intestate to the great inconvenience of his successor &c. As also of Bishops Thomas Talbot and Charles Berington dying intestate so that Longbirch (I believe) or some other estate goes to an heir at law, viz. the son of William Berington under age.

The Rev. Thomas Smith from San Albano last February brings this to Tudhoe in his way to Croxdale to be chaplain to Mr [William Thomas] Salvin. John Gillow, your cousin german, saw your father and mother well and hearty, as he said when there 3 weeks ago. Also your two brothers Thomas and Richard both at Liverpool and the latter a master-builder, joint partner with another.

Mr Daniel the president is not come from France again, as I hear. I am sorry to understand the ruinous condition of Douai College as there be no universities in the Great Nation. I see no more advantage in having a college there than at Crook or Hazlewood. The Republicans, like Dutchmen, will become commersants and their motto will be [Seek money first, then virtue]. And so 'tis proper for our regnicoles.

You left a shirt here. I do not this year expect you now but the next you will fetch it I hope. Pray stay where you are and begin some other work of learning to employ your thoughts. I remain, in real haste, your most affectionate and dear Uncle, R. Banister

1. Rutter's life of Christ came out as *Evangelical Harmony*, (Keating, Brown & Keating, 1803, small 8vo, 2 vols.)
2. (Alias Carter) missioner at Newhouse, Goosnargh.
3. There were several priests named Barlow and Gerard who might have made such a bequest.

138. Banister to Rutter Mowbreck, n.d. [October 1802]

My dear Sir

'Tis true that on the first page of my last letter but one (for my last I sent with Mr Thomas Smith) I did but dissuade you from undertaking the office of an administrator, but on the second page I represented to you (and in lively colours) the unsettled state of St Omers College; I never approved of its establishment. If you can recover it (which I very much doubt of) I shall have no better opinion of it, nor even of Douai College, for I hear nothing of the re-establishment of universities, of persons being assigned to professors in the three faculties, of libraries being restored &c. But it seems to me that the rulers in France, where nobility is annihilated and equality established, have calculated their laws to promote commerce and trade and thereby to make riches to flow in abundance into all parts of the great nation. I also apprehend that by their new Code, Catholics will fail first in respect of the Sacraments (there being so few priests) and consequently in to a neglect of spiritual duties &c. Those riches flowing by commerce and trade will choke the good seed &c.

This is our present state and condition; quaerenia pecunia primum, Virtus post nummos, which Alexander Pope translates: 'get money, money still, and then let virtue follow if she will', it is the fittest motto for our country. The traders and merchants in Liverpool have very lately suffered an extraordinary loss there; 14 warehouses of 13 or 14 stories high are entirely burnt. No efforts of men and their water-engines could quench the flames; they could not throw the water high enough.

Omerian property ought to be employed for its primary intention, viz. either to educate boys or to pension masters. The Bishop came hither on Thursday 12th August to dinner; in the evening we debated with much freedom how the conveyance of Hazlewood should be made. I contended for joint-tenants; I told him that I had approved of that mode of conveyance for Ushaw.

In the first week of September there was a meeting of Messrs. [James] Brockholes, James Orrell, Joseph Orrell, Barrow of Claughton and Garstang, Dr Jo. Rigby, Mr Dennett and Mr Crathorne at Garstang. Accidentally our Bishop was passing that day through Garstang to Lancaster; with much entreaty they prevailed on him to stop and dine with them. And dinner being over he (the Bishop) desired Mr Brockholes to take the chair, which he did and opened the business for which they were come and met at Garstang, viz. concerning the purchase of Ushaw and the means of acquiring it. They repeatedly urged the necessity of choosing a committee, but they could never get any answer from his Lordship. Some of them made offers of contributing largely but on condition that the monies should be under a committee.

By your account he stayed ten days at Minsteracres and I am to guess what was the topic of conversation; I suppose it was the same as at Garstang and at Mowbreck. Mr Thomas Smith arrived at Croxdale on the evening of Friday 24th September; the Bishop was gone about an hour before, so he was going to execute that which you mention on Monday 2nd. I presume that Messrs. Eyre, Gillow &c. are joint-tenants with him, and I hope the written stamp will correspond with the original paper agreement, i.e., to Messrs Gibson, Gillow, Eyre, Melling and Croskell as joint-tenants in common and to the successors of them his heirs and assigns for ever.

Did I not say that the person who told me of some words as spoken by Mrs Silvertop was no well-wisher? I hear nothing about Mr John Daniel to be depended on as certain. I believe I seldom or never forget you in Sacrificio Missae; I am very well at present (thanks be to God) and I hear nothing to the contrary from Ormskirk. I remain your dear affectionate uncle, R. Banister

139. Banister to Rutter — Mowbreck, 20th December 1802

My dearest Harry,

His Lordship sent me a letter dated 13th inst. from Minsteracres and tells me you are well and send your duty to me. He says he has ordained 4 priests and deacons and subdeacons; in short, all that came from Douai College, so he seems to think that the reapers of the harvest will not fail. But he says not one word about Sylva Corylorum [Hazlewood]. He tells me to direct my letters to him at York so I presume that he entertains some hope of taking possession of Hazlewood either at or soon after Christmas, which would have been probably effected if Sir Walter had lived. The purchase was certainly made but (as I told him in my last letter) a formality is wanting (I fear) viz. a livery and seizin. Nevertheless, I do not know whether the want of that formality [(if all the rest were perfect)] will invalidate the whole.[1]

Did his Lordship tell you he has given me Dodding Green for an easy retirement in my old age, yet leaves me at full liberty to choose either to stay at Mowbreck or to go into Westmorland? You cannot conceive, my dear Harry, how much I am embarrassed in this choice. I keep the secret to myself for I well know that if I quit Mowbreck I must steal away by the pacquet boat to Lancaster and by the diligence or mail to Kendal. For I believe not a few would be better reconciled to follow me to my grave at Kirkham churchyard to lie by my father and mother than to bid me farewell, where you are going. Notwithstanding this, my chief and greatest object is to have little more to do than to prepare myself for a good death. And, although I cannot but pity the lamentation some may make, yet I owe charity to myself before others. We have known bishops and saints quitting their flocks to prepare themselves for eternity, and I certainly ought to do so by a far greater necessity.

Mr [Michael] Wharton tells me that the income is £100 or nearly p.a. He says that [Robert] Johnson and [John] Lonsdale boarded with the farmer, who was related to them. Upon this I have written to Mr [Thomas] Wilkinson to know whether I may not keep house myself.[2] But I intend, Deo volente, to set out by the pacquet to Lancaster on Monday 10th January next, and the day after to Kendal. I desire you to meet me there. You can come, I think, in two days, but answer this for you have time enough. Mr [John] Lund of Cottam, to whom alone I have entrusted this secret, advises me before all things to visit the place before I determine my choice.

Are not the first volumes of your work to come forth next month? I remain your most affectionate dear uncle, R.B.

P.S. Evan Wearden died on Monday 7th inst. and was buried the ninth. Please to pray for him, he was about one year older than me. Please to say one Mass for all the faithful departed to satisfy my obligation which arises annually for one year's pension at Douai College.

1. Bishop Gibson prevaricated for a year over the offer of Hazlewood. It was not until 2nd November 1802 that he and his assistant Thomas Smith arrived at the castle to accept, but Sir Walter died suddenly the next morning before the deeds could be signed. Thomas Vavasour, his brother and heir, was interned in France, but on his repatriation he got the bishop to waive the church's claim to the estate in return for the payment of £60 p.a. to the priest at Hazlewood.
2. Wharton was missioner at Yealand Conyers; Johnson and Lonsdale were Banister's predecessors at Dodding Green; Wilkinson was assistant priest in

Kendal and Lonsdale's executor. In thanking William Brockholes of Claughton for his hospitality en route to Dodding Green, Banister said he found his new situation 'in no manner disagreeable'. [WAA/1803/Box A.52 No. 10 26 Feb 1803]

140. Banister to Rutter Dodding Green, 31st March 1803

My dear Harry,

I have now been in this retirement exactly 6 weeks and have spent at the least 15 guineas of my own and £5.12s. of that money which Mr Wilkinson, Mr Lonsdale's executor, put into my hands, which was £10.17s., being, as I understand, some residue now due to Mr Lonsdale who died 8th of last October; the half-year's rent being payable at Martinmas and the next in May. Mr Johnson first made himself a boarder of William Hogarth, and Mr Lonsdale in like manner. Thus the house and all utensils in the kitchen and brewhouse and cellar and buttery were delivered up to the farmer's use, as likewise bed-stocks, feather-beds (of which there are six) and sheets (a poor few of which are found for me). The two Mr Roydons[1] kept both the house and land in their own occupation with servants, both men and women, and Mr Johnson followed the same plan for several years.

I have no inclination to take and occupy the land but I am quite averse to boarding with the farmer. On this account I have changed Mr Lonsdale's sitting-room (which he made for himself out of the old hall) into a kind of kitchen by setting up a proper grate, a perpetual oven of cast iron &c which, with workmen's wages, amounted to £5.14s. I have only below stairs my parlour and kitchen, and above stairs I lodge over the parlour. The farmer and his wife lodge over my kitchen and Helen Laytham lodges with the farmer's daughter over the buttery. The chapel is part over the farmer's kitchen and back kitchen. There is an extensive garret over all the house and chapel; this I am willing to leave to the farmer to accommodate and fit up as he pleases for his own use, but as to the rooms on the south end upon the first floor, which are but four, I cannot do without them; the farmer may still occupy the great kitchen, back kitchen, buttery and cellar.

I am afraid that we shall have altercations and vexations.[2] This farmer was highly befriended by Mr Johnson, Mrs Riddell's cousin german, so he may possibly keep me, by the intervention of Mrs Riddell, from doing as I wish. Yet if I am not egregiously mistaken, Mr Riddell is not the

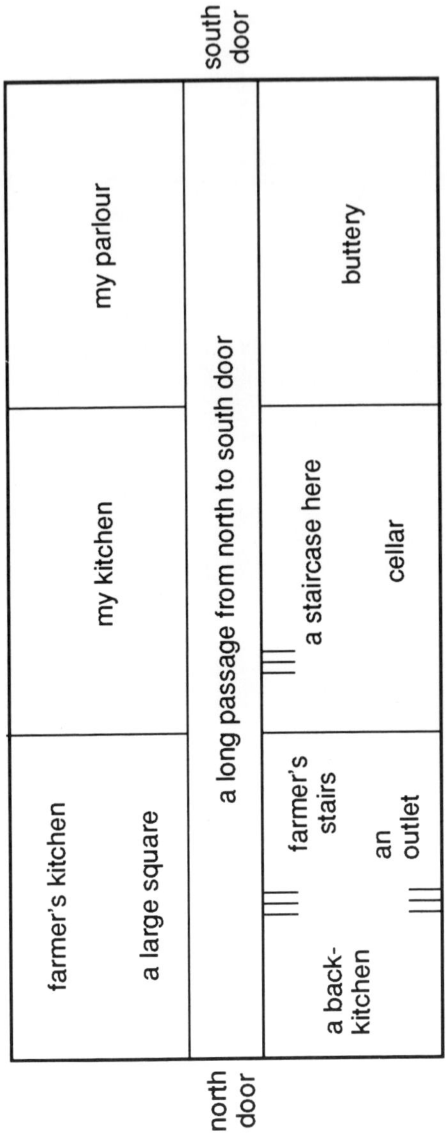
south door
my parlour
buttery
my kitchen
a long passage from north to south door
a staircase here
cellar
farmer's kitchen
a large square
farmer's stairs
an outlet
a back-kitchen
north door

setter or letter to farm this property. William Hogarth never had a lease of it, I know not his terms or conditions on which he holds it. I know not (for he has never told) whether I have any right to wood, peats, &c; nay, I do not know whether I have a right to set peas and beans and sow kitchen seeds &c in a part of the garden which faces the long shades, of which half is taken down to raise the barn. However, I have employed one Edward Derom of Kendal to delve, set and sow in the said garden. There is no inventory of goods belonging to the incumbent to be found. Mr Lonsdale has left a very imperfect catalogue of the books, but books will not feed and clothe me.

However, I assure you that William Hogarth is willing to bring us from Kendal whatsoever things we want. His wife is a good sensible woman and most obsequious to her husband. I wish I knew some in Lancashire of the same disposition. I do not frequent their house or kitchen, have little to say to either son or daughter. The least said is soonest mended. I presume you know their two sons, William and Robert Hogarth, at Crook Hall, they have been 5 years there.

Mr Francis Riddell commonly comes here at or about Easter. What his errand means I do not know. What shall I do if he lean to the farmer's grasping and if he take upon himself in his mother's name to let the farmer have all the land at the former rate and oblige me to pay both poor-taxes and window-money? Mrs Riddell told you that the rent is £130 but Mr Wilkinson still asserts that it is only £121. Mr Lonsdale raised the rent £5, have I not then a right to advance it as well as he? But assure yourself that I wish well to the farmer and intend to be as moderate as possible. But I think it is a duty of incumbents of benefices to take as much or more care of them than of their own property. Read St Francis of Sales answer to the Bishop Bellay Camus when he asked him what you do if a law suit were set on foot for your demesne? 'I am but a trustee for my successor'.

What a strange inverted system is here? The farmer puts the priest out of his (the priest's) house but builds not another for him. Mr Salvin, Mr Clifton, Sir William Gerard &c put the priest out of their own houses but built or found another for him.[3] If you ever see Mrs Riddell of Cheeseburn Grange before her son sets off hither, you must make my great and humble respects to her and if you can insinuate my distressful situation for want of conveniences to entertain (as hospitality requireth so much recommended by St Paul, and so much practised by all good men) the priests who have every where and every year visited me, and above all our Rt. Rev. Bishop who once stayed 3 weeks with me. I say if you can insinuate this into her mind, it may do me service.

Mr Correy, Mrs Ann Parker's second husband, came and dined with me on Wednesday 23rd of March. They left the George Inn in November last and now live at a house in Fishergate, newly built by him on his own purchased premises. For he is a master builder in partnership with one Wren. They built a house of God, Preston-chapel, and last year (for the great Preston Guild) a most spacious theatre, which I have seen in passing, but never entered. But several of our gentlemen honoured the performers by their presence. Our Rules published in 1753 ought to have been republished and enforced several times within these last 50 years.

I am of opinion that Hazlewood purchase will fall into nothing and that some beginning of a building will be talked of, at least perhaps some bricks and stones prepared on Ushaw, but nothing finished during the life of our present Vicar Apostolic. Can you give me any account of the causes of his declared oppositon to Mr Thomas Eyre? In his last letter to me he says that spiritual jurisdiction without temporal will little avail. There is in some cases real truth in his observation; the temporal strengtheneth the efficacy of the spiritual in many occasions. But how often are both these powers when united in one hand lying dormant?

Evan Wearden died the 10th of last December. The young boy, John Laytham, who lived two years with me, is bound apprentice to your brother Thomas for seven years. Many tears shed among my people upon my leaving them. And for my part I reckon it an image of death when a total separation from friends and acquaintances will be made. I balanced much between staying and leaving but my age and last year's illness and the example of holy bishops and venerable curates who have quitted their dioceses and parishes (with due permission) to live retired and to prepare themselves against the day of strict and severe scrutiny, moved me to come hither where I find a very small congregation. Mr Wilkinson is at Kendal a constant resident.

Do you think or surmise that Mrs Riddell expects from me any letter of thanks, as if I owed this place to her presentation? I believe the Bishop is the sole nominator; about a week after he had given me full power to choose, I wrote to him and thanked him and said I would enquire about it first. He told me in the next letter that the income was very good. However, I wrote first to Mr Wharton and then to Mr Wilkinson, who said there would be no objection to my keeping house and, not daring to go out so far in the cold frosty month of last January, I sent Helen Laytham to view the premises, She came back with great satisfaction in what she had seen and heard and was very willing to come with me and is now in the eleventh year of her service with me.

I now finish this on 2nd of April; we have had fine, warm, calm weather this entire fortnight. I believe the atmosphere of this Dodding Green is more salubrious than that at Mowbreck. I remain, my dear Nephew, your most affectionate uncle. R. Banister

1. Both called Thomas and both previous incumbents of Dodding Green.
2. This and subsequent letters are a foretaste of the long running 'Dodding Green Dispute' that arose long after Banister's death between the Riddell family and the Vicar Apostolic over the right of presentation to the living.

141. Rutter to Banister Minsteracres, 11th April 1803

My dear Uncle,

I return you many thanks for your kind letter which informs me of your arrival at Dodding Green. I had heard before that you were there in January and that after examining the premises you had resolved to stay in Lancashire. I was somewhat dubious whether I should set out to meet you at Kendal, but, however desirous I might have been, the boisterous weather rendered it absolutely impossible. The two first days of that week proved most destructive to the shipping on this coast as you might observe from the news papers. I easily conceive that you would be a good deal embarrassed about leaving Mowbreck but think all well approve your determination except your dear little flock which you left behind. They certainly had reason to lament your departure on several accounts.

I am sorry to find that you are pinched for room in your new situation but I hope the inconvenience will soon be remedied. I shall make it my business to go over to Cheeseburn Grange this week in order to state to the Riddells the propriety of your having all the accommodations which you mention. As Mr Riddell's eldest son [Ralph] is going to be married to Miss [Isabella] Widdrington, she is about to leave the Grange to settle at Leyburn, her own family place, with her son Francis.

Mr [George] Silvertop is now in London and Mrs Silvertop [his mother] sets out this week to go to Winchester where she has a sister a nun. I shall therefore be at liberty to go and see my friends and if I can finish my Easter business, propose being at Kendal towards the end of next week. As you have no room either for man or horse, I can easily walk from Kendal to Dodding Green and return in the evening. I have had a touch of the influenza and afterwards of the opthalmia but, thank God, am now better. Few have escaped in these parts.

You ask me what the reason is of the Bishop's declared opposition to Thomas Eyre. I believe you know it as much as I do. About 10 days ago I had a long letter from his Lordship but its contents are not very interesting. I have returned an answer which I believe will not afford him much pleasure because in favour of Mr Eyre. He desires to remove him from his office as President but without assigning any solid reasons. I refer his Lordship to Barbosa, where he says: [One canonically elected to the administration of a seminary ought to have it permanently and not be removed except for legitimate and just cause, referring to Galet's The Office and Power of Bishops.]

Keating has finished the 1st volume of the Life of Christ. The subscriptions, though liberal, are not sufficient to defray the expense of printing. But in the hope of seeing you soon I shall be short and subscribe myself, Your dutiful Nephew, Hen. Rutter

---

142. Banister to Rutter Dodding Green, 27th April 1804

My dear Nephew,

I have received all 20 volumes of your Harmony for which I subscribed, and also two more, your gratuitous gift, for which I return you my grateful thanks. You have, I think, made great improvements upon your first copy. I attribute this to your pure intention and ardent desire to promote amongst the faithful a clear and perfect knowledge of the life, actions and sufferings of Our Redeemer. Continue still to pray that all who shall read your harmony may imprint Jesus on their heart and retain his words and documents in their memory but forget the person who set forth the regular series of Our Saviour's life on earth. For Rodriguez says that those sermons are the best which excite contrition and a holy fear in the auditors and move them to a sincere repentance and confession of their sins. But when they go home full of encomums upon the preacher and do no more, such sermons are unprofitable to the hearers and dangerous to the preachers whose whole reward will perhaps be nothing more than human praise. You have read, I presume, the life of St. Francis of Sales by a canon of Usez and may recollect that when the saint had printed and published his Introduction to a Devout Life, it was deservedly praised and commended by all; nevertheless a preacher of a strict religious order inveighed against it, and burned it too, in presence of his audience. This was told to the saint but excited not in his mind or heart or tongue the least resentment. I think the preacher was of the saint's diocese, consequently liable to a reprimand from his bishop but the saint had built his house upon a rock and therefore neither the malignant blasts of envy nor the pains and sorrows of many encomiums and panegyrics could move it.

Mr James King (alias Green) who died lately at Rome was my Master in Divinity annis 1751 and 1752. I suppose him to have lived full 60 years. Mr John Taylor was a school-fellow of Mr Cliffe, 4 years below me. Our Bishop was here in last November 3 days and nights. I cautiously declined the least mention of Mr Eyre or of Hazlewood or of Crook, Ushaw or college-building, &c. I was not at our Clergy-meeting the last August. Mr Broomehead, Kenyon, Haydock and a few more resolved to contribute and to get contributions to enable the Bishop to build. Mr Broomehead wrote me a letter to invite me to contribute but added that he desired no answer if I refused, so I sent no answer. How very infirm is our Bishop in his limbs yet very cheerful and conversable. He said: Mr Rutter does not like Mr Eyre nor I. I said nothing, nor asked why or wherefore and he added no more.

Mr Eyre, not long after my coming hither, informed me that he expected a dismission from Crook. I encouraged him to be firm and to appeal 1. to the clergy, 2. to the Propaganda. I mentioned to him what you quoted out of Cabassutius and sent to the Bishop. Probably that citation deterred the Bishop from his design of disgracing Mr Eyre so peremptorily. Thomas, who is generally conscious of his Lordship's secrets, told Helen, my servant, that Mr Eyre arraigns his Lordship for a large debt. I remember that Mr Eyre informed me that he advanced £90 towards the incumbents who claimed dividends on the interest of that money which purchased Ushaw.

Do you think Crook College maintains itself by the sole pensions of the students? That is, supposing that there are 25 students who pay each for bed and board and learning £25 p.a. and their own clothing: 25 persons x £25 = £625. Will £625 maintain 25 students and 3 masters, 1 prefect, one manservant, 3 women servants, their salaries and wages too; house and land rent also, and we must not forget the President. If £625 can suffice for all these burdens, I will not compare it to the feeding of the 5,000 with 5 loaves of bread but I cannot but say it somewhat similar.

Dear Sir, I pray you let me know how you do and give me your nouvelles if you have any and believe me to be your most affectionate Uncle, R. Banister

143. Banister to Rutter Dodding Green, 21st April 1804

My dear Rev. Nephew,

I long expected a letter from you, for you have usually returned me an answer in a short time. I send this by Lancelot Hogarth to Durham, the postage will not, I presume, be much.

So Arthur Storey and six other confederates have agreed to subscribe £500, not their own property, or if some shares be their property, 'tis only for their lives or their respective residences and must go to their successors. But perhaps the Bishop is to pay the interest, equivalent to that accruing from stocks? Mr Eyre informs me that by selling the money in the stocks to buy Ushaw the Brethren have lost annually about £16. To build houses or colleges by borrowing money is a strange undertaking and not much better to buy land unless in part. But if Mr Eyre and his confederates subscribe £500 which is the property both of the present and future generations, 'tis in my opinion a flagrant injustice and not much better to change the certain security and punctual payment of stocks for a precarious and variable security and payment. For whilst our noble Rural Deans lent our Fund-monies to tradesmen, needy farmers, shopkeepers &c they frequently at the meeting told the Brethren non fructificat viz illa vel ista pecunia Dos. As now all our monies are funded, we hear no more of those hateful sounds, non fructificat.

I am of opinion that our Lancashire Brethren will not even bear to hear a proposal to sell out and to lend the money for building a college. At the meeting in August at Preston (I was not there and intend to go there no more) Broomehead, Kenyon, James Haydock and a few more called aloud for a subscription (not of fund monies) but from each man's private property. The greatest part had skulked away and Mr [William] Irving was marching off but the Nuns Rev. Father R. B[lacoe] set his back to the door and compelled Mr William Irving to stay and subscribe.[1] Broomehead wrote to me for my subscription saying it would be levied by six instalments but if I did not accede he would take my silence for my negative. I was and am still silent.

Our Bishop came to me at my invitation (of which I understand he was very glad) 21st November, 1803, Monday to dinner. He confirmed 29 on Tuesday 22nd, stayed all Wednesday and, after breakfast, on Thursday set out to Brough because he would not go to Lartington late in the evening. I entertained him on Tuesday with a Gross jest, on Wednesday with some Gibier, &c. Not a word of the building, nor of Crook; he only once said: 'Mr Rutter does not like Mr Eyre nor I', to which I made no reply nor questioned why or wherefore. He probably alluded to your objecting to sign away the above mentioned £500. He appeared to side with some of the French bishops who protest against the Pope's authority and power to take from them their jurisdiction. He also hinted something about Cardinal [Giovanni Battista] Caprara as a man obsequious to the First Consul in prejudice of the deposed bishops.[2] But his discourse is often so desultory and vague that for my part I can scarcely tell what he means to say or assent.

You intend to call a meeting at Newcastle in the course of a fortnight. I therefore fear that this will not arrive before you have summoned it. Such meetings seldom do any good. To your first question, I have above given my answer, viz. that they cannot alienate the Fund, nor a part of it, without a flagrant injustice. To the 2nd question I say that this building of a college is no reason at all, much less a sufficient reason, for alienating the funds originally destined to maintain the missioners. The Bishop himself is to erect his college or seminary; he is also every year to pay an income tax, as the priests of his chapter and of his district and diocese, lest the seminary or college fail for want of a sufficient revenue. But if the Bishop of our District allege his inability either to build or to pay a yearly revenue to his seminary, much more reasonably our missioners may plead a total inability to build a college and a present inability to pay any income tax to it. Our Bishop has most probably monies in the funds or at interest. Can he justly give any part away and alienate it from his successor?

You write that 'provided the Bishop will agree to a fixed plan of the building and nominate 2 or 3 persons to superintend the management of it, let us all unite &c.' Make no such provisions, he will not bear them and you yourself know it by long experience. Again you write 'Let the Bishop be requested to send an Address to every part of his District, &c.' A printed letter will do no good at all. He sent one about the country 10 years ago or near it, signed by himself and Douglass and Walmesley. I know no good that it did. The Bishop himself, and a chaplain or two (but all three ought to be men of courtesy, of amiable manners, of easy address) should visit every gentleman and gentlewoman, especially devout widows, and through every county. When such a tour is undertaken I shall have some hope of a college. But do not mention what I now write except to a person of great confidence. In short, I judge it to be quite useless to propose anything to our Bishop, but stand firm in refusing both to sell out and to lend the public monies either to the Bishop or to any other. Can not Ushaw transaction open your eyes?

As to St Omers, you must in conscience pay live-rents and debts but not out of Bishop Talbot's thousand, unless you suppose (which I do not) that [Richard] Cornthwaite[3] and Talbot were in partnership like two tradesmen; and when the live-rents and debts are paid, if Cornthwaite's thousand be left, I think Mr Milner has the best title to it. Our Bishop and Douglass can have none.

It is indeed surprising that Mr Thomas Eyre has given £100 to the Bishop, but is it not, think you, to hedge in the sum which he advanced for the Bishop. See his words to me in his letter dated 27th June, 1801:

> His Lordship is to refund out of Ushaw every half year £98.2.7. to make the Brethren 1 half-year's interest, equal to what it was every half-year before, viz. £104. Last Martinmas 1800 the Bishop should have made the 1st half-year's payment and I, being the agent for the Brethren, bona fide advanced to them £98.2.7. never doubting but the Bishop would refund that money from Ushaw. But to my great astonishment his Lordship has not so much as paid 1s. Nay, so far from making any apology for having so long withheld the money after my sending 2 or 3 letters, to which he did not deign to give an answer until the other day, when, instead of paying to me £98.2.7. and advancing the 2nd half-year's payment of £98.2.7. which was become due last May-day 1801, he wrote as follows: 'all I received from the farm must be paid away for new stock (of cattle, I presume) and I have been drawn on for payment'. Thus the Brethren are laying out of their small salaries at a time they can but very ill afford it. Mr Smith has repeatedly endeavoured to persuade his Lordship to remit the money but all his Lordship replies is that on that head he has made up his mind and therefore he need not give himself any more trouble by speaking to him about that subject.

So far Mr Eyre to me. Do not let him know that you received this intelligence from me, but you can ask him whether the Brethren can be certain and sure of receiving their dividends as now they do from the national stock.

I cannot find in this trumpery library the Council of Trent. I know it gives to bishops great powers for erecting their respective seminaries but let it be remembered that the capitulares, clerici and beneficiati were all endowed in re immobili terra firma. Many of them had a plentiful income, they could, without little abatement to their menage, pay both to the erection of a seminary and also an annual pension to its support and entertainment. A very infirm man of 66 years not worth above £200 a year is going to build an edifice which will cost him £8,000; he will want £8,000 more to fulfill his splendid plans. I do not believe all the funds of Lancashire, Yorkshire and Bishopric amount to more than £15,000 in the stocks; let us sell all out and give the Rt. Rev. William Gibson £8,000, it would not be enough. I am ever yours, R.B.

1. Irving was Banister's successor at Mowbreck; Blacoe was chaplain to the Benedictine nuns of Ghent, now in Preston.
2. Caprara was a career diplomat, but, when Nuncio in Vienna, he did not defend the church's interests against Emperor Joseph II as vigorously as he might. When the Concordat between the Holy See and the French Republic was concluded in 1801, Bonaparte obtained the cardinal's appointment as Papal Legate to France knowing his reputation and Caprara's conciliatory approach to the First Consul did embarrass Pope Pius VII.
3. Procurator at St Omer's college from 1782 to the Revolution.

144. Rutter to Banister Minsteracres, 28th November 1807

My dear Uncle,

I avail myself of the present opportunity to send you a copy of a small tract which I have lately published and which is entitled The One Thing Necessary. I showed it to you some years ago and the opinion you seemed to entertain of it was not very favourable. As it has, however, been somewhat improved and appeared to me to contain some good thoughts, I was willing to flatter myself that the publication might be of some use in awakening Christians to a sense of their duty. Keating has printed 700 copies, 500 of which I give him to defray the expense of paper and printing. I have also another small treatise ready for the press entitled Meditations on the Passion of Christ for Every Day in the Month. The work is a translation from the French and appears to me to be well calculated for common people, to teach them how to meditate on Our Saviour's sufferings. It is my intention to have it printed at Newcastle and to superintend the press myself. As Keating will have no concern in it, I shall rely on the encouragement of my friends and of such as are devoted to the Passion of Christ.[1]

My father and mother were both tolerably well when I last heard from

Lancashire.[2] My sister Dolly is gone to attend them in their old age. I was extremely hurt at the melancholy account which my brother Thomas sent me of my brother Robert's death. What can be done for his poor children? I wish very much to procure for them a Catholic education but I do not know how to accomplish it. I have written to Mr [Joseph] Hodgson[3] to see whether they can be admitted into any of the Catholic establishments in London where they might be brought up like Christians, but as yet I have received no answer.

It is certain that Mr Smith's name stands first of those who were sent to Rome and not Mr Gillow's as I had imagined.[4] Mr Smith was in a very bad state of health but I hear he is now much better. Our Bishop gave orders on St. Joseph to 4 of Crook Hall and is surprisingly well.

I fear the new college at Ushaw will not be ready for the reception of the Crook students so soon as the nuns of Haggerston wish.[5] The Bishop in his letter to me complains much of the Gentlemen not coming forward with their subscriptions. However, he has got more and done more than ever I imagined he would be able to effect.

I wish you a happy Easter and remain, dear Uncle, your most dutiful Nephew, H. Rutter

1. Gillow gives a publication date of 1806 for Rutter's *One Thing Necessary*, which makes his gift to Banister a little late. His *Meditations* are from the French of Abbe Coubon and came out in 1807.
2. Rutter wrote to his father in 1805: 'My cousin Hodskinson at Haggerston is pretty well. They have had grand doings there lately in consequence of Miss [Mary] Haggerston's marriage with Sir [Thomas Massey] Stanley. They are but a young couple but I hope the blessing of God will attend them. I see no prospect of Mr [George] Silvertop marrying, which I am sorry for, he is now of a proper age and a good wife would induce him perhaps to stay at home. I do not expect to see him at Minsteracres for the next half-year; he is now at Doncaster with a hunting party and Mrs Silvertop is with her friends in Yorkshire, so that I am left alone. I usually avail myself of these opportunities to make a spiritual retreat, which I am about at present. Mr [William] Hurst has left Cliffe, he does not seem calculated to live in a Gentleman's family. I often see Mr John Fletcher of Hexham; he is a great favourite with this family.' [Hurst moved to the extremely poor mission at Berwick in 1803 but he soon found himself 'quite bewildered and absentminded in his parochial functions' and had to be relieved within the year.]
3. Chaplain to the girl's school at Brook Green. Hodgson was 'a clergyman of deep learning, surnamed the 'Walking Library''.
4. As William Gibson's coadjutor.
5. Gibson's prevarications over the new college had an unexpected effect. In

1795 Sir Carnaby Haggerston (V) loaned Haggerston Castle to the Poor Clares as a temporary residence. To earn a living, the nuns opened a girl's school in the castle 'to form the good Christian and the industrious housewife', taking poor children gratis. When eight years had elapsed and the nuns had shown no sign of moving on, Sir Carnaby let it be known that he wanted to carry out major alterations to the castle and they would have to leave. The nuns could not move out, however, because they intended to occupy Tudhoe Academy when the students had transferred to Ushaw, and that was not yet possible. In some exasperation Sir Carnaby sent his architect up to prepare for the renovations at Haggerston and told Bishop Gibson that he could no longer accommodate the nuns; but they were still there a year later. Sir Carnaby therefore ordered work to begin; when it became apparent that the roof was about to be removed from over their heads, Mrs Jane Silvertop of Wooler offered to buy umbrellas for the nuns, observing that however bad the inconvenience to Sir Carnaby, it could hardly justify the exposure of the community to the elements. At this point Sir John Lawson intervened and obtained alternative premises at Scorton in the North Riding and the nuns moved out in November 1807. [Gooch thesis]

---

145. Rutter to Banister Minsteracres, 31st December 1807

My dear Uncle,

It gave me great pleasure to hear lately from my cousin Hodskinson that you were very well and it would have been an additional pleasure to have received this information from yourself. Your long silence, however, gives me but little reason to expect the favour of a letter and perhaps I ought not to expect it considering your great age.

I have but little news to communicate from these parts. With respect to the Bishop, everything goes on as usual. His coadjutor Mr Smith was here not long ago and informed us that his title is Episcopus Bolinensis. I could not find Bolina in my maps but I believe it is at no great distance from Acanthos. The letters from Rome concerning his ordination have not yet come to hand, though according to Mr Smelt, they were sent six months ago. It is highly probable that Bonaparte has seized them and that we shall never hear more of them, and how to get them renewed is the difficulty when all communication with Rome seems to be entirely cut off.[1]

You probably know that the Bishop has built 3 wings of the college at Ushaw but for want of money he cannot go on. I must confess that his Lordship has got foward better than I expected and I suppose for £300 the present building might be made habitable for the Gentlemen at Crook. They are much crowded and wish to remove to Ushaw as soon as possible, but I see little prospect of it unless money can be raised to finish what is absolutely necessary for their accommodation. If application were made to each congregation, I think a sufficient sum might be easily collected for the purpose. The Bishop indeed would have us sell out of the funds but, as far as I am concerned, I shall always object to it as I have always done from the beginning. After all that has been done, however, it would be a pity not to do the little that remains.

My cousin will doubtless have informed you of the removal of the Haggerston nuns to Scorton near Catterick. Sir John Lawson has had the chief management of the business. As my cousin is now staying at Newcastle on account of Mother Abbess who has a sore leg, I stand a chance of seeing her if the weather will permit.

I have nothing particular to say respecting myself. In order to promote the devotion of the faithful to the Passion of Our Lord, I have published a small work on this subject in the way of familiar colloquies.[2] I would have sent you a copy sooner had I found an opportunity, but as this does not occur, I will send it by the carrier next week, enclosed to Mr Wilkinson, to whom I beg my respectful compliments.

Mr Warrilow died a few weeks ago at Newcastle and I hear of no successor from Stonyhurst to supply his place. Mr Hull from Stella was here last week and seems to be in pretty good health. He expects his patron Mr Towneley to reside at Stella during the summer season. I wish you many returns of the season and remain, dear Uncle, your most dutiful Nephew, Hen. Rutter

1. He was not consecrated until March 1810.
2. Presumably the *Meditations* referred to in No. 144.

Postscript

Banister enjoyed nine years in retirement before he died in May 1812 in his eighty-seventh year. Rutter, too, was growing old; in 1820 John Lingard said he was 'very subject to infirmities and therefore wishes to have a house of his own, his own servant and to be his own master' [Ushaw College Mss., *Lingard Correspondence* No. 104, 17 May 1820.] He was then sixty-five years old, which was hardly an age at which to be thinking of taking over a public mission for the first time. The old priest wanted to spend his last years independently, however, and in 1822 Bishop Thomas Smith appointed him to Yealand in Lancashire. Twelve years later he moved to Dodding Green, just as his uncle had done, to spend his last days in a quiet undemanding mission. He died suddenly of a stroke in September 1838, aged eighty-three, while going to meet his nephew, Alexander Goss, a student at Ushaw College who afterwards became Bishop of Liverpool. By way of a valediction, we may note that it was Goss who was responsible for the preservation of these letters.

Bibliography

(of works cited frequently)

G. Anstruther, *The Seminary Priests* (4 vols., Ware, Durham, Great Wakering, 1968, 1975–7), IV 1716–1800.

D. Bellenger, *English and Welsh Priests 1558–1800* (Bath, 1984).

M. Bence-Jones, *The Catholic Families* (London, 1992).

J. Bossy, *The English Catholic Community 1570–1850* (London, 1975).

M Buschkuhl, *Great Britain and the Holy See 1746–1870* (Dublin 1982)

G.E. Cockayne, *The Complete Peerage* (2nd ed., London, 1910–59).

Stephen & S. Lee (eds.), *Dictionary of National Biography* (21 vols., London, 1908/9).

J. Gillow, A *Bibliographical Dictionary of the English Catholics* (5 vols., London, nd [1885–1902]).

L. Gooch, *From Jacobite to Radical: The Catholics of North East England, 1688–1850* (unpub. PhD, University of Durham, 1989).

P.R. Harris (ed.), *Douai College Documents 1639–1794* (Catholic Record Society LXII, London, 1972).

J. Kirk, *Biographies of English Catholics in the Eighteenth Century* (London, 1909).

J. Lenders, *Minsteracres* (Rochdale, 1932).

D. Milburn, *A History of Ushaw College* (Durham, 1964).

L.G. Pine (ed.) *Burke's Landed Gentry* (London, 1952).

F.J. Singleton, *Mowbreck Hall and The Willows* (Bolton, 1983).

Anon., 'Ushaw Papers XII-XIV: Letters of Robert Banister to Thomas Eyre 1797–1804', *UM* vols. 24/5 (1914/5).

B. Ward, *The Dawn of the Catholic Revival in England 1781–1803* (2 vols., London, 1909).

Westminster Archdiocesan Archives.

Index of Persons

(references are to letter numbers)

THE NORTH-EAST

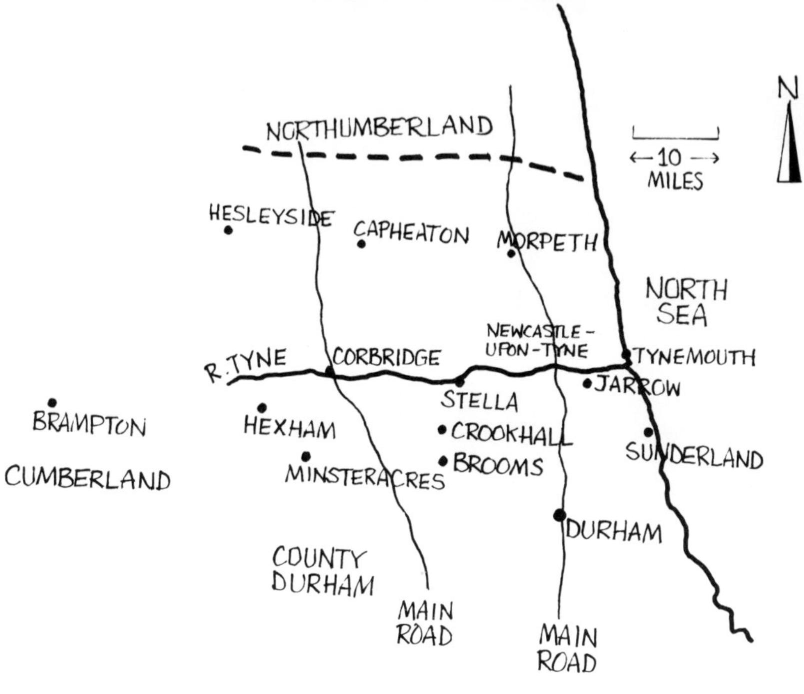